JUGGERNAUT

ALSO BY SUSAN DELACOURT

United We Fall, 1993

Shaughnessy: The Passionate Politics of
Shaughnessy Cohen, 2000

JUGGERNAUT

PAUL MARTIN'S CAMPAIGN FOR
CHRÉTIEN'S CROWN

SUSAN DELACOURT

Copyright © 2003 by Susan Delacourt

All rights reserved. The use of any part of this publication reproduced, transmitted in any form or by any means, electronic, mechanical, photocopying, recording, or otherwise, or stored in a retrieval system, without the prior written consent of the publisher – or, in case of photocopying or other reprographic copying, a licence from the Canadian Copyright Licensing Agency – is an infringement of the copyright law.

National Library of Canada Cataloguing in Publication

Delacourt, Susan, 1959–
Juggernaut : Paul Martin's campain for Chrétien's crown / Susan Delacourt.

Incluces index.
ISBN 0-7710-2605-6

1. Martin, Paul, 1938– 2. Liberal Party of Canada. I. Title.

FC635.D44 2003   324.27106   C2003-904278-2

We acknowledge the financial support of the Government of Canada through the Book Publishing Industry Development Program and that of the Government of Ontario through the Ontario Media Development Corporation's Ontario Book Initiative. We further acknowledge the support of the Canada Council for the Arts and the Ontario Arts Council for our publishing program.

Typeset in Minion by M&S, Toronto
Printed and bound in Canada

This book is printed on acid-free paper that is
100% ancient forest friendly (100% post-consumer recycled).

McClelland & Stewart Ltd.
The Canadian Publishers
481 University Avenue
Toronto, Ontario
M5G 2E9
www.mcclelland.com

1 2 3 4 5   07 06 05 04 03

CONTENTS

JUGGERNAUT

PREFACE

ON SUNDAY, JUNE 24, 1990, the day after the Liberal leadership vote and the
official death of the Meech Lake constitutional accord, the Palliser Hotel in
Calgary was crawling with battle-weary Grits.

I was at the hotel to interview Newfoundland Premier Clyde Wells, one
of the authors of the Meech defeat, who had flown to Calgary just in time
to cast a ballot and exchange a famous hug with the new Liberal leader,
Jean Chrétien.

After the interview was completed, I ran into a new friend, Shaughnessy
Cohen, a lawyer and defeated Liberal candidate from Windsor, Ontario. As
we walked and talked, we bumped into the two Paul Martins, Sr. and Jr.,
who were also out for a stroll.

The bar in the hotel was closed, but some gracious employee – or maybe
he could see the future and was prematurely politically savvy – opened the
doors and let the four of us in to chat over late-afternoon drinks. The
subject soon turned to the personal nature of political defeats, and it was
one of the most interesting discussions I have ever heard among politicians. Three people at that table had felt the sting of political loss. Both
Martins had experienced the failure to win the leadership – Junior just the

day before; Senior most recently in 1968, in the Liberal contest that brought Pierre Trudeau to power.

They talked about how a politician cannot live through any campaign unless he or she believes, even against incredible odds, that victory is possible. They explained to me that the best part of running for office was working with the team: the friendships forged, the war stories accumulated. But the best part can also be the worst when defeat arrives. Inevitably, they said, the supporters are more devastated than the losing candidate.

That was why, Paul Sr. explained, he was taking his son's loss in 1990 worse than he had his own in 1968. "Right," said Martin Jr. – and that's why he was crushed after his father lost to Pierre Trudeau but sanguine on this day, less than twenty-four hours after losing the leadership to Chrétien. Martin was most worried about how his little team, and especially his father, was taking the loss.

Over the past decade or so, I have gone back to that Palliser Hotel conversation many times in my mind. I wish I had taped it, although a tape recorder on the table would probably have inhibited the candour. I wonder what I would have thought if the waiter had leaned over at some point and told me that I would be writing books about two of the people at this table within the next thirteen years. One, Shaughnessy, is now dead, though not before finally winning – twice – the Commons seat that was once Martin Sr.'s. He too is now occupying whatever spot is reserved in the afterlife for former politicians. The other book subject, Paul Martin Jr., as he was then called, is about to become Canada's next prime minister, barring a catastrophe.

This book is the result of travelling along many roads, over many years, with Martin and his team. There are other journalists who were there before me, others who watched him far more intensely at certain points of his career, and I think I'm writing this book now only because I just never really did go away.

One of Paul Martin Sr.'s main pieces of advice to his son when he went into politics was, "Find yourself a good newspaperman." By *good* I think he meant someone friendly and complicit – someone apt to show the politician in the best possible light. More than once in the fifteen years or so since I first ran across Martin Jr., me as a rookie political reporter, he as a novice politician, I have worried that I was pegged as just that person. "Please, please, don't pick me," I wanted to plead.

Certainly, it will be evident from this book that Martin and his people have offered a generous amount of access over the years. I am grateful for that, but I have never felt beholden. If anything, I am more indebted to the various newspapers for which I have worked, not to mention their readers, who have deemed Martin an interesting-enough fellow to justify this long pursuit of his story. Moreover, as will also be obvious from these pages, Martin really opens up only when he is challenged or told flat out that he's wrong. There would be no story to tell here if I or any other reporter had simply followed along, smiling and duly recording what we were told to write. I like to think we've all learned something from this ride, which was sometimes bumpy, sometimes all but abandoned in the heat of mutual frustration. There were times when the natural tension between journalist and politician spilled over, as of course it would.

The book tells the story of Martin's struggles with Jean Chrétien, and by choice and necessity, it is viewed for the most part through the eyes of Martin and his people. First, let me deal with the matter of choice: by the time this book is published, the tension between Martin and Chrétien will have waned, if not disappeared. Grudges are a big part of politics, but they usually evaporate upon victory. There will be a huge temptation on the part of Liberals – and especially Martin and his supporters – to simply forget a struggle that was a fascinating and important ingredient of his all-but-inevitable success. Even as I did some of the last interviews in this book, I found people already eager to dismiss some intense, internecine fights as minor tiffs. By telling the story through the eyes of the victor, I'm hoping the book stands as a record of all the personal and political forces, petty and significant, that led Martin to where he is today. They have shaped the leadership he promises to provide.

The necessity comes out of the fact that Martin has always been more open and accessible to me, from the time of his first leadership campaign, when Chrétien was the cautious front-runner. Chrétien chose not to be interviewed for this book, though several people close to him were, and I'm grateful to Eddie Goldenberg, Peter Donolo, David Smith, Percy Downe, Warren Kinsella, and Francie Ducros for taking the time to ensure that I heard the other side of many of the Martin team's stories. I was impressed with how few times the facts of the tales failed to match up; where the disagreement lay mostly in the interpretation.

It's worth mentioning here that there is a lot of one reporter in particular in this book – Joan Bryden of Southam News (now known as CanWest News, though Bryden is no longer with the media outlet.) Bryden, who arrived on Parliament Hill to cover politics on exactly the same day I arrived to do the same for the *Globe and Mail*, brought a conviction and dedication to Liberal coverage unmatched by anyone else in the Press Gallery. People who don't know either of us well wanted to assume we were rivals, paralleling the politicians we covered most closely: Martin for me and Chrétien for Joan. Nothing could be farther from the truth. We are not the people we cover, as the crusty old editor-in-chief tells his upstart managing editor in the movie *The Paper*. Bryden's reportage, not to mention her friendship and counsel, was crucial to me in putting this book together.

I also know that for every one of Martin's friends and supporters with whom I did speak, there are dozens of others who could boast an influential role in his career. I was struck as I travelled with him over the past year just how large his circle has grown since the 1980s. All over Canada, there are pockets of people who can legitimately claim to have played an important role in his success. To all of those people, a sincere apology if you fail to find yourself mentioned in the tale. I could have filled the book with just the list of your names alone. It seemed a better idea to tell the story.

In telling that story, incidentally, this book doesn't aspire to meet Martin Sr.'s test. In journalism and book writing, sometimes it's better to be fair than good. If nothing else, this book will have done its job if it's seen as a fair account of one of the most fascinating character duels we've seen in Canadian political history.

OFF CENTRE

DURING THE LIBERALS' years in power after 1993, the seat of government authority and the still point of Prime Minister Jean Chrétien's far-reaching control were known by a single moniker: the Centre.

The Centre was a place and it was a state of mind; it was a cadre and it was an individual. It was where the buck stopped and started. It was both the maker and breaker of political careers. Cabinet ministers flagged vital instructions to aides with the warning, "This comes from the Centre."

But in the early months of 2002, political spectators began to see a weakening of this omnipotence. As William Butler Yeats observed, "Things fall apart; the centre cannot hold."

The erosion was nearly painful to watch. Chrétien had to shuffle his cabinet repeatedly to replace ministers touched by conflict-of-interest controversies. Every day in the House of Commons the opposition raised allegations of scandal over how the government had doled out federal advertising contracts in Quebec. The Liberals lost two traditionally safe ridings in spring by-elections, while the Canadian Alliance, under new leader Stephen Harper, was patching up old quarrels and pulling itself together. The prime minister, by contrast, seemed more easily rattled than

before, his testy pronouncements in caucus shared with reporters by mis-
chievous MPs. In public too, Chrétien seemed perpetually irritated, defiantly barking back at his critics. In one of his more memorable lines that
difficult spring, the prime minister appeared to be offering his resignation
in return for a media truce: *Leave me alone, maybe I'll go*. It had come to this.

The Centre's deeper rift was far more personal: it was about leadership,
the L-word, the ambition that dare not speak its name. Chrétien's most
daunting challenge, which neither he nor anyone in his government would
openly acknowledge, was the belief of many of his fellow Liberals that the
prime minister, now sixty-eight years old, had passed his best-before date.
The obvious heir apparent, Finance Minister Paul Martin, was waiting – and
waiting – in the wings. Since his strong second-place showing in the 1990
Liberal leadership contest and during twelve years as the right hand of Jean
Chrétien, Martin, now sixty-three, had attracted a devoted following. And
though levels of impatience varied in intensity among the "Martinites," for
most the appetite for change had become a consuming hunger.

At the beginning of the last week of May 2002, Parliament was in
session, but the prime minister wasn't in the capital. He'd shuffled his
cabinet on Sunday – for the second time that year – then flown to Italy for
a North Atlantic Treaty Organization (NATO) leaders' summit meeting.
So it was that Chrétien found himself an ocean away when the final
unravelling of his leadership began.

A small group of representatives of the building-trades unions held a
dinner on Monday, May 27, 2002, at Tosca, a cozy Italian restaurant on
Metcalfe Street in Ottawa, not far from Parliament Hill. As the group settled
in with pre-dinner drinks, two familiar members of Parliament announced
their arrival with hearty hellos and handshakes. Joe Fontana, from London,
Ontario, was a seasoned Liberal backbencher, a parliamentarian since 1988,
and chairman of the government caucus from 1996 to 1999. He'd brought
along another MP, his good friend Stan Keyes from Hamilton, Ontario, a
former television reporter who was the current chair of the Liberal caucus.
Beyond their common political experience on the backbench, Fontana and
Keyes shared a number of pursuits: they both were keenly interested in

transport issues, were members of the True Grits MP rock band, and were vocal supporters of Paul Martin. Only a couple of years earlier, Fontana and Keyes, with a clutch of others, had gained notoriety when they had publicly, unabashedly, called on Jean Chrétien to step down.

During dinner, the conversation turned to the government's troubles and the cabinet shuffle of the day before, which saw Don Boudria demoted from Public Works and Defence Minister Art Eggleton punted out of cabinet. Fontana, a tad triumphantly, recounted how many of Chrétien's most loyal ministers had been scorched by controversy over the past few months. Each new revelation from the press or the opposition touched the very people on whom the prime minister most depended for organizational support, especially in Quebec: Justice Minister Martin Cauchon had been singled out for his fishing trips with advertising contractors. His predecessor as Quebec lieutenant, Alfonso Gagliano, had been dumped from cabinet in January after allegations surfaced of his political interference in government business. Immigration Minister Denis Coderre was also going to tumble, Fontana said. With his inner circle crumbling around him, how did the prime minister intend to stay in power?

"Chrétien's going to go down too," Fontana predicted.

The more politically sophisticated around the table knew that what they were hearing was malicious glee, not unusual in Chrétien's fractious caucus. To at least a couple of political naïfs, though, Fontana's remarks sounded alarmingly like malicious intent, evidence that Martin's loyalists were not only delighting in Chrétien's troubles, but feeding them.

Late that night in Montreal, Coderre was at his riding office when the phone rang. It was one of the union men from the restaurant, who recounted Fontana's remarks to the incredulous minister.

At thirty-nine years old, Coderre was one of the youngest cabinet ministers, but he was also a hard-knuckle politician and a veteran of two decades of intense ground fighting in Quebec Liberal politics. Coderre saw himself as a protégé of Chrétien, a politician made in the same image. His jaw dropped when he was told what Fontana had said. "So that's how low we're going to go," fumed Coderre.

Knowing that his mentor was out of the country, the minister placed a telephone call to Chrétien's chief of staff, Percy Downe. Furious at the apparent duplicity of a Liberal backbencher and the implied threat to his own career, Coderre demanded that the prime minister be informed immediately. Downe, true to his low-key reputation, was more cautious. Rumours whipped around Ottawa all the time and it wasn't Downe's practice to pass them on, unverified, to his boss. Downe told Coderre that he'd do what he could to confirm what was said before he went to Chrétien with the disturbing tale.

Still, this report of Fontana's outburst was just the latest in a series of rumours about dirty-war tactics that had been buzzing through the political grapevine and the news media. The Prime Minister's Office (PMO) was receiving other reports that appeared to point to all-out internal warfare. A Martin supporter in British Columbia had been overheard boasting that Natural Resources Minister Herb Dhaliwal, a Chrétien loyalist, would be the next target of media and opposition allegations of controversy. The *National Post* had recently made public a fundraising letter sent out by the Friends of John Manley, supporters of the deputy prime minister's leadership aspirations. Written by Toronto lawyer David Gavsie, it solicited contributions as large as $25,000 and advised would-be donors that they might try, "at their own risk," to write off the gifts as business expenses. Given that the letter was sent out only to Liberals, it stood to reason that the leak had come from within the party.

The prime minister's NATO trip pushed the regular Tuesday meeting of cabinet to Thursday morning. Just before the full cabinet was due to convene, Coderre slipped into Chrétien's office for a private word. He was still agitated.

"You'd better wake up," he told the prime minister. "This is serious. Are you going to do something about it, or are you going to leave it to me?" Coderre got his answer within minutes.

At 10 a.m., the prime minister walked into the cabinet room, radiating rage. He took his seat, banged his fist, and levelled his gaze down the table, where, as it happened, Paul Martin sat directly in his line of vision. In a steely voice, Chrétien declared that leadership infighting was feeding the disruptive atmosphere in the House of Commons. He said he regretted his own permissiveness in allowing ministers to build campaign organizations. Cryptically, he talked about "double-crossers" in his own party, referring obliquely to union leaders and restaurants. Coderre, glancing around the table, knew he was one of the few ministers who fully appreciated Chrétien's meaning. Then, abruptly, the prime minister declared that he was staying for his full four-year term and all leadership organizing had to cease immediately. Oh, and if anyone didn't like it, they could resign from cabinet.

Other ministers chimed in. Human Resources Minister Jane Stewart lamented the party's tattered unity and said it was time for the Liberals to come together as a family again. Intergovernmental Affairs Minister Stéphane Dion demanded to know whether anyone was actively plotting to displace the prime minister. Martin said nothing.

When the meeting adjourned, reporters were waiting outside, as usual. Chrétien, chin up, eyes flashing, strode defiantly to the microphones. In response to a relatively mild question about the ad-contracting controversy, Chrétien launched into a rant, using much the same language he had employed inside the cabinet room. But now his heat was directed at the reporters who, he seemed to suggest, may have conspired with those disgruntled, "double-crossing" Grits.

"If you want to have a good story, give me the names of the guys who are leaking to you. . . . If you are lacking things for your headlines, give me the names. You will have a lot of fireworks and you will have very easy stories for many months to come."

Asked what he would do to the "double-crossers," Chrétien could only repeat himself: "Give me a name and you'll have your answer right away. . . . Give me the names of the bureaucrats too who would do that. . . . Give me the facts and I will pass judgment. . . . You will have a lot of good stuff on TV."

Martin, meanwhile, had returned to his office, two floors above the Prime Minister's Office and the cabinet room. Like some other ministers, he wasn't sure what to make of Chrétien's tirade. On the way out of the meeting, Martin had confided his puzzlement to Health Minister Anne McLellan, wondering whether this meant he would not be able to speak at fundraisers for Liberal friends or fulfill speaking engagements he'd already booked in various MPs' ridings in the coming weeks and months. Indeed, he was due to appear at a fundraiser the next evening in Toronto for rookie provincial candidate Nellie Pedro.

Martin called his executive assistant, Tim Murphy, into his office and presented him with a scrap of paper – scribbled points from Chrétien's lecture. Murphy did a double take; it was not like his boss to make notes during cabinet meetings. In fact, Martin's aides had a long-running joke about his debriefing abilities. Asked how a meeting had gone or begged to recount details of an important conversation, Martin was likely to answer with cheerful but stingy summations: "fine" or "great" or "interesting." On this occasion, though, Martin had written down the essence of Chrétien's scolding. Four items were recorded: (1) no more leadership campaigning; (2) the ethics controversy was a result of leadership politics; (3) the prime minister is staying for his full four-year mandate; and (4) new, stricter conflict-of-interest rules were being introduced to cabinet, forcing ministers to disclose any and all financial contributions to their leadership campaigns.

Just as they were beginning to sift through the implications of Chrétien's dictates, especially the prospect of his staying on as prime minister, Murphy was summoned to take a call from the Prime Minister's Office. It was Percy Downe, who said that Martin should rethink his plans to attend the fundraising event in Toronto on Friday night. Downe was uncharacteristically brusque. He had double-checked the travel schedule that Martin's office had filed, as required. Since the September 11, 2001, terrorist strikes, the Centre had been more scrupulous about ensuring that a critical number of ministers remained near the capital, and that all were reachable in the event of an emergency. The itinerary filed by Martin's staff showed that the finance minister would be in Hamilton on Thursday night and Friday morning, then returning to his home in Montreal late Friday evening after some "private" time in Toronto. Downe wanted to know why Martin had neglected to mention this fundraising appearance before one thousand Liberals – and asked how it qualified as "private" time. Murphy tried to extricate himself from the conversation with a vague promise to discuss the situation with his boss.

Martin, content to leave that dispute to Murphy, turned his attention to the speech he was to deliver Friday morning at a convention of the Federation of Canadian Municipalities (FCM) in Hamilton. It was intended as a major address on the future of cities, one of Martin's policy pre-occupations that spring. Martin was notorious for agonizing over speeches, putting his staff through countless drafts and redrafts, and this was a significant address. He had been flagging his intention to focus on revital-izing cities for several weeks, picking up on the phrase favoured by the *Toronto Star* – "a new deal" for cities – and running with it. Other ministers had been talking about a renewed federal interest in all things urban as well.

Ominously, at least in the eyes of Martin's advisers, there had been an undercurrent of tension with the PMO over this speech. Chrétien was reluctant to make sweeping promises to the cities, and his office had demanded to see the text. Many ministers were due to speak to this con-ference on municipalities and the PMO wanted the cabinet to speak with one voice. But Martin's office was not accustomed to having his speeches vetted by the prime minister's staff and bristled at the request. Only at the eleventh hour did Martin's communications people reluctantly pass the text to the PMO. On Wednesday, the day before the cabinet meeting, Murphy had been told that two words in particular – *new deal* – were troublesome. Paul Genest, the prime minister's policy and research direc-tor, had asked that the words be excised.

"Couldn't you pick another phrase?" Genest asked Murphy. "Maybe something else by Roosevelt?"

Murphy gave a noncommittal reply: "I'll see what I can do."

The attempt to edit his remarks unnerved Martin's people, but the specific change baffled them. Wasn't *new deal* a relatively benign term? Hadn't Martin already used those words in public? Yes, perhaps, but the prime minister had not.

Now, a day later, the Centre had a fresh bone to pick with Martin. Not only had his staff failed to give notice of the Friday fundraiser, but it conflicted with a speech that Chrétien was supposed to deliver in Toronto the same night. The prime minister would address the annual gathering of the federal Liberal party's Ontario wing around 7 p.m. at the Regal Constellation Hotel near Pearson International Airport. Martin's speech at a union hall just fifteen minutes along Highway 401 was set to take place at

7 p.m. as well. The PMO worried: What if the media decided to portray this as a duelling match? What if Ontario MPs felt torn about which event to attend? Transport Minister David Collenette had alerted the PMO, arguing that the last thing the government needed right now was for Martin and Chrétien to make competing appearances in Toronto.

Downe had to settle this matter as quickly as possible. Immediately after he relayed his frustration to Murphy, he called David Smith, a Toronto lawyer and a Liberal minister in the 1970s, who could have been recruited from central casting to play the part of a backroom political operative. Gravelly voiced, a fount of campaign war stories and ribald jokes, Smith was a formidable election campaign overseer and an adept negotiator of internal Liberal family feuds. With tempers in the backrooms rising by the hour, Smith was brought in, as Downe put it, "to give everybody a collective group hug."

Smith was on friendly terms with Martin and most of his people, including John Webster, president of the Maple Trust financial group and the organizational brains of the unofficial Martin leadership team. Smith explained to Webster that the PMO was miffed about the Friday-night event; it had not approved Martin's appearance at this fundraiser and the timing and optics were bad. It would be better if the finance minister, "as a show of loyalty," chose instead to appear onstage with the prime minister at the Regal Constellation. Webster listened, then said he wasn't sure he liked the idea of Martin having to ask permission to do provincial fundraisers. Smith leaned a bit more heavily. "I'd tell him to do it," he said, "or else."

Those last words stuck in Webster's craw. Or else what?

In Ottawa that Thursday, it was party night at Wallis House, a sprawling, Tudor-revival hospital-turned-condominium complex on Rideau Street. The building was home to some of Paul Martin's closest advisers, notably David Herle, a public-opinion strategist at Earnscliffe Research and Communications. David Brodie, a young staffer in the finance minister's office, who had recently become engaged, also lived at Wallis House. A celebration to mark Brodie's engagement was underway at his apartment.

Herle was at the party, but he was on edge. Earlier that day, he had been told that CTV News and the *Globe and Mail* had been given an account of what happened in cabinet that day. Herle had phoned Martin: "Why am I hearing this first from reporters?" Martin said he hadn't been sure what to make of Chrétien's order; he didn't know how it would work in practical terms. Herle suspected something more ominous: a general offensive was being mounted against Martin.

The news coverage that night would settle the question. If the leak portrayed Martin as having been disciplined, Herle would read it as a declaration of war. Herle left the party shortly before 11 p.m. to catch the CTV news. A small clutch of people joined him, traipsing into his apartment, lined with CDs, cluttered with music magazines, and sparsely furnished with a sprawling leather couch and big-screen TV. As the familiar chimes of the theme music sounded, they all fell silent, awaiting the lead item. It was billed as a CTV exclusive, an insider's report on what had happened at cabinet that morning. Parliamentary bureau chief Craig Oliver delivered the piece, calling it the prime minister's acknowledgement of a "civil war" going on within the governing party.

"Jean Chrétien walked into his weekly cabinet meeting and laid out his future for his astonished colleagues. This is the way it is going to be, he told them, 'I'm not quitting.' Ending months of intense speculation about his future, Chrétien announced that he will work his full mandate out and that he will face a review of his leadership at a convention of the Liberal party in February. Looking directly at Paul Martin, Chrétien said he expects each of the cabinet ministers and their delegates to support him fully. Liberal ministers left the cabinet room under orders to stop tearing each other apart. Chrétien told his potential successors to end their leadership campaigns and to stop their fundraising efforts."

Chatting at the end of the segment to news anchor Lloyd Robertson, Oliver portrayed this meeting as a moment of truth for Martin.

"Mr. Martin now has to make a difficult decision: Whether or not to put his future and his ambitions in the hands of Mr. Chrétien and hope for the best; or whether to take his future and his ambitions into his own hands and do something decisive, which might include having to quit and fight Chrétien from the outside in the way John Turner did to Trudeau and then Chrétien, by the way, did to John Turner."

The story confirmed Herle's suspicions: someone unfriendly to Martin wanted this version of events to make the news, to force a confrontation. Martin himself hadn't felt personally targeted by Chrétien's admonition, but it was being portrayed as a blunt message to Martin to get in line or get out.

Karl Littler, a senior Finance aide and a central organizer for the leadership team, watched the broadcast from Herle's leather sofa with the rest of the gang. As soon as the others had straggled back to the engagement party, Herle and Littler telephoned Martin at his hotel room in Hamilton, where he was fine-tuning the cities speech he was to deliver the next day.

Herle gave Martin a précis of the CTV story and his interpretation. Don't forget, Herle reminded him, that David Smith had used the words *or else* in his warning to Webster. Littler took the phone and spoke more frankly. "You see what's happening, don't you?" Littler asked. In less than twenty-four hours, Martin was being told to amend one speech, cancel another, shut down his leadership campaign, and submit to disciplinary drubbings in front of his cabinet colleagues and the country at large.

"If you buckle to the request to show up and introduce the prime minister, you'll be letting down all those MPs who are counting on you to stand up to Chrétien, who've put their necks out to support you," Littler said, employing what was usually a fail-safe appeal to Martin. "I know these MPs. I know they want you to stand up to him. They're depending on you to stand up to him."

Still, the finance minister was hesitant. He mused about cancelling the Toronto appearances, just bypass the city altogether and avoid both obligations. He was worried about the implications of defiance for himself, for his people, for his position in government. Littler and Herle told him he was coming down to a decision, like it or not. To allow the allegations of disloyalty to go unanswered would only prolong the humiliation.

The next day, the Chrétien-Martin story began to spill into the media. The *Globe and Mail* carried the news of the cabinet meeting across its front-page banner, strengthening convictions in the Martin camp that someone wanted to pin the blame on Martin for all the prime minister's troubles.

"Prime Minister Jean Chrétien threw down the gauntlet to Finance Minister Paul Martin yesterday, ordering his leadership rival to shut down his campaign organization and fundraising efforts. In a tense cabinet meeting, Mr. Chrétien confronted Mr. Martin and other leadership hopefuls and told them their underground campaigns are tearing the party apart, cabinet sources said."

Martin only glanced at the *Globe*'s coverage. His main concern was the Federation of Canadian Municipalities speech, which he delivered as written – with sixteen mentions of a new deal for Canadian cities, the phrase brazenly set out in bold capitals in the text distributed to media and delegates.

Chrétien, meanwhile, had made his way to Toronto to announce a major cultural aid package for the city. It was a last-minute addition to his itinerary. No one in the Prime Minister's Office had been sure that Ontario Premier Ernie Eves would be able to attend. Pleading a bad cold, Eves went back and forth on whether he could make a public appearance that day. At 9:30 a.m., he confirmed his presence and plans proceeded for a press conference at Roy Thomson Hall later that day. As these public events preoccupied the central characters, attempts at mediated diplomacy between Martin and Chrétien were stepped up.

Every political party has its good cops and its bad cops; so it was with the Chrétien and Martin squads. The aggressive face of Team Chrétien was personified by Warren Kinsella, a lawyer, author, and occasional adviser to the prime minister. Kinsella's approach to politics is best summed up in the title of his 2001 how-to book on strategy, *Kicking Ass in Canadian Politics*. Martin's hardball player was John Webster – the man who had taken the call from David Smith the day before.

Adversaries though they were, Webster and Kinsella were on cordial-enough terms personally to negotiate. While their leaders were very publicly estranged, these two held a conciliatory lunch meeting on Friday at Acqua Ristorante in downtown Toronto's BCE Place.

Kinsella came to the lunch with a mission: to secure assurances that the Martin people weren't planning a coup against the prime minister. Webster had a goal in the same vein: to find out if Chrétien was trying to push Martin out of cabinet.

The two men made a little small talk about families and the state of the world before turning to the particulars. Kinsella wanted Webster to guarantee there was no coup plot afoot, a vow that Martin's chief organizational man was happy to provide. No, a thousand times no, the Martin team was not scheming to force Chrétien out of office or plotting anything else that might destabilize the government. No, the Martin team was not stoking the flames of the ethics controversies. Martin himself had been on the phone to Denis Coderre a couple of times, assuring him that Fontana's remarks were not evidence of any dark scheming between Martinites and the opposition.

Webster had his own questions, revolving around why the prime minister would want to go through the leadership review in February 2003 as he claimed. In Webster's view, it was a pointless and destructive exercise if Chrétien intended to leave office anyway at the end of this government's current term. Kinsella assured Webster that the prime minister had no desire to leave the party depleted and fractured, a mess for a future successor to inherit.

They parted amicably. Webster went back to his office to rejoin the chorus of Martin advisers who were now busily chatting non-stop on conference calls with each other. Kinsella made his way to Roy Thomson Hall to link up with Chrétien and pass along Webster's words of reassurance.

David Smith was already there. Having been drawn into mediation duties the day before, he had a sense of how much tension existed between Martin and Chrétien, but it wasn't until he arrived at Roy Thomson Hall that he could see for himself how provoked the prime minister had become, whatever the message from Kinsella. Chrétien was cursing Martin and his inability to control his double-crossing caucus supporters.

Chrétien waded into yet another scrum with reporters at the end of the cultural-aid announcement, ratcheting up the public rhetoric another notch. If anyone had trouble with his ban on leadership organizing, they knew what to do, he said, "They will have plenty of time to organize because they will not be ministers any more." Then he hinted again that he might stay in office longer, just to spite those who wanted him out. "They can try. I love a fight. . . . You know, for me, for thirty-nine years I never ran away from a fight, so I'm not about to start at my age."

Smith's good-cop counterpart on the Martin side was Richard Mahoney, a gregarious Ottawa lawyer with an impressive array of friends in all quarters of the party. Mahoney had served as executive assistant to Martin in his 1990 Liberal leadership bid but had since gone into private law practice – with David Smith's law firm – and was now a familiar face on television as a Liberal spokesman.

Just as Smith had rushed to Chrétien's side, Mahoney made his way to Hamilton to be with Martin. The rising temperature of this feud was such that the good cops were less concerned with negotiations than with offering counsel and support to their battling titans. Mahoney found the finance minister prepared to consider a change in his plans for Friday evening – if the prime minister made the request personally. All that Chrétien had to do was call, Martin said, and he'd consider altering his schedule. But there was the prime minister on television, repeating the message that if ministers didn't accept his ban on leadership campaigning, they could leave the cabinet.

While Martin awaited some conciliatory gesture, he and his aides proceeded robotlike through the public events of the day, meeting and greeting municipal leaders at the FCM conference and touring a local industrial facility. The minister held a scrum with reporters. Anticipating a question about his deteriorating relationship with Chrétien, Martin was prepared to utter a few noncommittal lines, carefully sketched out in advance. No one asked the question. One reporter made a faint allusion to the leadership issue as the scrum broke up, but Martin was already walking away. In the meantime, Martin's aides considered the possibility of finding a stand-in for the evening's fundraiser appearance, even putting out a few feelers to likely candidates. They talked about shifting the time of the speech, to remove any appearance of competition with the prime minister's address. But Martin insisted that nothing would change until he heard from Chrétien personally.

By early evening, the Centre's silence was eloquent, and wounding.

Martin was due to arrive at the union hall at 5 p.m. for a private reception before the larger event. Toronto MP Joe Volpe, the dean of Martin's supporters in the Liberal caucus and one of the few MPs who had been with him in the 1990 leadership, wandered about the reception, assuring guests that the finance minister would be along shortly. Finally, at 6:15 p.m., Martin appeared, distracted and in a bad temper. He worked the reception for about ten minutes, then huddled in a backroom with his growing entourage around him. All were glued to their cellphones, plugged into conference calls with others in Martin's network of friends and advisers. Martin dipped in and out of the group discussion, weighing the decision before him.

Volpe pulled Martin aside: "This is the Rubicon. You've got to cross it." In Volpe's view, if Chrétien succeeded in getting Martin to do this "show of loyalty" at the Regal Constellation, it would be the end of the struggle. "He'll know he can browbeat you all the way to another term in office."

Martin had reached the same conclusion. It was time to declare where he stood. Or, more precisely, where he would stand no longer.

At the Regal Constellation, word was spreading that Martin was due to make an announcement to the media over at the union hall. Reporters who hadn't intended to cover Martin's event were now leaving the hotel, abandoning the prime minister's event just as David Collenette had warned.

Chrétien was about to step onstage when he got a call from his communications director, Françoise Ducros, who relayed rumours of a Martin statement, possibly his resignation. Cabinet ministers onstage were passed notes from their aides, with cryptic scrawls about Martin preparing to quit. Down on the floor, MPs were rounded up to join Chrétien onstage. A couple of busloads of Liberals had arrived, carrying hastily made signs of support for the PM. Four More Years, the signs read. A few boisterous Grits tried to cut the tension in the room with applause and cheers, which hung awkwardly in the air.

At the back of the crowd, Kitchener-Waterloo MP Andrew Telegdi stood with his arms folded, his face clouded. Telegdi was one of many in caucus who felt they owed their election in no small measure to the finance minister's popularity. He could not believe the situation had degenerated to the point where the party was about to lose its most powerful asset with voters. His teenaged daughter Erin urged him to mount the stage with the other caucus members. "No," Telegdi's wife, Nancy, gently chided. "Dad is making a statement."

At around 9 p.m., Martin finally broke away from his huddle and strode into the recreation room in the basement of the union hall to face reporters. The idea was to make as brief a statement as possible and take only a few questions. One photographer had positioned a large reflective shield right in front of the microphone, bouncing light into Martin's eyes. He could not see the reporters he was addressing without craning his neck awkwardly and squinting past the glare. As a result, he seemed to be speaking to no one in particular, saying little and looking hugely uncomfortable. The set-up made the encounter even more bizarre than it already was – Canada's finance minister, in a shabby basement, announcing that he'd come to the end of his rope with the prime minister.

"Some time ago, the prime minister stated that it was fine for people to organize for the leadership. In fact, he even encouraged some candidates to present their candidature. . . . Now it would appear that he's changed his mind. That's his prerogative. I just really don't know how this is going to work. I don't know what it means. Does it mean that potential candidates shouldn't go to fundraising dinners? Does it mean they shouldn't go to party functions? Does it mean they shouldn't go to riding meetings? These are all things which will have to be determined.

"Let me just say that I'm obviously going to have to reflect on my options. But when I do so, I'm not going to do so only in the context of a leadership race. There's something far more important at issue here. That's the government and the country. We have effected a remarkable turn-around as a nation in the course of the last six or seven years. We really are now at the point of takeoff. And we have some very, very important decisions to make. And I must say that I have to reflect, given the events of the last couple of days, on my capacity now as a member of the government to have an impact on those decisions, matters that I feel very strongly about. And the question is, Will my continuation in the cabinet, given these events, permit me in fact to exercise the kind of responsibility and influence that I believe a minister of finance must have?"

And with that question left dangling, he was gone. Reporters rushed to their cellphones and laptops, not entirely sure what story they were filing. Martin "reviewing his options"? Buried in the text of his prepared statement, though, were all the code words pinpointing Martin's discomfiture. It wasn't about the leadership race, it was about the prime minister's lack of confidence in his finance minister. Martin appeared to be leaving the door open to some future clarification, but the magnitude of the issues he raised, plus the fact that he'd chosen to make his unease known to the national media, said it all. There seemed to be a double-edged meaning behind the sentence: "We really are now at the point of takeoff."

At that moment, those closest to Chrétien decided Martin was gone, that he had quit in every way except officially. Eddie Goldenberg, the prime minister's long-time policy adviser and frequent bridge between Martin and Chrétien, felt a stunned hurt as he watched the news at his hotel in Vancouver. CTV carried a special broadcast on "a government in crisis," going live to the Regal Constellation Hotel, where shell-shocked Liberals milled about the lobby and adjoining bars.

Chrétien was on his way back to Ottawa, but most of the Ontario ministers remained behind. Tim Murphy was pacing the hotel lobby, jokingly distributing his business cards as souvenirs. "Here," he offered, "these are going to be collectors' items soon." Richard Mahoney and David Smith, the good cops, met in the restaurant. Smith was distraught. "Why has he done this? Do you realize what he's done?" Mahoney remained grim. "What else did you expect him to do?"

Martin rushed to the airport to catch the 10 p.m. flight to Montreal. His wife, Sheila, was waiting to drive him to their farm in Quebec's Eastern Townships, about an hour from the city.

Sheila was fully aware of the day's events. She had been in touch with her husband by phone throughout the day and evening. When he stepped into the car, she asked simply, "Well, what now?" Martin, weary, could only reply: "I don't know, Sheila. I just don't know."

For the next two days, Martin holed up in his study at the farm, a cordless phone never out of his hand and a bottomless mug of coffee always at his elbow. The phone rang from early morning to late at night: family, friends, political colleagues, and long-time supporters calling to contribute to Martin's review of his options. Eddie Goldenberg had left messages at all of Martin's residences and with almost all of Martin's closest advisers on Friday night. Having managed the Martin-Chrétien relationship since 1995, when the agonizing fights over a historic, deficit-cutting budget ended any collegial bonds between the two, Goldenberg was the obvious candidate to try to broker an eleventh-hour compromise. Alex Himelfarb, the newly minted clerk of the Privy Council, was also called into service.

Goldenberg's phone rang early on that Saturday morning. It was Martin, understatedly opening up the line of communication to Chrétien.

"Hi," he said. "What's new? What's going on?"

Goldenberg laughed out loud. "What's going on? What's new? You tell me."

The two talked about what it would take to set things right. Martin listed his grievances, the signals that he was mistrusted by the prime minister. He could not see how he could do another budget for Chrétien with such suspicion hanging over his every move. Martin had felt increasingly marginalized by the prime minister in recent months. Goldenberg tried to remind him that it had been possible for the two of them to work together all these years. Why did it have to come apart now?

Another man who should have been in a position to serve as a mediator between Martin and Chrétien was John Manley. The deputy prime minister had long been regarded as a fiscally conservative Liberal, much in the same mould as Martin. His steady, earnest response to the September 11 attacks had enhanced Manley's image and standing in cabinet and he was regarded as a serious leadership contender himself. But Manley's rise in stature appeared to have occurred at the expense of his formerly warm relations with Martin. The two had locked horns repeatedly on a whole range of issues and their friendship was badly bruised by the spring of 2002.

Still, Manley felt duty bound to place a call to Martin on Saturday to see if there wasn't something that could be done. Unable to get through, he left a message among the myriad piling up on the Martin answering machine that day.

Anne McLellan, the health minister and a Martin supporter, did get through that Saturday to register her annoyance. Never reticent with her opinions, McLellan lectured Martin on what she saw as career-ending recklessness, telling him that if he wanted to keep his job as finance minister, he should put his pride aside and place a call to the prime minister.

"No way," Martin said. "He has to call me."

Saturday night, Chrétien observed tradition by attending the annual Press Gallery dinner. Cabinet ministers and MPs who would normally be back in their ridings for the weekend were expected to gather with journalists at the National Arts Centre for an evening of schmoozing and light-hearted pokes at each other in the formal speeches.

Martin had studiously avoided the dinner since 1997, when his leadership ambitions had been the favourite butt of jokes. Chrétien, though, always showed up, as did most of the cabinet. At the last minute this year, however, due to the leadership crisis, all of the Ontario ministers decided they should remain at the Liberal convention in Toronto and sent their regrets.

Aides to Martin were the most popular figures at the dinner that night. Everyone wanted to hear the "real" story of the impasse and get the goods on whether Martin was in or out of cabinet. One of Manley's assistants was spotted haranguing one of Martin's senior advisers, also arguing that this showdown would end badly for everyone. The tension in the room was palpable, yet no one would discuss it openly.

The dinner's organizers had prepared a video presentation, including a segment featuring the song "Backstabbers" by the O'Jays, with Martin's beaming visage filling the screen. The soundtrack was interspersed with snippets of Chrétien's angry "double-crossers" scrum a few days previously. The crowd guffawed nervously. A tight smile played across the prime minister's face.

When it came time for him to speak, Chrétien made only a glancing allusion to the drama unfolding around him. He quipped that he had asked Martin to undertake a diplomatic mission to Afghanistan. It seemed the time for humour on the subject of Martin's fate had passed; anything he might say would be interpreted as a message to the conspicuously absent Martin.

A number of cabinet ministers had to be up on Sunday morning to attend an all-day retreat at nearby Meech Lake, Quebec, on the topic of health care. But the more critical ailments of the government kept intruding into the day's proceedings. Manley, who was chairing the meeting, was pulled out mid-morning to take a return call from Martin.

The two men's conversation would remain a point of contention for months. Manley came away with the impression that Martin planned to quit by the end of the day. Martin insisted that he told Manley he hadn't yet made up his mind.

Manley spoke to the prime minister, who then summoned Goldenberg back to Ottawa from the Meech Lake retreat. Goldenberg tried one more call to Martin. He got him on the line, through scratchy cellphone reception. Goldenberg asked, "Is there anything that can be said? Anybody else who should be called? I don't want to read tomorrow in the paper that there was something we could have done that we didn't do."

"No," Martin said. "This is about a loss of confidence by the prime minister in his finance minister."

Goldenberg arrived at Langevin Block to find the core PMO group assembled in a nondescript conference room in Percy Downe's offices. Chrétien was there, impatient to get this done. Francie Ducros, his communications director, was on hand. Alex Himelfarb was hunched over the square boardroom table. Downe had returned early from Charlottetown, where he commuted home each weekend, to be at Chrétien's side. By now the group was hearing reports of unusual goings-on at Finance. The lights were burning that weekend and document shredders were churning. The political staffers were clearing out their offices.

Goldenberg sat down in one of the black-and-chrome chairs and gave his view of the hopelessness of the situation. Himelfarb offered the same assessment. "It's over," they said. Chrétien, having heard from Manley as well, agreed that Martin's exit was imminent. But what were they to do? Just wait for his next move?

Ducros insisted that they make a formal statement, explain that after consultation with the Bank of Canada governor and market experts, it was the prime minister's responsibility to replace the finance minister for the sake of economic stability. Her suggestion was nixed by the others. No one wanted to feed the perception that Martin was being pushed out. The best option, they agreed, was for the breakup to be presented as a mutual decision. Goldenberg set to work on a draft of the statement.

By late in the morning on Sunday, Martin had decided to go back to Ottawa and prepare to make his departure official. He would stop at his Montreal townhouse first. On the hour-long drive to the city, he stayed on the phone, consulting with a team of about a dozen people, David Herle and his long-time partner, Terrie O'Leary, chief among them. O'Leary, who had served as Martin's executive assistant in the 1990s, was Canada's representative to the World Bank, a job that kept her in Washington during the work week. She was in Ottawa on Sunday afternoon, awaiting Martin's return. She and the others knew that he would have to quit within hours, by Monday morning at the latest. He would need his closest friends around him.

Soon after he walked into the Montreal townhouse at around 2 p.m., Martin spoke with Goldenberg again. He stood in his downstairs den, Sheila hovering protectively nearby. This time, though, Goldenberg had the prime minister on the line. Finally, the two men would speak directly to each other.

Chrétien sat in the gloomy conference room at the Langevin Block, his advisers arrayed around the table. A fuzzy satellite photo of Canada hung near the small oak stand that held the telephone; behind him a window gave view to a dim alley.

No pleasantries were exchanged. Chrétien said that all the reports – from Goldenberg, from Himelfarb, and others – weren't encouraging. "So what's going to happen here?" he asked.

Martin said, "Well, we've got a problem, and it's pretty serious." Martin told him he hadn't made up his mind about whether to leave cabinet; he needed more time to think. The prime minister then began talking again about Martin's people, about the restaurant scene earlier in the week, about disloyalty and double-crossers.

"I'm sick of having my loyalty questioned," Martin said.

"You can't control your people," Chrétien retorted. Then, abruptly, "Eddie's going to read you a letter."

Suddenly Goldenberg was back on the line. "The best thing is if we do this mutually," Goldenberg said and began to read his draft statement. It stated that Martin would no longer be part of the Chrétien cabinet because the two men's disagreements over Liberal party politics meant they could no longer work together.

Martin interrupted. "Forget it," he said. "This hasn't got anything to do with the Liberal party. Our problems are a lot more fundamental than that. That's the first thing. But the second thing is I'm not signing any mutual letter, this is no goddamn mutual letter. Forget about that."

He told Goldenberg that any further discussions about a letter should be held with Tim Murphy, who would call him shortly. He hung up and said to Sheila, "Come on. We're going to Ottawa."

In the car, behind the wheel, Martin stayed in touch with Herle, Murphy, and the others. They developed two statements: one a resignation announcement; the other a response to a firing. In mid-conversation, he heard whoops and yells in the background. "You've been fired!" Herle shouted. "I just saw it on Newsnet. There's a cabinet shuffle at five-thirty."

Martin turned on the car radio. It was *Cross-Country Checkup* on CBC Radio, and host Rex Murphy was announcing the scheduled shuffle. "I don't believe it," Martin said into the phone. "I just got off the line with Chrétien. He didn't say anything about this."

The shuffle itself happened without joy or much ceremony. The prime minister and John Manley appeared on schedule at Rideau Hall. Alex Himelfarb, acting in place of the absent Governor General, Adrienne Clarkson, made the move official and then Chrétien and Manley emerged to face reporters. Manley spoke about how he had briefly believed he would be finance minister for a few days back in 1993, before Martin decided to take the job. The prime minister said his goodbyes to Martin through a written statement, essentially the same statement that Martin wouldn't sign, portraying their falling-out as a partisan dispute.

Dear Paul:
It is with sadness that I confirm that you are leaving the cabinet. As I told you, I will always be grateful to you for your remarkable work as Minister of Finance. There are very few Canadians who have ever served in a cabinet with such distinction.

Together we have achieved a great deal for Canada and Canadians. The success of the government's economic policy has situated Canada very well for continued growth and prosperity. Your contribution as Minister of Finance will be a continuing source of pride for you and for me.

You and I have worked extremely well together, ever since we took office in November 1993, on all matters relating to government policy. We have always been in full agreement on economic and fiscal policy.

But, unfortunately, matters unrelated to governing have gotten in the way of our working together on government policy. As such, we both understand, with real regret, that it is in the best interest of the government and the country that you step down from the cabinet.

As prime minister and on behalf of all our colleagues in cabinet, I thank you for a job very well done. Aline and I wish you and Sheila all the very best.

A small contingent greeted Martin at his Ottawa condominium while others of his inner circle, including Mahoney, Murphy, and Herle, fanned out to give radio and television interviews. On behalf of the other camp, Eddie Goldenberg granted a rare television interview to CBC's Don Newman. When he spoke of Martin not being in cabinet any longer, he seemed close to tears.

"Are we going to miss Mr. Martin? Everybody will miss Mr. Martin. Is anyone going to replace him? No."

Martin's own statement had to counter the prime minister's assertion that party politics was the cause of the crisis. Scott Reid and Brian Guest, Martin's two trusted communications aides, put the final touches on the document prepared in the car, presented it to Martin, and waited for his usual felt-pen massacre of their draft. Reid, Guest, and O'Leary sat with him in the Ottawa condo's master bedroom while Martin read the statement one more time. Surprisingly, he made only two minor changes. "Okay, that's it," he said. He and Sheila got back in the car and headed to the National Press Theatre, where a mob of cameras and reporters waited.

There, Martin sat down at the desk onstage, cleared his throat, and read his statement:

Good evening.

Thanks to the hard work and the sacrifice of Canadians, we are now in a position to make great strides as a country. With courage and with vision we can confirm Canada's place among the leading nations of the world for decades to come. We can build an even stronger economy, we can build an even more fair society.

What I also know, however, is that in order to achieve this objective the cabinet must be united in its vision. Certainly the prime minister and his finance minister must be working in common cause and with a shared perspective on the most basic questions of direction and approach.

For a long time the natural tensions between my views and those of the prime minister were well within the manageable, even healthy, range that is customary in a sound, working relationship. In fact, we were always able to resolve disagreements working issue by issue.

Unfortunately, in recent months, and certainly during the last few days, the working relationship between myself and the prime minister had deteriorated. It was therefore threatening to impede our focus on the very important choices that confront us as a nation.

As I indicated on Friday, I intended to reflect on my options. That is now a moot point. I am no longer a member of the cabinet. And John Manley is now the new minister of finance. The nation already has full confidence in his skills. He is tremendously well qualified and will do an outstanding job, and I wish him the very best.

I also wish to express my genuine appreciation to the prime minister for the opportunity to serve as finance minister for the past nine years. It has been a great honour to serve my country.

Now before concluding, I'd like to emphasize a few things. First, while these have been certainly a difficult few days, I feel passionately about the future of this nation and about the opportunities that are before us. I feel strongly with the Liberal Party of Canada into which I was born and raised. And I believe very much in our caucus and cabinet. They are an outstanding and dedicated group of individuals motivated by a desire to make a great nation greater still.

Second, I will continue to sit as the member of Parliament for LaSalle-Emard, an active member of Parliament.

Third, I want to thank the many friends who called or sent messages in recent days. I'm enriched by their friendship and their support. In that respect, I want to thank above all others Sheila and my family for their patience and their advice.

As a final note, I would like to urge financial markets to keep in mind the extraordinary strength of the Canadian economy. GDP growth in the first quarter of this year was nothing short of remarkable. We're the only G7 nation in surplus, and job creation continues to be very strong. When markets open tomorrow, these are the facts that should be weighed.

Ministers of Finance come and go. I leave knowing that our economy is very robust. And now I look forward to the work and the challenges that lie ahead.

Thank you.

The next morning, Monday, June 3, Martin awoke as an ordinary MP. No departmental meetings scheduled, no speeches to give, no preparation for a major meeting with his international counterparts.

Sheila Martin thought she might learn to enjoy this new freedom. Bright and early, the Martins called David Herle and Terrie O'Leary – How about breakfast? Martin began his first full day as Canada's best-known backbencher with bacon and eggs at Nate's Deli on Rideau Street.

Martin insisted at breakfast that this was the beginning of the end of his political career. Only obscurity awaits a politician willing to walk away from his job. But every time the former finance minister tried to make the point to his companions, another passerby or fellow diner would approach the table. "Go for it," they said.

Less than a day after leaving Chrétien's cabinet, the challenge lay there in front of him. Now was the time. The prime minister's crown was within his grasp. The juggernaut was ready to start rolling toward 24 Sussex Drive.

2

INSIDERS VERSUS OUTSIDERS

EARTHQUAKES, POLITICAL AND geological, happen when long-contained pressure is released along ancient fault lines. In recent Liberal party history, the ground shifts roughly every twenty years. Two decades is about enough time to generate the kind of heat that can rock a party to its foundation.

To understand what happened on that fateful weekend in June 2002, when the earth shook under Jean Chrétien's government, it is instructive to look back to a moment twenty years earlier when the Liberals were nearing another serious upheaval.

On the first weekend of November 1982, Richard Mahoney, a Liberal of one month's standing and a first-year law student at the University of Ottawa, wandered through the ornamented halls of Ottawa's Château Laurier Hotel. He was in search of the meeting room where a dynamic, young businessman from Montreal, Paul Martin Jr., son and namesake of the legendary Liberal cabinet minister, was due to give a speech.

For the past few days, Mahoney had been nursing doubts about this whole business of joining the Liberal party. The people he had met so far had struck him as, well, a little geeky. They were all so earnest, so in awe of the Liberal regime of the day and Prime Minister Pierre Elliott Trudeau in particular. But after a couple of sessions at his first national party convention, the prospects were definitely looking up.

The posters aimed at youth, for instance, were kind of cool, he thought. Bold black-and-white graphics declared: "You're young. You're committed. You have ideals. You want to shake up things in the Liberal Party. We dare you."

There was definitely some attitude at this convention. At one of the early sessions, a young law student named Alf Apps slapped a piece of paper down in front of Mahoney. Apps had turned the sentiments of the poster into some bold black-and-white text of his own. Mahoney looked over the resolution that Apps was planning to put on the floor of the party's youth gathering, which preceded the weekend's bigger full-party convention.

It described Liberal backroom brokers as "a cancer" on the party and condemned what it called a prevailing attitude "that party loyalty requires loyalty to a certain narrow and intolerant Liberalism or group of persons within the party." It called for the Liberal grassroots to take back their beloved party from the cynical operatives in government. Though Apps didn't name his targets in the resolution, he was happy to tell reporters that he was referring to Senator Keith Davey, the "Rainmaker," and Trudeau's principal secretary, James Coutts.

Mahoney could hardly believe his eyes. Liberals don't do things like this, he thought.

Not in the past, perhaps, but change was coming. By the fall of 1982, Canada's "natural governing party," as it was immodestly named, had been in office for all but six months of the past twenty years. Right around the time of this convention, two major political books were being released, testaments to the Liberal dynasty and its main achievements in this decade. One was *Grits*, by Christina McCall-Newman, an intimate look at the people and forces behind Pierre Trudeau's Liberals. The other was *The National Deal*, an account of Trudeau's successful patriation of the Constitution, by *Globe and Mail* reporters Robert Sheppard and Michael Valpy. McCall's *Grits* was selling briskly outside the convention hall.

The Liberals' long reign in power, the subject of these tomes, had come at a price. The government's books were in a mess; spending during the

Trudeau years had been reckless to the point of obscene. His patriation of the Constitution had cost the party its support in the all-important stronghold of Quebec. The separatist Parti Québécois government of René Lévesque had refused to sign and even the federalist Liberals in the Quebec National Assembly had voted against it. The province's dissent had cast a shadow over what should have been a triumphant, symbolic act, when the Queen put her signature to the new Constitution on April 17, 1982.

Anti-Liberal sentiment was running high in the West too, thanks largely to the National Energy Program (NEP), which had been introduced to bring made-in-Canada prices to the oil industry. Instead, it bankrupted many in the resource sector when international oil prices fell dramatically. Liberals were demonized in Alberta, with one Calgary mayor, a plain-talking fellow named Ralph Klein, suggesting that those "Eastern bastards" be left to freeze in the dark. A cauldron of Western discontent bubbled under the Château Laurier this convention. "I'm called a complainer, but I'm tired of losing," Greg Schmidt, a young Alberta Liberal, told reporters.

Idealistic young Liberals were feeling isolated. The pivotal event for many had come a year earlier, when Trudeau hand-picked the quintessential backroom boy, James Coutts, to run in a by-election in the Toronto riding of Spadina. Coutts was defeated in a New Democratic Party upset. Indeed, the Liberals had lost a couple of by-elections recently, always a sign of bigger trouble on the horizon for a governing party.

The three separate pockets of disaffection within the Liberal regime – in Quebec, in the West, and among young people – were giving rise to a mood of broad discontent in the party. The Liberals' political culture was developing a fault line between outsiders and insiders, between the old party establishment and the Grits who wanted to "shake up things." Roaming the halls of the Château Laurier that weekend in November 1982 were two men who would eventually find themselves on opposite sides of that fault line: Paul Martin Jr., the unlikely outsider, and Jean Chrétien, the improbable insider.

Jean Chrétien, with his rough-hewn demeanour, mangled syntax, and street-fighter reputation, appeared very much the anti-establishment figure. He certainly didn't fit the intellectual image of Trudeau Liberalism and there were plenty of signs that the erudite, worldly prime minister regarded Chrétien as a bit too homespun. Yet there was no minister in Trudeau's cabinet who more aptly epitomized all that his government had accomplished and stood for over the past two decades. In a few months, Chrétien would mark his twentieth anniversary as a member of Parliament, his political career as solid as the current Liberal dynasty.

Its achievements and policies belonged to Chrétien in personal ways. A unilingual francophone when first elected in 1963, Chrétien embraced Trudeau's promotion of official bilingualism to help him achieve the heights of cabinet appointment. As justice minister during the recent round of constitutional negotiations, Chrétien had become a national figure: a Quebecer bold enough to be a strong federalist and a man willing to take on the separatists in his own home province. Newly installed as the energy minister, Chrétien had inherited the NEP so hated in the West. In the week before the national convention, newspapers reported that the minister was due to make a statement soon on oil and gasoline prices. The reports also noted, as a given, that Chrétien openly aspired to succeed Trudeau. And why would he not? Jean Chrétien was already comfortably situated at the very centre of power.

Paul Martin Jr., as he was then known, was in a different position at this convention. His pedigree seemed to be that of a Liberal insider, but his experience and his voice placed him well outside. The only son of the venerable Pearson-era politician, Paul Martin Sr., the younger Martin felt the influence of party politics and government service all his life. His very birth had been organized around his father's ministerial schedule. Nell Martin, expecting her first child, had her doctor induce labour on August 28, 1938, so that Paul Edgar Philippe Martin could come into the world a few days before his father was due to sail to England. When young Paul was diagnosed with polio at the age of eight, his father was summoned from a cabinet meeting and flown by government plane to his child's bedside in Windsor.

Yet the Martin progeny, Paul Jr. and his younger sister, Mary-Anne, had also managed to carve out lives far removed from their father's. Paul spent his summers working on fishing boats and in later years aboard deep-sea vessels plying the Beaufort Sea and the North Atlantic Ocean. He went to the University of Toronto, studied philosophy, and then obtained his law degree. Not a particularly stellar student, Martin was more interested in sports and partying. He had a wild streak too and once served a night in jail after getting into a rowdy scuffle outside a Liberal rally in Toronto. Working as a roustabout in the Alberta oilfields, he was fired when he "borrowed" a company truck to attend the Calgary Stampede.

He settled down when he became involved with Sheila Cowan, daughter of one of his father's law partners who lived down the road from the Martin's expansive home in Windsor's old Walkerville district. Sheila was a close friend of Mary-Anne and liked to hang out at the Martin household because it was so different from her own strict home. Mr. Martin was usually away in Ottawa; Mrs. Martin would often be occupied with the parade of visitors that passed through the rambling, former rum-runner's mansion. The Martin children came and went as they pleased. Paul Jr., five years older than his sister, was mostly away at university in Toronto. Sheila and Mary-Anne had almost free run of the house.

Sheila first met Paul when Mary-Anne, in a fit of teenaged rebellion, ran away from home at the age of seventeen. Her brother came back to Windsor to help track her down. With Sheila's assistance, he looked for clues in his sister's bedroom, any notes or diary entries that might lead to her whereabouts. The runaway incident was brief and soon forgotten, but the encounter between Sheila and Paul had a more enduring effect. A year or so later, Paul offered Sheila a ride to the Martin family cottage, along with another couple who spent the entire time necking in the back seat of the car. Sheila kept her eyes forward in the front seat, one hand clutching the armrest of the car door. Paul, driving, was interested only in the shy brunette beside him. He still remembers what she was wearing that day – a crisp, pink dress. It would be two years later, though, before he summoned up the nerve to ask her out, after they ran into each other Christmas shopping at Simpson's department store in downtown Toronto. They were married in Windsor on September 11, 1965, and their first son, Paul William, was born on their first anniversary. Two other sons followed: James (Jamie) in 1969, and David, in 1974.

Martin carved out a career as a young executive with Montreal's influential Power Corp. of Canada, owned by the politically influential Desmarais family, and then on his own as high-flying owner of Canada Steamship Lines. It was Maurice Strong, then president of Power Corp., who persuaded the young law graduate to move to Montreal in 1967 and enter the corporate world. Martin spent his first few years as a corporate troubleshooter – he would be parachuted into one of the firm's shaky holdings to return it to profitability. The young Martin suffered from no lack of confidence. Strong nearly fired him early on after a meeting with U.S. business leaders, at which the young executive-in-training believed it was his place to hold forth on his views too. Still, he brought an exuberance and toughness to the task that impressed Power's executives; they made him a vice-president within three years. The only real break Martin took from climbing the corporate ladder in these years was in 1968, when he arranged a six months' leave to help out in his father's final, unsuccessful Liberal leadership campaign against Pierre Trudeau. Martin attacked that mission with zeal as well. Though he would claim later that he was unmarked by the experience, he would never be a fan of Trudeau, and he retained vivid recollections of the personal scars that political contests can inflict. "I felt very, very badly for my father," he said in more than one media interview in subsequent years.

In 1971, he left Power Corp. to work at Consolidated Bathurst Inc., only to return to the firm after three years to deal with problems at Davie Shipbuilding Ltd., another of Power's transportation holdings. By 1974, he was president of Power Corp.'s CSL group, and considered one of Montreal's business elite. Sheila and the boys were comfortably housed in Westmount, while Martin, fully bilingual, moved freely between French and English communities. The family bought an old farmhouse in Quebec's Eastern Townships and spent most weekends and holidays in the bucolic countryside near Knowlton, swimming in the slough and puttering about the land.

In 1981, Martin took a high-risk gamble to buy CSL for $189 million in a leveraged buyout with a single partner, Laurence Pathy of Fednav Ltd. in Montreal. With no great financial reserves of his own, Martin borrowed against the assets of his future company and staked his personal wealth as part of the collateral. The day the ink was drying on the deal, interest rates in Canada climbed to an all-time high of 22 per cent. American financial commentators had been predicting that rates would eventually climb as high as 30 per cent. Martin had a hunch that rates would fall, however, and he staked it all to buy CSL. Sure enough, interest rates dropped to 14 per cent over the next year. CSL began an ambitious reorganization, transforming itself from a domestic Great Lakes shipping entity into an emerging multinational shipping firm.

Martin had found his niche, a job that blended his love of business and all things nautical. His passion for ships dated back to his summer jobs on fishing boats near the family's cottage in Southern Ontario. When he travelled to other cities on business or pleasure, he'd stroll down to the docks to inspect the vessels, begging invitations on board to tour the engine rooms.

But politics was percolating in his blood too. His desk at CSL was littered with social-policy papers and readings on the important issues of the day. His father's published memoirs, *The London Diaries*, reveal a son wrestling with his ambitions in the political sphere even as he was advancing in business. On a fishing boat on a summer holiday in 1977, the young Paul sought the elder's counsel: "With his head on a seat cushion, he opened the 'old question': Why should he not run in the next election, if he was assured of a cabinet post? He has the bug, I'm afraid." Paul Sr., according to the diaries, repeatedly advised his son to establish himself in business and wait until he was at least forty-five years old.

The "bug" was almost certainly planted by his experiences during the 1968 leadership campaign. But the younger Martin would always insist that his own ambitions were not about righting any wrong – to say that, in fact, was to insult his father, who had no apologies to make for his legacy. "My father didn't need to be prime minister to have a distinguished career as a politician," Martin would say.

One year ahead of his father's suggested schedule, Martin was feeling the lure of politics strongly enough to make his debut speech at a Liberal convention. He had been a regular fixture at Liberal events all his adult life, attending party gatherings and serving on various panels and boards set up by the party. But the November 1982 speech would be his first keynote performance.

Martin perfectly straddled the insider/outsider divide that troubled the party's youth wing. At age forty-four, he seemed the picture-perfect model for a new generation of Liberals. His father's legacy as one of the architects of Canada's social safety net connected him to the Liberals' expansive heyday, but his business acumen suited the more fiscally restrained future. These were the early 1980s, when successful business figures were celebrities. He wasn't part of the government, but he moved in lofty party circles. Through John Rae, another bright light at Power Corp., he had been introduced to Jean Chrétien, once Rae's boss in government in Ottawa. In company with other high-ranking Liberal players, Chrétien and Martin occasionally took golfing or hunting trips together. It was not unusual for Chrétien to pop by the Martins' Westmount house for brief visits. Sheila Martin remembers a dashing figure in an expensive trenchcoat, always in a hurry, always confident and charming.

The invitation to speak at the youth convention had been extended to Martin by three young Liberals in their early twenties: Theresa (Terrie) O'Leary, who served as a youth director in the central party office in Ottawa, Peter Donolo, president of the party's youth wing in Ontario, and Alfred (Alf) Apps, a law student and Liberal activist from Toronto.

Together, they paid a call on Martin at CSL headquarters in Montreal. They asked for half an hour of his time and were ushered into an impressive suite of offices, with arching windows overlooking Old Montreal, expensive rugs on the floor, and Krieghoff paintings lining the corridors. O'Leary was impressed and a little intimidated too, though it wasn't her style to reveal it. Martin sat them down and asked what he could do for them. They explained their mission: Would he come to Ottawa and speak to the young Liberals?

He was warm, friendly, and surprisingly curious, peppering them with questions about their concerns. Donolo criticized Trudeau's decision to run Coutts in Spadina – a move that exemplified cynicism and backroom control run amok, he thought. Martin stopped him short: "Jim Coutts is a good friend of mine," he said. Donolo's heart sank. So much for their attempt to find a Liberal outsider. O'Leary kept looking at the clock, convinced that this busy captain of industry would shoo the kids from his office. Three hours sped by before the meeting ended, with the trio having secured Martin's agreement to speak at their convention.

Public speaking wasn't Martin's strong suit in those days. Any training he had received was purely by osmosis. He could hold his own around the boardroom table and he wasn't afraid to pipe up at social gatherings. But when Montreal's corporate heavyweights got together and it came time for the big speech of the evening, the task usually fell to the president of the Iron Ore Company of Canada, Brian Mulroney. Martin marvelled that Mulroney leapt enthusiastically to any public-speaking opportunity, using that sonorous voice to seduce his listeners. Everyone knew that Brian was keeping the voice in tune for his next run at the Tory leadership, which was less than a year away.

On the day of Martin's presentation at the convention, his delivery was somewhat wooden and he was obviously nervous. Nevertheless, he had done careful research for this debut political appearance and knew what the kids wanted to hear. They wanted reassurances that the Liberals still stood for strong economic nationalism. Richard Mahoney listened closely and felt relieved. New Liberalism was all well and good, but no one wanted to disavow totally the Trudeau legacy. Mahoney noticed that Martin appeared to be more at ease during the bracing question-and-answer session. With about three hundred young Liberals in the room, Martin endorsed the program that was Chrétien's headache. "I support the thrust of the National Energy Program and I support Canadianization," he said.

He also put his business backing behind the Liberals' controversial Foreign Investment Review Agency (FIRA) – with a caveat. "[With FIRA,] I think they went too far too fast, but I'm proud to have been part of the party that brought it in. FIRA does nothing more than what other countries do behind closed doors – anyone who's ever tried to buy a business in the U.S. will recognize that." Rest assured, he told the young Liberals, "the Canadian business community supports economic nationalism more than many might assume."

Richard Mahoney was impressed by Martin's maiden convention speech, but he was genuinely delighted by the new friendships he was making that weekend. Bruce Ogilvie, a short, handsome young Westerner, was the nephew of Liberal cabinet minister Otto Lang. Originally from Humboldt, Saskatchewan, currently a law student in Calgary, Ogilvie was head of the Alberta Young Liberals association and a candidate at this convention for national youth president. Here was a fellow more in keeping with Mahoney's image of the ideal politician-to-be – relaxed, charming, sincerely interested in everyone he met. "Bruce was what you'd call 'inclusive' today," Mahoney said. "He remembered your name, asked a lot of questions, and wanted to introduce everyone else around." One suchintroduction was to a boisterous fellow who seemed to be Ogilvie's sidekick – David Herle, a twenty-year-old bearded student from Saskatchewan, whose fashion tastes, running to simple white shirts and double-knit slacks, slightly alarmed Mahoney. There was also Herle's fondness for Elton John, who was definitely uncool in these days of punk rock's surging popularity. Still, Herle had an easy laugh, a reckless sense of humour, and he was obviously a great pal of Ogilvie. Any pal of Bruce had to be a good guy.

The two Saskatchewan boys had bonded at a provincial Liberal youth gathering in Saskatoon in the fall of 1981. As always, the meaningful work and the real fun were found after the meetings were over, in the hospitality and hotel suites. One evening the more raucous partiers engaged in a game of beer-bottle tossing, aiming their missiles out the window and toward a distant field beyond the Holiday Inn parking lot. Herle got into the act, putting his best football-throw spin on the bottle. But a gust of wind veered his projectile suddenly sideways toward a line of guest vehicles, where it landed with a godawful smash. A wary reconnoitre a couple of hours later led to the discovery of a broken windshield on a 1972 Plymouth Valiant – Herle's own car.

The Saskatchewan meeting gave Terrie O'Leary her first experience with Western Canada and western Liberals too. O'Leary, the daughter of Irish-Canadian parents, raised in the same Toronto neighbourhood as Mahoney, attended this convention in her capacity as a youth worker with the party's national office. Petite, blonde, with a rapid-fire style of speaking and take-charge manner, O'Leary was responsible for tracking youth activities and membership for the federal Liberals. After the Saskatchewan meeting, she changed her travel plans to join Bruce Ogilvie and other members of the Alberta delegation in a van back to Calgary, instead of returning directly to her office in Ottawa. Ogilvie told her she had to see the Prairies, and O'Leary, like Mahoney, found his enthusiasms infectious.

The big news out of the 1982 convention was the youth wing's bid to unsettle the party's old guard. Alf Apps's youth convention resolution made it to the full party convention on Saturday afternoon, as Resolution 40. Party delegates voted overwhelmingly in favour of the anti-backroom protest. To the media, party elders praised the youngsters for their chutzpah, even if privately they cursed their upstart ambitions. Monday-morning headlines in the major newspapers focused on the grassroots' appetite for renewal and reform.

For the next couple of years, the group around Bruce Ogilvie stayed in touch, despite their distances. Herle went back to Saskatchewan, Ogilvie returned to law school in Calgary. Mahoney remained in Ottawa, also in law school, while O'Leary moved to Montreal and McGill University in the fall of 1983 for a degree in economics. O'Leary was a prodigious collector of useful information – articles, research papers, or cartoons – which she would methodically copy and mail to her buddies. All remained dedicated members of the Liberal party. Ogilvie was president of the youth wing, and Herle and Mahoney became members of his elected executive.

Summers would find them working together in Ottawa, thanks to a student-job program that employed sixty young Liberals in various ministers' offices. In those days, it was not a sin to land jobs through partisan connections and this was a blatantly Liberal-friendly employment scheme. But even as these young Grits moved closer to the inner workings of Liberal government, they felt their outsider status no less. They hadn't lost their desire for renewal in the Liberal party and in the government, which seemed to grow more tired and unpopular with each passing month.

Brian Mulroney had won the Progressive Conservative party leadership in June 1983. He was positioning the Tories as the true advocates of disaffected Canadians, painting the Liberals and their policies as out of touch with the real values of the nation. Mulroney's denunciations resonated with the public; they reverberated even within the Liberal party. Ironically, it seemed that a Conservative was ultimately destined to shake up things in the complacent Liberal regime.

In early 1984, with Trudeau's resignation anticipated and new leadership increasingly the preoccupation in Liberal circles, the "outsider" sentiment began to coalesce around one candidate, John Turner, the former finance minister, who had parted ways with the Trudeau government in 1975, retreating to private law practice in Toronto. For the past several years, Turner had lurked at the fringes of the party, where he remained a saviour-like figure in the eyes of many. He aroused hopes for a fresh vision that would harness those streams of discontent in the West, in Quebec, and among young Liberals. Herle and Mahoney especially were keen on the idea of a Turner-led Liberal party and looked for opportunities to support him. They had become enchanted with the Turner so glowingly described in McCall-Newman's book – "a Liberal dream in motion," she called him. Herle had gone to a Turner speech out West a couple of years earlier and quizzed him on his opposition to the National Energy Program. How could Turner buck a policy so integral to the Liberal firmament in Ottawa? "Young man," Turner told him, "the Liberal party is a big tent, a big tent."

Trudeau finally took his walk in the snow on February 28, 1984, and the battle to succeed him began at once. Turner declared his candidacy, then Jean Chrétien joined in, followed by no less than five other Liberal cabinet ministers, albeit with significantly lower national profiles than either Turner or Chrétien. There was Don Johnston, the minister of state for economic development; John Roberts, minister of employment; Indian Affairs Minister John Munro; Justice Minister Mark MacGuigan; and Agriculture Minister Eugene Whelan. Turner was the only candidate not in the government, making him the immediate favourite.

Bruce Ogilvie was by then working in John Roberts's office, and he persuaded Herle, O'Leary, and Mahoney to come on board his boss's leadership campaign. Roberts was earnest and patrician in bearing. Like Johnston, he talked a lot about reinjecting vitality and ideology into Liberalism. Though they all knew that Roberts's chances of victory were slight, given his limited campaign resources and name-recognition outside

Ottawa, they were attracted by the chance to do serious political work: travelling, strategizing, making decisions. Had they gone with the front-runner's campaign, they would have been relegated to the thankless dog's-body duties that fall to inexperienced partisans – packing rallies, stuffing envelopes, serving as on-cue noisemakers.

Paul Martin, meanwhile, had felt it necessary to issue a news release to counter media speculation about his potential candidacy in this leadership race. "I strongly believe in the ideal of public office and it is my hope to serve in some capacity eventually. However, because of other personal commitments, that time is not now, nor can it be in the near future." As he would explain later, one of those prime "commitments" was CSL and his enormous financial stake in the shipping enterprise.

However, he did have a high-profile assignment in this leadership campaign, one which put him conveniently above the fray but at the centre of attention. Martin was chosen to moderate the leadership debates, rendering him officially neutral. This suited Martin's disposition perfectly: he could be active in the process and friends with everyone. Eddie Goldenberg, Chrétien's right-hand man, found Martin helpful when his candidate's team needed a few CSL-owned Voyageur buses or introductions to Quebec business leaders. Turner's people saw Martin as a kindred spirit in the cause for a new, business-friendly Liberalism. Even Don Johnston's campaign crew thought themselves connected to Martin through Jamie Deacey, one of Johnston's organizers, who had known Martin since childhood.

Onstage during the debates, Martin's role as moderator earned him a positive public profile and some early fans. Pundits noted how quick he was on his feet, how graceful his handling of an unwieldy stage crowded with large egos. Author Norman Snider, in his 1985 book, *Changing of the Guard*, wrote admiringly, "Martin has all the platform smoothness that Turner is lacking. He has a distinct resemblance to the movies' Bill Murray and an easy humour. Martin was the kind of new face the Liberals sorely needed."

Martin benefited from comparison to his stage-mates. Turner was emerging as a stiff performer, slightly rusty on the campaign circuit, much to general surprise. Chrétien, on the other hand, rose from low expectations to be Turner's most serious challenger, with his folksy "straight from the heart" rhetoric. Don Johnston's campaign was also unexpectedly energetic, having attracted another group of young rebel outsiders. Still, Johnston and the other contenders were regarded as little more than also-rans. The race was shaping up to be one between Turner, representing businesslike, pragmatic renewal and change, and the more emotional Chrétien, representing the sentimental heart of the Liberal party.

Turner's victory seemed assured by the time the convention was called to order in June. But the contest was close enough, or the field wide enough, that no candidate was likely to win on the first ballot. Turner's red-and-gold signs dominated one end of the sweltering arena at Ottawa's Landsdowne Park; Chrétien's team waved a sea of white signs at the other. In between, the rest of the candidates and their workers occupied sections of noisy chaos.

John Roberts at least had high spirits on his side. His section of the stands was the loudest, belting out endless repetitions of a campaign song set to the tune of the big-band classic "Pennsylvania 65000." Mahoney, Herle, and Ogilvie were leading the chorus, punching the air, belting out "R-O-B-E-R-T-S" in place of the 6-5-0-0-0 refrain. O'Leary, never an enthusiastic participant in loud, partisan displays, hung back more discreetly in the stands.

The first-ballot results were announced mid-afternoon: 1,593 for Turner, 1,026 for Chrétien. The five other candidates shared about 800 votes between them, which could prove decisive, if they moved as a block. Four of the contenders – Whelan, Munro, MacGuigan, and Roberts – promptly dropped off the ballot. All of them, except for MacGuigan, walked down to Chrétien's end of the arena.

Roberts's decision to join the Chrétien side came as a disappointment to some of his workers. Herle, Mahoney, and Ogilvie were not about to follow him and instead dove into the red-and-gold crowd of Turner supporters for the next ballot. O'Leary, though, went the other way, joining the throngs with Chrétien. Independent and single-minded, this would not be the last time O'Leary would show more willingness than her friends to drift closer to Chrétien's cause when the situation demanded. Herle and Mahoney would always keep a deliberate distance. As for Martin, he remained near the stage, prominent but determinedly neutral throughout. He did not cast a ballot in either the first or second round.

Turner triumphed decisively on the second ballot, with 1,862 votes compared to Chrétien's 1,368. Party president Iona Campagnolo famously declared that Chrétien came "first in our hearts" – a phrase that would echo through the next six years of Turner's troubled leadership.

Almost immediately after becoming prime minister, Turner plunged the country into a general election campaign. That meant another summer of deep politicking for the eager quartet. Herle and Ogilvie were working in the office of Finance Minister Marc Lalonde. O'Leary too spent some time in the Finance offices, working on a new system of budget consultations designed to allow more public involvement. Once the election was called, however, Herle and Ogilvie were keen to get out and help campaign in their home province of Saskatchewan. One of Lalonde's former assistants, Doug Richardson, was running in Saskatoon East and the finance minister happily agreed to the boys' request to lend him a hand. "You can't leave me behind!" O'Leary lamented when she heard the news. Somehow, she wrangled Lalonde's permission to join her buddies on the campaign trail.

Mahoney stayed behind in the capital, serving as co-chair of the national youth campaign for the election. The four talked constantly on the phone, trading campaign gossip and speculation. Though the polls held in the Liberals' favour in the early days, it seemed much of the Grits' energy had been spent on the leadership contest and internal party wrangling. It sometimes felt like the election was a mere afterthought. Brian Mulroney and the Tories started to make inroads where the Liberals were the most vulnerable, in the West and in Quebec.

Around 5 a.m. on July 13, the phone rang at Mahoney's apartment in Ottawa. David and Terrie were on the phone, terribly distraught. At first, Mahoney didn't grasp what they were trying to say, and told them to call back later when he was awake. Then he absorbed their horrible news: Bruce Ogilvie, their centre of gravity, their compass, was dead, killed in a car crash on a bad patch of road in rural Saskatchewan.

Everything else that followed in the campaign, including the Liberals' humiliating defeat, paled in significance for the three friends. O'Leary,

Mahoney, and Herle were now bound together by mourning and a lasting sense of loss. They helped set up a scholarship in Ogilvie's honour, with seed money contributed by Martin. On September 4, the mighty Liberal Party of Canada also learned a lesson in loss – voters returned only forty Liberals to the House of Commons. The wilderness years were about to begin, years that would pit the party establishment in Ottawa against the increasingly defiant grassroots.

Jean Chrétien won his seat in 1984, but the result was bittersweet. The bruised feelings of the leadership defeat were still evident. Sitting in Shawinigan with Roy MacGregor of the *Ottawa Citizen* while the results came in on September 4, Chrétien kept a tense vigil to see whether Turner would be among the scores of Liberal casualties. MacGregor described that scene vividly in a column he wrote much later.

"A single twitching muscle in his right cheek betrays his anxiety. He waits with a certainty that John Turner will fall in Vancouver and fall forever, but finally, when even the toughs have ceased to prowl, the news comes that Turner has taken the lead in Quadra. Without a word, Chrétien rises and heads toward the open door. When he reaches it, he turns briefly. 'I might be back,' he says, then stabs his hands deep into his pockets and heads off down the street."

Chrétien lasted a little more than a year under Turner's leadership before he decided to abandon the Commons seat he had held for almost a quarter-century. It was a black time for Chrétien, as biographer Lawrence Martin revealed in his book, *The Will to Win*. Chrétien was constantly marginalized by the man who had bested him in the leadership race. He had to get approval for his every move from junior-level staffers around Turner. Chrétien's pick for the Quebec party presidency, Francis Fox, was rejected by Turner, in what Chrétien condemned publicly as a double-cross. As Lawrence Martin noted, Chrétien's wife, Aline, was as angry as her husband at his treatment by the party. "He doesn't have to take this shit," she said in a chippy aside to CBC interviewer Jason Moscovitz when Chrétien finally announced his resignation in 1986. Chrétien, after a quarter-century inside the Liberal power establishment, would now relegate himself to outsider's status. It was a strategy that had worked for John Turner and Pierre Trudeau; now he would try to make it work for him.

While Chrétien was moving toward his exit from front-line politics, Paul Martin began to consider seriously making an entrance. He had now reached the magic age of forty-five, the age at which his father deemed it appropriate to consider changing careers, and "the bug" was taking hold. In 1985, in a wide-ranging interview with a business reporter at the *Montreal Gazette*, Martin mused candidly about his career-change options. It was either serve in the Third World or go into politics. "I really am torn between the two," he said.

Martin would claim that he was a reluctant, late convert to politics in the mid-1980s, but as newspaper interviews and his father's diaries showed, the decision to enter politics was more inevitable than he liked to admit. He was preoccupied with making a mark on the world. "He eloquently explained that, 'if at the end he had not done something to help his fellow men, let us assume in the underdeveloped world, he would be unhappy,'" his father recorded in *The London Diaries*.

Martin often said that in a perfect world, he would have become a research scientist; this, in his mind, being one of the higher callings in a modern era. He devoured books by science writers and even sought out Nobel laureate Stephen Hawking for a personal audience to discuss his theories. Lacking a scientific aptitude himself, however, Martin fixed on politics or Third World aid as his new, mid-life frontier. The interest in the Third World was fed largely by his old mentor, Maurice Strong, who was beginning to expand his international influence in the 1980s as secretary-general of the United Nations Conference on the Human Environment. The interest in politics was rooted in his father's career, unquestionably, but it was encouraged by the people with whom Martin was choosing to surround himself at Canada Steamship Lines.

David Herle had joined CSL in the fall of 1985, at the age of twenty-seven. Earlier that year, while still living in Saskatchewan, Herle had persuaded

Martin to speak to a party gathering there. Boldly, Herle walked up to Martin after the speech, ostensibly to introduce him to his mother, Magdalena. He took the opportunity to declare to Martin: "If you decide to run for the Liberal leadership, I'll work for you."

Martin laughed. "I'll keep that in mind," he said. A few months later, Herle wanted to move east, to be closer to a young woman from Montreal he was seeing. Boldly again, he got on the phone to Martin and asked if he could work at CSL. After some weeks Martin offered him a job, which, though corporate, had a political flavour. Herle's main task would be to build a coalition of interested parties around the shipping industry. Believing that the Association of Canadian Shipowners was not broadly based enough to be sole spokesman on issues relating to maritime commerce in Canada, Martin wanted Herle to draw others – farmers, municipalities, manufacturers – into a larger organization. The effort culminated in the formation of the Chamber of Maritime Commerce, where Herle eventually served as general manager.

Dennis Dawson was a former Liberal MP from Quebec City whose career in elected office ended in 1984 when he was just thirty-one years old. Martin had phoned him the day after his defeat and offered him a job if he decided that the business world was attractive. Dawson had pursued a master's degree in business administration and ended up on the staff of CSL in 1985. Dawson's job involved the CSL-owned Voyageur bus lines and stick-handling its problems through the provincial government. Pierre Deniger, another defeated Quebec Liberal, also worked at the shipping firm.

For these young politicos, CSL provided an excellent introduction to the corporate world. Martin was a friendly, if sometimes volatile, boss. They came to understand his tendency to heated outbursts and they learned how to deal with them: yell back and then forget the argument the next day. Everyone who had ever worked with Martin appeared to have mastered this technique and few walked away. Martin's family operated the same way.

Herle and Dawson also learned useful business skills. But whatever Martin was teaching these young Liberals about business life, they were teaching him twofold in matters of politics. Dawson introduced Martin to more members of the provincial Liberal party, already a very different creature from its federal counterpart and much more Quebec-nationalist-leaning. Herle kept Martin connected to the West. Throughout the late 1980s, Martin organized fundraisers in Montreal on behalf of Saskatchewan's penurious Liberal party, then led by a young politician named Ralph Goodale, who held the only Grit seat in the legislature. In a single evening, Martin's business connections could net as much as $50,000 or more for the Saskatchewan Liberals, enough to finance almost entirely the leader's office budget. Dawson and Herle, active on Turner's behalf federally, were also keeping Martin in close proximity to the tumultuous events unfolding inside the natural governing party – which found itself in the uncomfortable position of not governing at the moment.

As required by the Liberal party's constitution, John Turner's leadership faced a review vote at the Liberal convention planned for the fall of 1986. Chrétien's loyalists, plus many members of the old Trudeau establishment, were agitating for the leader to be dumped. The former backroom operators resented their declining influence; others, like David Collenette, the former multiculturalism minister from Toronto, chafed at what they saw as ungracious behaviour in victory by the new Turner team. Publicly, Chrétien did all he could to keep his profile high, releasing his best-selling memoirs, *Straight from the Heart*, and appearing at every rubber-chicken event that would have him. Quietly, Chrétien's former leadership team built support on the ground to challenge Turner.

Richard Mahoney was now the president of the federal young Liberals, a job he inherited upon Ogilvie's death and earned himself in an election in 1985. Herle was running to succeed him when his term ended at the 1986 convention. Fully committed to Turner, Herle and Mahoney became charter members in the Friends of John Turner movement, a group formed specifically to mount a defence against this rear-guard assault on the leader from the likes of Chrétien or the former party establishment.

It was a rough but enlightening initiation in the arts of internal party warfare. The fight was for leadership convention delegates – who could claim more in each riding. Herle threw himself into pitched battles at the riding level all over the country. Mahoney was also fighting for Turner in his capacity as youth president, especially in Ottawa, where he could see some of the most senior Chrétien operatives in action. At one meeting in the capital to select delegates for the convention, Eddie Goldenberg approached Mahoney just as the voting was due to begin. It was Mahoney's job that evening to get out the pro-Turner vote. Goldenberg, smiling, came over and shook Mahoney's hand and kept shaking it, asking about the young law student's future plans. Would he be interested, perhaps, in prospects at Lang Michener, where Chrétien and Goldenberg were now based in private practice? Mahoney, agitated as the voting deadline ticked down, didn't know whether to pull away rudely to do his political duty or stay and talk about his career plans. He finally freed himself at the last moment to cast his own vote at the meeting, where Turner's forces prevailed.

As Martin's friends in the party rushed to the leader's defence, the CSL owner came to be seen as a Liberal more in the Turner mould. Martin wasn't particularly close to Turner personally, but both were perceived as more business-friendly than the Liberals drawn to Trudeau or Chrétien. Martin was growing ever-more active in the Turner party establishment and made hundreds of phone calls on his behalf, before and after the leadership review.

Turner won the review vote by a convincing margin of three to one. David Herle was elected youth president of the party. But the convention itself had produced scars and deepened divisions between Chrétien and Turner forces. David Collenette, the national director of the party, who was supposedly above the fray, aroused the enmity of Turner's people when he stepped in to act as a bodyguard for Chrétien in the midst of one wild scrum. The tactics used on both sides, the rough stuff and the sneaky techniques, sharpened enmity among Liberals. Inside Turner's circle, no one believed that the pro-Chrétien team was totally vanquished, but it had been stalled for now.

Turner had asked Martin to head up a candidate-recruitment effort, to find new and promising Liberals to replenish the MPs' ranks depleted by the devastating 1984 loss. Martin travelled the country, meeting and evaluating dozens of individuals and duly recording the details in what came to be known as "the black book." He would write down the person's name, then make notations to remind him of everything from the particulars of spouses, children, and hobbies to details of conversations he'd had. If the

person was a former Liberal MP, the abbreviation S.A.L.D would sometimes appear beside the name. This was Martin's curious way of noting the
type of sympathy call he had made to Dawson in the wake of 1984 election.
It stood for "spoke after last defeat." The abbreviation showed that Martin
was learning the finer details of political networking – powerful organizations are built on just such attention to personal outreach, especially when
potential allies are feeling down.

Herle and Dawson would pore over the book in the offices at CSL,
imagining a dream team of Martin supporters for the time when their
boss took the expected plunge into politics and a leadership campaign.
These young Grits were still preoccupied with party renewal. Dawson was
one of the founders of a Liberal ginger group known as the Grindstone
Liberals, named after the island near Kingston where they met annually.
The group was the brainchild of Blair Williams, the party's national direc-
tor, who conceived it as almost a spiritual retreat for reform-minded
Liberals. Martin loved the whole idea of Grindstone – even its rustic,
camp atmosphere – and was an enthusiastic participant in the early
years, contributing financially to the launch of its newsletter, *De Novo*.
Other original members included Rick Anderson, the son-in-law of Blair
Williams, who would become a key strategist in the Reform party, and
Mike Robinson, a lobbyist and chief financial officer of the Liberal party,
who would serve as campaign boss of Martin's leadership organization in
1990. The fact that it took place outside strict party structures made the
discussions more freewheeling – just Martin's style.

Those who came to know Martin in these circles had no doubts that he
had no doubts he would someday run for the leadership of the party; it was
just a question of when. So casually was it assumed that neither Herle nor
Dawson – nor even Martin – could recall the specific moment of decision
to run for office or to seek the leadership. The two goals were twinned in
their mind and in Martin's.

When he turned seriously to the possibility of running for office, Martin
did his usual mass consultation by telephone, canvassing widely on whether

and how he should enter elected politics. He received plenty of encouragement. Friends told him he would be seen as a prize Liberal catch and an obvious successor to Turner. Indeed, his name was already being bandied about some circles as a contender. His name had crept on to some of the polls circulating at the time of the 1986 leadership review as a potential alternative to Turner or Chrétien. Closer to home, however, Martin was getting very different advice.

Neither his mother, Nell, nor Paul Martin Sr. were delighted by the notion of their son entering politics. "My father thought that my life was pretty good and why the hell would I give it up for politics? My mother never liked politics," Martin said later. Sheila wasn't enthused either. She knew that it would take a toll on his time with his family.

In the midst of this deliberation process, Martin and Chrétien ran into each other and had a candid conversation about leadership prospects. Chrétien advised Martin not to run in Montreal at all; if he had leadership designs, he should run as a candidate in his hometown of Windsor. Chrétien reminded Martin of the Liberals' policy of *alternance* between leaders from French and English Canada. By this reasoning, it was Chrétien's turn next time, since Turner was from English Canada. When Chrétien left, after a couple of elections, Martin could step up as the English-Canadian successor from Windsor.

Martin thought the idea was ridiculous. He had, after all, lived in Montreal for twenty-five years. He cast about for a riding, subjecting the decision to his usual obsessive concentration and massive consultation. Traditionally "safe" Montreal seats, such as Notre Dame de Grace and Mont Royal, were out because they were already held by Liberal incumbents. Martin didn't want to pick an overly affluent area either, wanting to temper his reputation as a rich man's Liberal. In the end, Martin picked Lasalle-Emard, a riding on the lower eastern tip of the island of Montreal – not one of the city's more picturesque districts. It had a mix of anglophones and francophones, as well as sizable Spanish- and Italian-speaking communities. The average household income was $35,000. More than any other riding in his home city, Lasalle-Emard reminded Martin of Windsor. (He bought a townhouse in the riding in 1987, to prove that he wasn't a parachute candidate, but he never did fulfill his promise to move into the home and it was eventually sold in the early 1990s.)

The 1988 Liberal election campaign began poorly. A few days after the official kickoff, John Turner, nursing a bad back, hobbled into Montreal to announce the party's day-care policy. All the local candidates were there, including Paul Martin.

After Turner outlined the main points – 400,000 new day-care spaces over seven years, plus tax breaks and tax credits for working families – reporters began to examine the numbers. The hastily produced handout did not explain how the program would provide double the Tories' promised spaces for the same $6.4 million. Worse, no one around Turner could explain the day-care plan in detail. Red-faced aides tried to handle the media's aggressive questioning but were unable to salvage the event. Martin looked on, taking it all in. How could the party be so ill prepared? Whose idea was it to unveil a policy that no one could properly explain?

Stumbling on, the Liberals' only hope was to stake their fortunes on a larger issue. In 1988, that issue was free trade. Turner had positioned the entire party squarely in opposition to Brian Mulroney's proposal for a Canada-U.S. free trade deal. "Let the people decide," was one of his favourite refrains.

John Webster, the blond, boyish-looking Toronto Grit, was the Liberals' election campaign manager in 1988. One of the key strategists behind Turner's leadership and leadership-review victories in 1984 and 1986, Webster was also closely tied with the Ontario Liberals, then in power under David Peterson.

Among his many problems in this campaign, Webster was getting grief from the first-time candidate in Lasalle-Emard, who refused to stay on script when the focus shifted to free trade. While Turner was waging what he called the "fight of his life" against Mulroney's trade deal, Paul Martin was talking up the virtues of free trade in principle. The media picked up on the contradiction, wondering what this said about Turner's ability to control his candidates.

With every news article that showed Martin off message, Webster would pick up the phone and dress him down. Martin, with all the confidence of a rookie, would not be restrained. "When I'm prime minister, you're never going to be my minister of external affairs," he'd say to Webster.

"Don't worry," Webster would reply. "At the rate we're going, neither of us has to be concerned."

Chrétien was not a candidate in the 1988 campaign, but he and his band of disaffected Liberals were players of a different sort. Chrétien's supporters had made a last-minute, desperate bid to depose Turner in the months leading up to the election. In April 1988, Senator Pietro Rizzutto, Chrétien's Quebec organizer from the 1984 leadership, had circulated a petition that was eventually signed by twenty-two members of the Liberal caucus, imploring Turner to resign. That revolt was quashed, but the Liberals' lame performance in the early days of the campaign stirred rebellion again. It built quietly, but came to light just as Turner was starting to prepare for the television debates against Mulroney.

CBC-TV had learned, it said, that Turner's core election organizers had asked him to step down in the middle of the campaign. Senior journalists Don Newman and Peter Mansbridge revealed how a mutiny building in the ranks, fed by Liberals who wanted Jean Chrétien at the helm, had turned into a high-level coup attempt. Spooked by the party's shaky start, the party's senior organizational team got together October 14 to review possible salvage efforts. The election co-chairs, Senator Alasdair Graham and André Ouellet, were at the meeting, as were John Webster, Senator Michael Kirby, and Mike Robinson. The group discussed Turner's bad back, the obvious pain he was enduring, and the negative media coverage received by the campaign. They also discussed whether Turner, facing these realities, might offer to step down.

For Webster and Robinson, firm Turner supporters, this was just idle speculation. But the next day, André Ouellet paid a Saturday-morning call on Turner's chief aide, Peter Connolly, and briefed him on the discussion, including the part about Turner voluntarily stepping down. Ouellet explained that Chrétien, more popular in the polls, would serve as acting leader through the election campaign, after which an official leadership vote could be held. Turner could announce his departure as leader immediately, in the interests of his health. Connolly, skeptical, nonetheless delivered the message to Stornoway. A furious John Turner dismissed the idea as preposterous and declared he would do no such thing.

The whole incident might have blown over, but then word leaked to the media. The explosive story painted a picture of a Liberal party reduced to a state of total dysfunction, unfit even to knit its insider-outsider battles into a unit capable of governing. This, and a negative advertising campaign launched by the Tories to exploit Turner's weak leadership, helped sink the Liberals' fortunes.

Martin's friends, many of them diehard Turner supporters, were infuriated by the coup attempt, but the rookie candidate only nodded distractedly at news of this mid-election drama. Martin was fretting, worried he would lose in Lasalle-Emard. Now that he was in the game, he was entirely immersed and on edge. Dennis Dawson, helping to run his local campaign, fought off repeated efforts by Liberal party headquarters to tour Martin to other ridings. Martin believed any minute away from Lasalle-Emard would cost him precious votes.

Already, Dawson sensed a certain ambivalence in the party establishment toward Martin. While he was regarded as a star candidate and a valuable asset in 1988, Martin was also viewed with some suspicion by Turner and by Chrétien's forces. They saw Martin's ambitions as a threat, Dawson realized. Martin himself was perplexed by the tension, not understanding what he had done to invite it. He was beginning to learn that it was impossible to be in politics and be everyone's friend.

He was also taken aback when his old business colleague, Brian Mulroney, waltzed into the riding in the last week of the campaign to help boost the Tory candidate's chances. Naively, Martin had assumed that Mulroney would keep a gentlemanly distance while he made his bid to join the ranks of the elected. Instead, the prime minister came to LaSalle-Emard to denounce the Liberals as "Luddites" for resisting free trade. "Anti-investment, anti-trade, anti-business, anti-American and anti-progress – this kind of attitude would cripple Quebec's growth," Mulroney said.

This high-level intervention was worrying. Martin figured that Mulroney wouldn't have bothered with the riding if it were a lost cause for the Tories. He spent the last days of the campaign at a nervous, fevered pitch, infecting everyone around him with the fear of defeat.

Sheila Martin could barely watch the results come in on the night of November 25, an aversion she'd retain through subsequent elections, even when Martin's victory was assured. This first election, though, justified some of her jitters. The result was painfully close: Martin won, but only by about a thousand votes. Conservatives sailed to a second majority government, but the Liberals could take some comfort that Martin, along with thirty-nine other new MPs, had doubled the party's seats in the House of Commons to eighty-two.

It was over for John Turner, of course. Just a few months after the election, in May 1989, he announced he was stepping down as Liberal leader. Chrétien was waiting, having earned his heir-apparent status while out of government. Martin decided he would not hesitate, and joined the queue as well. Another insider-outsider battle for the party's leadership was about to begin.

Within days of Turner's resignation, Martin hired a new executive assistant, none other than Richard Mahoney. He had finished law school by then, and had joined the Toronto law firm run by former Trudeau cabinet minister David Smith. In Mahoney, Smith saw a younger version of himself, a man who liked to be a player but who didn't take himself or his grudges too seriously, a kindred spirit for the fun side of politics.

Mahoney had tried to enlist Smith's support for Martin in early 1989, but Smith told him flatly that it was Chrétien's turn this time. (Smith had supported Turner in 1984.) They agreed to disagree. Several months later, Mahoney went back to Smith and said he had a chance to work full-time for Martin, to be his right-hand man through the leadership campaign. Smith understood completely and sent Mahoney off with his blessing.

Mahoney had come a long way from the young Liberal recruit at the 1982 convention. Thanks to an innate charm and a self-deprecating wit, he was well connected with Liberals all over Canada, keeping up to date on the latest gossip and political chitchat. This was precisely the kind of person that Martin, no expert in those arts, needed to help smooth the glad-handing required of a leadership candidate. Martin joked that Mahoney sometimes forgot he was hired to put that charm to work for the candidate. "Richard was supposed to stay with me as I worked the room. The problem was that I always accompanied him while he worked the room."

The opening skirmish between the contestants revolved around the convention's timing. A brief leadership campaign would favour Chrétien, whose five years of effort had given him an impressive strength among the party rank and file. Anyone who wanted to be a serious contender – namely Martin – would need a long time to accumulate any significant challenge. Chances were good, though, that the Turner-controlled party apparatus on the national executive would look favourably on a long race to beat back Chrétien, whom they saw as the scourge of their years in power. Strategically, Chrétien's gambit to take the leadership from outside had earned him heir-apparent status, but on this issue, he was now at a disadvantage.

In mid-June, the Liberal party brass met to decide the date. By early afternoon on the day of the national executive meeting, various members were telling reporters waiting outside that the Turner-Martin forces had prevailed: that a long leadership race was in the works, with the date of the convention likely to be June 23, 1990. Some of the reporters blinked at their calendars: June 23, 1990, was the deadline for the ratification of the Meech Lake constitutional accord.

Meech was a pivotal and explosive issue within the Liberal realm, provincially and federally. Signed by Mulroney and all ten premiers in spring 1987, it was a constitutional accord designed to make Quebec a signatory to the Constitution. Under the deal, which all provinces would have to endorse in their legislatures within three years, Quebec would be recognized in the Constitution as a distinct society, with guarantees of greater influence in federal institutions, while all provinces would have greater flexibility to opt out of federal spending programs. It was supported by all parties in the House of Commons, including the Turner-led Liberals, who were still trying to reconcile the old Trudeau-era schisms between federal and provincial Grits in Quebec.

But the official Liberal party position in favour of Meech did not go over well with grassroots Grits outside Ottawa and Quebec, especially after Trudeau weighed in to voice his opposition to the deal. Two provincial governments – Newfoundland and New Brunswick – had turned Liberal since Meech's signing as well, and the deal was imperiled in those two legislatures, as well as in Manitoba, where a Tory government held a shaky minority in co-operation with anti-Meech New Democrats and Liberals.

Chrétien drew a lot of his support from Liberals who opposed Meech, Grits who believed that he would have stood up much more forcefully for the Trudeau vision of Confederation than Turner did. Meech promised to be a major issue in the leadership campaign. But the party's national executive, many of them sympathetic to Martin, did not seem to recognize that the constitutional deadline could have an impact on the contest. It would not be the first time that the Martin team miscalculated on the Meech front.

Over the summer and fall of 1989, Martin pulled together his campaign team and set up headquarters at an office tower just off the Sparks Street Mall in Ottawa. Martin liked to surround himself with people who were gregarious, who networked, and who were fond of spontaneity and risk.

"There are essentially two kinds of people," he says, "those who do, and those who don't. Those who don't never get into trouble. And I don't think you really want them around. Those who do occasionally get into trouble. And when they get into trouble, you say let's not do that again, but if you come down on them like a ton of bricks, then they basically won't do anything any more."

David Herle was named national campaign director and decided to put his law education on hold for a year. (He had left CSL in 1988 to get his law degree at the University of Saskatchewan, though he worked at the shipping firm in the summers.) Terrie O'Leary was with Merrill Lynch in Toronto, but she left her job to serve as the director of organization.

Mike Robinson was a respected consultant in Toronto who had been serving in a voluntary capacity as chief financial officer for the Liberal party, trying valiantly to pull it out of the massive $3-million debt it had accumulated while in opposition. He was thirty-nine years old in 1989 and comfortable enough financially to consider an unpaid stint as Martin's campaign manager. His skills as a no-nonsense political operative who could play hard politics with a smile on his face were well known, and soon tested.

Robinson recognized that he had a lot of work to do to turn Martin into a solid leadership contender. Early in the days of the campaign, Robinson held a dinner at his home to introduce the candidate. Martin was called upon to say a few words. As he spoke, he absentmindedly bent over several times to pick lint balls off the carpet. His audience wasn't sure which was more fuzzy – Martin's words or the little lint collection still cupped in his hand at the end of his speech. More than one person in the room that night wondered if this fellow could be a serious rival to Chrétien.

Robinson had managed to recruit John Webster into the Martin fold, though not without resistance. Webster insisted he had enough scars from fighting the Chrétien team in 1984, when he was a Turner strategist, and through 1986 to 1988, defending Turner's leadership against Chrétien challenges. "I don't need any more pissing matches with them," Webster said. Martin flew to Toronto, to make a personal pitch at John Turner's favourite haunt, Winston's restaurant. The would-be candidate pressured Webster with his enthusiastic embrace of business-friendly Liberalism, the same kind of thinking that had attracted Webster to Turner and to David Peterson. By fall 1989, Webster was on board, helping steer the show in Toronto, where he remained deeply involved with the Queen's Park Liberals.

Two communications aides rounded out the core team at Ottawa headquarters: Jamie Deacey, Martin's childhood neighbour, now a lobbyist with Liberal connections, and Daniel Despins, who had served as the Liberal party's communications director in recent years. Many of Turner's former advisers were with Martin: Mark Resnick, policy director in the Official Opposition Leader's Office, became head of policy for Martin's leadership bid, and Kaz Flinn, a young Nova Scotia Liberal, came over from the party office to work as his Atlantic organizer.

Dennis Dawson oversaw operations in his home province of Quebec. The official Ontario organizer was Tim Murphy, a twenty-nine-year-old lawyer and contemporary of Richard Mahoney, who had come into the party as a Turner supporter too. Most of his Liberal credentials were established at Queen's Park, where he'd served as an aide to Attorney General Ian Scott.

His conversion to Martin's cause was rapid. In October 1989, Murphy was still casually considering the leadership alternatives being bandied about in federal party circles. He attended a meeting organized by John Webster at a dingy Travelodge hotel, and met the tiny crew of Toronto Liberals who had joined the Martin campaign. Heather Reisman, later to become the head of Indigo and then Chapters Inc., was among them. A few weeks later, seized by the chance to get in on the ground floor of a rookie campaign and organization, Murphy arranged a leave of absence from his job at Blake Cassels and was running Martin's Ontario operations out of his apartment. Murphy's roommate, a Conservative supporter, was jarred to come home one day and find Ontario riding maps pinned up on the walls and the phone constantly ringing. It wasn't until January that Murphy moved Martin's Ontario campaign into full-fledged headquarters deep in the heart of the financial district at 2 Toronto Street.

The campaign co-chairs were Iona Campagnolo, the former party president, and Jean Lapierre, a Quebec Liberal MP with a tough reputation and nationalist leanings. As for a platform, Martin drew heavily on the ideas of renewal and reform to appeal to those familiar bands of discontent: young people, Westerners, and Quebec Liberals. He would be the candidate of a new, economically savvy Liberalism, grounded in policies to support employment growth, research and development, the environment, and education.

Many of the core ideas were generated by Martin himself, then filled out into briefing books by a tiny cadre of policy wonks: Alan Alexandroff and Jim de Wilde, business academics from Toronto, were two key contributors behind the scenes. With the help of a brainy history expert and New Democrat–turned–Liberal partisan named John Duffy, Martin produced a policy document extolling an outward-looking, trade-and-aid-obsessed new Canada, one that would push "nationalism without walls." Martin memorized numbers and facts, statistics and case studies. He could rattle off the points of his complicated platform for anyone who asked. What he lacked, however, was a linking theme for all these ideas. The media filled the vacuum, describing him as a "business Liberal" or a "blue Grit."

The number-one issue on the minds of Liberals, however, was the Constitution – not a subject for which Martin had an aptitude. Just a couple of months after he was first elected, at a Liberal caucus retreat in St. John's in January 1989, he had blundered into the debate over whether Meech could be fixed with a "parallel accord," arguing for it, then reversing himself. New Brunswick Premier Frank McKenna was championing this "parallel accord" idea as a way to answer Meech critics while leaving the original accord intact. Turner and Quebec Liberals were dismissive of that plan from the start, but Martin believed, at least for a while, that the idea had merit. At an April 1989 gathering of the old Grindstone group at Montebello, Quebec, where criticism of Meech was the primary topic of conversation, Martin delivered a vague, shaky performance in group discussions, with no one sure what he was trying to say. *Globe and Mail* columnist Hugh Winsor described Martin as "dithering" before the microphones.

Martin's leadership campaign was officially launched in January 1990 with what was intended as an ambitious three-city event. It would start early in Montreal, to emphasize Martin's Quebec connections and local strength. At midday, he'd fly to Toronto to capture the national media based in Canada's largest city at a big-splash announcement at Glendon College. From there, he would head to Windsor to wrap up the day with a rally in the town where the name Paul Martin was still spoken with reverence. The idea was to put the two Martins on display, surrounded by all the loyal supporters who wanted to vault the next generation of the family to high office.

On the appointed day, January 17, Martin arrived at Montreal's Queen Elizabeth Hotel to execute part one.

"Let's be clear. I unconditionally support the Meech Lake Accord with or without a parallel accord," he said to the assembled press.

These words fixed Martin as the pro-Meech candidate in a party that, outside Quebec, was largely opposed to the deal. He didn't utter them mindlessly. Dennis Dawson had encouraged him to adopt a position that would draw Quebec Liberals to his side. The Mulroney years and the constitutional dramas seemed to have reduced the federal Liberal presence in the province to scattered outposts of elderly and anglophone voters. A pro-Meech stand might reinvigorate support for the Grits. Strategically, however, this position would obscure any other substantial differences he had with Chrétien. He would spend most of his time defending his Meech position rather than confronting Chrétien on what he viewed as outdated leadership and policy approaches.

Outside the Queen Elizabeth Hotel, the weather was turning foul. Martin and his team, along with the throng of media following him, raced to the airport to catch their flights to Toronto. But almost all flights were grounded; Dorval and Pearson International Airports were paralyzed by a midwinter fog. Everyone scrambled to change flights, Martin securing himself a spot on a City Express plane to Toronto's Island Airport. Once aloft, however, the flight plan went awry. After some futile circling in the skies, the plane landed late at Pearson. The Glendon event was scrapped, as were all his scheduled interviews with the major TV networks. Martin and his entourage disembarked at the still-unfinished Terminal Three, where passengers were mistakenly streamed into the customs lineup. Martin had to produce evidence of his Canadian citizenship before he was permitted to rush, well behind schedule, to his final engagement of the day.

Down in Windsor, Martin's hometown supporters had resorted to an open bar by early evening in a bid to keep the crowd in the hall. Richard Mahoney just gave the bartender his credit card and decided to let the chits fall where they may. Shaughnessy Cohen, a Liberal lawyer who had run unsuccessfully in the city in 1988, was onstage, pushing Paul Martin Sr. and others to make speeches to keep the crowd entertained.

Martin finally arrived well after most media deadlines. The hope of presenting him as a figure who travelled with ease between Canada's two solitudes got lost in the fog. It was not an auspicious start.

Chrétien's launch the following week was all control and polish. No tri-city extravaganzas for the front-runner, but simply an announcement, carefully delivered, at the Château Laurier Hotel, the very hotel where Trudeau had welcomed Canadians to the 1980s and his party had denounced his backroom operators a couple of years later.

The most impressive feature of Chrétien's campaign launch was the caucus support he could claim – about 40 per cent of the Liberal representatives in the Commons and Senate. Most of these thirty-one MPs and twenty-four senators stood onstage beside a beaming Jean Chrétien, reinforcing his image as the obvious heir and accepted choice of the party's establishment. Martin had only a handful of sitting MPs supporting him.

Chrétien's platform was far simpler than Martin's complicated, numbers-laden program. It had accessible themes: strong leadership and a revival of faith in the federal government. "The central issue in this campaign is none other than leadership itself. This country is thirsting for leadership, for a national leader who can inspire Canadians to dream dreams and strive toward all we can be."

He also used the event to signal his acceptance of the prevailing attitude in the party on the Meech Lake Accord. Meech's failure, he said, "won't be the end of the world. Quebec will have the same powers afterward as it does today." At a subsequent news conference, Chrétien famously compared the Meech impasse to a car stuck in the snow: a situation one could resolve simply by rocking back and forth.

The first of the Liberal leadership debates on January 28, 1990, set the pattern for the months ahead. This was going to be a contest about Meech, about the polarized positions of Martin the New (naive, to the critics) and Chrétien the Familiar (worn, in the eyes of his detractors). It would be another manifestation of the insider-outsider Liberal culture, but one in which Martin found himself on the wrong side of the history now being written.

On the main stage of the Metro Toronto Convention Centre, with respected law professor Bill Graham acting as moderator, the candidates rolled up their sleeves and began the fight. Chrétien and Martin were the front-runners in a large field. Two of the other candidates were members of the Rat Pack, a gang of brash young MPs who enlivened the Liberals' early years in opposition. Sheila Copps, feisty and loud, made it clear at this first debate that her intentions were serious. This was her second precocious run at leadership, having gone against David Peterson for the Ontario leadership in the early 1980s, when she was not yet thirty. John Nunziata was the other Rat Packer in the race. Unlike Copps, he did not position himself as a Turner Liberal, coming out of the gate to condemn the party's support of Meech. Tom Wappel, a rookie MP like Martin, hailed from Scarborough, Ontario, and made no secret of his dedication to the anti-abortion campaign that had fuelled his political career to date. Clifford Lincoln, a former cabinet minister in the Quebec legislature, was onstage for the first debate, but he would pull out of the contest within a month.

All the candidates targeted the high-profile Chrétien. Martin did his fair share of goading. Pointedly, he asked Chrétien whether he believed he could get Quebec to come to the negotiating table in any future constitutional talks. Chrétien accused Martin of trying to have it both ways on Meech, calling for improvements to the deal but saying it should be supported. "I'm not talking on both sides of my mouth on that."

Chrétien ran a classic front-runner's campaign, saying little and giving almost no media interviews. When he did talk to selected reporters one on one, as with Joan Bryden of Southam News, he made no significant statements. The interview with Bryden was conducted by telephone from Florida where Chrétien travelled mid-campaign to take a break. So confident was he of victory that he didn't believe he had to wear himself out with endless appearances.

Martin, on the other hand, was completely accessible and always on the move. At the Liberal leadership forums, held on weekends, Martin was eager to sit down with reporters in sessions where he would invariably end up asking more questions than he answered. He was curious about the journalistic trade: who writes the headlines, who edits the stories, how does a reporter decide how much to write and what to put in the first paragraph? In the evenings, Martin and his people would almost routinely round up a crowd of participants, including reporters, for a dinner and a night on the town. Martin was less host of these events than a bemused straight man for Richard Mahoney's tales of mishaps, miscues, or missed opportunities on the road. Martin would be laughing the loudest, clapping his hands, urging him on. He would have to be dragged away eventually to get a good night's sleep – he was the Candidate, after all – while his team stayed out until all hours.

If Chrétien was having such dinners, the media didn't know about them. The front-runner's organizers moved almost shadowlike through these weekend gatherings, appearing en masse. Chrétien would rush in, surrounded by a phalanx of assistants, and disappear just as quickly into a suite of rooms in the hotel off-limits to reporters. His formal scrums were tidy, brief affairs, light on information and tightly scripted.

Meech was the lead issue at each of the leadership forums, starting in Toronto, then in Yellowknife, Vancouver, Winnipeg, Halifax, ending in Montreal.

The Martin team's strategy was to build momentum early in Ontario, then consolidate that strength with the backing of Quebec Liberals, put off by Chrétien's opposition to Meech. The first stage of that strategy worked reasonably well. Because Ontario had so many ridings, it began delegate-selection meetings two weeks before the rest of the country, in mid-February 1990. Windsor, Martin's hometown, was to be the site of the first meetings. Though there were tough battles with the Chrétien supporters and local Liberal bigwig Eugene Whelan, the Martin team did establish a beachhead in Windsor St. Clair – Martin Sr.'s former riding.

Over the next two weeks in Ontario, the Martin team continued to rack up victories. On March 2, campaign manager Mike Robinson sent a note of congratulations to Tim Murphy. "What a great start," Robinson wrote, recounting what he hastened to point out were the "very honest" results of the first barrage of delegate-selection meetings. Martin's people were already becoming notorious – especially Mahoney and Herle – for exaggerated boasts to the media: "We're winning everywhere." This private correspondence showed that Martin's team did have reason to celebrate. Of the 273 delegates selected in Ontario, Martin had 121, double Chrétien's 61. Sheila Copps was running a respectable third, with 35 delegates, while another 60 or so were undecided, neutral, or yet to be named.

The second part of the strategy – the appeal to Quebec – was less successful. Chrétien had impressive tacticians in the province, the mastermind being Pietro Rizzutto, and the operative, Denis Coderre. Complicating matters was Sheila Copps's surprising appeal in the province. Copps was dating a Quebec Liberal cabinet minister, Lawrence Cannon, and he loaned his organizational resources to her campaign. Organizer Marc-Yvan Côté had also joined her team. (For Dennis Dawson, this was an enormous personal disappointment; he'd believed that his friends, Cannon and Côté, would support Martin.) Copps was giving Martin a run for his money in his home province. The media was impressed with her French, her spunk, and her enthusiastic pro-Meech position, which she articulated far more forcefully than the cautious Martin.

The early surge ended almost as soon as it began. Once voting for delegates started across Canada on March 1, Chrétien's numbers surpassed Martin's everywhere outside of Ontario. His deep roots in the party and his overwhelming caucus support simply swamped the rookie Martin boat. By mid-March, rumours circulated that Martin was out of the race. Onstage at the leadership debates, he stepped up his attacks against Chrétien on the Meech front. Behind the scenes, Martin attempted to broker a truce with the Chrétien team – let's keep Meech off the table, debate other issues. "Rifts within the country should not have been part of the leadership," he argued. Besides, whoever won this contest would not be in a position to do anything about the constitutional deal. It would either be dead or the law of the land by June 23, when the new leader took over.

The Chrétien forces weren't interested in any deal. "I can't imagine how you keep the single biggest public-policy issue of the day off the leadership convention," Eddie Goldenberg said.

Privately, Martin's team knew that the game was lost by April. At the farm one spring weekend, Paul and Sheila sat the boys down and explained that defeat was inevitable. It was one of those classic parental talks about sportsmanship: the fun is in the playing, not the winning; look at all the friends we've made, the people we've met, and the places we've visited. This had been a great adventure for the boys, especially for the eldest, Paul, known as Paul W. to his new friends in the Martin camp. It had also brought father and son to a closer relationship, one result of which was that Paul W. decided to take up a career in the shipping industry. The Martin boys weren't overly distressed by the prospect of defeat, as long as Mom and Dad were okay with it. Jamie didn't like politics at all, anyway. David, only fifteen, wouldn't get hooked until he was older.

The more difficult conversations about the looming defeat were between Martin and his father, who regarded himself as a senior partner in this enterprise and had come to see his son's ambitions as a family project. He worried that by warning his son away from politics all these years, he had kept him from the necessary experience that would harden him to the personal blows that all politicians must learn to weather. Paul Sr. would be up at dawn every morning in Windsor, on the phone with Mahoney (whom he persisted in calling "the organizer" in his daily calls to the office) or with Shaughnessy Cohen, who had somehow become an unofficial minder of the candidate's father in Windsor, ferrying him around on his daily political errands. Paul Sr. was no fool; in his heart, he knew his son was going to lose, but he was determined that it would be a noble fight to the finish.

With the outcome a virtual certainty by April, the Liberal leadership race slipped off the front pages and out of the early lineup of items on the nightly news. The country turned its attention to the perilous state of the Meech Lake Accord, and its rough ride in three provinces: Manitoba, New Brunswick, and Newfoundland. Brian Mulroney had set up a special Commons committee to explore the "parallel accord" compromise proposed by Frank McKenna, but its work was hampered by hardening positions on both sides. Politicians such as Newfoundland Premier Clyde Wells were wary of any compromise forged by the same government that authored the deal; Quebecers didn't understand how a compromise could be anything but a retreat from the basic tenets of the accord. Emotions were rising, fed by dark media predictions and overheated political rhetoric. The assumption in the country was that Quebec would move toward separation if this historic opportunity was lost and this chance to put the province's signature on the Constitution was missed.

Chrétien, meanwhile, was being demonized in Quebec for his opposition to Meech, which he reiterated at every appearance at the leadership forums. Then in early June, on the eve of the final debate, Chrétien gave an interview to *Le Devoir*, in which he was quoted as saying of Meech: "I hope it passes." Though he later claimed he had been misquoted, evidence of his change of heart was apparent behind the scenes, where Chrétien allies such as Goldenberg and Newfoundland MP Brian Tobin were beginning to exert pressure on Newfoundland Premier Clyde Wells and Manitoba's Liberal Leader Sharon Carstairs to end their opposition to the deal.

Shaken by the crisis atmosphere building over the potential collapse of Meech, Chrétien and his team realized that the accord's death could leave any future prime minister with a massive national-unity mess. Tobin, at

Mulroney's behest, had been pressing this message home to Chrétien and company to help lower the temperature over Meech.

Martin and his organization were incredulous at Chrétien's apparent volte-face. After hammering Martin and Copps for the better part of six months on their support for Meech, Chrétien suddenly seemed to be coming over to their side and paying no political price for his inconsistency. There was no hope now for Martin to win the Liberal leadership, but the frustrated team was determined to show Chrétien for the unprincipled opportunist they believed him to be. They decided that the final leadership debate, in Montreal, was an opportunity to wind the campaign to a close with a bang, not a whimper. Martin huddled with his speechwriter, John Duffy, and came up with some hard-hitting lines to portray Chrétien as an inveterate, cynical waffler.

This last debate competed with the larger drama of Meech's final scenes on the same weekend – another unlucky double booking by the Liberals. Brian Mulroney had summoned all of Canada's premiers to Ottawa to try to get around the Meech impasse. On the same Sunday that the Liberals staged their debate in Montreal, Canada's first ministers were at the Museum of Civilization in Quebec, just across the river from Parliament Hill. Most of the national media were camped outside the first ministers' meeting; only a small group of political reporters made the trip to Montreal to watch the Liberal show.

But what a show it was. As usual, the Martin youth could be counted on to kick up a clamour. Jean Lapierre had dragooned a noisy mob of young Quebecers to pack the hall and Martin's squad came with reinforcements from outside the province. Several of the provincial youth presidents – Ontario's Nick Masciantonio, B.C.'s Bruce Young, and Alberta's John Bethel – had brought delegations in mini-buses from Ottawa and Toronto. They swarmed into the room, some of them standing on chairs, and started swaying and chanting, "Le Flip, Le Flop." As the chant grew louder, the swaying became a stadiumlike wave. "Le Flip, Le Flop, Le Flip, Le Flop." Chrétien grew visibly agitated, stabbing his finger in the direction of the mounting chorus. A hard-line gang of Copps's Quebec supporters joined in.

Then, the ugliest chant of all: "Chrétien! Vendu!" Translation: Chrétien,

Sellout. Not all the young Martinites knew what they were saying. The non-French speakers from the West believed for some time, even after the event, that they had been yelling "fondue."

Mark Resnick, standing in the Martin section with a walkie-talkie, was smiling at the kids' spirit, impressed that their candidate's dim chances hadn't dulled his followers' enthusiasm. Suddenly, the walkie-talkie crackled. Liberal party president Michel Robert summoned Resnick behind stage and berated him. "Shut them up! Shut it down!" he warned. Resnick went back into the hall, took one look at the chanting mob, and decided it was impossible to restrain them.

Martin didn't descend to name-calling in the debate itself, but he and Copps went after Chrétien's stand on Meech. "Jean, for the love of God, you want to become prime minister of Canada but you give us no indication where you're going," Martin said. "You have not understood Quebec and you are gambling dangerously with the survival of Canada." The kids kept up their chant. Chrétien glared. He insisted he hadn't changed his position but that Meech needed to be changed. The chanting carried on: "Vendu, vendu." Just offstage, Eddie Goldenberg felt sick, so did John Rae. They stood there, asking themselves – not for the last time – why can't Paul control these people? The fact that Martin wouldn't take responsibility for the display sowed the first seeds of a deep resentment among Chrétien and his people, which would come to poison their entire relationship in years to follow.

Later, this incident would assume mythic status as the beginning of all of the animosity between Martin and Chrétien. Yet at the time, no one, not even Chrétien, acknowledged any lasting damage from the Montreal dust-up. The newspapers buried accounts of the debate in their back pages. In a next-day interview with Mike Duffy of CTV, Chrétien shrugged off the encounter. "I have been in very stormy situations ten times worse than that in my political career," he said. "They have to import big mouths from Toronto, bus them to Montreal to make sure that there was noise. . . . It was not traditional in the Liberal party, but it gave me a chance to perform." He was the front-runner to the end, never betraying a hint of vulnerability.

The country's attention was on Meech's shaky fate, now upgraded to a constitutional emergency. Mulroney's Sunday-night dinner party with the first ministers had turned into a marathon negotiating session lasting a further six days at the Government Conference Centre across the road from the Château Laurier.

The federal Liberals were little more than spectators to this crisis, though highly interested ones. Their provincial cousins, especially the Liberal premiers in Quebec, Ontario, New Brunswick, and Newfoundland, were the real players. Goldenberg was now paying calls on Newfoundland's Premier Wells, trying to use the soon-to-be leader's good offices to soften Wells's hard line of opposition. Tobin was also doing shuttle diplomacy with Wells on behalf of Chrétien and Mulroney. Manitoba's Sharon Carstairs, one of Chrétien's strongest allies, was close to nervous collapse in the face of pressure to approve the deal.

So great was the Meech tension, however, that Chrétien's apparent reversal was a mere footnote to larger national events. The flip-flop chanting squad drifted on to Ottawa, where their overworked vocal chords were pressed into service to cheer Ontario Premier David Peterson and boo Clyde Wells outside the Government Conference Centre. Masciantonio said the gang was keen for any role, even as background noise, in the country's dramas.

Over the next two weeks leading up to the June 23 deadline, the Liberals coasted toward the foreordained conclusion of the leadership race, while Meech's fate was far from certain. A national-unity crisis gripped the political class and the country. If Meech died, the pundits and politicos were saying, Quebec would almost certainly separate. Television news broadcasts and the press were giving Meech massive coverage, churning out specials and supplements that were riddled with disaster warnings: "A nation hangs in the balance"; "Unity at risk." In the end, neither the Newfoundland nor Manitoba legislatures were prepared to pass the accord and Meech died on June 22.

That same day, the Calgary Saddledome was the site of a strange sideshow to the main event gripping the nation. The Liberals carried on their leadership convention as though nothing had happened, even though every TV in the hall was tuned to developments elsewhere. Images of the devastated Meech crusaders – an angry Quebec Premier Robert Bourassa, a grim Prime Minister Brian Mulroney – flickered in all corners of the stadium. Meanwhile, in the corridors, Pierre Trudeau, sporting a golden-rod coloured shirt and casual slacks, sailed through adoring throngs, signing autographs. The leadership candidates' advisers bustled about the stage in the centre stadium, going through a rehearsal for the next day's vote and finale.

Martin watched the day's developments from his trailer. Huddled with Herle, O'Leary, Mahoney, Dawson, and his communications team, he lamented the demise of Meech as a "tremendous opportunity lost." He placed calls to Bourassa and other premiers to register his sympathy. His campaign co-chairman, Jean Lapierre, and Dennis Dawson were heartsick, sure that this meant the province would see another resurgence of sepa-ratism, another ugly period of division. Martin's aides came up with a material way to register their sentiments: black armbands. Several of them rushed out to nearby stores to buy lengths of black ribbon, which they then cut and tied around the arms of Martin's delegates in the hall. Thus bedecked, the Martinites sat glumly in the hall that night, listening to the candidates' final speeches.

The surreal atmosphere persisted through the next day. The song "Don't Worry, Be Happy" blared through the loudspeakers as Liberals waved their signs and danced in the Saddledome. Cynics in the Martin camp joked that someone was playing Chrétien's Meech theme.

Martin's supporters donned bright pink baseball hats and fuchsia-framed sunglasses and frolicked about the stadium with the rest. Some were still wearing their black armbands, but most had come to Calgary for a leadership party and they weren't going to spend this day in mourning. They sang and waved their arms to the cheesy campaign song, intoning, "Paul Martin stands for Canada, he stands for you and me." High in the upper seats, two lone Martin supporters carried a huge Quebec flag, with Martin's face in the middle. The message was that Martin was the real Quebecer among the leadership candidates.

As the crowd waited for the results of the first ballot, the whole stadium broke into a chorus of "Happy Birthday" for Paul Martin Sr., followed by a rousing chorus of "For He's a Jolly Good Fellow." Martin turned eighty-seven at this convention, but he was denied his birthday wish – a leadership victory for his son.

Finally the results were announced. Chrétien won on the first ballot with 2,652 votes. Martin had garnered less than half that number: 1,176 votes. Copps had come in a solid third with 499 votes, putting her far ahead of the single-issue candidate, Wappel.

In the Martin stands, Paul Sr. leaned over, kissed Paul Jr. on the lips, and said, "Sorry, son." Two of Martin's three sons, Jamie and David, wept. Paul W. stood stoically beside his grandfather. Sheila Martin held tightly to her husband's hand and began the walk with him to the stage.

As soon as the results were known, Jean Lapierre announced to the media he was leaving the Liberal party, as did Gilles Rocheleau, another Liberal MP from Quebec. Martin's Quebec supporters cared not a whit about grace in defeat or the new leader's feelings.

The bitterness on the floor of the Saddledome was not carried onto the stage. All the candidates linked upstretched arms and strode forward together. As the outgoing leader, John Turner, took to the podium, Martin and Chrétien chatted amiably; Martin offered his sincere congratulations and pledged to be helpful in the coming days. "I can work with Jean," he told reporters. "Jean and I are old friends and I'm sure we will able to work out differences of vision. We are both Liberals and we both want the best thing for this party."

When Martin turned to the crowd to make his concession speech, he began in French, mindful of Quebecers' sentiments in the wake of Meech's defeat. Then, in English, he addressed his disappointed supporters.

"We have built a new coalition for this party. We have formed friendships, and let me tell you, we have formed friendships that are going to last the rest of our lives. For me this is victory."

That was indeed the legacy of the race. Martin would learn to rely on those friends in the years to come. The adventure was just beginning.

3

SAME PARTY,
DIFFERENT PEOPLE

IN THE DAYS immediately after the 1990 leadership convention, Paul Martin and Jean Chrétien went their separate ways. Chrétien returned to Ottawa, where he busied himself with the leadership transition, getting a fix on the state of the Liberal party and summoning those supporters whose loyalty would be rewarded with jobs in the Opposition Leader's Office (OLO).

Martin took off for a holiday in Portugal with Sheila, apparently putting the last months of campaigning behind him with ease. He joked that the only devastation he had suffered was the sight of Richard Mahoney, his executive assistant, sprawled out naked in the adjoining hotel room the next morning, sleeping off the effects of the raucous defeat party. Sheila was convinced he wasn't dealing with the loss. "It's like a shutter he puts up," she says. "It's like it never happened."

The circle closest to Martin settled back into positions that reflected their individual personalities. O'Leary had few qualms about joining a Liberal team led by Jean Chrétien and went to work in Martin's parliamentary office, taking over Richard Mahoney's job as executive assistant. Mahoney and David Herle, still nursing bruised feelings from the leadership defeat, stepped back a few paces from the party and sought out careers in the private sector. Martin, echoing his own father's long-ago advice, was heartily in favour of that move, encouraging the two young men to see politics as something to do after they made their own way in business or legal circles.

Herle resumed his law school studies, this time at the University of Ottawa, before going on to article in Toronto. He maintained only minimal contact with Liberal politics in the capital. He got a dog, a border collie named Shadow, and devoted himself to the puppy's training. Mahoney settled down with his new wife, Kathy, in Ottawa's Glebe neighbourhood. He considered provincial politics and a run for the presidency of the Ontario Liberal party, which was now sitting in opposition, thanks in part to an anti-Meech backlash that had cost David Peterson the premiership. Mahoney stayed a bit closer to action at the federal level than Herle did, setting up a legal and lobbying practice at a firm called Association House, run by Jamie Deacey, Martin's former communications aide.

Though a Martin supporter since first meeting him in 1982, Terrie O'Leary had kept a respectful distance till now. When she stepped into the position of his chief aide, the two got to know each other and developed a unique and irreverent rapport. At first, Martin didn't remember that she'd been among the Liberal youth delegation that had invited him to the 1982 convention. He started to tell her the story one day, trying to remember the names of the young men. "And there was a young woman too," he said, before the penny dropped. "Oh wait – that was you!"

O'Leary was unperturbed by Martin's poor memory and had always been content to work out of the limelight. But while she eschewed attention for herself, she understood it was important that Martin have well-honed people skills. It was O'Leary who prodded him to become better acquainted with MPs and to forge relationships with journalists. She encouraged Martin to dine with selected reporters so they could meet the relaxed and interesting private man behind the awkward, somewhat vague public performer.

Eddie Goldenberg, who had been at Chrétien's side since the 1970s, joined the Opposition leader's staff, in the position of principal policy aide. Warren Kinsella was hired too. Kinsella had supported Chrétien's opposition to Meech and he'd taken a leave of absence from his Ottawa law firm to help out in the leadership campaign. After the convention, Goldenberg had offered him a job in the OLO, working on speeches and caucus relations. Kinsella refused at first, but Chrétien appealed to his sense of adventure. "You can always be a litigation lawyer, but how often do you get to have fun in politics?"

That summer, Chrétien made moves toward reconciliation with his old leadership adversaries, with mixed success. Some nerves on both sides were still raw. Richard Mahoney ran into Martin and John Rae that summer at an Expos baseball game in Montreal. When Martin slipped out to buy refreshments, Rae levelled his gaze at Mahoney. "You were at that debate in Montreal, weren't you?" he said, referring to the flip-flop protest. Mahoney just gulped. "You've done a lot of damage," said Rae.

In Toronto, a month after the leadership convention, Chrétien convened the principals of all the leadership teams in Ontario for a dinner at Old Angelo's restaurant, a favourite downtown Liberal haunt.

John Webster was one of the Martin-team invitees. When he arrived at the restaurant, Chrétien was standing at the entrance. "I hear you like to smoke cigars at Stornoway," he said, smiling at his old foe from battles with Turner and Martin. "I'm not a fan of Stornoway. Don't intend to stay there long. I like 24 Sussex much better." Webster had a feeling that this wasn't meant as a future invitation to either official residence. Before he could reply, he was pulled aside by one of Chrétien's strongest caucus supporters, Toronto MP Sergio Marchi, who warned Webster: "Just don't say anything."

After the dinner, Chrétien spoke briefly, extolling the importance of party unity and the need to leave leadership divisions behind, then opened a question-and-answer session. Finding the crowd rather subdued, he singled out Webster. "You've been too quiet. Don't you have a question?"

Webster had been in the middle of a gossipy session with his tablemates about who was having an affair with whom in the news media world. He looked up and declared, "I don't have a question because I was told to keep my mouth shut."

Chrétien, unfazed, said, "Well, I'm inviting you to ask a question." Webster responded, asking the new Liberal leader, in rather raw terms, if he knew who was sleeping with a certain national TV news personality. No stranger to coarse language, Chrétien was known nonetheless as a strict conservative on matters of sexual morality. Webster had crossed a line and demonstrated a gauche lack of deference to the leadership. The incident helped cast Webster as one of the hawks in Martin's camp.

There was plenty of hawkishness to be found among the young people who had been such a spirited part of the Martin leadership team. It was evident hours after Martin's defeat, when the kids had drowned their sorrows with shooters and beer at a raucous party at Winston's on Calgary's Electric Avenue. The Martin defeat party turned out to be the most popular bash of the leadership convention, with Liberals of all stripes lining up to pack the bar and second-floor patio. Late in the evening, after Martin had left the premises, a few young Martinites turned up with a bag of potatoes. "Trouble," predicted some of the cooler bystanders. Potato-head was the young Liberals' nickname for Chrétien. Hurling the potatoes to the floor, they bellowed their frustration, declaring: "Leadership Review in '92."

The exuberance of youth makes victory all the sweeter and defeat almost unbearable. So while Martin and his more experienced campaigners tried to get past the disappointment of defeat, the youngsters weren't eager to forget. Around the first anniversary of the convention, in 1991, some of Martin's former agitants staged the First Annual Potato-Head Golf Tournament. The winner was Nick Masciantonio, one of the ringleaders of the flip-flop brigade. On the precise anniversary, Masciantonio and a clutch of similarly devoted Martinites holed up at a cottage in Northern Ontario, celebrating what they dubbed Bitterness Weekend 1991. Paul W. Martin was among them, having formed lasting friendships of his own with his dad's youthful supporters.

The younger Liberals were determined to keep the torch of Martin's leadership hopes aloft. Unlike their seasoned elders, they were unfazed by the prospect of a long wait for the fabled "next time." What are six or ten years when you're in your teens or early twenties? Moreover, they had joined the party when its fortunes were on the rise, when bodies were needed for election organizing and there were plenty of opportunities for young volunteers to play a role. After 1990, while Chrétien's more experienced colleagues moved ever higher in the Liberal ranks, the young people, mostly Martinites, contributed their energy and enthusiasm on the ground. That divide, one with historical precedents, worked against attempts at reconciliation.

So too did Chrétien's shaky performance in his first year at the helm. Even as the country was still recovering from the collapse of Meech, another crisis exploded at Oka, Quebec. Armed Mohawk warriors set up a blockade in early July on a parcel of land due to be turned into a golf course, land the natives claimed as their own historical property. Quebec Provincial Police had attempted to storm the barricades with assault rifles and tear gas in a bloody altercation that left one officer dead and the militant natives holed up behind the blockade. The siege dragged on for weeks, then months, while the governments in Quebec and Ottawa seemed too shell-shocked to end it.

At a Parliament Hill rally mid-crisis, Chrétien issued a bizarre suggestion: End the standoff, let the native militants go, and the police could catch up with them later. The problem, he said, was that the situation had become dangerously overheated – an echo of his Meech position.

"They should let them go home," he said of the militants. "The moment they get out of that house, they will be arrested right away." How would the authorities find the warriors once they had fled? "We have their names," Chrétien replied. His critics sniggeringly described this as the "head-start" solution. The Opposition leader's views were no longer solicited by the media as the blockade dragged on to its conclusion in September.

In early fall, the nation's attention shifted to the more mundane matter of taxation. The Tory government had unveiled a new tax, called the goods and services tax, which would replace the old manufacturers' sales tax and add a 7 per cent surcharge to virtually every commercial transaction. Chrétien had been cautiously silent on the GST during the leadership campaign, while Martin had vowed to scrap it.

Newfoundland MP Brian Tobin, ever alert to the winds of public opinion, sniffed opportunity in the air and argued spiritedly in one of the first fall caucus meetings that the Liberals should become the anti-GST heroes. They would fight the unpopular tax from their platform in the Senate, where they still formed the majority, thanks to years of Trudeau appointments. The Senate became the battlefield in the last months of 1990, and a crowded one when the Tories stacked the chamber with a flood of fresh appointees and then used their sudden majority to throw out the rules Liberals were using to block the legislation. The Liberals responded with a display of rebellion, blowing kazoos and inviting the media to roam about the chamber.

Chrétien was almost invisible throughout the GST drama, leaving it to Liberal senators to articulate the Opposition position. He didn't seem to know how to function in opposition after decades of experience on the government side of the House. Every one of his attacks on the Tories went awry. As Canada was hurtling toward war in the Gulf in early 1991 and Parliament debated whether to commit Canadian troops to the American effort to end Iraq's invasion of Kuwait, Chrétien offered this policy position:

"Of course, if there is no war, our forces should stay there," he said. "If faced with an act of war, we say on this side of the House that it is premature and that our troops should not be involved in a war at this moment, and our troops should be called back if there is a war, unless we decide to be in a war."

Such equivocation was similar to his earlier Oka pronouncement. Both statements reflected Chrétien's instinctive embrace of ambivalence and an aversion to firm positions – by himself or anyone else. Though a useful skill in the complex task of governing, or at least managing government, prevarication was not desirable in the role of chief government critic, which requires blunt talk and sweeping assertions. According to Goldenberg, Chrétien could never muster the indignation to accuse the government of deliberate wrongdoing or evil motivation, as Opposition leaders must often do.

He was frequently overscripted as well. His handlers were trying to teach him to speak from a teleprompter and sending him to remedial English lessons. They insisted Chrétien be tutored in basic English pronunciation. "I spent a whole morning learning to say TH-UH, TH-UH," Chrétien joked at a dinner held with his Toronto supporters at Christmas 1990.

A group of caucus members was dispatched across the country to assess, discreetly, whether Chrétien's leadership was a problem and why. Joe Fontana, from London, Ontario, along with a handful of others found in their travels that the new leader was seen as remote, out of touch, "yesterday's man," as the pundits were fond of calling him.

Chrétien was also suffering health problems. A tumour on his lung, believed to be benign, was deemed serious enough to warrant surgery. In

February 1991, he announced he was taking several weeks off for the procedure and some rest. Sheila Copps was named acting leader in his place. He didn't return until April that year, leading many to speculate whether the long absence was proof of deeper problems with his leadership.

Like Chrétien, Martin had a hard time expressing unqualified disdain for the government benches. He was still shy and uncomfortable before the cameras. He dreaded the daily "troll" through the Commons foyer after Question Period. For opposition MPs, this media circus is a much different experience than it is for cabinet ministers or government members, who can count on being in demand when they emerge into the glare of the television lights. Those in opposition cannot assume that the media will want to talk to them. Instead, they linger in the foyer, like wallflowers at a school dance, waiting to be singled out for attention. Martin detested this duty, but O'Leary insisted he endure it.

O'Leary was worried that her boss was bored. He had asked to be the party's Environment critic, which appealed to his fondness for research science, but it wasn't job enough to keep him fully engaged. Beyond asking questions in the House and doing constituency work, there isn't much that an opposition MP can do to make a difference in the affairs of the nation. Martin needed a project to occupy his hyperactive curiosity. After several conversations, O'Leary and Martin hit on the perfect idea: he would ask to write the platform for the next election campaign. He would bring to the exercise a method and a discipline unprecedented in the party's past practices. During the Trudeau years, the platform was usually developed by the wily Cape Bretoner and cabinet veteran Allan MacEachen, who would scribble down its essential points a few nights before the campaign began. On-the-fly election promises had gone out of fashion, though, as Martin understood after the disastrous day-care announcement in 1988.

He wasn't thinking of using this assignment to build connections for a future run at the leadership, though O'Leary and Herle saw the long-term wisdom in keeping Martin in conversation with the Liberal rank and file. Besides, said Martin, it wasn't like he had to compete for the job. "There weren't forty other members of Parliament saying, 'I want to do it.' Nobody thought it was a very significant thing because, historically, these platforms had never been important before."

In Chrétien's office, Warren Kinsella had some initial reservations, fearing that the Liberals might simply construct an easy target for their foes. Kinsella possessed a sometimes over-the-top fixation on enemies and a great fascination with ultra-right-wing, neo-fascist underground movements. (He was then gathering material for what would be two books on these subjects: *Unholy Alliances* in 1992 and *Web of Hate* in 1994.) He also had an abiding interest in the rougher type of political game played in the United States, and had observed how independent presidential candidate Ross Perot won credibility in the early 1990s with a comprehensive platform. Weighing strategic worries against the evidence of changing attitudes toward detailed election promises, Kinsella calculated that a carefully crafted platform was a "terrific" idea.

Goldenberg had fewer reservations and was sold almost immediately. He found Martin a co-chair, Chaviva Hosek, former Ontario cabinet minister and social-policy expert now ensconced as an adviser in the Opposition Leader's Office. For the next year, they would travel the country, soliciting views from Liberals and from policy experts, hammering out a platform they hoped would be a trail-blazing document.

Many of the broad themes for the early drafts of the platform were identified at a pivotal party conference, a session convened in part to bridge the acknowledged divisions between insiders and outsiders, and between the right and left wings of the party. Liberals gathered at Aylmer, Quebec, just across the river from Ottawa, in the fall of 1991 to hammer out a modernized ideology and fresh policies. This meant grappling with such concepts as globalization, productivity, and innovation – buzzwords for the decade ahead. The signature statement of the event came from Chrétien: "Globalization is not right wing or left wing. It is simply a fact of life." A key speaker on productivity was Lester Thurow, from the Massachusetts Institute of Technology. Peter Nicholson, a former Liberal finance critic in the Nova Scotia provincial legislature, then an executive with the Bank of Nova Scotia, laid out a six-point program for bringing the party's policies in line with modern, bottom-line demands for economic efficiency.

The Aylmer conference drew a lot of attention, with skeptical Ottawa pundits wondering whether there could be a true reconciliation between the right and left wings. The schism was personified by two individuals: on the right, Roy MacLaren, an unapologetic free-trade fan and business-minded MP from Etobicoke; on the left, Lloyd Axworthy, former cabinet minister and the party boss in Manitoba during the Trudeau years. As the Aylmer event wound down, MacLaren was quoted as saying: "Eat your heart out, Lloyd Axworthy," a statement interpreted as proof of the triumph of the right in setting the next Liberal agenda.

Of course, the MacLaren-Axworthy rivalry was seen as the Martin-Chrétien relationship in miniature, and all the patching and gluing at Aylmer an attempt to contain their differences inside one coherent Liberal package. The Aylmer conference had a profound effect on Chrétien's thinking. For the first time since he assumed the leadership of the party, he had a clear sense of mission. One of the biggest problems of his first difficult year, many close to him argued, was that no one seemed to know what he wanted to do with the leadership he'd fought so hard to win. Now he had a goal: a new, modern Liberalism that would tie the traditional left and right wings of the party together. Martin had already been seized with that notion, but the Aylmer conference crystallized his thinking as well. Nevertheless the two leadership foes were seen as extremes on the Liberal spectrum, even though each man's deeper political influences blurred those distinctions. Their respective mentors, for instance, might have had the same initials, but they had very different philosophies.

Chrétien had learned much of what he knew of government at the feet of Mitchell Sharp, the venerable former Liberal finance minister who was strongly identified with the fiscally minded right of the party. It was Sharp who had taught his young parliamentary secretary, Jean Chrétien, the importance of balanced books.

Martin's mentor was Maurice Strong, who had given him his summer job in the Calgary oilfields and then his first real job at Power Corp. in Montreal. Strong, a friend of Paul Martin Sr., was a well-connected Liberal who travelled high in corporate circles, but whose passions ranged across traditionally left-wing concerns, especially foreign aid and the environ-ment. He was once quoted as saying that the Depression of the 1930s had left him "very radical." In the 1970s and 1980s, Strong was assuming ever-more-influential roles internationally and with the United Nations, serving as secretary-general of the UN Conference on the Human Environment and as the first executive director of the UN Environment Program in Nairobi, Kenya.

What Martin learned as he worked with Goldenberg and Hosek was that they were of similar minds on the basic ingredients for platform emphasis: education, training, and research and development. "Each of us had our slight differences, but all of us had roughly the same biases," he recalled later. O'Leary was similarly inclined, and she brought her well-grounded common sense to the process.

Researching and developing the election platform forged a productive working relationship between the Martin and Chrétien camps within the Liberal government. Martin and O'Leary proved themselves to be reliable team players; Goldenberg undertook the early bridge-building work that would be so crucial in good and bad times ahead.

Goldenberg was initially impressed simply by the way O'Leary spoke to her boss. It showed she could be counted upon for candour and clear judgment. Her propensity to collect bits of political information, once used casually to keep her friends in touch and informed, now had a professional outlet. Her work in the early 1980s on democratizing budget consultations also gave her some ideas on how to make this policy process more responsive to Liberals at the grassroots. Martin and Hosek spent a lot of time consulting with Liberals in community halls and living rooms across Canada.

They worked well together through the next year, meeting regularly in the capital to trade ideas around a conference table at the Opposition Leader's suite of offices in the Wellington Building, across the road from Parliament Hill. Naturally, their discussions would spill over into evenings and weekends too, though none felt the overtime a hardship. Goldenberg would find himself at his cottage, writing drafts of various proposals long past midnight. At other times, Martin, O'Leary, and Goldenberg would traipse over to Hosek's apartment to haggle over policies and programs until the early hours of the morning.

Martin's enthusiasm sometimes ran up against Goldenberg's trademark caution. Like his boss, Goldenberg worked on the principle of keeping options open, avoiding grand gestures that could turn into political traps.

Martin, for instance, wanted the platform to promise a doubling of federal dollars for research and development. But Goldenberg balked. Such commitments made by parties out of government and in ignorance of potential pitfalls could defeat them before any election, he feared.

Nonetheless, Goldenberg was happy to boast that a strong and effective liaison now existed between Chrétien and Martin, though he would always stress that there was only one boss in the end. Yet it was at this point that another notion began to take hold – the idea of the Liberal Opposition as a joint Chrétien-Martin enterprise. On one level, this wasn't a bad concept to promote. It spoke to the Liberals' ability to overcome internal rivalries in favour of a greater goal and to the magnanimity of both men. But the partnership idea also fed an underlying tension. It drew on an oversimplification – Martin as the brains of the operation, lending depth to Chrétien's humble charisma. To the immense frustration of Chrétien's people, it perpetuated the image of their man as a simpleton, ignoring the fact that he had a mind of his own and formidable experience in the game of politics.

In the summer of 1991, Chrétien made two new appointments to the Opposition Leader's Office. The new chief of staff was Jean Pelletier, an old college friend and a former mayor of Quebec City. Possessing a stately, dignified grace, Pelletier was the soul of discretion, a valued asset in Chrétien's tight clique of advisers. "You don't do your cooking in the living room," was one of Pelletier's favourite expressions, to explain why it was fruitless for reporters to ask him about matters of political strategy. The other new recruit to the Chrétien circle was Peter Donolo, the same young man who had accompanied Alf Apps and Terrie O'Leary in 1982 to Paul Martin's CSL offices. He was named communications director, moving to Ottawa from Toronto, where he had been working as an aide to then mayor Art Eggleton. Some of that youthful rebellious Liberal spirit still survived in Donolo and he had kept up his friendship with O'Leary through the previous decade.

The first noticeable effect of Donolo and Pelletier's arrival was a turn away from leader-centric organization to the Liberal team as a whole.

Donolo's most successful strategies started with the belief that Liberals should speak with a collective voice. In some ways, he made a virtue of necessity, since the party had not been faring well when it was seen as Chrétien's show alone. Donolo spread around the communications job, delegating segments up and down the party chain of command. He set up a system of "talking points" for all Liberals on every major policy announcement or news development. He and another Chrétien aide, Michael McAdoo, also established Infofax, which transmitted the Liberal spin by facsimile machine to partisans all over the country. This co-ordinated communications strategy accomplished two goals: it ensured that the Liberals were singing from the same song sheet, and, even more important, it made rank-and-file Liberals feel connected to the leader's inner circle.

Donolo loved it when reporters got their hands on the talking points, treating them as leaked documents, obtained from shadowy sources in Liberal backrooms. He would read his spin points framed in front-page stories and chuckle, "Thanks for the assist."

The team approach turned into a road show in 1993, when Prime Minister Mulroney announced his resignation and the Tories' mandate neared the end of its fifth and final year. Chrétien began to travel the regions by bus, with the media in tow. MPs and would-be MPs hopped on the bus during different legs of the trip to introduce themselves and their ridings to the leader and reporters. These excursions gave the appearance of a party on the move, talking with one voice, all members travelling down the same road.

And what's a team without pride? The combined Donolo-Pelletier formula also emphasized the importance of self-confidence. They abandoned efforts to "professionalize" Chrétien with the teleprompter and English lessons. Chrétien told CBC-TV interviewer Hana Gartner that his mangled syntax endeared him to ordinary Canadians and Donolo dressed him in blue-jean shirts for the campaign posters. The pride strategy extended to the party and was evident in early May 1993, when the Liberals held a week-long "candidates school" on Parliament Hill.

"We, the Liberals, are not ashamed of our previous leadership and our record," Chrétien told the current and future MPs jamming the huge ballroom in the West Block of Parliament Hill. While Tories would spend the next election ducking their past, Liberals would present themselves as the proud heirs to the legacy of Pearson, Trudeau, and Turner. Yes, even Turner. Chrétien could afford to be magnanimous in his new position as Turner's successor.

Following a get-acquainted reception at the candidates school, Martin's friends from caucus and Liberal backrooms went to a nearby restaurant in Ottawa's Byward Market, where Paul and Sheila Martin were hosting a dinner. A Toronto rookie named Allan Rock, a corporate lawyer who was planning to run in Etobicoke, was invited to the dinner at the last minute. Walking the short distance to the restaurant, Rock talked about how keen he was to meet Martin, how he'd always admired him from afar. Martin had saved a spot at the centre of the table for Rock, so the two could chat. They hit it off as soon as Rock shed his formal and deferential demeanour, exchanging good-natured jokes while Martin shared the benefit of his political experience to date. Lesson one: It's harder than it looks.

For Richard Mahoney, the 1993 candidates school was a psychological turning point in healing the old leadership rifts. For the first time since Martin lost in 1990, Mahoney felt a surge of hope about the Liberals' prospects. He felt part of the family again. It had taken almost three years, but gradually the Liberal family had been knitted together. David Herle had returned too, moving back to Ottawa to take a job in the polling and research section of the powerful Earnscliffe lobbying group, at that time an influential Tory-connected firm. He harboured his reservations about Chrétien, though, fearing that Martin was being drawn into a docile complicity while distracted by the election platform.

That enterprise, meanwhile, was taking shape in a first draft. One of Martin's speechwriters from the leadership campaign, John Duffy, was responsible for crafting this early version. John Godfrey, a former *Financial Post* editor, soon-to-be Liberal candidate in Toronto, was also working on wording. Duffy was closeted in a room at the Delta Hotel in May, wading through the hundreds of policy pieces that Chaviva Hosek and Martin and company had accumulated. Liberal research staff kept dropping off more notes, more pieces of the puzzle.

Duffy's first draft seemed a little too breezy for the platform authors. They wanted something weighty and substantial, "like an annual report,"

O'Leary said. More drafting and redrafting followed, the costs of the programs tallied and retallied for several more weeks. These Liberals were not going to get caught out by haste or carelessness.

In June, the governing Progressive Conservatives chose a new leader and Canada's first woman prime minister, Kim Campbell. Throughout the summer, rank-and-file Liberals were made anxious by her popularity in the polls: Was it possible that Campbell could reverse Tory fortunes and shut out the Liberals for a third consecutive time? Neither Chrétien nor Martin thought so. For different reasons, both were relaxed and confident.

Chrétien's equanimity was based on instinct and experience. He had no patience with those MPs who openly expressed their fears of being blindsided by the Tory leadership race and a possible resurgence of Conservative strength.

In a foreshadowing of lectures to come, Chrétien told reporters that fear was an unattractive feature of some Liberals' personalities. "I'd like to have their names so that I can put some backbone in their backs," he said. "There are always nervous Nellies in any organization. . . . The best way, if they are afraid, is to work and that way they will win. But if they cry, they will be seen as crybabies and the people don't vote for crybabies."

Martin's pre-election confidence was based on intense preparation, the only cure for nervousness, he believed. The platform was finished, waiting to be unveiled in the forthcoming election campaign. It was a document teeming with provocative ideas and novel approaches, heavy on education and innovation, laced with proposals for making the federal government relevant and respectable in the eyes of Canadians. New programs, such as child care and infrastructure, would be joint projects with other levels of government, ushering in a new style of co-operative federalism – a sharp contrast from the confrontational us-versus-them attitudes that had characterized the Mulroney years.

The Liberals decided to keep the details of the platform under wraps until an election was called. Well-chosen hints would be dropped to the media, preparing the ground for policies the Grits intended to put forward. O'Leary met with selected reporters during the late-summer months, talking up the central themes.

When Kim Campbell called the election for October 25, the Liberals were ready. In mid-September, about a week after the campaign began officially, the Liberals rolled out their manifesto – 112 pages, titled *Creating Opportunity*, which would be known thereafter simply and accurately as the Red Book. O'Leary came up with the idea of releasing it to the press in a budget-style lock-up with reporters. The press gathered in one room, no cellphones or outside communication allowed, to pore over the document for a few hours before its public release. Although no financial markets would be affected or state secrets violated if the Red Book's contents leaked out before the press conference, the tactic lent a note of urgent authority to what amounted to a campaign event. Chrétien, Martin, and Hosek appeared onstage together at Ottawa's Delta Hotel ballroom to promote their ambitious agenda. The would-be prime minister vowed that it was a tool of accountability – Canadians could come back to a Liberal government in four years and measure the record against this written set of promises.

The presence of Martin and Chrétien together again added to the image of the Liberals as a partnership, one that went over well with the public and the chattering political classes in Ottawa.

In keeping with his inclusive, team approach, Peter Donolo had set up an advisory group of lobbyists with Liberal ties, hoping to solicit their input on campaign strategy. He knew that lobbyists can be a cynical breed, quick to criticize. Several had served as aides or assistants or politicians in previous Liberal governments and they were prone to measuring their successors' achievements against nostalgic recollections of their own days of influence. Donolo figured that if they were made to feel as though they were inside the current Liberal tent, they would claim some ownership for their party's approach.

A meeting of this group was scheduled a few hours after the Red Book was launched. They gathered, as usual, in the Opposition leader's suite in the Wellington Building. At 9 p.m., Donolo turned on CBC's *Prime Time News*. The report on the Red Book was glowing, the commentators' reviews positive. At the end of the segment, the assembled lobbyists broke into applause. Even the most skeptical of the Liberal veterans were impressed.

The Liberals sailed to victory on October 25, buoyed by voters' fierce resentment of Mulroney's Tories and the persuasive presentation of the Grits as a team ready to govern. This latter perception seemed confirmed by the Red Book. When it came time for Chrétien to choose his cabinet, Martin's contribution was acknowledged with the gift of choice. While others were handed their cabinet assignments, no questions asked, Martin was given a few days to think over what portfolio he wanted. Chrétien urged him to take Finance, but Martin was more keen on Industry, which the new prime minister also said he could have if he chose. The pressure was heavy for him to take Finance, however.

A year earlier, the party's pollster, Michael Marzolini, had canvassed the views of representatives of the major banks, most of whom were nervous about the prospects of a Liberal regime. The business community feared a return to the free-spending Trudeau era. Marzolini had said to the bankers: "What if Paul Martin is finance minister?" The mere question had a soothing influence. "Oh, well, I'd be comfortable with that," said one, the others nodding in agreement. Now, the Liberals were about to assume power and needed to establish credibility with Bay Street as quickly as possible. Goldenberg had been telling fellow Chrétien staffers days before the election that reassuring the markets would be one of the new government's first priorities.

Martin returned from his meeting with Chrétien to the small condominium apartment he was renting about a block away from the Hill, where Sheila was waiting to hear what job was in store for her husband. The Martins phoned David Herle and Terrie O'Leary and asked them to come over to talk about the choices. Told that Martin had been offered Finance, the three responded enthusiastically. But Martin held out. He wasn't sure he liked the idea of Finance – it seemed like career suicide. He had been struck during the Red Book consultations by how many people, especially in the West, cited Allan MacEachen's 1981 budget as their main gripe against the Liberals. Finance ministers, Martin had learned, were either remembered for how little they did to rein in the economy or for how much damage they had done. As a rule, they did not become much-beloved politicians, and Martin was still uncomfortable with the idea of having enemies.

Martin conducted his customary consultation process. The especially influential voices he listened to were those of Arthur Kroeger, a former senior deputy minister in government, and Ed Lumley, a one-time "minister of everything" in Trudeau's cabinet, who had known Martin since they were teenagers working as Coca-Cola delivery boys in Windsor. With their endorsement of the idea, Martin was persuaded to take the Finance portfolio. (His mother, Nell, hovering near death at her home in Windsor, managed to regain consciousness enough to chide her son on his decision when he went to pay what would be his last visit. "Why, Paul? Why Finance?" Nell gasped.)

Once Martin had decided, Ottawa MP John Manley was dispatched to Industry. Allan Rock, the newcomer, got the powerful Justice post, and Lloyd Axworthy moved to Human Resources, where he would be charged with a massive overhaul of the social-security system, as promised in the Liberals' Red Book.

On November 4, Donolo put a populist, thrifty spin on the swearing-in ceremony. New ministers were ferried to and from Rideau Hall by bus; no limos for this crowd. The early reactions justified Chrétien's desire to have Martin in Finance. "CONFIDENCE IN CABINET BOOSTS DOLLAR; SPECULATORS WHO PREDICTED A FALL AFTER ELECTION ARE EATING THEIR LOSSES," proclaimed the headline in the *Edmonton Journal*. "BLUE LIBERALS CONTROL AGENDA," read the headline above a column in the *Ottawa Citizen*, which revealed that both Paul Martin and John Manley had been talking to corporate leaders in the months before the election, establishing their bona fides as fiscally responsible politicians.

Chrétien was ready to govern because he had been confident he would win. For the previous year, David Zussman, a University of Ottawa academic and expert in public administration, had prepared a transition plan for the Liberals that covered everything from ministerial organization to the number, salaries, and training of ministerial staffers. It was a plug-in-and-play kit for government machinery: all the new prime minister had to do was take it out of the box and push the start button.

In the Commons the Liberals had won a huge 177-seat majority and, as a victory bonus, a fractured, dysfunctional opposition. More newcomers were elected to this Parliament, from all parties, than at any other time in the history of the country. The rookies themselves had impressive credentials: Bill Graham, the law professor and leadership-debate moderator, now represented Toronto's Rosedale district; John Godfrey, former journalist and Red Book drafter, took one of the city's two Don Valley ridings while David Collenette, back in elected politics, represented the other. Shaughnessy Cohen won her seat in Paul Martin Sr.'s old riding in Windsor; Anne McLellan, a law professor from Edmonton, won a rare Alberta seat for the Grits by just eleven votes. The country was awash with shiny new parliamentarians of the Liberal stripe, from Herb Dhaliwal, a Sikh businessman in Vancouver, to Allan Rock in Toronto, to Marcel Massé, a former senior bureaucrat, elected in Hull, Quebec. Chrétien had an embarrassment of caucus riches from which to choose his cabinet. He would boast that his B team was every bit as talented as his A team.

The Official Opposition was the Bloc Québécois, a separatist party with no aspirations to be a government in waiting. Behind it in number of seats was the ragtag Reform party, led by Preston Manning. The once-mighty Tories had been reduced to two seats, the NDP to nine. Neither of the Liberals' traditional adversaries could claim official party status.

This didn't mean that governing through the next mandate would be a cakewalk. The Liberals had inherited a serious financial mess – a deficit of $45 billion and growing. Chrétien had vowed during the election campaign that he wouldn't plead surprise at the numbers once he came to office, but the rest of his ministers weren't bound to hide their shock. Martin was even more stunned to discover Canada's lack of credibility in the international financial community. Soon after he issued a quick, poorly received 1994 budget, he went on a tour of world financial capitals and came to the realization that Canada's reputation was badly sullied. In business, Martin had been accustomed to dealing on trust, making deals and letting the paperwork follow later. No such trust or credibility was being extended to his own country. International financiers would simply shake their heads skeptically when he outlined how Canada intended to handle its economic situation.

"There's a difference between knowing something intellectually and knowing something in your gut," Martin says. "They're looking at me and they say, 'Don't give me your predictions, I've met six of your prede-cessors, all gave me the same line of crap, and I don't believe it.' That's when I felt it."

Much later some people around Chrétien alleged that Martin and his people deliberately aggrandized their minister's role at the cabinet table and in this government – at the prime minister's expense and with a view to future leadership. It was true that Martin became a media darling in the first year of government, partly because he and his people were well liked in press and political circles. Unlike Chrétien's crowd, who tended to keep to themselves, Martin's gang had a reputation for informality and not taking themselves too seriously. O'Leary certainly had a magical touch with the media and was clever enough to dispense spin in unpredictable ways.

Six months into the Liberals' tenure and just before the summer break in 1994, O'Leary sent out a hefty brown envelope to selected friends and a few national reporters. It was a sheaf of pages from Hansard, with a brief cover note: "Thought you might like to see some of Paul's finer moments in the House." Had it come from any other minister's office, one might have been tempted to toss it away as just another over-the-top promo-tional piece. But a riffle through the pages told another story: O'Leary had methodically pinpointed every incidence of Martin forgetting a question, flubbing an answer, tripping over his words, or otherwise making a fool of himself in the hallowed chamber of parliamentary debate. It telegraphed a disarming message: Martin was endearingly un-perfect and his staff unafraid to acknowledge it. Martin wasn't running a ministerial shop on the force of intimidation.

His managerial style became the subject of gossip when word spread of his conduct at the meetings known as CMOs – pronounced See-Moes – at the Finance Department. The name was inherited from the legendary, 1970s-era deputy minister of finance, Mickey Cohen, and it stood for "Cohen, Minister, and Others." Martin's sessions were rollicking affairs between an impressive array of political people and some of the govern-ment's sharpest bureaucrats. On the political side, Martin would be accompanied by O'Leary, his parliamentary secretary from the Commons (Winnipeg MP David Walker and Toronto MP Barry Campbell in the early years), as well as David Herle and Elly Alboim, a former CBC-TV Ottawa bureau chief, from Earnscliffe. Karl Littler, a whip-smart, confident aide who worked for Martin on policy and legislation, was a regular at these meetings too, as was Ruth Thorkelson, a young Alberta Liberal who worked in Martin's office. To earn admission into Martin's side of the table at these CMOs, an adviser had to be sharp, quick, and willing to talk back to the minister.

On the bureaucrats' side were David Dodge, the deputy minister, and an array of well-respected senior economic analysts from the department: Scott Clark, Ian Bennett, Don Drummond, and Susan Peterson. Peter Nicholson, the Bank of Nova Scotia chief who had impressed so many Liberals at Aylmer, had temporarily joined the Finance Department in the first year as a visiting fellow.

Every Finance policy decision was debated at the CMOs, where opinions were freely offered and freely refuted, without regard to hierarchy or delicate sensitivities. No other ministry in government had such meetings. No parallel certainly existed in the PMO, where Chrétien's meetings were short, pointed, get-down-to-business affairs.

The bureaucrats at Finance were initially shocked at the heated exchanges between O'Leary and Martin. O'Leary, for her part, was surprised to learn that her boss was acquiring a reputation in the department as a yeller. Don't people understand that with Paul, you get to yell back? she wondered. Soon enough the bureaucrats learned, and within months the CMOs were high volume on both sides of the table.

CMOs often had no fixed hour for adjournment. Participants would file into the room in the morning, looking for the stainless-steel steam tables that meant the meeting would carry on well past the dinner hour. Martin led the discussion by prompting, urging, and listening. He believed it was his job to speak last, because he was the one who would have to make the final decision on the policies being discussed. He wanted to leave himself free to change his mind too, after hearing the debate.

This tendency of Martin's – to change his views – would earn him a reputation beyond these rooms as indecisive. He dismissed the label as "crap," blaming it on outdated, simplistic ideas about what's involved in making a decision on matters of complexity and nuance.

"I make a decision when I have to make it. And I won't make the decision before. Normally what I would want to do would be to begin the debate well ahead of time, because my own view is that in nine decisions out of ten, if you argue them out, the decision becomes very evident."

The management style that Martin set up in these years was rooted in his past experience in business and would emerge again later in the set-up of his leadership organization. He believed hierarchies to be a waste of time. "The only thing that these people are doing is checking the person below them. And nobody's doing a goddamn thing except checking to make sure the person below him or her is doing it. You rank your power by the number of people reporting to you. And you don't get anywhere."

Herle and Alboim took an unprecedented role in these proceedings. Earnscliffe had been given the contract to handle Finance's communications strategy during the Tory government's last months, but it was under Martin that it came to be known as almost an adjunct of the department. Their influence was first noticed with the slick, professional presentation that Martin delivered to the Commons finance committee in late 1994, to prepare the ground for the 1995 budget. The professional style of this event and its signature phrase – "come hell or high water" – underlined the credibility that Martin hoped to restore to Canada's fiscal house.

Earnscliffe was divided into two operations: one did more traditional lobbying and consulting work with industries and private-sector interests; the other, the research arm, worked primarily with government departments and ministers' offices. Its private-sector clients included energy industry giants such as the B.C. and Ontario Hydro corporations, Petro Canada, Mobil Oil, and communications firms such as AT&T Canada and Microsoft. Mike Robinson, Martin's leadership campaign chairman in 1990, was attached to the lobbying side of the firm; Herle and Alboim worked on the research side.

The two functions made Earnscliffe powerful – and controversial. Through its doors passed both clients who wanted certain things from government and bureaucrats or politicians who could deliver them. In other words, you could go to one side of Earnscliffe to lobby for an item in the budget, fully aware that the other side was deeply involved in preparing that budget. Several reporters started sniffing around the firm, trying to see if this represented a monumental conflict. No one ever managed to make any controversy stick. Earnscliffe's partners insisted that a "Chinese wall" separated the two sides; that there was no traffic between the firm's different functions.

During the first, intense year of the Liberal government, the CMOs grappled with the realities of the eroding fiscal situation in Canada, prompted by the $45-billion deficit and international developments such as the Mexican peso crisis, which rocked financial markets around the world.

Martin was largely motivated by the lack of international confidence in Canada, which he'd experienced in his early ministerial travels abroad. He was determined to bring order to the country's economic affairs with the same enthusiasm he had long ago used to tackle problems at Power Corp.'s troubled holdings. Even the Tories, in their dying days, had recognized the need for fundamental restructuring and rethinking of government. Martin, to his great fortune, found the public service primed for an overhaul. It would make the road ahead a little easier. So would the help he got from his boss.

Chrétien was more than an ally in this effort. Belying his image as a holdover from the free-spending Trudeau era, the prime minister was insistent on bringing order and discipline to Canada's finances. Martin was willing to do the tough detail work on making the sweeping cuts that would be necessary, while Chrétien was willing to use his power to back the effort, warning ministers that he would punish dissenting departments with even harsher cuts.

There was every reason to believe that Martin and Chrétien would be able to work closely together. Their first important achievement in the working partnership had been the replacement of the Bank of Canada governor, John Crow, in December 1993. It did not take Martin long after he arrived at Finance to realize he was going to be at odds with Crow over his fixation with inflation above all else. Personally, Martin and Crow clashed too, even on matters as mundane as speaking style. (Crow once indiscreetly compared Martin's conversational technique to a teenaged girl's, filled with gushing overstatement.) On Martin's recommendation, Chrétien chose not to renew Crow's term, and a new governor, Gordon Thiessen, was named.

"Changing the governor of the bank is not an easy task," Goldenberg said. "That was done by the prime minister and the minister of finance – by the two of them together. It could only be done by the two of them."

Earlier, Chrétien and Martin had established a workable partnership in the development of the election platform, which would serve as the template for the massive 1995 budget undertaking. Everything that the Liberals had learned through the making of the Red Book was applied to the development of the 1995 budget. Martin's and Chrétien's teams came at the question of government finances as they had with party policy in 1991, subjecting every notion to an exercise known in the bureaucracy as "program review." Ministers and their departments were forced to do line-item analyses of their spending programs and cut whatever was deemed to be wasteful or ineffective.

David Zussman, architect of the transition plan, was brought in as an assistant secretary to cabinet to help direct the program review. Marcel Massé, a public servant turned rookie politician who now was Treasury Board president, helped steer the task, because he knew the labyrinth of bureaucracy they would have to navigate. But it was the other three M ministers – Martin, Anne McLellan, and John Manley – who really drove the exercise. In the process, the three became close allies and friends. David Dodge, Martin's deputy, assumed a leadership role as well, ensuring that its ultimate aim would be the bottom line of the government's books.

Martin looked outward, talking to MPs and consulting public-administration experts, relying on Earnscliffe to analyze public opinion and recommend ways to shape it. Herle and Alboim developed a process that would become the standard structure for all of Martin's future budgets and major policy declarations, a formula that reflected Martin's own decision-making method.

There were four steps: first, a "diagnostic," or a description of "where we are now"; second, an explanation of the implications of the situation – in other words, what happens if we do nothing; third, an examination of the options available; and fourth, a conclusion, or plan of action.

In 1995, this was the diagnostic: Canada was in a good-news, bad-news situation. Economic growth, the trade surplus, business confidence, and job creation were up. The projected deficit, though, was $35.3 billion, and interest rates were expected to be higher than originally forecast, meaning that debt charges would threaten future deficit targets. If the government had any hope of getting out of this mess, it would require about $7 of spending cuts for every $1 of new tax revenue.

The second part – what if nothing was done – was daunting to contemplate. Without serious cuts, the deficit would balloon by $5 billion more than the original target and $10 billion by 1997. The downward spiral into the red would continue. If spending wasn't cut radically, confidence in Canada would be further eroded, which would only inflict further damage on investment, trade, and interest rates.

The third part, the options available, forced Martin and the government to back down from a fundamental Liberal economic position: it just wasn't enough to keep the debt to 3 per cent of the gross domestic product. That option was closed. The only choice was major cuts across all of government.

The fourth step was the most jarring: almost $30 billion in cuts would be required over the next three years. The program-review exercise would yield about $18 billion in cuts over three years. Lloyd Axworthy's social-program overhaul would have to be primarily concerned with saving money. Many of the federal cuts would be concentrated in federal transfers to the provinces for such crucial items such as health, education, and welfare. A contingency reserve was needed, probably around $2.5 billion.

The Red Book's media techniques were also applied to ease the landing of the 1995 budget. Through targeted leaks, O'Leary and Donolo got the word out of a massive budget "restructuring" to come. The team approach was put in play: Ministers were dispatched on budget day to carefully chosen destinations, in Canada and abroad, to explain various aspects of the budget to members of the financial community. The talking points were prepared in the PMO, to ensure that the budget carried the imprimatur of the entire Liberal government, not just the Department of Finance.

Donolo believed in what he called the Holiday Inn approach to budgets – no surprises, as the hotel chain advertises. Neither the media nor the business community appreciate the unexpected; it was better to deliver bad news before it was perceived as a disaster. Hence the need, in spinners' parlance, to manage expectations. Donolo's motto was: Build low expectations, then exceed them. If the situation called for tough measures, get the grapevine humming with expectations of drastic measures. He deliberately encouraged rumours in 1995 about possible tax increases, for instance, knowing that the government was determined not to put them in this budget.

The advance spin also emphasized the democracy of the cuts being contemplated. No one would be spared the Liberal knife. No regions, no constituencies would be favoured.

In that spirit, Martin and his team decided that pension reform should also be tackled in 1995, proposing cuts in benefits to seniors earning over $40,000 annually and increasing payouts to those whose income fell below that line. Chrétien and other senior ministers, including Sheila Copps, then the deputy prime minister, balked, mindful of the perils of tampering with old-age pensions. Conservative Finance Minister Michael Wilson had been forced to retreat from a similar proposal in the early years of the Mulroney government. Martin was sure he could finesse the seniors' reforms this time, going as far as paying a call on the famous pensioner, Solange Denis, who confronted Mulroney with her "goodbye Charlie Brown" warning in 1985. Martin won the elderly woman's approval of his winners-and-losers reform scheme, but he got nowhere in his efforts to persuade the prime minister.

At first, Chrétien put off Martin's overtures with vague, non-committal replies. Martin wanted a clear answer; instead, he would be subjected to Chrétien's rambling, cautionary anecdotes. The prime minister wouldn't budge, but Martin was determined that if pension reform didn't happen in this budget, it would never happen at all. The only time seniors could be persuaded to take a cut in their pension, Martin reasoned, was when they saw every other group in the country taking a financial hit as well. As late as ten days before budget day, the standoff was serious enough that Martin considered resigning.

Eddie Goldenberg salvaged the situation and the political marriage. He viewed the issue as a difference of predictions, not basic opinions. Both men were concerned, he believed, with how the budget would be received against the backdrop of Quebec's looming referendum on sovereignty.

Chrétien believed the budget was very close to the limits of Canadians' tolerance. If public acceptance was lost, so too would the federalist vote in Quebec be squandered. Martin worried that the financial markets would take a dim view of a budget that shied away from pension reform. Such a loss of confidence in the federal budget would also weaken the federal cause in Quebec. It was, in essence, a standoff over what constituted credible federalism.

"So here you have Martin saying, If I don't do it, we will be in trouble in the referendum, and Chrétien saying, If you do it, we will be in trouble in the referendum, and both of them having the same objective – we don't want trouble in the referendum," Goldenberg said. His trademark solution was to defer the decision to a future date and leave all options open. "What I was able to do was come up with a bit of a compromise. We won't do it now, but we will say that we will look at doing this next year."

In retrospect, Martin and his budget team recognized that this was probably the right way to go, especially since the budget was generally well received. Even so, Martin came to regard this dispute as the first sign of his deteriorating personal relationship with Chrétien. "What I do remember recognizing is that it wasn't going to work. From then on, in subsequent budgets, I would essentially do the budgets, make the decisions that I thought I had to make, sit down with Eddie, and Eddie would essentially play the role of intermediary between the two of us," Martin says. That process had reverberations beyond the Martin-Chrétien relationship, in ways that no one in Finance or the PMO could have predicted. While Goldenberg's intervention was the symptom of a gulf between Martin and Chrétien, other cabinet members perceived it as evidence of the finance minister's favoured status at the Centre.

Goldenberg acknowledged that this reality just "evolved." Thereafter, every meeting between Martin and Chrétien was preceded by extensive negotiation beforehand. "I would go to the prime minister and try to organize the meeting before it happened," he said. Fundamental problems between Martin and Chrétien were finessed or deferred by Goldenberg, who bore the weight of the differences on his shoulders.

The centrepiece of Martin's budget preparation was the speech. Martin organized his thoughts and confirmed his decisions in the process of writing any speech. In crafting a public address, he arrived at his position. All of the intensity of the previous months of program review and government overhaul were poured into the words he would speak in the Commons on the appointed day. The speechwriter, Larry Hagen, once a wordsmith for Joe Clark, was present from the start of the budget-making process. Every idea was test-driven. Martin, his feet on the table, his countenance twisted in thought, would articulate the proposal in various ways, the sound and impact of the words measured and analyzed by the group of irreverent critics from the bureaucracy and his political office. For Martin, it was as much an intellectual exercise as a delivery check, a way of thinking through complexity. He could not relax about the speech, believing he would be judged by history for the words he spoke.

On February 27, 1995, Martin arrived in the Commons to deliver the distillation of his work. It opened with an appeal: "There are times in the progress of a people when fundamental challenges must be faced, fundamental choices must be made – a new course charted. For Canada, this is one of those times."

Martin then laid out the program in terms of the four-step formula developed by Herle and Alboim. It was a sweeping plan to put the nation's finances on a more secure footing at the expense of many of the Liberals' sacred social legacies: radical cuts were made to health and education transfers to the provinces, other transfers to the regions, and to national spending programs. All for the sake of confidence and credibility.

Ironically, after the hours and sweat poured into the speech itself, Martin ended his performance with some remarks about the inadequacy of mere words. "This government wants Canadians to be able to judge it not on its rhetoric, but on its results; not on more promises made, but on real progress secured."

At the end of the speech, Chrétien walked over and warmly shook Martin's hand. This was his victory as much as it was Martin's, no matter what scuffles had taken place over pension reform or personal relations during the budget's creation. He had not only stood by his finance minister, but he had used his authority to make sure that his will was done.

The budget odyssey was captured in the 1996 book *Double Vision*, by authors Edward Greenspon and Anthony Wilson-Smith. *Double Vision*, as a book and a concept, went further in sealing the idea of the government as a joint enterprise, even if people around Chrétien were fond of saying "there's only one prime minister." The notion of Martin as the senior partner, if not the brains of the operation, stuck in popular political consciousness long after the 1995 budget, which was overwhelmingly embraced by the markets and the media pundits. As one minister close to Chrétien explained: "If you ask me, it's the whole *Double Vision* idea that really ticked off Chrétien. What other prime minister in history has tolerated the view of his government as a partnership? What other prime minister has been that generous?"

The Prime Minister's Office certainly wasn't averse to the idea of a government organized around the creative give and take between the prime minister and his finance minister. Nor was Canada alone in having this dynamic at the cabinet table. Later, in Britain, Prime Minister Tony Blair and Gordon Brown, his chancellor of the exchequer, would grapple with a similar tension. It would be the same in Australia between Prime Minister John Howard and his finance minister, Peter Costello.

It may have become a phenomenon of post-modern parliamentary democracies for a simple, practical reason: by and large, it worked. Goldenberg was a firm believer in the idea of two strong figures playing off each other at this level. Experts in governance also saw the wisdom. "I don't think it's a bad thing for a prime minister and his finance minister to have a bit of tension between them," said David Zussman, author of the transition plan.

Even Martin agreed. "There is a natural tension between a prime minister and the minister of finance. And if that tension isn't there, it's probably because one or the other isn't doing their jobs."

Goldenberg resisted the overly simple descriptions of Chrétien and Martin's working relationship as a marriage between right and left, the risk-taker and the risk-averse. On many matters of policy, Goldenberg viewed Martin and Chrétien as cut from the same cloth.

"Often, you would be surprised who was on which side. The corporate tax cuts and the capital gains tax cuts were the prime minister's. Paul would say, 'I don't want to have a rich man's budget.' They very rarely disagreed. . . . They are both incrementalists. Paul makes speeches about how we have got to be the best in the world, but in order to become the best in the world, they both believe in a step at a time."

It was true that Martin didn't want to do budgets for rich men, nor did he want to be remembered simply for shredding social programs to ribbons. He was, after all, the son of Paul Martin Sr. But beyond that, even in the very early days of his tenure at Finance, Martin sought out social-policy thinkers to challenge the government's cost-cutting philosophy. He wanted to hear from these people before he heard from his own economists, believing that Finance already had enough of that perspective within the department. He kept in close touch with the policy debates at leading social-policy think-tanks such as the respected Caledon Institute of Social Policy or the Canadian Council on Social Development, and some of their ideas found their way into his budgets. So-called "green funds" to help municipalities guard the environment were an example of Martin's openness to new social-policy ideas.

Outside his immediate entourage, Martin was building more and more friendships within caucus during these early years of government, even as he was getting more distant personally from the prime minister. The MP from Lasalle-Emard, though, was not the only one to operate at remote distance from the Centre, nor was he the only minister in that position.

Apart from Peter Donolo's outreach efforts, this was not a PMO that paid much attention to relations with its MPs and partisans. No matter how unpopular Brian Mulroney had been with Canadians during his tumultuous years in power, Conservative MPs remained loyal to him. Chrétien, by contrast, dispensed with much of the PMO machinery that Mulroney had put in place to address the needs and concerns of caucus members. Well-paid senior Tories had served in Mulroney's PMO on powerful regional desks. Chrétien kept the regional-desk system but filled the positions with junior Liberal employees who were expected to do double duty on advance venue-scouting missions for the prime minister's trips. Without clout, these regional-desk staffers came to be seen as more interested in representing the PMO to MPs instead of the other way around. Many caucus members soon learned to ignore them, taking their problems directly to Eddie Goldenberg or Jean Pelletier.

Chrétien made a few attempts to build connections with the caucus, hosting periodic lunches for groups of MPs at 24 Sussex Drive. But little warmth was generated at any of these encounters and, as often as not, the MPs would simply resume their grumbling as they walked out the door.

In Martin's office, a young policy assistant named Ruth Thorkelson looked to the old rival's model. Thorkelson was the sister of an Alberta Tory backbencher from the Mulroney era, Scott Thorkelson. He told her about Mulroney's simple yet highly effective gestures: the congratulatory or sympathetic phone calls, the invitations to dinners and get-togethers. With O'Leary's encouragement, Thorkelson organized breakfasts and dinners for Martin with groups of MPs. She made sure his schedule included a canvass of all of them in the early stages of budget preparation. And she kept her ear tuned to the grapevine so that Martin would know when MPs were celebrating the births of children and grandchildren, or mourning the loss of a parent. Twice a year, Martin hosted a dinner for the House of Commons finance committee. More often, he'd pick up the phone at the last minute to invite a caucus member or two out for a meal at a local restaurant.

The finance minister was everywhere and accessible; the prime minister was remote. Their opposing styles were already becoming entrenched: it might well have been called a case of the CMO versus the PMO.

The distance between the PMO and the Liberal caucus became even more evident in the months leading up to the other major event on the 1995 calendar – Quebec's referendum on sovereignty. Parti Québécois Premier Jacques Parizeau had called the vote for October 30, fifteen years after Trudeau had defeated René Lévesque with Chrétien at his side.

Following the release of the 1995 budget, there was a sense in the government that its troubles were in the past; the hard part was over, the tough decisions had been faced. Perhaps this is why so few in Ottawa seemed fussed by what looked like a spent sovereigntist force in Quebec

City. They believed Parizeau was holding the referendum more to fulfill a promise than out of any expectation he could win. The national-unity debate felt like an anachronism, so Mulroney, so Trudeau. The federal agenda was now run in the hands of pragmatists who weren't interested in plunging the nation into abstract, constitutional debates. Chrétien, acting largely through Goldenberg, intended to handle the referendum in low-key fashion, no melodramas, no angst, no fuss – it would be treated as a management problem.

Instead of engaging Donolo's team approach, the prime minister kept with his go-it-alone instincts. Months before the referendum, MPs and non-Quebec ministers came to understand that the federalist strategy in Ottawa was strictly a PMO project: a speech here, an announcement there, a refusal to be drawn into the more extreme rhetoric coming from Parizeau. It seemed to be an excellent tactical approach until Lucien Bouchard, the charismatic leader of the Bloc Québécois, came on to the field.

Bouchard was a compelling figure in Quebec, if not all of Canada, by this point. In his first year as leader of the Official Opposition, the one-time Tory and friend of Brian Mulroney had surprised the country with his expert handling of the job. Though the Bloc didn't pretend to speak for anyone outside Quebec, it was the most forceful and eloquent critic in Ottawa of the Liberals' deficit-cutting measures. In 1994, Bouchard had been felled by flesh-eating disease, almost losing his life before one of his legs was amputated. The Bloc leader was treated with sympathy across the country and as a hero at home. With the separatist effort flagging in the early weeks of the PQ campaign, Bouchard rallied the cause. Almost immediately, the federalists in the province were on the run, while the seriousness of the challenge had yet to be acknowledged in Ottawa.

Martin was due to make a pro forma appearance or two in Quebec to pitch the economic case for federalism. Like every minister, he followed the schedule set by the Centre. A speech was prepared, playing to his strength as a credible, sober voice on the economic benefits of federalism and the financial perils of separation.

On October 17, Martin addressed an audience of Quebec City businessmen, during which he declared, "Ninety per cent of our exports would be threatened, close to one million jobs." His comments were quickly seized upon by separatist critics as scare tactics, hyperbole born of desperation.

Parizeau indulged in some hyperbole of his own and exploited Martin's statement beyond its clear intent, dismissing it as federalist hysterics. The PMO, especially Goldenberg, who had reviewed the speech beforehand, thought the rap was unfair. Nonetheless, it seemed that once again Martin had dipped his toe into the national-unity waters and once again he'd been toppled by heavy breakers. On every other issue, Martin came across as smooth, sophisticated, and savvy. When he opened his mouth on Quebec, he seemed accident-prone. He became even more reticent on the subject.

Chrétien harboured broader concerns about Martin's approach to federal-provincial relations, especially as it applied to Quebec. In candid moments with confidants, the prime minister would accuse Martin of being soft on separatism and too eager to grant concessions to the provinces. Martin had supported Meech, after all, and its decentralizing features.

Just ten days before the vote, private and public opinion polls showed the federalist side faced the real prospect of defeat. The Liberals' pollster, Michael Marzolini, contacted the PMO, warning that some immediate action was needed to persuade Quebecers to stay in the country. Fisheries Minister Brian Tobin, with the help of his passionately federalist assistant, Françoise Ducros, organized a huge No rally in Montreal, so that Canadians outside Quebec could display their desire to keep the province in the federation. On the final Wednesday before the referendum vote, Chrétien bared his soul to his caucus, acknowledging his fear of losing the country. Before stunned MPs, he broke down in tears. Jane Stewart, the caucus chair, rushed to his side to throw a calming arm around his shoulder. Several caucus members began to let the tears flow freely as well. After such a promising start to the Liberal years, this would be the legacy for all of them – the loss of the country.

The fear and the emotion forced Chrétien out of the shadows at last. He spoke at a rally in Verdun, Quebec, where he issued a vaguely worded pledge to address the province's demands to be recognized as a distinct society in the Constitution and to have a veto over future amendments. He addressed the nation by television, assuring Canadians that the country would not be lost without a fight. On referendum night, the results were agonizingly close: the No side won with 50.6 per cent of the vote. Had a few thousand votes gone the other way, Canada might have been lost – on Chrétien's watch.

Some caucus members thought that Chrétien was changed by the referendum, that his confidence took a blow. Some blamed the unsettling effects of a break-in at 24 Sussex Drive just days after the referendum, when Aline Chrétien surprised an intruder in the hall outside the master bedroom.

The evidence accumulated in subsequent months of a prime minister slightly off his game, his famed instincts failing him. For a couple of weeks in the referendum's immediate aftermath, Chrétien appeared to be reneging on his promises concerning Quebec's distinct-society status and constitutional veto. He challenged the opposition in the House of Commons to "read the text" of his Verdun speech, bragging that it was written with plenty of wiggle room. Then he appeared to relent, serving up a weak, distinct-society "resolution" for the Commons, which was little more than a non-binding declaration of goodwill. The government slapped together a more substantial piece of legislation, which required the approval of every one of four regions in Canada before Ottawa would approve any changes to the Constitution. This in effect lent Quebec a veto, because it was one of the four regions. But the four-region concept of Canada had died in the 1970s; British Columbia's growth had given it regional status alone. Further, Chrétien's own constitutional position in the early 1990s had recognized five regions. The government was forced to change the legislation to reflect the five-region reality, but only after a howl of outrage from British Columbia and resurgent Western alienation.

Then there was the marketing element of the post-referendum strategy. There was a plan to "rebrand" the Canadian identity in the province of Quebec, following observations by Goldenberg and others during the referendum campaign that the Canadian flag was conspicuously absent throughout the province. Brian Tobin and Sheila Copps, the one-time Rat Packers who appreciated the power of icons, were particularly keen to fight separatism with showy patriotism. The federal government declared February 15 Flag Day, in honour of the adoption of the maple-leaf design as Canada's official flag on February 15, 1965, and Chrétien travelled to a park in Gatineau, Quebec, just across the river, for a small ceremony. The presentation was disrupted by protesters. As soon as Chrétien had finished speaking, he leapt from the stage and made his way into the crowd. Encountering one of the protesters, a man named William Clennett, the prime minister raised his elbows, grasped Clennett near the throat with a combat-style manoeuvre, and pushed him to the ground. The photographs strained credulity: Chrétien, looking like a gangster in sunglasses, throttling a small man in a woollen cap.

Still, there remained enough public goodwill toward Chrétien, enough faith still in the little guy from Shawinigan, to overcome what could have been a career-killing blunder by the prime minister. A few years later this bizarre incident was recalled to support a very different perception of the man, but for now, Canadians rallied to his side, believing that the protester, for whatever reason, had provoked the prime-ministerial throttling.

In the spring of 1996, the country's attention was once again diverted from national unity to the issue of taxation. Toronto MP John Nunziata, a leadership contender in 1990, started to make noise about voting against Martin's latest budget because the government had not kept its promise to scrap the GST. The media recalled that during the 1993 election campaign, Sheila Copps had vowed to resign if the Liberals failed to kill the tax.

Pickering MP Dan McTeague, also a bit of a renegade in caucus, was talking to reporters about his constituents' simmering anger at the Liberals' hypocrisy. Citizens were buttonholing him on the street and berating his government for its political cynicism.

Martin and his officials at Finance had looked for ways to keep the promise to eliminate the GST. At CMO after CMO, they brainstormed for a solution: how to keep the much-needed stream of revenue but get rid of the hated tax.

They considered finessing it through a communications strategy: rename it, for instance, or harmonize it with provincial taxes to make it less visible. Maybe they could streamline its administration, reducing the extra bookkeeping headaches that were such a headache to business. If people didn't notice the GST as much, would it be a case of out of sight, out of mind, and therefore scrapped? Nope, that wasn't going to work. Herle and Alboim shook their heads at each wacky, obfuscation proposal – the public wasn't that stupid.

Finally, at a meeting attended by Eddie Goldenberg and Peter Donolo, the collective threw up its hands. The tax could not be scrapped. Better to face the music and admit the folly of the promise, however vague it might have been, however Chrétien may have tried to couch it with words about the need to replace the revenue.

Earnscliffe's polls suggested that the voters might forgive a broken promise if Liberal politicians simply came clean and acknowledged their error. Here was a novel idea – tell the truth – based on an old public-relations truism: Better to have one bad day than many of them.

The proposed resolution couldn't come too soon. The *Globe and Mail* was relentless in its calls for Copps's resignation, running a daily editorial. The opposition delighted in her embarrassment, targeting the deputy prime minister every day. McTeague was getting ready to join Nunziata in all-out revolt against his party.

One evening, McTeague heard from Martin. The two weren't particularly close. In fact, McTeague had been an aggressive organizer against Martin's leadership in 1990 and helped humiliate Martinites in at least twenty ridings in Southern Ontario. The last thing he expected was a one-on-one telephone call at this juncture. But Martin was by now adept at reaching out to individual MPs.

"Dan, just hold tight," Martin told him. "I'm going to do something to fix this. I promise you won't have to leave caucus. I'm going to try to make this right." Over the previous days, Martin's office, working closely with Goldenberg and Donolo, had cobbled together an apology to the public that they hoped would get them out of the GST quicksand.

The next day, Martin made the statement in the House of Commons, declaring the government's intention to harmonize the GST with provincial sales taxes in the Atlantic provinces. Then he put the broken promise on the table.

"We know that many Canadians believed we would be able to do more than we are announcing today. Indeed, we had hoped we would be able to do more. However, there is something Canadians deserve above all else and that is government that is responsible in its management of the economy and honest in what it does. . . .

"During the election campaign we were right to criticize the GST. It created overlap and duplication among governments. It was costing small business time, energy, and money; the price paid for having to keep two sets of books, to track two sets of transactions, and to deal with two tax collectors. We were right to say that all that was wrong. It still is. However, we were mistaken to have believed that once it was anchored in place a completely different alternative would be within reach, responsibly. It has not been.

"The honest truth is that for two and a half years we looked at virtually every conceivable alternative. Some were not possible or desirable because of their economic impact, others because of the nature of our federation. What we have arrived at is not the best alternative conceivable; it is the best alternative possible and it is in keeping with our Red Book commitment."

Martin then crossed the street to the National Press Theatre to say his mea culpas in front of the journalistic pack. It wasn't the most comfortable of news conferences, but it was necessary. Martin and his team waited to see whether it would work. The next day's headlines played up Martin's comment that it was an "honest mistake." Brows were wiped. A mistake it was, yes, but an "honest" one.

While McTeague was grateful for Martin's intervention – gratitude that earned the finance minister a new loyalist among the MPs – Nunziata refused to back down on his threats to vote against the government. Chrétien, true to his word, expelled him from caucus.

On April 25, Nunziata held a news conference. It was a startling display of discontent with a PMO that had previously kept a pretty firm grip on internal dissent. Judged against complaints that would surface in years to come, Nunziata's condemnation of Chrétien looks prescient.

"I think Mr. Chrétien is going to have to seriously consider the people that he has in the Prime Minister's Office. They clearly do not have the support of the caucus; the national Liberal caucus," he said. Nunziata mentioned Eddie Goldenberg and Jean Pelletier by name, saying they were leaving Chrétien ill served and isolated from the MPs and Canadians who thought this prime minister was one of them. "Too much power is concentrated in the hands of unelected people in this country," Nunziata said.

The same day, cracks started to appear in Martin-Chrétien unity on the "honest mistake" line. In the House, the prime minister backed away from any talk of an apology. Instead, he insisted that the harmonized tax was the fulfillment of the Red Book promise. This was the communications strategy explicitly rejected at the CMOs as too insulting to Canadians, an explanation that would never wash with the public. Goldenberg and Donolo had agreed with that diagnosis.

The Reform party picked up on the discrepancy, asking who spoke for the government: the prime minister or the finance minister?

Martin reached for a rather dubious denial of any discrepancy whatsoever. "The statements that I made the other day stand. The statements made by the prime minister today stand. The statements made by the deputy prime minister stand. The fact is, this government speaks with one voice."

This of course was simply unity for the sake of appearances. There was deep frustration in Martin's office that Chrétien was not going along with the come-clean approach. Now they seemed to have the worst of both worlds: they had admitted a mistake and yet, thanks to the prime minister's stonewalling, they were being accused daily of denial.

Nor had the heat been lifted from Copps. Behind the scenes, Copps argued to all who would listen, including Chrétien, that Martin deliberately undermined her, inflicting another jab in an old rivalry. Publicly, she attempted a half-apology herself, saying she had been too quick with her words during the campaign, a "slip of the lip," she said. But the cries for her resignation continued.

Joe Fontana, the caucus chair, met weekly with the prime minister for a private chat on caucus issues. He arrived at his regular Tuesday-afternoon session on April 30 to find Chrétien in a foul humour. Martin was the subject of a lengthy rant, liberally sprinkled with curses, before they could turn to other subjects. According to Fontana, Chrétien thundered, "That fucking apology. That fucking Martin."

Early the next morning, while Liberals prepared for the weekly caucus meeting, Sheila Copps flew to Hamilton East and announced she was stepping down to run again for her seat in a by-election. A few hours later, Chrétien told the caucus he was sorry Copps had to resign, but "Paul, you know, he caused us some problems." While the caucus meeting was still going on, Terrie O'Leary received a call from Windsor MP Shaughnessy Cohen. It might be a good idea for her to come over, Cohen said, since Martin was sitting off in an anteroom, steaming mad. He could not believe that Copps's problems had been laid at his feet, especially since the PMO and Finance had arrived jointly at the come-clean approach.

Martin's people's mood was not improved when they heard what PMO officials had quietly been telling reporters in the wake of Copps's forced resignation. "We are wondering, in retrospect, whether that was a good idea," Donolo said, anonymously, in one news report. "I don't know whether we'd do it again." Wait a minute. Hadn't this been a joint decision?

After caucus, talking to reporters, Chrétien carried on with the idea that it was a mistake for Copps to have made such a concrete promise. Implicitly, he seemed to be saying that this vindicated his time-honoured approach of saying as little as possible, as ambivalently as possible. Straight talk, whether in making promises or acknowledging mistakes, was just buying trouble.

"Sometimes, in the course of a mandate, you're faced with a situation where you cannot deliver. You have to have some flexibility . . . because acts of God come in the administration. And no politician can see everything happening," he said.

By the Friday of that long week, Donolo was desperate to contain the damage of the GST debacle. Then he remembered one of the harsher realities of political life: the only thing that ends controversy is the start of another. "You can't balance bad news with good news. Only new bad news trumps bad news," he reminded his colleagues. Luckily, he had the ingredients close at hand to build just such a distraction: legislation to amend hate-crime laws, which would add homosexuals to the list of people protected under the act. The government had been sitting on this long-awaited legislation, much to gay advocates' frustration, awaiting a chance to slip it through the Commons with as little fuss as possible. The Centre had to scramble to find the appropriate ministers to introduce the legislation into the Commons that weary Friday. But it was worth the effort. The Reform party's hard-core members rose to the bait, condemning the legislation with ill-considered words of protest. The Liberals then counterattacked, characterizing such objections as proof of the intolerant heart of Reform party ideology. Preston Manning had been struggling to change that perception of Reform and moved quickly to silence the critics, temporarily banning them from caucus. In the midst of all of this dust-up, the Liberals' GST fiasco was forgotten.

"It worked like a charm," Donolo said.

Still, Chrétien was not done with the controversy. Later that year, he again dug in his heels and refused to concede that the Liberals had broken a promise. On this occasion it was an ordinary citizen, a waitress, who raised the question in the course of a CBC town-hall broadcast shortly before Christmas 1996. He maintained that no mistake had been made, honest or otherwise. Privately, he told his advisers he regretted the whole strategy of admitting to an error, but Donolo insisted that it was the best exit strategy from the GST mess. It took Chrétien a week to admit publicly that perhaps the Liberals were responsible for the impression they had created on scrapping the GST.

In early 1997, Chrétien began to consider a spring election, to capitalize on an opposition that was still fractured and the relative good fortunes of the Liberals. Though the party's shiny image had been dulled somewhat over the past two years, it remained high in the polls. Moreover, a spring election would be a gift to his grumpy caucus members. If he waited until fall, MPs would lose their summers to pre-election campaigning. "If I go now," he told one of his golf partners, "then I'll be giving them the summer off. They could use that. They deserve it."

As the strategists geared up for a spring campaign, they considered the advantages of the team approach in this election. Party pollster Michael Marzolini had tracked Paul Martin's popularity for almost a decade, ever since he worked on his leadership campaign in 1990. (It was a testament to the conciliatory spirit of the post-leadership period in the early 1990s that Marzolini was chosen to be the Liberals' official opinion-tracker.) He urged the Liberal marketing gurus to feature Martin in the party's advertising. Martin's presence, he said, boosted Liberal popularity in traditionally weak regions, in the West and Quebec. It was already obvious to Marzolini that voters were attracted by the package deal: a vote for Chrétien now meant a vote for his successor – Martin – later. David Herle called it the "two-fer," two Liberal leaders for the price of one.

The election-strategy team for the 1993 campaign had included a healthy number of individuals from the Martin camp. Significantly, the more senior Martinites sat this one out. Herle was asked to do some polling, but told the PMO, "I'm not your guy." O'Leary also turned down a request to go on the campaign bus with the leader's team, as she had in 1993. She would stay close to Martin instead, who was expected to spend more than half the campaign travelling. But three staffers from Martin's entourage – Scott Reid, Ruth Thorkelson, and Karl Littler – were recruited to work at Liberal command central at the party's Metcalfe Street offices in Ottawa, or "the war room," as it was popularly called.

The writ was dropped in early May 1997 for a June 2 election, just as Manitoba's Red River overflowed, causing massive, record flooding over large areas of the province. Proceeding with the election in the midst of this natural disaster was a risk for a prime minister who had been tarred with allegations of insensitivity. It exposed him once more to the accusation that he was out of touch, inconsiderate of the regions. The old Liberal fault line was threatening at least two fronts through the last half of his first mandate. Here was a prime minister who had gravely miscalculated on Quebec, and was now running into trouble with the West again.

But as the campaign unfolded, it wasn't in these areas that the Liberals started to feel vulnerable. For all the wisdom of positioning Martin as a star of this regime, it was the policy with which he was most associated – the deficit fight – that was risking the government's future. Liberals who had resented Martin's influence in the first mandate felt vindicated, especially those who believed that the finance minister had become a captive of the fiscally obsessed bureaucracy and forgetful of real people. They considered Martin unquestionably competent, but lacking true Liberal political instincts.

Nine days before the vote, Marzolini warned campaign headquarters that the voters in Atlantic Canada were turning against the Liberals, largely because of their cuts to employment programs. Campaign manager John Rae launched Operation Save Majority and called on the big guns in the region – premiers Brian Tobin in Newfoundland and Frank McKenna in New Brunswick – to come to the aid of the party. Despite these efforts, voters in the four Atlantic provinces reduced the number of Liberal MPs from thirty-one to just eight, and turfed out two leading cabinet ministers: Human Resources Minister Doug Young and Public Works Minister David Dingwall. Nationally, the number of Liberal seats fell from 177 to 155. There was grumbling in the PMO and some partisan circles that in the first mandate the government had strayed too far from its traditional Liberal roots, and that the next term should be devoted to putting a fresh coat of bright red paint over the blue-hued Liberalism championed by the likes of Martin.

There were hints too, even on election night, that the Martin forces were getting ready to widen the distance between themselves and the Chrétien wing of the party. As in 1993, the party had booked the World Exchange Plaza in Ottawa for a lavish celebration. But in a move that Donolo would describe as "hurtful" and "sending all the wrong messages," the Martin workers from the war room – Thorkelson, Karl Littler, and Scott Reid – broke away to join closer comrades. The Chrétien and Martin camps celebrated separately that evening.

The partnership had produced two election victories, and for many on both sides of the Martin-Chrétien divide, that was just about enough.

4

VEILED AMBITION

IN JULY 1997, with the election behind them, David Herle and Terrie O'Leary made a trip to Montreal. This wasn't purely a pleasure excursion. They planned to link up with Paul Martin and, over dinner, initiate a discussion they believed was overdue.

The three met at a sidewalk café on Rue St. Denis, a lively magnet for tourists, street performers, and the chic, local set. Herle opened the conversation.

"Paul, it's time to start thinking about the leadership," he said.

Herle and O'Leary told Martin that he had accomplished the near-impossible during the first mandate; he'd become a successful and popular finance minister. Canadians, and especially Liberals, regarded him as a jewel in the cabinet crown. He was now positioned as a credible, if not the most credible, candidate to replace Jean Chrétien, when and if that day ever came. Martin listened carefully to what both had to say.

During the previous four years, there had been developments on a personal level between the three people at this café table. Herle and O'Leary had become a couple and had built a country home together on a lake in the Gatineau Hills, where their cottage neighbours included Elly Alboim, Peter Mansbridge, and Richard Mahoney. They had also become the closest friends that Martin had among his team of advisers.

Of all the people in the constellation of Martin supporters, David Herle was the North Star, a beacon and a compass. While others' fervour for Martin's leadership hopes might fade or waver over the years, Herle's commitment only deepened. Virtually everyone in Martin's inner circle had come to it through Herle. His great strength, according to Martin, was his ability to recognize a defining moment, and the finance minister relied heavily on him for advice and comradeship.

Only Terrie O'Leary could claim equal or surpassing closeness to the man who would be prime minister. She and Martin were now virtually inseparable, as friends and colleagues. Martin valued her ability to balance competing views and her astute assessments of political friends or foes. The finance minister rarely made a move without soliciting her advice and almost never went against it. O'Leary's interest in education or disability issues were Martin's as well. He had come to regard Terrie's family as an extended version of his own, especially her younger, mentally handicapped brother, Stephen, who often came to Ottawa to stay with his sister in the summer.

Martin was no stranger to disability: his own childhood bout with polio and Sheila's nephew, Douglas, who was confined to a wheelchair, had given him intimate knowledge of the challenges of physical impairment. Meeting Stephen O'Leary, though, provided him perspective on the needs of the mentally disabled and their families.

During Stephen's visits to Ottawa, Terrie brought her brother to work. Martin's Finance office, which he turned over to Stephen, would be a riot of crayons, shredded paper, and other of Stephen's diversions. The minister himself would fetch breakfast, dutifully making a return trip to the cafeteria if he forgot the syrup for Stephen's favourite pancakes.

There were advantages and disadvantages to Paul Martin treating his close staff as family. On the upside, it meant being warmly welcomed at the Martin household, where Sheila Martin entertained guests with a relaxed hospitality. On the downside, it meant there was no escape from Martin's relentless curiosity. In O'Leary's case, the boss's inquisitiveness often collided with her fiercely guarded privacy. Terrie's sister, Karen, once popped in to say hello to the finance minister, only to be surprised by a knowledgeable grilling on the state of her love life.

"How does he know all that?" Karen challenged her sister later.

"I'm sorry, I can't help it," Terrie apologized. "He needs to know the details of people's personal lives. I'm not giving him any of mine, so I threw your stuff at him to keep him happy."

Before their dinner with Martin on Rue St. Denis, Herle and O'Leary had plotted only the broad, preliminary steps of a future leadership campaign: where to position Martin and how to take the lessons of the 1990 contest and turn them into a winning formula for the next one. They were determined that, just as Jean Chrétien had won in 1990 with impressive strength at the grassroots and with solid caucus support, so too would Martin. But unlike Chrétien, Martin would have to build his victory within the caucus, as a loyal member of the Liberal team in Ottawa. Memories of the Turner-Chrétien schism in Opposition were still painful for the Martin team, many of whom had backed Turner in those difficult years. As for the organizational nuts and bolts, they could think of no one better than John Webster, who had worked with Herle as far back as those Friends of John Turner days. For more than a year, Webster had been arguing that it was important to keep the old Martin team together. He had a longer-term objective in his sights, well beyond the next leadership convention.

Webster hadn't forgotten the nightmare of 1984. Turner had won the leadership contest but lost the election just months later. The reason? Turner's troops had lain dormant and disconnected through the late 1970s and early 1980s while they waited for their man's chance at the top job. They leapt into action to grab the immediate goal, but lacked the cohesion to transform their success into an election win. They had been trained for one mission only. Webster also looked to the example of the U.S. presidential primaries. By the time the six-month race began officially, candidates had been running for two years or more. Political victories, he maintained, were built on deep and enduring foundations.

Webster believed that a long-haul team had to be developed for Martin, one that could learn to accumulate consecutive victories, from the riding level to some future, far-off general election. Never bedazzled by the Parliament Hill bubble, Webster insisted this had to be done from the outside; Herle and O'Leary were too preoccupied by the up-close world of politics. In that world, Martin's strengths were exaggerated, and he was too far removed from the fickle grassroots. "No campaign, run exclusively out of Ottawa, has ever won an election," he said, citing the examples of Kim Campbell in 1993, John Turner in 1984, and Pierre Trudeau in 1979.

O'Leary was reluctant even to consider these questions while the government was in its first mandate. "Let's have one more election," she would say when Webster raised the subject. "Once Chrétien has his two majorities, then we'll talk about what to do down the road."

In the summer of 1997, the moment had arrived. Martin sat listening to Herle and O'Leary's pitch. David and Terrie weren't asking him to do anything different, simply more of the same. The hard strategizing and organizing would be done by others, as Martin preferred.

"I don't lie awake at night, overjoyed with the whole political aspect," Martin once explained. "I have never had a lot of time for those people who say, 'I have gone into public life, but I am not a politician.' To which my answer is: Then don't go into public life. Go home, become something else, become a nun. . . . I am quite proud to be a politician and I understand the organizational side of politics. I just don't happen to be wildly interested in it."

David Zussman, the man who designed the architecture of Chrétien's governing machine, found Martin to be one of the few ministers who actively sought out new ideas during the first term. Ironically, another minister who impressed Zussman this way was Lloyd Axworthy, who often butted heads with Martin during the deficit-cutting years. Former Liberal cabinet minister Warren Allmand, who became head of the Canadian Human Rights Institute when he left politics in 1993, said Axworthy and Martin were the only ministers who, in his experience, looked for opportunities to exchange ideas with non-governmental organizations.

For Martin, political life was essentially a civically responsible way to indulge his intellectual curiosity. "You've got to ask yourself: You could be at the farm. You could be messing around the world. . . . I'm not doing it because I like politics. I'm doing it because there are certain issues that really grab me, and the best way for me to do something about them is through politics."

O'Leary knew this was Martin's true enthusiasm and she played to it heavily over dinner. She talked about how the budget would soon be balanced, how the government could start to stretch itself on new issues and policies. At the end of the spiel the wineglasses were empty and O'Leary's ashtray was full. Martin leaned back in his chair, a sea of possibilities and wish lists swirling in his head. For the moment, all he could feel was flattered by their reviews of his performance to date.

"Well, this is kind of nice," he said.

Nothing about this conversation in the summer of 1997 felt premature to the people around Martin. Even Chrétien's inner circle believed that he'd probably call it a day after two decisive triumphs at the polls. This prime minister had defied expectations and matched Brian Mulroney's two-majority record. He would be leading the Liberals, like Wilfrid Laurier had a hundred years earlier, into a new century at the end of his second mandate. In two years, he'd reach the customary retirement age of sixty-five.

The prospect of this being Chrétien's last term in office gained strength when Liberal MPs returned to Parliament that fall. Two of their former colleagues – one defeated in June, and one who resigned – were special guests at the first caucus meeting in September. They came to preach to the mostly converted: Let's vote for Jean Chrétien. In about seven months, the federal Liberal party would hold its national convention in Ottawa. Under the terms of the party's constitution, there had to be a vote on Chrétien's leadership. The membership is allowed to render its verdict at the first convention following every general election.

Ron Irwin, the former Indian affairs minister and a long-time friend of Chrétien, had resigned from politics before the 1997 election. He told his former caucus colleagues that he would be spearheading the effort to win Chrétien a ringing endorsement. "He deserves our thanks," Irwin declared. Pierrette Ringuette, a New Brunswick MP defeated in the gun-control backlash of the June campaign, was at Irwin's side. She too talked up the need to generate a solid vote of thanks for all Chrétien had done for the party.

To some, including several cabinet ministers, this sounded like scene one of the final act. Not a moment too soon, said a few of Chrétien's critics. Ontario MPs especially had heard rumblings of discontent with the prime minister when they had knocked on doors in the election campaign a few months earlier. He had obfuscated on the GST and dangerously miscalculated the separatists' strength in his own province. Worse, there were signs that the little guy from Shawinigan had a bit of a mean streak, as evidenced by the Flag Day throttling incident. Dr. Carolyn Bennett, running for office for the first time in the Toronto riding of St. Paul's in 1997, had learned of Chrétien's falling popularity from her campaign workers. They would return from canvassing duties with reports that voters wanted reassurance that this was Chrétien's last term in office. Martin, on the other hand, appeared to be a doorstep favourite. "It wasn't so much that anyone wanted to push Chrétien out, but that they were impatient for the next thing," said Bennett. "Paul was the obvious next thing."

In the fall of 1997, Allan Rock, newly installed as health minister, met for a serious discussion with Cyrus Reporter, his executive assistant. In Rock's office in the Tunney's Pasture area of the capital, its wall of windows looking over the Ottawa River and the Peace Tower on the distant horizon, they tried to divine the long-term political future.

Reporter had been promoted to the top job in Rock's office a few months earlier after four years as his communications chief. He had come to appreciate the minister's potential leadership material. Underneath a rather stiff public persona was a quick sense of humour, an easy intelligence, and an irreverent attitude toward political sacred cows. Rock had been touted as a potential prime minister since his entry into politics, notably by the notorious Rainmaker of the Trudeau years, Keith Davey.

Reporter was the first to broach the topic of leadership with Rock. He told him that with talk of Chrétien staying for only two terms, it was time to decide whether he would be a candidate in the next leadership race.

Rock listened to Reporter's pitch, the possibility twinkling before him. He liked the idea of positioning himself to the left of Martin, and being the candidate who would champion the more traditional Liberal values. Rock felt that he had laid a credible groundwork for that style of campaign with his work in Justice in the first mandate, and that now, as health minister, he had more opportunities to paint himself a social Liberal.

"Let's open that door," he told Reporter. "Let's just say for now that I'm open to the idea."

On one level, running for the leadership seemed an enormously precocious notion for a man so new to politics. Rock had joined the party in the early 1990s and had never even attended a leadership convention. Vaulted from idealistic rookie candidate to justice minister in 1993, Rock had received a swift, sometimes cruel education during four years on some of the government's most troublesome files.

While the Liberals tilted to the right in the deficit-cutting exercise of the first mandate, Rock and the Justice Department were burdened with championing the leftish side of the government's program: gun control, gay rights, and hate-crime legislation. These were all matters of Liberal principle that were presumed to be relatively inexpensive – at least at the time.

Rock had also achieved a certain notoriety during Brian Mulroney's Airbus lawsuit, when he was pursued by the former prime minister between 1994 and 1996. Mulroney sued the attorney general when he learned of a letter the Justice Department had written to the Swiss government in 1994, alleging he had received bribes in exchange for Air Canada's purchases of Airbus airplanes while he was in office. Rock was pegged as the perpetrator of this libel by the sophisticated lawyers and public-relations experts who fought for Mulroney's reputation in the courts and in the news media. In early January 1997, the government settled with Mulroney. The former prime minister, as part of the settlement, explicitly exonerated Rock from any role in sending the letter to the Swiss government or in launching the RCMP's investigation in the first place. Still, an impression lingered that Rock was somehow responsible for the whole mess.

Rock had relied on Earnscliffe for communications advice during the Airbus controversy. David Herle and Elly Alboim had coached him on what to say to the media and on how to handle himself and the department in negotiations. Now they were helping him navigate the shoals of yet another hot issue: government compensation for people infected with hepatitis C through tainted-blood donations. Reporter had to deliver a hard truth: if Rock intended to run for the leadership, he could not lean any more on help from Earnscliffe.

"The biggest problem we're going to face is you being taken seriously as a candidate," Reporter told Rock. "If you say you're running against Martin but are still using his closest advisers as strategists, you won't be taken seriously. You'll be seen as Martin's protégé."

The annual Press Gallery dinner was held in November 1997, postponed from spring because of the June election. The jokes at the gallery dinner are always a good gauge of the buzz on Parliament Hill. No surprise, then, that this event was packed with gags about leadership, most on the theme of Martin grasping for Chrétien's job.

New Democratic Party Leader Alexa McDonough quipped that a recent poll showed that only 60 per cent of Canadians knew that Chrétien was prime minister, but he should be relieved by this, because only 40 per cent thought Paul Martin was the PM.

Jean Charest, Kim Campbell's successor as Conservative leader, described the kind of hard-nosed politician who could unite the right. "Someone who is bloodthirsty. Someone whose every move is calculated to undermine his superior. Someone who can forget every one of his previous principles." Pausing for effect, Charest said, "There is only one conservative in all of Canada who is qualified to unite the right. Paul Martin, rise from your seat."

Even Chrétien picked up the theme, joking that he had recently commissioned Liberal MP John Godfrey to do a psychological profile of certain politicians with identity problems. He found that many of Canada's top politicos wanted to be someone else. B.C. Premier Glen Clark, for instance, wanted to be Brian Tobin. Brian Tobin wanted to be New Brunswick Premier Frank McKenna. Frank McKenna wanted to be Paul Martin.

"And Paul Martin," said Chrétien, gazing mischievously at his blushing finance minister. "I forget . . . who is it you want to be?"

It would be Martin's last press gallery dinner for a long time.

Joe Volpe, a Toronto MP since 1988 and a Martin supporter in the 1990 leadership campaign, didn't deny he was pleased by the rumours of Chrétien stepping down after two terms, but he wasn't entirely sure that Martin was considering another run. He had seen no evidence of a leadership organization – and figured he ought to know. Could it be that Volpe wasn't as important to the future Martin team as he assumed he would be?

One day in late fall 1997, Volpe caught up to Martin in the Commons lobby.

"Paul, are you interested in the leadership?" Volpe asked.

"Yes, of course I am," Martin replied.

"Well, look," said Volpe. "Is there an organization out there? Because if there's a team and I'm not on it, that tells me something. And if there's no organization, that tells me something too."

Martin was quick to respond. Yes, it was true that Herle, O'Leary, and Webster were doing early, exploratory work, but everyone was being very circumspect. "I've been concentrating on my job. If I were to do anything else, it would be seen as trying to undermine the prime minister."

Volpe, a veteran of the Turner-Chrétien struggles, had to agree. Back in 1985, when Volpe was an administrator at the Toronto School Board and only dabbling in Liberal politics on the side, Chrétien, then an opposition MP under Turner, had come to Toronto to meet with him. Chrétien had a proposal for Volpe, which was that he should run for president of the Liberal party's Ontario wing. Volpe, whose strength was organizational knowhow, didn't understand why Chrétien would want him in that position. Chrétien explained, "Once you win, you can ask Turner to step down." Volpe demurred. Toppling the Liberal leader wasn't what he had in mind at this early stage of his political life.

With signals of Chrétien's departure in the air, however, it didn't seem too soon for Volpe to start thinking about reviving Martin's 1990 leadership organization. And Volpe knew where to start, with the most rudimentary tool in the political organizer's kit – a good list. Volpe had kept all the names from the 1990 leadership campaign: the donors, the volunteers, the party workers and officials. It was time to update and expand those lists. Terrie O'Leary had an impressive cache of her own Martin-friendly contacts to add, friendships across Canada nurtured quietly for years.

Meanwhile, Joe Fontana, chair of the Liberal caucus and another Martinite, knew the risks of trying to organize on the ground too soon, especially in ridings held by the party in government. If the member of Parliament was sympathetic to Martin, it could be seen as organizing against the prime minister, and the repercussions would be severe. If the MP was undecided or not particularly warm to Martin, organizing in the riding would be seen as provocative. But the Liberals held only 155 of the 301 seats in the Commons. That meant that almost half of Canada's ridings were potentially open to a new organization stepping in. Here it seemed safe to make forays on behalf of Martin's clandestine leadership hopes.

In the spirit of growing the party, Fontana had established a "twinning" program in 1997 between Liberal and non-Liberal ridings. The idea was simple: an MP would make contacts with Liberals in constituencies represented by other parties. Andrew Telegdi, from Kitchener-Waterloo, was twinned with the B.C. riding of Nanaimo. Stan Keyes was matched with an Edmonton-area riding that had a heavy industrial base and working-class demographic similar to Keyes's own Hamilton-area riding. The MPs would keep up to date with events in their "twin" riding, attending annual general meetings of the riding association and ensuring that local Liberals stayed in touch with the party establishment in Ottawa.

Fontana was happy to put the contacts he'd made in this program at John Webster's disposal, giving Martin's team a ready-made list of Liberal organizers across the country – many of whom might be delighted to participate in a future leadership bid. Fontana and Volpe put the "twinning" idea into practice within caucus as well. The half-dozen or so MPs who had been with Martin in the 1990 campaign decided to link up with prospective supporters on the backbench, one by one. New converts to the cause would in turn work on persuading others. It was like that television commercial for hair conditioner: I told two friends, and she told two friends, and so on.

In these ways a small band of MPs, very quietly so as not to arouse allegations of plots, started to make their moves. They weren't exactly Boy Scouts, but they were borrowing the motto: Be prepared.

This early leadership work coincided with the run-up to the April 1998 convention, where Chrétien was supposed to receive his party's hearty thanks. While Liberals were being lobbied to give Chrétien a resounding endorsement in the leadership-review vote, they were also being asked to think about his successor. The Martin and Rock teams had to be extremely careful that their own preliminary efforts were not seen as a challenge at the prime minister's leadership review.

Webster had been adamant that the Martin organization would not attempt anything resembling a coup. He'd had enough of that kind of drama during the 1980s. "I never believed in a civil-war scenario," he says. "We weren't going to do this through a leadership review. It was too bloody. Besides, Paul would never have gone along with it. That's just not him."

The Martin team kept a low profile at the April convention. They made no overt attempts to run a Martinite candidate for the party presidency, nor did they aggressively pursue elected seats on the national executive. The theme of this convention was "one big happy family" in the hopes that harmony would encourage Chrétien to leave on a high note.

The boosterism of Irwin and Ringuette paid off when Chrétien's leadership was endorsed by a whopping 90 per cent of voting members. Some were skeptical of that figure, given that ballots were counted behind closed doors by Chrétien's most loyal supporters in the party administration, including Terry Mercer, the executive director. But if 92 per cent was the incentive required for a graceful leave-taking before the next election, impatient Martin supporters in caucus and beyond decided they could live with it.

In the meantime, seismic shifts were being felt in Martin's Finance Department. One came in the form of an unexpected announcement in January 1998, as two of the country's largest banks, the Bank of Montreal and the Royal Bank, told Canadians they intended to merge. Martin knew the big banks were considering the idea. Anticipating such a merger proposal, he had appointed a federal task force, headed by Saskatchewan lawyer Harold McKay, to investigate the implications. But Martin was totally blindsided by the announcement and annoyed that the banks hadn't waited until his task force had reported. Finance was not amused.

The banks made another miscalculation in underestimating the growing clout of the backbenchers or, more precisely, the depth of Martin's connections with the Liberal caucus, carefully built over the first mandate through budget consultations and his office's outreach efforts.

Tony Ianno was a soft-spoken but hardball-playing politician from the Trinity-Spadina riding in Toronto with a daunting reputation as a Liberal organizer, especially in the Italian- and Chinese-Canadian communities. In 1998, he was heading a special caucus task force on bank mergers, filled with MPs who were eager to display that they had some clout with the financial institutions. In the wake of the 1995 budget, especially, the governing Liberals were accused of pandering to the financial markets at the expense of the voting public. Ianno wasn't intimidated by the banks or by the business agenda, as were some other MPs from suburban ridings where the Liberal vote tended to bleed toward the right. His own riding battles had been fought at the left end of the political spectrum, against the strong New Democratic Party presence in Toronto's urban core. His focus was on how well these big-business entities were serving consumers and the community. (Ianno, who had supported Chrétien in the 1990 leadership, had become one of Martin's stronger caucus supporters by 1998, and he lent his formidable network to Webster's leadership rebuilding efforts.)

Ianno's committee hearings had an important influence on Martin, whose political antenna twitched on the subject of multinational business and globalization. Voter concern with urban affairs and environmental issues was up, and young people – one of Martin's favourite constituencies – were becoming more vocal in their objections to big corporations. Martin had seen first-hand how the young anti-globalization protesters had seized the limelight at the World Trade Organization meeting in Seattle in 1996 and at the Asia-Pacific Economic Co-operation (APEC) summit in Vancouver in 1997. When protesters were pepper-sprayed at the latter,

Chrétien's folksy persona had taken another hit. The prime minister dismissed the police actions by saying, "For me, pepper, I put it on my plate."

"As the world is going more global, citizens are getting more local," Martin was saying in speeches devoted to the theme. He warned that multinational enterprises, such as banks or automobile manufacturers, had to balance their worldwide influence against community-based interests. In simple terms, he explained that this is why people liked car companies and loathed banks. Car dealerships had a presence in small towns; they sponsored baseball teams and raised money for charities. Banks were a diminishing presence, shutting down local branches and introducing more and more automated services. He carried this analogy with him to debates on globalization and development both at home and on the international stage.

In the early months of 1998, Martin prepared his fifth budget. This budget – billed as "the education budget" – signalled that the Liberal government was changing tack and reasserting its traditional, left-leaning belief that the federal government should act as a force for social change. It was also instituting the National Child Benefit, an ambitious joint project of federal, provincial, and territorial governments to alleviate child poverty and help low-income families with the costs of raising healthy, educated children.

There was another significant aspect to the 1998 budget. After four years of deficit-cutting, the government was projecting a small surplus, which meant that the budget would be balanced for the first time in decades. At this important watershed, though, Martin was far more cautious than the prime minister. Chrétien was sure that when the final numbers were available in August, the government would be in a surplus position. Martin hesitated to create that expectation before he saw the true figures. Yes, he was confident in predicting that the budget would be balanced next year and the year after that, but this year? He wasn't ready to say that with certainty.

Martin haggled with Eddie Goldenberg, arguing it was risky to proclaim a balanced budget now, before it had actually happened. The prime minister's emissary insisted, and finally, with the Finance Department's cautious assent, Martin agreed. He then convened to a CMO meeting to discuss how to announce a balanced budget while at the same time conveying his wariness about this year's numbers.

Speechwriter Larry Hagen, always present at budget-preparation meetings, rarely ever spoke. He scribbled, he listened, and he would occasionally punctuate the discussion with sharp, pointed questions. As he absorbed the CMO's excitement over the surplus, and how to best capture this moment in the speech and history, he spoke up.

"How does this sound?" he asked. "We will balance the budget next year. We will balance the budget the year after that. And we will balance the budget this year." Everyone around the table beamed. Martin's face broke into a smile. Hagen had captured his long-term optimism and short-term caution by putting this year's forecast last. "That's it," he said. Indeed it was, as the 1998 budget would be remembered for this clip. On the news that afternoon and night, the three-line phrase summed up a great achievement and a rosy future, for the government and for Martin. It was the bookend to that first memorable phrase in the Martin lexicon – "come hell or high water," the government had cleaned up its finances. Overnight, Paul Martin seemed to become a star, approached in restaurants and on the street by well-wishers.

Although those around him went to ridiculous lengths to pretend Martin's leadership candidacy did not exist, the reality flapped like a flag in the wind. By now, Martin had a communications director named Scott Reid, a quick-thinking, fast-talking young supporter from the 1990 leadership who was already known for rapid-fire repartee and hard, elbows-up defence of his boss. One day in June 1998, Martin took a trip to Belleville, Reid's hometown. Martin was paying a call on Loyalist College and the media was out in force. Cameras followed Martin and Reid as they made their way across the college campus. Suddenly, there came a cry from someone in the pack of reporters and onlookers. "Hey! It's the next prime minister of Canada."

Martin reddened and the quick-thinking Reid jumped into the spotlight. "See what a great hometown I come from? Did you hear what they called me?"

In retrospect, Reid and others would realize that this denial of the obvious was a foolish strategy, one that only fed the perception in Chrétien's world that ambition was synonymous with disloyalty. Naively, they felt they were contributing to Chrétien's success at the same time as planning for his succession. Martin didn't see any discrepancy between organizing for a future leadership and serving as a loyal Liberal under Chrétien, nor did his organizers. He thought that David Herle, whom the Chrétien forces were treating as an adversary, should be recognized for his contributions to the budgets and the overall success of this government.

It was certainly as a team player that Herle went to the caucus meeting in Shawinigan in the summer of 1998 to present the results of recent polls. Normally Michael Marzolini would give the rundown at these gatherings, but when Marzolini was unable to attend, Shaughnessy Cohen, a big believer in personal bridge-building, suggested that Herle be given a chance to take the MPs through the numbers. The prime minister and others could then see for themselves how he was working in the Liberal party's interest. Herle and Chrétien even sat at the same table at lunch, enjoying homemade butter tarts baked by former hockey great, and new senator, Frank Mahovlich.

Herle made a rare public appearance before the media at the Shawinigan event, summarizing the presentation he had given to the MPs. "Health care is the most important issue by far," Herle told reporters. "Canadians want an emergency system they can count on, and they want to know they can get to a doctor if they need to and they don't particularly want to hear governments talking about whose job it is to ensure that."

This was a hint of the theme, or "narrative," of the next budget, due to be delivered in early 1999. A health-care budget meant Martin and Rock would have to work together more closely, not an easy assignment for either. Now that they were known leadership rivals, their relations had turned frosty. Each blamed the other for the deterioration. From Rock's perspective, it looked like Martin just couldn't tolerate a challenge, that he was too thin-skinned to handle competition from colleagues.

Martin admits that it's hard to stay on good terms with a political rival. "It's a time of suspended friendships," he says. "It's just impossible to remain friends."

One level down, David Herle and Cyrus Reporter were trying to manage the same tension. The two had been roommates during the Liberals' first term of government and friends for years. Reporter had supported Martin in the 1990 leadership. Now Herle and Reporter were on different sides in the undeclared leadership contest.

It does happen that close friends, siblings, or husbands and wives find themselves divided by political rivalries. Ruth Thorkelson, the Liberal sister of a former Tory MP, was an example in Martin's office. The Anderson brothers of Ottawa were another: Rick Anderson was chief strategist for the Reform party and Canadian Alliance, while Bruce (who worked with Herle at Earnscliffe) was chief adviser to Jean Charest when he was leader of the federal Progressive Conservatives. Younger brother Jim was a Liberal.

It takes an ability to compartmentalize to maintain personal relationships through the fire of political battle. Herle and Reporter still socialized, but the Liberal leadership as a conversation topic was out. They talked instead of their other interests: dogs, music, and their beloved Montreal Canadiens.

The friendship between Rock and Martin proved impossible to sustain. Their simmering rivalry flared into outright hostility after Rock spoke out at a cabinet committee meeting in 1998. Martin wasn't at the meeting – the finance minister rarely attended them, leaving it to the secretary of state for financial institutions to represent the department. But Rock was there and used the occasion to vent his frustration over how Martin was deliberately not giving cabinet a true fiscal picture so that he could make debt reduction a bigger priority than spending. This, said Rock, was unfair. The finance minister held all the clout to accomplish his goals – balancing the books – before other ministers could tackle theirs.

"I don't think I was alone in feeling the frustration because of the process," Rock said later. He admitted that the nascent leadership campaign was also part of the tension, calling it part of a "quite natural human dynamic."

Martin was furious when he heard about Rock's remarks. He was less upset about the substance of the diatribe than the fact it was delivered when he wasn't present. "He might have told me ahead of time, and why would he wait for a cabinet committee meeting, when I'm not there?"

The making of the health-care budget in the closing weeks of 1998 and early 1999 was a strain on the Martin-Rock relationship too. The tension was tempered somewhat by the fact that David Dodge, Martin's old deputy minister, had now moved to Health to serve as Rock's most senior bureaucrat. Still, Rock remained frustrated by Martin's secrecy about the numbers.

Their relationship reached its nadir in a private room at the Ritz restaurant on Nepean Street in downtown Ottawa during the final stages of budget preparation. Martin was there with Ruth Thorkelson and his deputy minister, Scott Clark. Rock was there with Cyrus Reporter and David Dodge.

The two ministers exchanged testy remarks all through the dinner, circling the now-familiar issue of why Martin was being so stingy with the facts about how much money was available for health. As Rock pressed, Martin's famed temper showed itself. "Oh go to hell," Martin said. "Screw you."

As the Liberals settled into their second mandate, growing comfortable with being in power, there was restlessness in their backrooms. Key ministerial aides were starting to move on or move out, departures that would have major repercussions in some cases.

A change of the palace guard was inevitable, partly because of the way political staffing was handled in Chrétien's Ottawa. When the Liberals came to power in 1993, Chrétien wanted to reverse what he regarded as the dangerous and rampant politicization of government during the Mulroney years. Under the Tories, the number of political staff in ministers' offices had ballooned, some having as many as forty or fifty aides on their payrolls. Chrétien's transition adviser, David Zussman, had pared the number to eight or ten key positions in each office. Why create a whole new tranche of political advisers and aides when every minister had a perfectly good bureaucracy at his or her disposal? As a bonus, the bureaucrats would feel more valued and government work wouldn't be hampered by constant power struggles between the political and public-service arms of ministers' offices. There would be no chiefs of staff. Jean Pelletier, with his trademark subtlety, told an early meeting of Liberal aides: "There's only one chief of staff in this government." The top aide to a minister in the Chrétien government would be known as an executive assistant. Beyond this, budgets for political staff were radically reduced. Average salaries for ministers' staffers offices were between $40,000 and $60,000 a year, and Zussman had deliberately excluded pension benefits so that no one would be encouraged to become a career assistant. Zussman believed that Liberal ministers should have a high turnover in their offices, which would keep the staff contingent vital and energetic.

The compensation was attractive to thirty-somethings, but prohibitive to the forty-and-over crowd, who knew they could probably make more in the private sector, parlaying their government experience into consulting or communications jobs. The hours were punishing too. Ministerial staffers were always on call, working nights and weekends. It was no life for someone with family responsibilities. The more experienced hands began to seek regular jobs, with regular hours. They would be replaced by a younger crew; Chrétien's and Martin's offices were no exception.

In the spring of 1998, Peter Donolo went to lunch with Chrétien at 24 Sussex Drive and notified his boss that he was preparing to leave the PMO. "It's been seven years," he said. "Not many people have done this job for that long. It's time for me to move on." Donolo didn't think his timing would inconvenience the prime minister, whom he expected would serve no more than two terms.

Chrétien said, "What if I tell you that I have a consul-general's job opening in Milan next year? If you can hold on another year, the job is yours." Donolo agreed.

Over at Finance, Terrie O'Leary was having a similar conversation with her boss.

O'Leary was burned out, in every sense of the word. The lakehouse that she and Herle shared had been destroyed in a fire earlier that year, and they had lost many of their precious possessions. They were slowly rebuilding. She was tired of the hours and the tremendous energy that the job required and dreamed of a job that would not require her to be on call twenty-four hours a day, seven days a week. She had talked to some corporate headhunters, but many of the jobs they had floated her way would have put her in a conflict-of-interest position with Finance. O'Leary was not interested.

It was Scott Clark, then the deputy minister at finance, who talked to her about sitting on the board of the World Bank. Canada's representative is traditionally picked by the department and answers to the finance minister. Clark believed this position would give O'Leary a chance to stretch her horizons, while still allowing her to work for Martin – at a more reasonable pace. The job, which paid about U.S. $150,000, would require a lot of travelling, especially to Ireland and to Caribbean nations, as Canada also represented these countries on the board.

Martin thought the appointment would be ideal for O'Leary and got the process in motion. Chrétien merely had to rubber-stamp the decision, which he did. The announcement was made, O'Leary found an apartment in Washington, and Donolo threw her a going-away party in his backyard, which even Chrétien attended.

Ruth Thorkelson took O'Leary's place. Her style was much more low-key than O'Leary's, but she shared her predecessor's interest in keeping Martin connected with MPs and with Liberals across the country, especially young people. Closer to home, Thorkelson organized pub nights and barbecues around Parliament Hill to introduce the finance minister to younger Parliament Hill staff. She made sure that Martin's office – unlike many other ministerial offices – actually used its full $20,000 annual budget to hire summer students. Thorkelson hired student Liberals from all regions in a move reminiscent of the job program that had brought Herle, Mahoney, and O'Leary together in the 1980s. Many weren't Martin supporters, but she hoped that by exposing them to life in the capital and to the finance minister, she'd win new converts.

Another factor contributed to a change of tone in Liberal politics around this time – the newspaper wars. In late fall 1998, Conrad Black launched the ambitious *National Post*, an unapologetically cheeky and right wing daily newspaper. The grey *Globe and Mail* reacted in panic, trying to enliven its coverage with more columns and uncharacteristic gossip about the political class.

The backroom denizens soon learned to exploit the new media rivalry to their advantage. With heightened competition between the political reporters on the Hill, there was a rush to publish any and all tips or leaked information. It became far easier for strategists to plant their stories in the national press, sometimes just for mischief, sometimes to send messages to their rivals.

Percy Downe, a former aide to the late Prince Edward Island premier Joseph Ghiz, came to Ottawa to work in the ministerial office of Lawrence MacAulay, and in the second mandate became director of appointments in the Prime Minister's Office.

"A lot of the gossip was elevated to the front pages as news story," he said. "A lot of the MPs who might be on the margins were suddenly [seen by] a percentage of the Canadian public as spokespersons. . . . A lot of this talk that is always around Ottawa started to become conventional wisdom."

When this phenomenon touched the simmering but still underground leadership campaign, the result was explosive. The influence that restive backbench MPs lacked at the Centre was restored by speaking to the media. Private grumbling against the PMO's closed shop began to turn into a muffled but public chorus.

Martin was growing restless himself. With the budget balanced, the priority project of this Liberal government was complete. He still enjoyed the Finance portfolio, but he looked for new ways to do the job. Martin had become uncomfortable with the cabinet dynamic that had been set up during the deficit-cutting years, a modus operandi that reduced budgets to a deal hammered out by the prime minister and the finance minister. He believed that other cabinet ministers should be more than mere spectators, especially now that the government's economic fortunes had turned. He started to talk about the idea of more collective decision-making in cabinet. "You understand, when cabinet doesn't make the tradeoffs, the minister of finance ends up making them."

He paid a call on David Zussman, now with the Public Policy Forum, a think-tank that serves as a bridge between the private and public sectors. For a few hours, Martin and Zussman batted around ideas on how to share the finance minister's power around the cabinet table. Perhaps they could return to the old "envelope" system, by which departments or sectors of the government received a bundle of money, to be allocated according to priorities at the ministerial or department level. Neither the prime minister nor the finance minister would have to sign off on each and every item within the budget.

But the discussions didn't lead to any obvious solutions, partly due to inertia, partly due to an if-it-ain't-broke-don't-fix-it syndrome. Ministers such as Allan Rock bristled under the paternalist nature of the Finance-PMO compact, but, by and large, this model had a record of success. "They [Chrétien and Martin] fell into a pattern of behaviour that encouraged them to work it out themselves," Zussman said. "It was hard to change that pattern, especially because it had worked so well."

Martin turned in another direction, readjusting his own sights from the domestic to the international stage. Terrie O'Leary's experiences at the World Bank contributed to his interest, and his youthful impulses to contribute on the global scene were reawakened. There was a practical element as well: If Martin started casting around for a new domestic project, he would inevitably stumble onto another minister's turf. Worse, he might collide with Chrétien and risk the accusation of trying to upstage him.

Martin had already found that he could use Canada's good international reputation to be a broker between the United States and other, less powerful countries on issues of debt relief or currency stability. He had established friendships with his counterparts around the world and with key people in the Clinton administration.

His approach to the United States was rooted as much in his upbringing as it was in ideology. The boy from Windsor, who grew up in the shadow of Detroit, genuinely liked the Americans and enjoyed warm friendships with key figures in Washington. Yet, as Chrétien had learned, Martin could be frustratingly non-deferential toward power and enormously competitive. The prime minister had once complained to a Finance adviser, during one of the early tussles with Martin over the 1995 budget: "That Paul, he never has known who the boss is."

That streak revealed itself in one of Martin's earliest encounters with Clinton. In the late 1990s, the world economic community was rocked by the so-called Asia crisis, a rapid devaluation of currencies and national-debt defaults, which started in Thailand and spread like a contagion through Asia and into Russia. Clinton called it the worst international crisis in fifty years, a description that Martin viewed as overblown and unhelpful. Martin, in concert with his opposite numbers in the major industrial countries, including the United States, had been wrestling with new measures to make the world economy more stable.

At a meeting of the International Monetary Fund (IMF) in Washington in fall 1998, the Asia crisis was the dominant topic of discussion. President Clinton hovered around the gathering in a demonstration of his concern. Treasury Secretary Robert Rubin approached Martin at one of the early sessions and said that Clinton wanted to speak to some of the finance ministers. Martin grudgingly agreed to help round up a few people, believing that this encounter would serve as little more than a photo opportunity for Clinton, with international financial leaders as background props. Martin's patience was tested when he arrived for the meeting on schedule at 3 p.m., only to be told that the president wouldn't be there until 4:30 p.m. The ministers had been instructed to come ninety minutes early so that they could be checked out by the president's security detail. When Clinton finally did arrive, Martin fumed while the strains of "Hail to Chief" blared from the loudspeaker. Here were some of the world's leading finance ministers, kept cooling their heels for ninety minutes, subjected to an FBI search, and now ordered to stand and applaud a triumphal presidential procession.

Rubin opened up the discussion with a relatively soft question for the president. Martin launched a sharper salvo, designed to trip up Clinton on his knowledge of monetary policy. And then something interesting happened. "Clinton, for two hours, gave every bit as good as he got. He displayed a mastery of the subject that absolutely amazed all of us," Martin said. "Let there be no doubt about Clinton's brains."

Despite Clinton's impressive performance, Martin had his own ideas about how the world should be responding to the Asia crisis. His solution envisioned a forum beyond the G7 group of nations, one that would include the countries – "the emerging markets," as they were called – whose economies had proven to be so vulnerable during the recent collapse. The seed of this idea eventually produced an agreement in September 1999 to create the G20, an international forum of finance ministers and central bank governors dedicated to promoting stability in global economics.

These twenty nations or institutions represented more than 80 per cent of the world's economy.

One of the many people Martin consulted throughout this period was his old law-school colleague Bill Graham, who had headed up the House of Commons foreign affairs committee since 1993. Graham thought Martin's notion of enlarging the G7 concept was an innovative way of breaking what he called the "1945 syndrome" of foreign policy – judging all developments through the prism of the postwar world order.

Martin was instrumental in making the G20 a reality primarily by persuading the Americans to join. U.S. officials had been skeptical at first, but Martin appealed to his friends in Clinton's circle on practical grounds: It would be less costly to head off international economic crises in advance than to provide financial aid to debtor nations in the aftermath. Martin's lead role in this effort earned him the title of first chairman of the G20, a position he would hold until 2002.

For all his interest in multinational institutions, Martin retained much of the economic nationalism he had displayed at the Liberal youth convention in 1982. He believed in counterbalancing the United States' global dominance with strong collectives of nations and interests. He thought that Canada should stand firm in the face of its neighbour's overwhelming power – one of his motivations for buying Canada Steamship Lines in 1981 was to prevent it from falling into American hands. Martin's Windsor childhood was again influential. Growing up in a border town, playing basketball and baseball against Detroit teams, instilled an early determination not to be cowed by Yankee competition.

It was also through his distaste for American aggrandization that Martin met one of his closest foreign colleagues, Gordon Brown, chancellor of the exchequer in the United Kingdom. Martin was due to meet Brown formally for the first time at the G7 summit in Denver in June 1997. Their American hosts staged the usual splashy affair, heavy on special effects and politicking. President Clinton opened the event with a long-winded speech, introducing every one of his political friends in the audience. Martin ducked out of the room and returned to the air-conditioned bus used to ferry the dignitaries around the summit site. He pulled out his briefing papers and started to read. The bus door opened and in stumbled another escapee from the ceremonies, a young, tousle-haired Brit, clutching a briefcase crammed with papers. "Hello, I'm Gordon Brown," he said.

Martin knew Brown only by reputation. He was the most senior member of Tony Blair's New Labour regime that had swept into power in May on a bold promise to modernize the tired policies of the socialist Labour party. Brown's political career mirrored Martin's. He had competed with Blair for the leadership of his party but wound up as runner-up, in charge of finance. Like Martin, he was considered more business-friendly than his boss, and he had not abandoned his hopes of succeeding his former rival.

The two confessed their mutual exasperation with the opening proceedings and decided to skip the next session and hold their get-to-know-you meeting right there in the bus. They talked for the next two hours about policy and politics, discovering they were kindred spirits on the subject of education. Later, this mutual interest was channelled into efforts to increase funding for schooling in the Third World, a cause also championed, not coincidentally, by Terrie O'Leary's fellow board members at the World Bank. Oxfam International helped steer the education initiative championed by Brown and Martin, streaming more foreign-aid dollars toward schooling in the world's impoverished nations.

Carolyn Bennett, a well-known Toronto physician who had won her Toronto seat in 1997, took her interest in economic issues to a seat on the House of Commons finance committee.

The committee was loaded with Martin supporters: Maurizio Bevilacqua, the chairman, was seen as a Martin protégé; Tony Valeri, Martin's parliamentary secretary, was also a member. Bennett soon saw for herself how closely Martin worked with this committee and she was impressed that he would phone individual members and sound them out on issues or policies.

Out on the road for committee hearings in fall 1998, Bennett and Bevilacqua met for dinner after the day's sessions in Winnipeg. They chatted casually about the committee's forthcoming travels and in general about their colleagues. Delicately, Bevilacqua raised the L-word with Bennett. "Have you, um, thought about what you're doing on leadership?" he asked. Bennett had no hesitation: "I'm with Paul," she said matter-of-factly.

Then here's what she must do, Bevilacqua told her. Make an appointment with Martin to declare her intentions. That's how the leadership non-campaign was operating. Martin didn't ask for support – he merely accepted it. Bennett felt a bit silly. For a year now, she'd considered herself a Martin supporter, but she had no idea there were rules – a procedure, no less – for making it known formally to Martin

So she made the appointment. Walking into his fifth-floor office a few months later, Bennett sat down and blurted it out. She joked that she thought it was obvious she was on his team, then recounted her surprise at learning from Bevilacqua that she had to make the commitment in this deliberate fashion. "There was something therapeutic in saying it out loud," she later recalled.

Martin laughed, then thanked her for coming aboard, telling her that he was pleased to be judged by the company he kept if it included the likes of Dr. Bennett. Bevilacqua had added another caucus colleague to his list of declared Martin backers.

One of the original caucus supporters of Martin in the 1990 leadership campaign when he was barely thirty years old, Maurizio Bevilacqua had been a spokesman for youth issues, much as Dennis Dawson had been in the Trudeau days. Bevilacqua had been first elected to Parliament in 1988 in a closely fought election with a Conservative candidate in North York, then Canada's most populous riding. Elections Canada went back and forth for ten days before declaring the winner. Bevilacqua was sworn in as the riding's MP after a couple of weeks, only to find himself an ex-MP when the results were nullified two years later in 1990, after a long dispute and inquiry into the balloting. Bevilacqua's loyalty was sealed by the simple fact that Martin kept in touch, helping him in the 1991 by-election that returned him to the Commons.

Bevilacqua had been a tireless campaigner for Martin during the 1990 leadership contest, working closely with youth leaders such as Nick Masciantonio as well as the Italian-Canadian community. He had an entrepreneurial flare. Once, he landed in Edmonton, set up a headquarters at a neighbourhood Italian grocery store, and signed up almost four hundred new Liberal members to support Martin in the space of three days.

His encounter with Bennett was typical of those that he and Martin's other 1990 caucus supporters conducted quietly with their colleagues during the second mandate. Bevilacqua usually began his appeal with: "Look around, who do you see out there who could be a better leader?" Martin's talents spoke for themselves, he said. "It wasn't hard to sell Paul."

The scene was repeated with almost all caucus members between 1997 and 2000. At least a few dozen MPs made the suggested appointment, sitting down privately with Martin and pledging allegiance. The rule was: Martin won't ask for your support; you must offer it. Never should there be the suggestion that Paul Martin was actively soliciting Liberal MPs for his leadership organization.

There were other strategic considerations behind this approach. If Martin had to ask caucus colleagues for support, he would unavoidably accumulate IOUs. He would be playing into that most basic of political equations: you do something for me and I'll do something for you. This way, there was no obligation. MPs found themselves offering to help; Martin had only to show his gratitude, at least for the time being.

Joe Volpe, for one, says he never raised the issue of a quid pro quo with Martin, not future cabinet considerations or anything else. "If I did that," he explained, "everything I said would be seen through that prism. Paul would always think that everything I did for him was about trying to get something for myself."

The prospect of a quid pro quo was enough to make Stan Keyes nervous when he paid his call on Martin. Keyes, a Hamilton MP, had supported Sheila Copps, his hometown candidate, in the 1990 leadership, but he had grown to admire Martin in the budget-consultation process. As one of the class of 1988, Keyes believed he had been patiently riding the backbenches long enough. Going into his meeting with Martin, Keyes was a bundle of nerves. How could he say he wanted to be in cabinet someday without being seen to beg or make it a condition of his support for Martin's leadership?

Martin solved the problem for him. "Listen," Martin told him in a reassuring tone, no doubt well practised with others. "I know people will be looking to me for a fresh start, for fresh faces, for a new cabinet. I will be bringing fresh faces to cabinet."

It wasn't a promise, Keyes recognized. But it spared him having to raise the issue, even obliquely. This was all he needed to know – that Martin recognized his ambition and was promising to bring new blood into cabinet. It was more hope than any Chrétien had extended to Keyes in the five years the Liberals had been in power.

It was Richard Mahoney's job to attend to the care and feeding of the new caucus supporters, quietly meeting with them and keeping them informed. This mostly diplomatic function was perfectly suited to Mahoney's ample schmoozing abilities. Every month or so, he would invite a small group of MPs over to his offices at the Fraser Milner law firm, where he had returned in 1994 to work with David Smith once again, leaving Association House. He would order some gourmet takeout pasta from Fettucine's restaurant on Elgin Street, lay on a case of wine, and host the parliamentarians in for a casual evening of gossip. It would be an exaggeration to call these dinners strategy sessions, since it was far from clear how and when the leadership would come open. They were simply another way of keeping the Martin team connected and growing.

Just before Christmas 1998, the team suffered a devastating loss. On Wednesday, December 9, hours before the Liberal party's Christmas bash was due to begin, Windsor MP Shaughnessy Cohen collapsed in the House of Commons. She was rushed to the hospital with a ruptured aneurysm. Her roommate, Justice Minister Anne McLellan, accompanied her, as did more than a dozen of the popular MP's friends.

Cohen was close to Martin. She had been a friend to his mother and father, driving Paul Sr. around Windsor on political errands during the 1990 leadership and paying regular calls on Nell Martin before her death in 1993. Shaughnessy was wildly indiscreet, recklessly funny, and fiercely adoring of Paul Martin. The night before she collapsed, she had been sitting with Martin at the smaller caucus Christmas party, and when he had tried to leave, she insisted he finish a bottle of wine with her. Martin had tried to beg off, pleading that he needed his rest and time for reflection before announcing his decision on bank mergers in the days ahead. But she sat him down. "I'll tell you what you're going to do," she said.

The Martins kept a vigil at the hospital that night while Cohen hovered near death. Martin took charge, sending his car to meet her husband at the airport and delegating others to get in touch with her huge network of friends and family.

Grant Hill, a Reform Party MP and medical doctor who had tried in vain to resuscitate Cohen after her collapse, stood at the entrance to the hospital ward, watching Martin preside over the grief-stricken group. On his way out, he said to one of the MPs, "I had no idea how much you guys are like a family."

Martin stayed at the hospital until Cohen's husband arrived and the life-support systems were turned off. The next night, he hosted a dinner party at Mamma Teresa's for all of her friends in cabinet, caucus, and beyond. He delivered the eulogy the following weekend in Windsor, saying that two of Windsor's finest MPs – Paul Martin Sr. and Shaughnessy Cohen – were now in heaven, looking down on all the fuss, and undoubtedly arguing over who had been more important.

The bank-merger decision, the one that Martin had discussed with Cohen, startled many observers. Martin announced a few days after her funeral that Ottawa was refusing to allow the merger. Those who had expected this finance minister to buckle before the banks discovered that his connections to the Liberal caucus trumped any alliances he felt with Bay Street on this issue. Through his own consultations and in no small measure because of what he heard from Liberal MPs such as Tony Ianno and Shaughnessy Cohen, Martin said no to the proposed merger of the Bank of Montreal and the Royal Bank.

The decision was bolstered by other powerful influences too, however, including the real question of the impact on other banks considering mergers.

In April 1999, Allan Rock asked for a meeting with Jean Chrétien, to serve him formal notice of his intent to run for the leadership. Chrétien invited him to lunch at 24 Sussex Drive to talk things over.

In the second-floor den, which overlooks the Ottawa River, Rock assured the prime minister he was in no rush to see him leave, but wanted to let him know so there would be no suggestion that he was acting behind his back.

"Just remember, you're part of the team," Chrétien told him. "And do your job."

Rock told Chrétien that there were no worries there – he was busy at Health and wouldn't forget his priorities. He just wanted to have as long as possible to build an organization to rival Martin's.

If Chrétien was pleased that Martin would have a rival, he didn't let on to Rock. Nor did he offer him any help. The prime minister did tell Rock, however, that it wasn't too soon to start laying the groundwork of a campaign, since his plan now was to serve two terms and retire well before it was time for the Liberals to go to the polls again. That meant that the leadership campaign, for all intents and purposes, could begin in earnest within a year.

Operating on that assumption too, the Martin leadership campaign entered its next phase.

The organizing effort in the ridings was underway, thanks to John Webster, who was working with friendly MPs, and to a new campaign worker, Michèle Cadario, who operated out of the Maple Trust office.

Cadario was one of the strongest youth supporters of Martin's leadership, yet another Westerner with ties to those two pockets of disaffection that kept challenging the party establishment. As the first paid employee of the Martin organization, she energetically plugged herself into ridings all over Canada, making contact with MPs and local Liberals, becoming Martin's eyes, ears, and voice at the very grassroots. She was pulling together a version of the black book that Martin had filled with the names of potential Liberal candidates in the 1980s when he was at CSL. Hers was a much larger list of party members who would support Martin's future leadership.

Fundraising also became a priority of the team, under Webster's supervision. Martin was still doing the bulk of his fundraising for the Liberal party, but his advisers told him it was time to consider his own campaign too. This leadership run would be much longer and more expensive than the $2-million campaign they had mounted in 1990. Ruth Thorkelson had started to add one or two political events to each of Martin's ministerial trips across the country.

There was little immediate need for cash. It was more important to collect promises of money than to accumulate real dollars and cents in the bank. Lloyd Posno, a young Martin worker in the 1990 campaign, now at Ernst & Young in Toronto, established a blind-trust account, under the name Project 2000. The very name conveyed a telling expectation. Gerry Schwartz of Onex Corp., who had done a little fundraising for Martin in 1990, concentrated on the corporate world, mining the business community for promises and contributions.

No rules existed to govern leadership fundraising. Martin was relieved when he was told the blind trust was being established, knowing that it gave him a way to extricate himself from conversations with businessmen who were even now offering to bankroll his leadership bid. He could just clap his hands over his ears, figuratively speaking, and say this wasn't his responsibility.

Karl Littler happily moved into a more active role on the organizational front. During the government's first term, Littler had served as policy adviser in Finance's junior ministry, the Secretary of State for Financial Institutions, though most of his work was in the service of the finance minister. Bright, brash, with an impressive grasp of detail, Littler could dissect complex tax policy or the minutiae of Liberal party rules with equal facility. In his spare time, he competed aggressively in pub-trivia contests around Ottawa and wherever his work took him in Ontario. He would walk into local establishments and take on whole teams single-handedly, rattling off arcane tidbits of knowledge on subjects ranging from medieval history to current pop culture.

In the summer of 1999, Littler decided to do a study of the Liberal party rules surrounding leadership selection. There had been important changes since 1990 and his first mission was to understand and make use of a system that gave greater influence to the individual party member. The Liberals would still hold a convention of delegates, but delegate numbers would be apportioned among the leadership candidates on the one-member, one-vote approach at the riding level. For instance, if 60 per cent of the riding association membership voted for Martin as leader, then 60 per cent of the riding's twelve delegates would be sent to the convention as Martin supporters.

Littler's thirty-page paper, which became an annotated guide for Webster's operation, was roughly 80 per cent description, 20 per cent prescription. Addressing strategy, Littler suggested that the first objective was to get Martin-friendly individuals in executive positions at Liberal party associations across the country. That goal was within reach, thanks to the efforts of Webster and Cadario. At the convention for the Liberal party's Ontario wing in September, Martin people ran for – and won – most of the key positions. This feat was being repeated in other provinces and territories, and in Liberal women's and university clubs all over Canada.

There was a reason that attention to executive positions was step one in the strategy. Everything revolved around membership forms. Fears that Liberal riding associations would be taken over by single-issue interest groups, such as the anti-abortion squads so active in the 1980s, had forced the party to clamp down on wide-open sales of Liberal memberships. Distribution of membership forms was strictly controlled by the presidents and officers of local and provincial riding associations. If the Martin team wanted to boost its numbers with membership sales, it had to ensure its access to the precious forms.

Of course, no one knew when a leadership campaign would begin officially. Most, including Rock and Martin organizers, assumed they were working toward a convention within twenty-four months – at the outside. Rock's own conversation with the prime minister earlier in the year supported that assumption, as did informal exchanges with Chrétien intermediaries.

In early fall 1999, David Smith dined at Opus in Ottawa with Richard Mahoney and Karl Littler. He guessed that Chrétien would leave within the year. Goldenberg was putting out much the same message. He said that the prime minister did not intend – emphasis on the word *intend* – to run for a third term. While his potential heirs were not delighted by the uncertainty, they could understand the ambivalence. It was Chrétien's trademark. He would say he was staying right up to the moment he left, that was how he worked. Chrétien always left doors open, and his chief aide, Eddie Goldenberg, always preferred to defer a deal than to close one.

True to his word, Chrétien awarded Peter Donolo the consul general's position in Milan in June 1999. The woman picked to succeed Donolo was a surprise. She was Françoise Ducros, a lawyer and a daughter of the late Jacques Ducros, a Crown prosecutor in the trial of the FLQ terrorists charged with murdering Quebec cabinet minister Pierre Laporte in the 1970s.

Ducros was a federalist and Liberal who flirted with several leadership campaigns in 1990, once backing Toronto MP Dennis Mills before he withdrew from the race. She'd ended up a Chrétien supporter. In 1994, she was working in the bureaucracy at Indian Affairs when she came to the notice of Brian Tobin, then fisheries minister. Tobin hired her on the spot to serve as his executive assistant. When Tobin left in 1996 to become the premier of Newfoundland, Ducros moved over to serve as top aide to Stéphane Dion, the new intergovernmental affairs minister. In this job, with its intense focus on the post-referendum strategy in Quebec, Ducros fell into the orbit of the Quebec-fixated PMO. She shared Chrétien's tough, unapologetically federalist approach and she believed that government positions should be embraced unequivocally and advanced aggressively.

In June 1999, Ducros received her orientation from Donolo. The two got along well, working side by side for a few weeks before Donolo left to take up his posting in Milan and Ducros went off to Newfoundland's northern peninsula for a summer vacation.

During this quiet summer period, Chrétien considered a midterm shuffle of his cabinet. As usual, even the whisper of a shuffle sent backbenchers' hopes soaring. It's said that there are two kinds of MPs on the government benches: those who are members of cabinet and those who believe they should be members of cabinet.

Sergio Marchi, a long-time Chrétien loyalist, had decided to leave elected politics, and a plum appointment awaited him at the World Trade Organization in Geneva. His departure created an opening in cabinet for an Italian Canadian from Toronto – and there were plenty of those. Most were Martin supporters from 1990. With the exception of Ralph Goodale from Saskatchewan and Martin himself, no one else in cabinet had been on the Martin team.

Ducros was a very different person than Donolo, less comfortable with ambivalence, highly dedicated to clarity in purpose. She brought to the PMO communications office the same head-on approach she had taken with national-unity politics when she was in Dion's office: the best line is a clear one, drawn in the concrete, articulated with authority, and argued from strength. So it was that Ducros wanted to present Chrétien's leadership at this six-year mark in his rule. His control could not be seen to be wavering; there should be no hint that a turnover in cabinet represented a rollover in the prime minister's ultimate authority.

Goldenberg had been hobbling around most of this year on a broken leg, which he had shattered in a skiing accident. In July, in a terribly timed mishap at home, he broke it again and was laid up once more. Ducros returned early from Newfoundland, paid a call on Goldenberg, and then prepared to handle the cabinet shuffle – her solo flight as a political spinner. She knew precisely the message she wished to convey. "My view was that you do say the prime minister is going to run again. You say, This is the prime minister's cabinet that he will be running again with in the next general election. That was the hard spin," she says.

Ottawa's pundit class interpreted it as a sign that the people who were keen for Chrétien to leave, namely the Martinites, would no longer be indulged with ambivalent hints that their dream was within reach. Moreover, the shuffle seemed to indicate that backbenchers who supported Martin would pay the price for it, through continued exclusion from the government's top jobs.

Maurizio Bevilacqua was one who believed he might have a chance; some of Chrétien's advisers were sounding him out and Martin himself had made an appeal on his behalf. Tony Ianno thought he might get a turn this time too. But when the new ministry was unveiled, the more obscure, less experienced Maria Minna from Toronto was chosen to be minister of international co-operation. Four other newcomers were welcomed into cabinet as well and not a Martin supporter among them: Robert Nault from Kenora went into the Indian Affairs post; Elinor Caplan from Toronto got Immigration; George Baker of Newfoundland was given Veterans Affairs; and Denis Coderre, a youthful Quebec backbencher, was named to the new post of secretary of state for amateur sport. Chrétien also promoted some of his loyalists: Jane Stewart was moved up to the daunting Human Resources Ministry; Martin Cauchon, another young Quebecer, was promoted to Revenue; B.C.'s Herb Dhaliwal was given Fisheries and David Anderson, also from B.C., got the Environment post he had long coveted.

Another message was being delivered with this cabinet shuffle. It seemed that the prime minister, with his budget balanced and surpluses on the way, was ready to return to centre-left Liberalism. He placed similarly minded individuals in key positions to help tilt government priorities in that direction. But the media was fixated on the leadership issue – what the shuffle meant to Martin's prospects and what it said about the prime minister's own intentions.

In the *Toronto Star* the next day, reporter Tim Harper weighed in with an analysis, sprinkled with anonymous quotes from Liberal insiders. Well down in the story, but not so far down that Ducros didn't notice, was a line from an anonymous Martin adviser, scathingly dismissing the PMO's spin on the shuffle in scathing terms.

"With Donolo gone and Eddie Goldenberg in the hospital, there's a lack of adult supervision in the PMO right now."

Ducros was deeply wounded by the remarks, or so she told every journalist for weeks afterwards. She was first convinced that Scott Reid had been the source responsible, but later learned it was David Herle. She saw no way to take the slur but personally. Here she was, new on the job, and the Martinites were lying in the weeds, taking shots at her. More than once she wondered aloud whether she'd be similarly dismissed if she were a man.

Ducros barely knew Herle; they had encountered each other socially a few times and had no professional dealings. Yet he quickly became the vessel for all her insecurities and resentments toward the Martin camp. Herle was like a knot in her conversational string, one that she would tug tighter every time she spoke about the tension between the two teams over the years. If she happened to be talking to someone who was on good terms with Herle, she'd invariably toss in a gratuitous reference. "Well, what does *your friend* David Herle say?" Ducros's colleagues found this became hard to take.

The new dynamic wasn't lost on Martin, who could not help but see Ducros's hand in an increasing number of media reports about how the PMO was at odds with the finance minister's team. Unlike Goldenberg, Martin felt Ducros had no intention of making the relationship work. "I saw it all over the place," he said.

Littler and others were beginning to regard the PMO as split into two camps, loosely divided between the Chrétien PMO and the Next Play PMO. The people in the Chrétien PMO, they figured, comprised all those people whose main interest was in serving the prime minister and protecting his interests. This camp didn't bother the Martinites. Who wouldn't be loyal to the man who had hired them, promoted and protected them through the years? The Next Play camp rankled people around Martin; these were the people who wanted to keep Martin as weak as possible to the benefit of future leadership rivals. They considered Ducros in this latter group, accusing her of actively promoting Brian Tobin, her former boss who seemed to be keeping a hand in federal politics as well.

Given the gradual polarization of their forces, it was unlikely that anyone close to the prime minister would come to Martin's side in a future leadership contest. Before 1999, however, it was in no one's interests for the government to be divided against itself. Now, as leadership became the battleground, internal bickering was increasingly the norm.

In the fall of 1999, the Liberals' powerful Ontario caucus chose a new chairperson, Brenda Chamberlain, a blunt, no-nonsense former union leader from Guelph. Chamberlain was hardly an establishment candidate and her election as chair was another signal that backbench MPs were feeling increasingly aggressive and independent-minded. Experience had taught Chamberlain a lot about bargaining tactics on both sides of the negotiating table. All these pronouncements about Chrétien staying on from Ducros and others sounded to her like the opening salvo from the management lawyer. What else was he going to say? Her job, she decided, was to speak for the collective will of Ontario MPs, and stand firm in the face of intimidation.

The first test of her resolve came early. In a meeting of all the regional chairpersons within the Ontario caucus – MPs who spoke for the Greater Toronto Area (the GTA), Northern and Southwestern Ontario, and other regions – complaints were raised against the presence of PMO officials at the caucus meetings, which had been a standard practice since 1993. It was seen now as evidence of a domineering PMO, and MPs felt they should be free to speak critically of the prime minister behind closed doors without the details being reported to him. Chamberlain worried too that these emissaries for the prime minister were distorting the positions taken by the Ontario caucus when they reported back, softening the members' views to prove that their presence in the room kept MPs in line. "Basically, they weren't giving Chrétien the straight goods. I do believe they were telling him what he wanted to hear," Chamberlain said.

The regional chairs voted unanimously to ask that the PMO representatives not be sent to Ontario caucus meetings in future. Chamberlain personally informed Cate McCready, head of the Ontario desk for the Prime Minister's Office, that she would no longer be welcome at gatherings of the province's MPs. McCready stared at her, then said, "I'll just tell you, you'd better not do this." Francie Ducros then waded in, chiding the Guelph MP for creating dissent. "I found her abrasive, that's the best word for it," Chamberlain said. "She also seemed to have a mean streak." Then came a summons to the office of Jean Pelletier, the prime minister's chief of staff. The charming Pelletier chatted amiably with Chamberlain but soon cut to the point: Was she going to reverse this decision?

"No," Chamberlain replied. She was speaking for the caucus, not herself, and this was a decision, democratically reached, by the Ontario members.

"You, Brenda, have made this mess," was Pelletier's chilly reply. "And I will be waiting for your call to fix it." Chamberlain never called, but she began to realize that dissent was being viewed as treachery. If you criticized the prime minister, you were ipso facto an agent of Paul Martin. This baffled caucus members, who wondered why they had to choose between the two men. "I honestly thought I could like both of them," Chamberlain says.

The idea that his supporters were regarded as bad Liberals or that they would punished for endorsing him weighed heavily on Martin. "There was an inability to recognize someone who supported me as a good Liberal. Whether it was his office or whether it was him, it was hard to say. It was very clear that if you were not there for him in 1984 or 1990, there was a problem," Martin says.

In private conversation, Jean Chrétien had been known to refer to them as "Martin's Italian cabinet." Others nicknamed them the Spaghetti Caucus or the Martinis. Among the most ardent Martinites in caucus were Joe Volpe, Joe Fontana, Tony Valeri, Tony Ianno, Albina Guarnieri, Maurizio Bevilacqua, Joe Comuzzi, and Nick Discepola.

Their leadership sentiments aside, the healthy contingent of Italian Canadians in the Liberal ranks reflected a significant aspect of the party's demographic makeup. It had long been a berth for new Canadians, thanks to its immigration-friendly policies in the 1950s and 1960s. Historically too, the Liberals were regarded as the more natural repository for Roman Catholic votes. (Chrétien and Martin are both Roman Catholic, as were John Turner and Pierre Trudeau before them.)

Italian Canadians gravitated to the Liberal party much as Irish Canadians had done a generation earlier, and as Indo Canadians and other newly arrived ethnic groups were doing in the 1980s and 1990s. Their political activism would follow a pattern: First they would be recruited en masse to fill halls and stack meetings, then they would be invited into the backrooms as organizers within their communities. Eventually, and not without difficulty, they would make the leap into elected politics and, perhaps, leadership roles. This wasn't a purely Canadian phenomenon: Irish and Italian politicos marked their progress with the same steps in the United States, a journey that took John F. Kennedy to the White House in the 1960s and people such as Mario Cuomo and Rudolph Giuliani to high office in New York in the 1980s.

Martin's leadership campaign had attracted a disproportionate number of Irish and Italian Canadians. A roll call of his closest, backroom advisers revealed several Irish names: O'Leary, Mahoney, Dawson. His most dedicated caucus followers included a generous sprinkling of Italian Canadians.

Late in 1999, Mississauga MP Carolyn Parrish complained to Southam reporter Joan Bryden that Martin's so-called Italian caucus was cooking up trouble at the transport committee, deliberately trying to undermine the minister, David Collenette. Parrish connected the dots: "Mr. Collenette is very close to the prime minister . . . and I think the perception is that if you make him look bad, maybe this is another shot at the prime minister." This same week, Nic Discepola had been defeated in his bid to become chair of the federal caucus.

Over one of their regular dinners at Casa Calarco, the so-called Martinis decided it was time to unravel the twisted threads of discrimination they were feeling. Were they being targeted because they were close to Martin or was ethnic prejudice holding them back? Joe Fontana requested a meeting with the prime minister.

Fontana gathered up all the Italian-Canadian Liberal MPs he could find, calculating that a large group would in itself send a message. He button-holed stragglers as the party made its way into Chrétien's offices. Tony Valeri, the quiet and hard-working member who was Martin's parliamentary secretary, ran into them at the entrance to the Centre Block. Reluctant to make waves with Chrétien, and not someone who had been a player or even a Liberal party member during the last leadership contest, Valeri hesitated, then said, "Oh, what the hell," and joined in.

About a dozen MPs filed into the prime minister's office. Fontana opened the discussion, citing what he characterized as veiled attacks on Italian-Canadian MPs and demanding that they be stopped. It was wrong, it was prejudiced, and it was definitely contrary to the Liberal spirit.

Chrétien took his customary position with disgruntled MPs and assumed this was frustrated ambition talking. "I don't know why you're complaining. You've got to be on committees, be parliamentary secretaries. I haven't refused to give you anything – and you were all with Martin in 1990," he added. He pointed his finger at each turn. "You were with Martin," he said to Joe Volpe, "and so were you, and you, and you," he said to Guarnieri, Bevilacqua, and Fontana. "And you," he said, indicating to Valeri, "I don't know where you were in 1990."

Volpe snorted. As far as he could see, what Martin's 1990 supporters had received was the minimum this prime minister could provide without looking vindictive. At least half of the MPs in the room were eleven-year veterans of the Commons, part of the class of 1988. They believed that experience alone entitled them to the positions that Chrétien was portraying as generous favours.

Chrétien had digressed off into anecdotes about his own years as a back-bencher and the immense satisfaction he derived from introducing the bill to change the name of Trans-Canada Airlines to Air Canada.

Bevilacqua interrupted. "That's enough. We're not here to listen to your old stories. I've heard all these stories before. We came here to have a conversation."

Chrétien looked startled but returned to the issue: "Look. I'm a lawyer. I can't go and accuse anyone of discrimination when I don't have the proof."

Again, Bevilacqua spoke up. "I didn't come here to talk to a lawyer. I came to talk to a prime minister. This is a political issue and you're saying you can't do anything about it? I'm a backbencher, I can't stop this. But you can."

Chrétien sat scowling behind his desk. The others stiffened in their chairs, waiting for the explosion. Bevilacqua, feeling emboldened, suddenly stood up and approached the prime minister to shake his hand in farewell. "I'm leaving now. You go back to running the country." His colleagues rose as one and shuffled out behind him.

Once down the stairs and out the front door of the Centre Block, the delegation stood and stared at each other, then burst into relieved laughter. "Holy shit," Fontana cried, lighting a cigarette to shake off the icy chill of the meeting's abrupt end. "I can't believe how you gave it to him, Maurizio!" Tony Valeri, the reluctant comrade, was still shaking his head. The group agreed that Bevilacqua's fate was sealed. "You've done it now," they said. "You are *never* going into cabinet." Bevilacqua, a little surprised himself, ruefully agreed. "Guess not," he said. "But I don't regret it."

"Hey look," said one of the Commons security guards nearby. "It's the Italian caucus."

On a sleepy Tuesday in January 2000, while the Commons was adjourned for the holidays, Industry Minister John Manley called a press conference to announce that the government had come up with a bailout scheme for the financially troubled Ottawa Senators and other Canadian-based National Hockey League franchises.

This had not been Manley's idea. It was well known that the industry minister, no fan of government subsidies, was resisting the calls for help that had been received at the highest levels of this government. Ottawa Mayor Bob Chiarelli, a Liberal with close ties to Paul Martin, and Rod Bryden, another Liberal and owner of the Senators, were relentless in their quest for government aid. Over the Christmas break, the pressure worked: the PMO and the Industry Department came up with a scheme to offer financial aid to NHL teams, provided the provincial and municipal governments chipped in as well. It was standard Liberal procedure on financing, applied to everything from infrastructure to day-care spaces: federal dollars were dependent on a partnership with the relevant province. It was an amicable way to share the credit or pass blame if other governments declined to participate. In this case, the federal contribution to the NHL aid package would be capped at a maximum of 25 per cent of the cost. Rough estimates placed the federal commitment at the $3-million mark for all teams in Canada.

Manley was chosen to make the announcement because it was an Industry – that is to say, a business – bailout, and because his Ottawa riding made the Senators a local concern. But perhaps Manley was the favourite candidate because he'd earned a special place in the prime minister's trust as a loyal soldier, willing to put aside his own sentiments and ego to serve the PMO's interests. Manley looked uncomfortable, but gamely he went ahead and issued the statement.

Liberal MPs first heard the news like everyone else did, from the media. Unlike other government program announcements, this one came with no advance warning, and no widely distributed "talking points" had been issued. It seemed yet another example of the PMO cutting itself off from caucus and much of the blame was laid at the feet of Francie Ducros.

The angry MPs simply returned the snub, bypassing the PMO altogether and walking straight to the media with their protests. Brenda Chamberlain put it succinctly. "People [voters] are going crazy over this," she told reporters. "They are frustrated over the loss of services in health and education and they see a huge problem with farmers and homeless people. To people in my riding, it's a question of whether you fund wealthy hockey players or a hospital bed."

Sarnia MP Roger Gallaway, who had grown increasingly grumpy during this second mandate, released a copy of a letter he had written to Manley. "Quite simply, people are beyond furious. . . . Your proposal is nonsense and shameful," he charged.

Mississauga MP Carolyn Parrish this time added verbal arsenal to the caucus rebellion, lashing out at Senators owner Rod Bryden. "He used blackmail tactics to really put the heat on everybody. I don't approve of that, and I don't approve of giving in to it."

Within seventy-two hours, a red-faced Manley stood before the media again, informing reporters that the government had seen the light and would be reversing its decision. No bailout, no subsidies. He handled the reversal masterfully, with self-deprecating wit and ready acknowledgement of the healthy dose of crow he had been forced to eat that week. The controversy soon passed, proof that it was possible for the government to admit a mistake, contrary to the beliefs of those who had feared a similar admission on the GST would sink the Liberal ship.

A more enduring effect was the rush of confidence that had emboldened the disaffected Liberal MPs. They were growing more willing and less afraid to test their wills against the prime minister's. Soon enough, they would learn the limits of their new insubordination and the consequences of crossing Jean Chrétien on the larger question of leadership.

5

GOING NOWHERE

LESS THAN TWO weeks into the new millennium, Prime Minister Jean Chrétien celebrated his sixty-sixth birthday. But retirement seemed far from his mind. As wisecracking pundits would observe, most men retire from their jobs to play a little golf, ease up on stress, and spend more time with the wife. And that was exactly Chrétien's approach. Why bother retiring when he enjoyed those luxuries on the job?

Jamie Deacey, Martin's 1990 communications chief and a senior figure at the lobbying firm Association House published a bimonthly newsletter exclusively for the firm's clients that attempted to offer an insider's perspective on the issues of the day. In the first issue of the year, employing more tactful phrasing, Deacey offered a similar assessment of Chrétien's retirement prospects.

"He apparently enjoys the job he currently holds. He plays golf when he wants, where he wants, and with whom he wants. He travels in his own jet. He has a government-supplied mansion, servants, and security. His wife enjoys her position and carries it out well. . . . He has worked all his life to achieve where he is today and there is no one in another political party who is likely to unthrone him if he runs for a third term."

Deacey then laid out the case for Chrétien's departure, emphasizing internal Liberal unease with his open-ended reign. Deacey wrote plainly what most Liberals wouldn't dare say publicly: the prime minister might stick around just to ensure that Paul Martin did not succeed him. "I don't doubt that the PM has been stung for so long by the praise given to Martin, and not to the PM, for the fiscal policies and the successes of the government that Chrétien will attempt to give other potential candidates a leg up."

Deacey paid a price for his candour. His newsletter somehow found its way to the media, through anonymous sources who touted it as proof that Martin's people – of which Deacey was one in 1990 – were agitating for Chrétien to leave. Martin's office issued denials, saying Deacey did not speak for the finance minister or his team. It was the opening salvo in a skirmish that would become bloodier as the year unfolded.

The supposition of the Martinites' impatience became a favourite media theme in the early months of 2000. *Saturday Night* magazine gave the story cover treatment in its February issue. "The Non-Candidate: Power and Paranoia in Paul Martin's Ottawa" by freelance writer Guy Lawson portrayed an underground operation embarrassed by its own ambitions, carrying out its secret activities with amateur cloak-and-dagger tactics. An anonymous organizer meets Lawson in a seedy bar to warn him away from drawing attention to their machinations. Leaked talking points arrive in a brown envelope, purportedly instructions from the shadowy Martin organization on how to talk to Lawson. Much of the piece is devoted to the writer's efforts to get someone, anyone, to say on the record that Martin is running for the leadership.

The Martin gang collectively cringed when the article hit the newsstands. Herle, who had met with Lawson for an off-the-record interview (and discovered they had attended nearby high schools in Saskatchewan at the same time), realized how naive they looked. They'd believed they could bob and weave their way around any journalist; instead, they had received a very public slap for arrogance.

The mystery of Martin's ambitions was matched only by the uncertainty of Chrétien's plan for a third term. Ironically, amid all the murkiness of the leadership question, the major legislative project of the day was something called the Clarity Act.

In 1996 the federal government had asked the Supreme Court of Canada to rule on the legality of Quebec separation. Two years later, the court set out the terms under which a province could secede from the federation. It was a good-news, bad-news ruling. Yes, a province had the right to secede, but only after a clear referendum, with a clear question, and subsequent negotiation with the rest of Canada. Chrétien's Clarity bill was intended to make these principles an act of law, though the legislation itself didn't set out precise criteria for a clear question or a clear result. It was the final piece of Chrétien's post-1995 referendum strategy, designed to ensure that never again would the country be so ill prepared to deal with the threat of Quebec separation. There was plenty of nervousness around the cabinet table about the Clarity bill, with ministers worried about provoking Quebec separatists with its tough-love approach.

The only unconditional cabinet supporter of the act was Stéphane Dion, intergovernmental affairs minister, who had devoted the better part of his time at the ministry to a letter-writing campaign against what he called the myths of the separatists' arguments. Unlike other cabinet ministers who met infrequently with the prime minister, Dion saw him almost daily. He enjoyed a near father-son relationship with Chrétien.

A second strong advocate for the Clarity bill was Newfoundland Premier Brian Tobin, who remained in close touch with Chrétien after leaving the cabinet for provincial politics in 1996. Dion helped the prime minister make the legal, substantive case for the legislation; Tobin's encouragement was on a more visceral and personal level. For Tobin, the introduction of the bill represented an opportunity for Chrétien to regain his confidence, much as he had in his early days in Opposition. It was Tobin who had urged Chrétien to throw away the teleprompter, arguing that he shouldn't be hiding his natural charisma behind artificial gadgetry. Once, while rehearsing for the 1993 election debates, Tobin had broken into the prepared text of the teleprompter and scribbled, "Fuck this. You're on your own." Chrétien read the lines out loud in rehearsal before he realized what he was saying. He didn't appreciate the humour. It was the one time that Tobin feared he might have gone too far in his easy familiarity with the prime minister.

One person who connected well with Tobin, Dion, and Chrétien was Francie Ducros, who had worked for all three men. It was during the debates around the Clarity bill that Ducros came to be seen as a trusted confidante – a friend even – of the prime minister, more so than her predecessor, Peter Donolo. Less than a year into her tenure, it was acknowledged that Ducros was close enough to the Centre to be a reliable barometer of its proprietor's mood.

"I think that I had tremendous influence with the prime minister and I don't dispute that. And I think he's a great friend of mine, and I think he's a great, great prime minister," Ducros said later. Her admiration of his uncompromising federalism was fuelled by her childhood memories of soldiers guarding her family during the trials of the FLQ separatists.

"There were a lot of people, including my father, who took hits as being *vendus*," she said, explaining why Chrétien and other Quebec federalists took such umbrage when the epithet was tossed around by young Martin and Copps supporters at the infamous 1990 leadership debate. "It's a huge word – [it means] you're a traitor to your people. You have to fight through the hard, hard fight. And Chrétien fought all the way."

In pushing for swift passage of the Clarity bill, Ducros, Tobin, and Dion had encouraged the prime minister not to dither while cabinet ministers – including Martin – wrestled with their reservations. The trick was to get the principles on the table and before the public, Tobin advised. It was no coincidence that Chrétien introduced the bill in Ottawa in late November 1999, then jetted off to Newfoundland to talk it up at Tobin's side. The PMO and Dion also worked to have the bill supported by a resolution at a convention of the Liberal party's Quebec wing around the same time. The debate on that resolution featured a spirited argument on the convention floor between Dennis Dawson and Ducros. Dawson insisted that the bill was an "unnecessary provocation." Ducros argued that Ottawa had a duty to be the voice of strong federalism. Dawson stressed he was speaking for himself that day and was representing no one else's viewpoint. Dion would say that Martin's doubts were no different than those voiced by other ministers.

Martin bristled uncomfortably throughout the Clarity bill discussions, knowing that his block of Quebec support was strongly against it. He himself was ambivalent, professing to be frustrated by his inability to speak out. Yet it was not clear what he would say even if offered the opportunity.

Later he said, "I said there is no doubt that Quebec has to understand that they can't separate at their own whim. There is no doubt that I felt, as did Pierre Trudeau by the way, that the Supreme Court's decision basically said that. I didn't have any great objection to the Clarity bill. I voted for the Clarity bill. What bugged me more . . . is that [the PMO] said nobody is allowed to speak on the Clarity bill except the prime minister and Dion. And then the word spread: 'See? Martin won't speak on the Clarity bill.'"

His ambivalence was on full display November 25 during a scrum with reporters outside the Commons. He was asked, several times, whether he supported the Clarity bill. He would not be drawn into answering and he believed he should be allowed to walk away from these encounters once he had declined the same question twice. When reporters pressed, he said nothing and turned and raced up the stairs.

Goldenberg, who had his own doubts about the proposed legislation, found Martin's complaint of muzzling a little weak.

"They were told that only the prime minister and Dion would speak after one cabinet meeting. He wasn't told to run up the stairs when asked whether he supported the bill. . . . It doesn't mean that you are not allowed to say that you support a bill when you are asked."

There were Quebecers close to Martin who had been vocal in their opposition to the bill. Here was Martin dodging the obvious question and withholding his endorsement of the prime minister's pet project. Was this running away deliberate or simply another misstep on Quebec issues?

In February, as the annual convention neared, it seemed the prime minister was warming up to run for a third term. Herle wasn't surprised; he had always believed that Chrétien would linger as long as possible. "What prime minister in history has voluntarily left office?" was Herle's rhetorical question. This perspective tended to make him "a bit of a downer," as he puts it, in any conversation about how long Martin would have to wait for his chance. But if it was true that the prime minister had decided to go for a third term, Herle believed it was time for Martin to start thinking of leaving politics.

O'Leary agreed, for different reasons. She thought that Martin's reputation as a competent finance minister would be compromised if he stayed in this government much longer. She already felt that the Liberals were rudderless, without a clear purpose, and that as budget surpluses accumulated, Martin would be urged to create an agenda by loosening the purse strings again.

Herle was more calculating. He believed that Liberals would only recognize Martin's value if they faced the prospect of losing an election without him. Chrétien might not mind if Martin left politics, but Liberals would not stand for it. The prime minister would come under severe pressure to step down before a third term, Herle reasoned, if rank-and-file Liberals insisted he make way for Martin.

The two laid out their respective cases to Martin in several phone conversations in January and February 2000. He couldn't decide. Maybe it was a good idea, maybe not. In early March, with the convention fast approaching, Herle decided to take matters into his own hands. He contacted several influential political reporters and put the bug in their ears. Martin, he said, was thinking of leaving politics.

Precisely as Herle had planned, the unnerving news appeared in several leading media outlets. Jeffrey Simpson of the *Globe and Mail* wrote that Martin might be packing it in, as did Bill Walker at the *Toronto Star*. Lawrence Martin's column delivered the message in every Southam newspaper across the country. "Prime Minister Jean Chrétien and his cohorts are making a big mistake if they assume Finance Minister Paul Martin will be at their side to fight the next election campaign. This is the word from political insiders close to Martin, who made it amply clear Monday that their man is likely to be seeking other career options, possibly as early as the late spring." He added that the finance minister would not speak publicly about this before the annual Liberal party convention March 16 to 18 because to do so would be too "disruptive" – as though there would be no disruptive fallout from these rumours. He opined that Martin's likely destination would be the director general's chair at the International Monetary Fund, a seat that was vacant since the departure of Michel Camdessus. Eddie Goldenberg barely glanced at the reports, believing that if Martin were serious, he would have notified him.

Goldenberg may not have given any credence to the rumours, but there were enough Liberal MPs who did. Many of Martin's caucus supporters had long feared that rumblings of this kind would surface, and they privately bristled at Herle and others whom they suspected of trying to bring the matter to a head.

Joe Volpe was in Edmonton, meeting with fellow Liberals who might be helpful to Martin's cause. He telephoned Martin's office, demanding to know what was going on. Ruth Thorkelson made reassuring noises, then put Martin on the line. Volpe said, "Paul, I appreciate that we're not in a campaign or anything official, but would you mind telling me what I am doing out here in Edmonton if you're not planning to run for the leadership?"

Martin called the news reports rumours, nothing more. He asked Volpe if he'd heard that MPs with similar concerns were getting together with John Webster in Toronto over the weekend. Yes, Volpe recalled something about that meeting. Is that what it was all about? Persuading Martin not to leave politics? Martin said he didn't know much more than that; it was Webster's show.

Carolyn Bennett was flabbergasted by the notion of Martin's departure. She fired off a handwritten note to him, saying she couldn't imagine getting on a plane every week to make the trip from Toronto to Ottawa if Martin wasn't there in government at the end of the journey. "You're the only grown-up in the sandbox," she wrote. Bennett's office got a call: Come to the Regal Constellation on March 10 and sit down with John Webster and David Herle and company to discuss what all of this means.

Meanwhile, Herle's plants had generated the desired media buzz about the wisdom of the prime minister hanging around for a third term. Commentators opined that Chrétien was stretching the patience of his caucus and of Canadians. They noted that he had articulated very few reasons to stay on; his precious Clarity bill would stand as a legacy document; and Martin was poised and ready to assume the leadership he'd earned.

The Regal Constellation is not the most luxe of hotel establishments. The entrance is large and airy enough, but the warren of back corridors and meeting rooms appears to have been added as an afterthought. It was in one of these meeting rooms that more than two dozen members of Parliament gathered around the table. Most were from Toronto and Southern Ontario constituencies.

At the head of the table sat David Herle, John Webster, Richard Mahoney, Karl Littler, Scott Reid, Ruth Thorkelson, and Michèle Cadario. The Ontario MPs included Joe Volpe, Carolyn Bennett, Tony Ianno, Maurizio Bevilacqua, Albina Guarnieri, Tony Valeri, Stan Keyes, Paul Bonwick, Joe Fontana, Andrew Telegdi, Janko Peric, Brenda Chamberlain, Rick Limoges, and Walt Lastewka. Only a smattering were from other provinces, including Nick Discepola from Montreal and John Harvard from Winnipeg.

Mahoney, acting as chair, called the group to order and laid out the broad agenda. "As you've probably read in the papers, Paul is considering his future," Mahoney said.

This meeting, he explained flatteringly, was intended to gather Martin's closest friends in caucus and lay out the inside story for them. They would have a frank discussion about whether Martin should leave politics and the implications of that decision. Then he turned the floor over to Herle, who fired up his laptop and walked the MPs through a PowerPoint presentation.

First, Herle debunked the findings of other recent polling. Reports of the Liberals' strong standings were misleading, he argued. Underneath those numbers were some ominous trends: the public's tendency to vote against incumbent governments and the fact that when the national numbers were broken down regionally, the party was weak in important pockets all over the country.

Then he moved on to a current hot controversy. In the first few months of the year, the House of Commons had heard multitude allegations about mishandled money in Human Resources Development Canada (HRDC). The Auditor General had unearthed millions of dollars in misspent funds and the opposition's torment of Minister Jane Stewart was unrelenting.

Here too, Herle said, the polls were misleading. Although Liberals were doing well overall, 65 per cent of respondents in his polling called the HRDC controversy a "major" issue and there was potential for it to erode public trust in the government generally.

Then it was on to the next slide: Paul Martin and his prospects. The finance minister was, according to Herle, "the bedrock of credibility" for the government, with personal positive rankings in the polls twice as high as the party. He was extremely attractive to soft nationalists in Quebec and he was much more acceptable to the West than was Chrétien.

The penultimate slide laid out the problem in clear language.

Point number one: "We do not believe Chrétien has plans to resign."

Point number two: "We are operating on the assumption that he – like all before him – will hang on to power as long as he can."

Point number three: "Very few levers at our disposal."

Point number four: "Only the likelihood of losing the majority will make him [Chrétien] reassess. A proper reading of public opinion should give him real pause about his capacity to put together a majority."

This slide also read, "The convention offers no opportunity to make a difference." There was "no advantage in a blow that only wounds."

Herle's presentation drew to a close with four practical proposals. One, "Position Paul, not just as the heir apparent, but as the preferred option now"; two, "Control the [Liberal party] executive"; three, "Make sure the rules are fair"; and four, "Be as strong as possible organizationally."

The last slide was "Issues for discussion." Herle wanted confirmation that the MPs agreed with the positioning of Martin and how he was being perceived. Was there general agreement about the likely far-off timing of Chrétien's departure? And, as a final question, was there anything more that they could do?

Once the lights went up, Stan Keyes, the one-time television reporter, had an idea. Why didn't they develop some type of media line? Should members of Parliament be more forthright about their desire for Chrétien to stand down? Should they be more candid in expressing their fears about the prospect of Martin leaving? "What do we say to reporters?" Keyes asked.

The question was greeted with blank stares all around. Keyes had the uncomfortable feeling that he'd said too much, at least in this forum. He didn't know how to interpret the silence. It could be a quiet wink in favour of raising the volume; it could be disapproval of any further publicity.

Herle's expression gave away nothing – for good reason. The MPs were not aware that Herle had leaked the possibility of Martin's departure, but the news reports had created the level of nervous agitation that he had privately hoped for. He had led them through a slide presentation that demonstrated Martin's importance to their collective political future. He reminded them of the prime minister's intransigence in the absence of a serious threat to his majority. He ended by saying that they were helpless to do anything about it. The MPs could surely read between the lines. This was more of a cry for help than it was a strategy session.

Before the meeting adjourned, Webster said he wanted to underline something. It was not just that the team was considering Herle's instincts. "We've been told, by people close to the prime minister, that it's pretty certain he's staying on to run for a third term," he said.

Mahoney added that Chrétien could simply be keeping his options open as long as possible, but that he would certainly stay on if he felt Martin and his people were becoming too aggressive. "For some time now, they've been telling us that if we push too hard, he'll stay." This is why, Mahoney explained, the Martin forces had not put forward their own candidate for the Liberal party presidency. Running a pro-Martin Liberal for the top party job would be a provocative move – though one of the few the team would be able to make at this convention.

That did it for Volpe. On his way out, he said to Webster, "Okay, let me get this straight. We've met here to talk about doing nothing for a leadership campaign that isn't going to happen because the prime minister isn't going anywhere. Do me a favour. The next time you want to have a meeting about doing nothing for something that isn't going to happen, don't bother calling me." Bevilacqua wasn't sure why he'd attended the meeting either. "From a sheer strategic point of view, it was a screw-up," he says.

The next day, in Washington, Herle stood in Terrie O'Leary's kitchen and debriefed Martin on the meeting.

Martin sought assurances that the MPs had been calmed down.

"They don't want you to leave, Paul," Herle told him. "But don't worry. They're not going to do anything. The convention is not going to get messy."

"Good," Martin said. "We don't need that."

The dynamic of Ottawa's pack-journalism culture is not easy to dissect. Reporters don't conspire to pursue the same story or personality. There are no head-office directives distributed to members of the parliamentary press gallery, as conspiracy theorists might imagine. Rather, the media will be seized with a single idea simultaneously and spontaneously, and then collectively pursue it to death. Media competition exaggerates this tendency, as rival reporters scramble to outdo each other. One story begets a follow-up story. One question in a scrum leads to another along the same lines. The morning chitchat on the Sparks Street Mall turns into an item by lunch and an issue by pre-dinner drinks. Soon, the theme seeps into the wider culture. In March 2000, the preoccupying theme in Ottawa was Liberal leadership politics and two intertwined questions in particular: whither Jean Chrétien and whither Paul Martin. And every reporter was after the story, however he or she could get it.

The *Hill Times*, the independent Parliament Hill newspaper, appears every Monday and is often influential in setting the media agenda for the week ahead. It is a feast of news, gossip, and analysis for the politicos. On the Monday before the Liberal party convention, its front-page story quoted two Liberal MPs, both calling on Chrétien to step aside: Diane Marleau from Sudbury and Ovid Jackson from Barrie. Neither had attended the Regal Constellation meeting.

Television reporters rushed to tape Marleau and Jackson saying the same for the cameras, and they obliged. Watching the broadcast later, Stan Keyes decided to join the fray. He had come to believe that there was a virtue in forcing the issues that had been discussed at the Regal Constellation, and no one, after all, had specifically discouraged him from speaking out. Meanwhile, Southam's veteran reporter on the Liberal beat, Joan Bryden, had resolved that this week – amid the preheated atmosphere going into the convention – she would not allow MPs to remain anonymous when voicing their frustration with the prime minister. If they spoke in favour of Chrétien's exit, they would have to do so on the record.

She called Keyes, who said yes, his constituents were looking for change at the top. Bryden asked Keyes if he was sure he wanted to go on record with these remarks, offering him an out that he declined. "No, you can go ahead and quote me saying that," Keyes told her. To anyone who asked him the question on this Monday – Mike Duffy at CTV and Julie van Dusen at CBC – Keyes gave more or less the same answer about his constituents: "And they're saying, you know what? Jean, maybe you should step aside.

You've been there twice for us now; you've done great things for us. You're at the crescendo of your career. Pass the torch."

Reporters pursued Martin for comment, but he ducked any questions on his future or Chrétien's, using that reliable wiggle word, *intend*, when he spoke of his plans. "You know my answer this week is the same as my answer last week, is the same as my answer the week before that. In fact, it's the same answer I gave last year and the year before that. I intend to run again."

On Tuesday, other attendees of the Regal Constellation session joined Keyes in the public calls for Chrétien to step down. Though Herle and company had spoken of striking no blows, the MPs decided otherwise. First, Keyes's friends in caucus weren't about to leave him out there alone, where he'd be dismissed as a solitary radical voice. And second, there had always been a degree of tension between Martin's backroom operators and caucus supporters. MPs resist taking directions from unelected strategists; they believe they have earned the right from the voters to speak their minds when they choose.

Joe Fontana was the first to back up his friend Keyes. "If [Chrétien] decides to go, we'll understand," Fontana told reporters. Nick Discepola from Montreal also took the plunge, explaining to reporters that a changed political landscape called for a new Liberal leader. Borrowing directly from Herle's presentation at the Regal Constellation, Discepola said, "If the right is going to shift and support Stockwell Day, say for hypothetical reasons, then possibly we could lose quite a few seats in Ontario, seats that would be difficult to make up elsewhere, and thereby risk a minority government." Joe Volpe spoke bluntly to Radio-Canada, saying that yes, it was time for new leadership and, yes, he didn't mind putting that on the record.

Mahoney was visiting his brother in Toronto that evening. He clicked on the CBC News and watched the footage with growing alarm. The MPs had gone rogue; they'd taken matters into their own hands. The next day, three more from the Regal Constellation meeting – Paul Bonwick, John Harvard, and Rick Limoges – spoke out to reporters. By now, though, Chrétien's people were beginning to snap back. David Collenette suggested that dissident Liberal MPs shouldn't run in the next election if they couldn't support the leader. Mississauga MP Carolyn Parrish, who could be counted on in these days for colourful anti-Martin commentary, called her colleagues "toads," "dull, blunt clods," and "sneaking, snivelling shitheads."

Then later that night came the bombshell. On the same day that Chrétien's Clarity bill passed in the Commons, CBC's *The National* led its broadcast with news of the Regal Constellation meeting. Anchor Peter Mansbridge described "one of this country's most popular prime ministers ever" fighting to control his own party and to "crush suggestions tonight he should retire." He then introduced the CBC's chief political correspondent, Jason Moscovitz. After an overview of the latest declarations and denials in the Liberals' leadership non-race, Moscovitz unveiled his scoop.

"CBC News has found out that there was a meeting at this airport hotel in Toronto last Friday. Close to twenty-five MPs met with key Martin advisers to discuss leadership strategy. Richard Mahoney, a former executive assistant to Martin, who travelled with the finance minister the last time he ran for leader in 1990, chaired the meeting. John Webster, who helped run Martin's last campaign, was there. So was David Herle, a long-time Martin confidant. At the meeting Herle provided polling information on how Martin would outperform Chrétien in Quebec, as well as in Western Canada in the next election. Scott Reid, Martin's director of communications, was there as well. Everyone it seems but Paul Martin himself. As for the twenty to twenty-five MPs, they expressed the following concerns: Martin could quit if Chrétien stayed. Some could lose their seats if Chrétien stayed. . . . But when they left the room they agreed the best short-term strategy was to lay low and stay quiet during this weekend's Liberal convention. At least that was the plan."

The news item then replayed Keyes's comments, as if to throw doubt on the keep-quiet plan: "You're at the crescendo of your career. Pass the torch."

At Hy's Steak House that night, several members of the Italian caucus were standing in the adjoining bar (known as the Martini Ranch) watching the Moscovitz report with horror. "Uh oh," said Tony Valeri, his face darkening as he watched the screen. "This is going to mean trouble."

And at 24 Sussex Drive, Jean Chrétien was watching the news too. Francie Ducros had received a heads-up about the item when she was called for comment an hour before it went on the air. Aline Chrétien was in the room with her husband. Here it was, all the proof they needed of

Martin's treachery. Aline clenched her hand into a fist and uttered three simple words: "Four more years."

The next morning, March 16, the Liberal convention opened at Ottawa's Congress Centre with sessions for women, youth, and aboriginal delegates. Traditionally, cabinet ministers were called in to address these groups, a mark of the party's determination to stay in touch with its membership. Martin was due to speak to the women's group that morning.

Reporters were patrolling the halls, on the lookout for the MPs who had been at the Regal Constellation. Brenda Chamberlain, the normally outspoken Ontario caucus chair, got caught in the camera lights and turned evasive. "I don't wish to talk about that, thank you," she answered primly, when asked what had gone on at the meeting. Worse was Carolyn Bennett, who stood speechless, lips pursed, while the cameras rolled, then called it a "support group" gathering. The hourly newscasts ran the Bennett clip, awkward pause and all.

Martin had no idea while he spoke to the Liberal women at the Westin Hotel that reporters were lying in wait, eager for his statement. This in itself, he argued later, should have been proof that nothing nefarious was afoot. If he was plotting a coup, would he have been so obviously caught off guard when confronted with the suggestion? For that is exactly what happened.

Leaving the meeting room, he walked right into a pack of aggressive journalists. He wasn't accustomed to fielding questions about leadership politics; others had always done this for him. Up to now, Martin's scrums had been conducted under the pleasant fiction that his only concern was his work as finance minister. But the media appeared to have agreed, all at once, that this fantasy was over. It was time for Martin to speak up. A cacophony of questions surrounded him: "What about this meeting at the Regal Constellation? Did you know about it?"

Martin attempted to reassert the old rules of the game: I'm finance minister, politics happens elsewhere. "My staff meets with members of caucus all the time," he said. "It's the way we develop the budget. It's the way that we basically sell the budget. Those meetings take place all the time."

The horde was having none of this. Still, Martin insisted, "I don't know what went on at this particular meeting." There was no let up until Martin suddenly bolted for the escalator. About two dozen journalists and cameras chased behind, elbowing each other to capture his non-answers on tape. Sometimes refusing to reply, sometimes pleading ignorance, he fled the hotel like a fugitive. The whole spectacle was aired repeatedly, along with the MPs' clumsy denials.

Richard Mahoney and David Herle had been hiding at the Earnscliffe offices a block from the Congress Centre, wondering how they were going to show their faces at the convention. Their mug shots had been broadcast all over Canada in Moscovitz's report. (Herle's mother called her son to complain that the photo wasn't flattering. Mahoney's mother told him, "You looked like a criminal.")

The phone rang in Herle's office. It was Scott Reid, telling them to turn on the TV. Martin's flight down the escalator filled the screen, but there was no audio. As Herle lunged to adjust the volume dial on the set, he heard the sound of his leather jacket ripping all the way up the back. Not a good sign.

Eddie Goldenberg stared at his television in his office, watching Martin's very bad scrum. It was the guiltiest performance he had ever seen.

Martin returned to his office, fully aware that he had badly handled the scrum. He was angry, demanding that everyone turn their attention to fixing this mess. Scott Reid could suggest only the most basic of damage-control strategies: let's not do that again. He got on the phone to pass the word, "Here's the plan: no more screw-ups." After the staff huddled for a while, they concluded that the best course was to put Martin back in front of the cameras, armed with a fuller explanation. Wincing at each hourly loop of the escalator scene on Newsworld, they all hoped that a different scrum would replace this mortifying image, on the screens and in people's minds.

Martin emerged to face the microphones in the Commons foyer after Question Period. He tried to make light of the morning's fiasco.

"Well, we meet again. Didn't I see a lot of you on an escalator?" he joked. He tried to be more forthcoming, explaining that the Regal Constellation meeting was intended to quell rumours that he was leaving politics. But when pressed for more information, Martin turned evasive again: "I don't really know what the details of the discussion were."

MPs who hadn't been nabbed already by the TV cameras were stalked by reporters at the convention site or in the Commons foyer all that day. Those who were able to talk to Martin in the lobby or by phone were assured that the media's speculations would eventually be exposed as a "bum rap" against them. If the purpose of the meeting had been subversion, surely the conspirators – including himself – would have handled themselves with wily finesse. Outsiders would acknowledge this in time, and those who knew anything about him understood he would not sanction subversion.

In the face of this imbroglio, Martin's team decided to change course. Mahoney and Herle began to encourage MPs to join the chorus. There was no sense trying to hide disappointment at the suggestion Chrétien might stay on; to do so now lent credence to the alleged plot. MPs were urged to go before the cameras and say what was on their minds: that the prime minister had overstayed his welcome with the party. This recommendation, however, only added to the general confusion.

Maurizio Bevilacqua was one of a few MPs who didn't think it made any sense for the caucus dissidents to push the prime minister. He wanted to stick to Herle's script. When he talked to reporters, he said simply, "There's no dissent here." Challenged by his colleagues later, Bevilacqua complained that all the others were doing was hardening divisions between Chrétien and Martin. "How does this help Paul's agenda? How does this move him any closer to becoming prime minister?"

A special Thursday-night caucus session was called so that Liberals could air the angst of this week behind closed doors. The Martinites braced for a tongue-lashing. Speaking first, Chrétien lamented that he had expected the news coverage of the week to be devoted to passage of the historic Clarity bill – the piece of legislation closest to his heart in all his years as prime minister. Instead, he had to endure the exposure of a secret meeting of Liberals, conspiring against his leadership. MP after MP took to the microphone to denounce the "Brutus-like behaviour" of the Regal Constellation crew.

Most of the Martin supporters sat stoically, arms folded, taking the flak. Joe Volpe finally lost patience with the meeting's descent into a melodrama. "Okay, that's enough, all right already," he barked from the back of the room.

On Friday morning, David Smith was in Ottawa and due to appear at CTV's studios for an interview on the opening of the convention. He was leaving the Westin Hotel when a bright-faced young man approached. Smith had no idea who this fellow was.

"The prime minister is looking for you," the stranger said. "He wants you to come to lunch. Call John Rae on his cellphone. Here's the number." Sure enough, when Smith called Rae from a nearby payphone, he was ordered to 24 Sussex. He arrived at the prime minister's residence to find him railing against the treachery of the finance minister and his people. Smith had been named that week as co-chair of the Liberals' next election campaign. Witnessing the prime minister's rage, Smith had a feeling that the leader's contingency plans for a third term had just become reality.

That Friday Carolyn Bennett had a massive migraine. She couldn't walk through the convention corridors without someone stopping her to express pity or sarcasm about her dead-air performance the day before. Mahoney was asking her to go before the cameras again to echo the sentiments now being expressed more boldly by the other MPs. Bennett couldn't stomach the prospect. She left the convention, went home to her darkened apartment, and decided to skip the rest of the weekend's events.

Pain relief arrived for the rest of the Martin team on Friday morning when the *Toronto Star* carried a front-page poll by Goldfarb Consultants claiming that 45 per cent of Canadians wanted Paul Martin to lead the Liberals, compared to 37 per cent who wanted Jean Chrétien to stay on.

"That Goldfarb poll helped me get out of bed on Friday morning," Mahoney exulted. Copies of the *Star* were snapped up at newsstands near the convention centre and pressed into the hands of arriving delegates.

The team's damage-control effort focused on Martin himself and the need to restore his credibility as the voice of candour. O'Leary, staying in touch by telephone from Jamaica where she was attending to World Bank business, believed that the only solution was an honest statement of the facts. They had laboured too long to protect the facade that Martin was not organizing for the next leadership, when really, what was wrong with that? Attempts to hide or downplay their intentions had played directly into the notion that supporting Martin was tantamount to knifing Chrétien. O'Leary had pushed this message for as long as she had advised politicians. If you try to mask your actions, the media will assume malice and guilt.

When Martin waded into the convention on Saturday, rather than flee reporters, he sought them out. "I don't think it's a state secret that I ran for the leadership in 1990. It's not a state secret that if the possibility arose in the future that it's something I would consider. But one thing is very clear and that is one of the great strengths of the Liberal party is its unity, its loyalty to the leader. I learned that at my father's knee and essentially every person understands that our great strength is our ability to work together."

Martin was more or less on his own at the convention; Herle, Mahoney, and Webster were still lying low, stewing in a basement bar in Ottawa's Glebe neighbourhood, a good few kilometres clear of the convention. Mahoney ventured over to the site briefly only to run into Eddie Goldenberg.

"David Smith is looking for you," Goldenberg told him. Gesturing to the cast on his leg, Goldenberg added, "You see this? I think he wants to do this to you."

When Herle eventually skulked into the convention, trying to duck the cameras, he walked past Goldenberg, who was huddled with friends. Goldenberg tried to hail him, but Herle kept his head down and walked on. Goldenberg began to hobble in determined, if slow, pursuit. Herle had to turn around and face his accuser. Goldenberg was livid. The Regal Constellation meeting was absolutely wrong, proof of Herle's disloyalty and that of his friends.

"That's a bit rich coming from you, after what you did to John Turner," Herle replied.

Goldenberg told him there was a big difference between the protest of the 1980s and his antics: Turner was not the prime minister. Turner hadn't won two elections and brought his party to record high standings in the polls. Herle agreed that the situation was different now, that this wasn't a game, that people's jobs were at stake.

The two men soon became aware of a phalanx of TV cameras circling them and they put a brusque end to the conversation.

At the main event on the Saturday, Martin would have to stand onstage with Chrétien and his fellow ministers while party members lined up at the microphones to pose questions to whomever they liked. The "accountability session" was a standard feature of Liberal conventions; it's like Question Period, except with a friendly, cheering crowd. There are no tough queries and no bad answers.

It was a chance to showcase Martin as a loyal Liberal-team player. Karl Littler had scribbled out some questions, one on flat tax that would allow Martin to go after Ontario Premier Mike Harris. Better that he be seen battling an external rival than his own boss. Littler then sat down with Martin to work up his answers. They crossed their fingers and hoped for the best.

Once at the convention, Littler found the doors to the accountability session hall already open and delegates flooding in. He plucked two Martin-friendly faces out of the crowd and pushed them into line ahead of people already queued fifteen deep at the microphones. Littler didn't expect that anyone would deliberately embarrass Martin, but he did anticipate an attempt to make him invisible.

Littler's sharp elbows paid off: two generous questions were lobbed at Martin and he batted them out of the park. The audience gave him an enthusiastic ovation. At the customary Martin party that night at the Cave, a bar near Parliament Hill, the mood of the troops was one of cautious relief. The convention had started out badly, no question, but Saturday had been a good day. They might just get through this thing. The *National Post*, which had been tracking performances with a tortoise-and-hare graphic, decreed in a deliberate echo of Chrétien's billing that Martin had redeemed his "first in the hearts" reputation. "By the end of the weekend, those tepid chants of 'four-more-years' were starting to sound suspiciously like 'Paul-Mar-tin.'"

Any comfort taken by Martin and his chastened team turned out to be short-lived. On Monday, as the business of Parliament resumed, Martin was summoned to a rare meeting in the prime minister's office. The request came in the form of a formal note, delivered to him as he sat in Question Period. Uh oh, he thought. This thing isn't over yet.

Martin slipped upstairs to the prime minister's third-floor suite and walked in to find Chrétien glowering behind his desk, with Jean Pelletier and Eddie Goldenberg nearby. Martin was invited to take a seat.

Pelletier slid a sheaf of papers toward Martin. "What's this?" he demanded.

It was a four-page memo titled "Post Convention Conference Call" and had arrived in a brown envelope, addressed personally to the prime minister. The first page gave a list of participants in the call, with their phone numbers plus an agenda for discussion. David Herle was designated as the chair of the telephone meeting, his name shortened to DH in the minutes that followed. DH's overall feeling, according to the memo, was that the convention had been a success. "The PM is wounded and on the defensive. We now have control of the national executive which is the key to forcing a leadership change." The memo then went on to describe various post-convention strategies designed to force the prime minister to step down: suspending the Liberal party constitution, for instance, precipitating an election, or working one-on-one with friendly journalists to turn media coverage against Chrétien. "Efforts to keep the PMO press office off balance are under development," the memo concluded.

This missive was being taken very seriously within the PMO. Lloyd Axworthy, in his capacity as elder party statesman, had been called in to look at the document and recommend how it should be handled. Axworthy believed that Martin should be confronted with the damning document at once.

Martin riffled through the pages, then tossed them aside dismissively. "It's a fake," he snapped, "a phony. Somebody's making mischief."

Chrétien wasn't buying that explanation. Neither was Goldenberg, who could not erase the memory of Martin's suspicious scrum a week earlier. Goldenberg was convinced that the Regal Constellation meeting was called to plot a coup against the prime minister and that Martin was involved.

"You're calling me a liar?" Martin angrily retorted. He challenged the PMO to ask around all they liked, there wasn't a shred of credibility to this memo. It might have come from *Frank* magazine, for all they knew. Martin invited them to examine his staff's phone logs and e-mail records if they wished.

The next day was no better. The morning began with the weekly cabinet meeting, where Martin came in for a pummelling. Jane Stewart, who had been under siege in the Commons that spring for squandered job-training dollars in Human Resources, led the barrage. She called the more recent embarrassments "disgraceful" and beneath the party. Others joined in, telling Martin to pull his supporters in line and take control of his staff.

Martin, shaken, came out of the tense cabinet meeting to tell reporters, "There is no leadership race." He said his supporters had been told "we should all focus on one thing and that is the re-election of the prime minister." Scott Reid followed up with calls to reporters with the new modus operandi: "Paul said down tools and we're downing tools. This thing is over."

That night, Chrétien hosted a party for cabinet members at 24 Sussex Drive. Paul and Sheila Martin pasted on their best smiles for the festivities. At dinner, Martin was seated on one side of the prime minister, Jane Stewart on the other. Everyone behaved politely, like the good Liberals Stewart had implored them to be earlier that day. After dinner, the group gathered convivially for a singalong around the piano, Aline Chrétien playing. The ministers sang a favourite from *Casablanca*, "As Time Goes By," followed by a rendition of a French country song, "Madame la Marquise," in which a noblewoman returns home to find her horse gone, her estate in flames, and her husband dead by suicide. But apart from that, "all's well," went the chorus.

Paul Martin stood at the piano with the prime minister and the rest of the cabinet, belting out the lyrics with the others. "Tout va très bien, tout va très bien," he sang. All's well – apart from everything else.

6

AN UNEASY PEACE

PAUL MARTIN WON one tiny victory in the wake of the March 2000 convention and Regal Constellation dust-ups. After a brief investigation, the Prime Minister's Office conceded that the incriminating "Post Convention Conference Call" memo, with its talk of dark plots to unseat Chrétien, was indeed a fake.

"So let's call in the RCMP," Martin said bitterly when Jean Pelletier passed along word of his exoneration. "Let's get the Mounties to find out who did this." It galled him that the memo was received like an act of treason when it was viewed as evidence of a plot against the prime minister, but when it was confirmed to be a fabrication, its content a slander against Martin and his people, it was written off as a simple hoax. The PMO's failure to call in the RCMP told Martin one thing – that it had probably come from one of Chrétien's own loyalists.

It might have been that Chrétien was too distracted by a larger sense of outrage. His resentment of Martin was spilling out at inappropriate moments. In late March, for instance, former Israeli prime minister Shimon Peres came to Ottawa to address a fundraising dinner sponsored by the Canada-Israel Committee. Peres and Chrétien were head-table companions.

At the evening's close, just after Chrétien left the hall, Peres turned to one of his Canadian hosts and asked with concern, "Who is Martin?" Allan Greenspan, chairman of the U.S. Federal Reserve, found himself defending Martin to the prime minister in Washington a few weeks after the March convention. Martin ran into Greenspan at a subsequent international meeting. "Guess you've got some trouble there at home," Greenspan chuckled. Business leaders also reported how they had heard an earful from the prime minister on the subject of his finance minister.

Eddie Goldenberg was still simmering too. He was haunted by the image of Martin on the escalator and the conversation he'd had with Herle at the convention, an exchange that left him convinced that Herle and his cohorts were motivated by nothing more than the advancement of their careers. He began to tell people: "I bet you that if the prime minister were to fire everybody in the PMO and hire all those guys, they would drop Paul like a dirty shirt." He was suspicious too of the Goldfarb poll. It was the sort of tactic he'd come to expect, an orchestrated piece of business designed to influence public opinion against the prime minister.

In fact, the poll had been commissioned independently by the *Toronto Star*. Martin was popular, but his organization clearly lost points in the public-relations war immediately after the Regal Constellation controversy. The meeting was described in a *National Post* report as a "coup" attempt by an anonymous "member of the committee to re-elect Chrétien." Francie Ducros was fingered by the Martin team as a likely source, but the communications director vigorously denied that this was her spin. "The *coup d'état* line I absolutely did not say," she declared.

Southam reporter Joan Bryden's articles were always monitored closely by the Martin team for signals from Chrétien's camp. Bryden had long been critical of Martin, describing him in a news analysis two months after his election to the Commons as "a dud." With Chrétien, the tone of Bryden's pieces was invariably more forgiving, and she was viewed by most in the parliamentary press gallery as one of the prime minister's favoured reporters.

Bryden's first post-convention article highlighted the severe antipathy building against Martin personally within Chrétien's circle. Writing that "the nation's capital is not big enough for both the prime minister and his finance minister," Bryden reported that Chrétien loyalists would prefer Martin be ejected from cabinet. One anonymous source suggested it would be best if Martin just quit. Firing him, this person said, could make him a martyr.

"While loyalists acknowledge that Mr. Martin's departure would create a short-term crisis for the governing Liberals, they believe Chrétien could weather the storm if he appointed Industry Minister John Manley, who has impeccable fiscal conservative credentials, to the Finance post." The story noted too that Chrétien was being encouraged to punish Earnscliffe by ensuring it received no more government business.

No reporter would be calling it a coup, reasoned the Martin group, unless they were being told to do so by Chrétien operatives. Herle and Mahoney were certain that the PMO, mainly through Ducros, was making a concerted attempt to portray Martin and his people as traitors in the ranks. There was an irony in this perception. On the heels of learning just how hard it was to keep their own troops under control and on message, the Martin team seemed to believe that Chrétien's side possessed a singular mastery of its message delivery system. They ignored the reality that political reporters such as Bryden more often come to their own conclusions after taking a sampling of the political buzz.

In truth, both sides were floundering, trying to cobble together a workable truce in a highly charged atmosphere. Jean Pelletier called an informal meeting in his office late in March, inviting his counterpart on Martin's staff, Ruth Thorkelson, and Scott Reid, Martin's communications director. Goldenberg joined them. Pelletier's objective, he said, was to put this messy feud behind them and get back to the work of government. Though Ducros was not present, he spoke of the importance of resolving differences with her too, urging Reid to arrange a lunch or dinner with her.

"Sometimes the answers to these questions are best found at the bottom of a bottle of wine," Pelletier said. Reid and Ducros took his advice, meeting a week or so later in a quiet back booth of Suisha Gardens. The lunch began awkwardly, but as Pelletier had predicted, the two communications aides arrived at a détente. They ended the lunch laughing.

Goldenberg hosted a small clear-the-air session at his home some time later. Martin was invited to talk things out with Goldenberg and Chaviva Hosek over a dinner of takeout Chinese food. The conversation got off to a rocky start. Martin was angry that his loyalty had been questioned, that his word hadn't been accepted on the phony memo, and that the PMO had made no effort to identify the perpetrators. He was annoyed too that Goldenberg was singling out David Herle for particular criticism.

When Goldenberg and Hosek raised the matter of the scrum on the escalator, Martin offered his oft-repeated disclaimer: "Look, if I had been planning something subversive, would I have handled that situation so badly?"

By the time the paper cartons were emptied, the Red Book co-authors were back on a friendlier footing. Goldenberg and Hosek set aside their suspicions and Martin's indignation cooled.

The prime minister did some repair work with caucus too. Many of the Regal Constellation attendees paid a call on his office, most at his invitation. Andrew Telegdi, the MP for Kitchener-Waterloo, found Chrétien philosophical about the whole business, acknowledging that it may have been blown out of proportion. Walt Lastewka, from St. Catharines, was surprised by how much Chrétien seemed to know about the meeting. Windsor's Rick Limoges was lectured on why Martin had only himself to blame for his long wait for the leadership. Had he gone along with Chrétien's proposal to sit out the 1990 leadership campaign, and run in Windsor as a backbench MP, the job would probably be his by now.

At Brenda Chamberlain's audience, the prime minister wore the mantle of father confessor. "Brenda," he said, "A lot of people have come to me about that meeting at the hotel. A lot of people have told me things. You can tell me."

Chamberlain returned his gaze and gave him the same curt reply she had issued to the media. "I'm not talking about that meeting," she said.

Chrétien at once switched gears, lapsing into a monologue about himself, his experiences, his successes, which she dismissed as a summary of "how wonderful he was." Chamberlain's stare was steady. After three or four minutes, he abruptly declared the meeting over and dismissed her. "You can go now," he said.

Martin's supporters in caucus and beyond were on the alert for signs of vengeance, but there were no demotions, nothing overt. Occasionally, however, they thought they saw the signs of a continuing dirty-tricks campaign. One was a leaked letter that found its way to the *National Post,* alleging that Martin and the Earnscliffe group were conspiring to wrest $50 million out of the government for Canada Steamship Lines. In the words of the *Post*'s Robert Fife:

"The letter claims the Chamber of Maritime Commerce, run by Raymond Johnston, a former president of CSL, acts as a front for Mr. Martin's shipping firm and has been lobbying cabinet for $50-million to dredge the Great Lakes. The inland waters are facing historically low water levels, forcing the ship owners to carry less cargo, which means lower revenues. The document also alleges that Mr. Herle, a senior consultant at Earnscliffe Strategy Group, former CSL employee and past general manager of the Chamber of Maritime Commerce, is providing strategic advice to Mr. Johnston."

As Fife's story pointed out, all of the letter's allegations were false, easily disproved with basic investigative reporting techniques. The anonymous author had gambled that his "tips" would slip into print unchecked – a not unreasonable calculation given the rush-to-publish heat of the newspaper wars. It was a demonstration of why reporters had to be careful not to be used as the means of reprisal in this long-running feud.

It was at this time that Martin's critics became fond of dividing his leadership organization into hawks and doves. Webster and Herle were identified as hawks; Mike Robinson, Richard Mahoney, and those who had working relationships with Chrétien loyalists were said to be doves.

Mahoney wearied of hearing: "I like Paul Martin. It's just some of his people I can't tolerate."

"And what people are those?" Mahoney would ask.

Not him, he'd be assured. It was that mob of thugs who had organized the "coup" at the Regal Constellation.

"Oh, then you mean me," Mahoney would say. "I chaired that meeting, you know." Attempts to portray Martin's insiders as divided actually knit the team more closely together.

Tony Ianno, the Toronto MP whose caucus committee work had influenced Martin's decision to disallow the bank mergers and one of the Martinis, held a party fundraiser at the CN Tower in Toronto shortly after the convention. Martin was the star attraction. Some of Bay Street's biggest hitters grazed the trays of appetizers, sipped drinks, and exchanged intelligence about the tumultuous events of the past few weeks. The cocktail-party chitchat made its way into the newspapers, via Joan Bryden, who reported that Martin's advisers were being described in conversation as "bozos" and "clowns."

Ray Heard, a former communications adviser to John Turner then working at the Royal Bank, told Bryden that Martin had been "let down by some self-appointed self-promoters." Patrick Gossage, one-time press secretary to Pierre Trudeau, lamented that the hard-liners may have damaged their candidate's reputation.

Martin was infuriated by their suggestions that he lose some of these people for his own good.

"First of all, I owe them a lot. Second, they're really close friends. And whatever the hell they did, they didn't do it for themselves, they did it for me."

The charges against Herle and Earnscliffe particularly bothered him. "If I've been a reasonably successful finance minister, it's because of them. They . . . participated in those massive fights. . . . They're every bit as responsible for the government's success."

The down-tools order had hit the Martin team hard. Herle, Mahoney, and Webster felt defeated in the wake of the March debacles. Herle, always prone to brooding, had "gone to a black place," his friends said. Chrétien was running for a third term and the dreams of Martin at the top of the Liberal party were on hold again, maybe permanently.

As May turned into June and the House of Commons prepared to rise for the summer, the core group held a "where-are-we-now" session at a French restaurant in Ottawa's Byward Market. Martin had warned them not to hold a meeting-before-the-meeting, as they sometimes liked to do when they intended to gang up on the finance minister. This would be a CMO-like affair, an unbridled exchange of individual viewpoints on the subject of whether he should stay or go. Martin took the position of chairman and, one by one, asked them to give their opinions.

Once again, Herle and O'Leary were strongly in favour of Martin leaving, more convinced than they were earlier in the year that it was the only option. O'Leary reiterated that he should leave while he was at the peak. Herle insisted that Martin could win the leadership only as a private citizen, as Trudeau, Turner, and Chrétien had done.

Martin countered Herle's argument with the example of Michael Heseltine, once the darling of the Conservative party in Britain and heralded as prime minister in waiting, who faded into obscurity after he left Margaret Thatcher's government in a huff in 1985.

"I'll be another Heseltine."

"Who?" Herle asked.

"Exactly," said Martin.

Mahoney thought he should leave too, which surprised Martin. Indeed, everyone at the table delivered the same verdict – the hawks, Herle and Littler, and the doves, Mike Robinson and O'Leary.

Sheila Martin agreed; enough was enough. Her husband didn't look forward to more political bickering, and she resented the portrayals of Paul as merely a leader in waiting. She could barely read the papers any more, with their reports of shadowy machinations attributed to people she called friends.

Martin leaned in that direction for his own reasons. He understood that his ability to do his job had been severely undermined, that a finance minister must have the trust and confidence of the prime minister. Given the evidence, Martin no longer enjoyed either and whatever he could accomplish in future would be done with that tarnish upon him. Not without some misgivings, he had to agree with his team. He should not run in the next election.

"When would I announce this?" Martin asked.

"Now, tomorrow," said Karl Littler, calculating the strategic advantages. He reasoned that if Martin stepped down before the House broke for the summer, there would be tributes in the Commons, statements from the Opposition that could be stored for further use. Imagine Martin as Liberal leader, reminding the Canadian Alliance on the campaign trail of their warm words about his fiscal-management skills. Others endorsed the idea of an early announcement. The sooner Martin was gone, the sooner the

Liberal party – and Chrétien – would confront the party's electoral prospects without the popular finance minister. Besides, after the humiliation of the last two months, why would Martin want to help those who were revelling in his misfortunes?

In the end, Martin decided not to reveal his intentions until closer to an election, whenever that might be. The current betting was that the prime minister would drop the writ in about a year, maybe later. In the meantime, Martin wanted to accomplish all he could in the Finance portfolio and he worried he would be less effectual if his resignation plans were known or suspected. Nonetheless, word of Martin's anticipated departure gradually spread, reviving the media's speculations and the MPs' anxieties. Once again, Martin was caught in the middle of a tug-of-war between the elected and unelected wings of his leadership team. "The MPs believe I am too driven by those who are closest to me. And those who are close to me complain I am too driven by the MPs. And the answer is that both sides beat the hell out of me," he said.

Chrétien meanwhile seemed energized by the quest for a third mandate, inspired in no small measure by his wife's defiant "four more years" declaration. The couple didn't hesitate to share their indignation over the Regal Constellation scandal with friends and confidants.

Frank McKenna, the former New Brunswick premier, was well acquainted with Chrétien and Martin, largely through the 1990 leadership campaign and the concurrent Meech Lake Accord drama. McKenna had been a major player in Meech, starting out as the first dissenting premier and winding up on the pro side as the architect of the failed "parallel accord" idea. He had come to admire Martin in Meech's dying days, while his distrust of Chrétien grew. He believed Chrétien had played Meech for his personal gain in the leadership race and ended up voting for Martin at the convention. "I walked into that voting booth . . . not knowing what I would do, and ended up casting my vote for Martin," he said.

In summer 2000, McKenna was one of a number of luminaries whom Chrétien approached to run as federal Liberal candidates, dangling visions of leadership succession before them. Roy Romanow, former Saskatchewan premier, was another, but he politely declined the invitation to abandon his life-long dedication to the New Democratic Party. Chrétien's pitch to

McKenna and others always touched on Martin. The prime minister left no doubt as to his sentiments: with help and encouragement from the PMO, Martin would find himself facing strong competition in the leadership race.

Chrétien made no specific offer to McKenna, but he did muse aloud about a potential opening in the Finance portfolio. It would be good for Martin to take something other than Finance, Chrétien said, perhaps Foreign Affairs, like his father. That move would also keep Martin out of the country, not only out of Chrétien's sight but separated from his expanding base of support. McKenna rebuffed the appeal. He'd suffered a tough withdrawal period after leaving politics. Now, feeling like a recovered addict, he wasn't ready to become a junkie again – at least not yet.

Martin spent most of the summer at his farm in the Eastern Townships, playing golf and puttering about amid the chaos of a massive renovation project. The rustic old farmhouse was being transformed under Sheila's supervision into a graceful country manor, with wide, wraparound porches and spacious, airy rooms.

One steamy afternoon in midsummer, Eddie Goldenberg telephoned the farm. He was visiting friends nearby and wondered if he could drop in for a visit. When he arrived, Martin showed him around, pointing out the new foundation and explaining the particulars of the construction. After the tour, Goldenberg came to the purpose of his visit: He'd heard the rumours and he was there to persuade Martin to stay in politics, to run in the next election. Martin was noncommittal. "We'll see," he said. "I'm still thinking about what I'll do."

Goldenberg left after a few hours, unsure whether his pitch had made any impression.

Martin was genuinely torn about leaving a job that he was enjoying immensely. It was its international dimensions that afforded the greatest satisfactions, stretching his outlook, as well as his influence.

Martin and his British counterpart, Gordon Brown, had become close friends and together they contributed to an initiative known as Jubilee 2000, a U.K.-based scheme to relieve the staggering debts of struggling Third World nations. In government finance parlance, such nations were called HIPCs – heavily indebted poor countries. Much to the delight of

Martin's younger staff, this interest connected Canada's finance minister to the celebrity spokesman for Jubilee 2000, none other than Bono, lead singer of the Irish rock group U2.

In September 2000, Martin flew to Prague for a meeting of the IMF and the World Bank, at which aid for HIPCs was slated for discussion. Martin's speech for this event revealed Terrie O'Leary's influence. O'Leary's position at the World Bank required her to represent Ireland and the Caribbean as well as Canada. Martin singled out the former in his remarks, lauding Ireland's remarkable progress on the economic front, while offering more cautious optimism about the prospects for the Caribbean.

Accompanying Martin were Scott Reid and Ruth Thorkelson. As with all international forays, the work schedule was hectic, but so was the socializing. O'Leary was in attendance and the group intended, as Thorkelson put it, "to suck every moment of fun" out of this trip.

Bono had asked for meetings with all the finance ministers at this session to help push the debt-relief campaign. Martin, one of the longest-serving ministers at the gathering, was among his prime targets. Reid passed the news on to Thorkelson, a huge fan of U2. "Sister, you better get on your bicycle. Guess who's going to meet Bono to take him to Paul's room?"

A star-struck Thorkelson was directed to the appointed place, shook hands with the sunglasses-clad Bono, and accompanied him to see Martin at the convention centre. In the elevator, Thorkelson stood quietly beside Bono, barely breathing. To cut the silence, U2's lead singer hummed a little tune. Months later, when U2's new album was released, Thorkelson realized she'd been treated to an advance a cappella performance of "Beautiful Day."

Martin returned from Prague to find the Centre contemplating an early election call, just three years into its second mandate. Chrétien had been meeting with advisers in the first weeks of September, weighing the pros and cons of a fall campaign.

One gathering brought John Rae, Eddie Goldenberg, David Smith, and pollster Michael Marzolini to 24 Sussex Drive. Smith, the election co-chairman, was not convinced of the wisdom of going to the voters so soon, but gamely accentuated the positive every time someone raised a potential obstacle. "We don't have all our candidates in place," one said. "No problem, we'll get them," Smith replied. "We don't have a Red Book," another said. "No problem," Smith said, "we'll pull something together."

Marzolini had put his views on record in his column in the party's newspaper, *Liberal Times*, in which he argued in favour of a strike against the Alliance while its new leader, Stockwell Day, was still adjusting. "Electoral honeymoons are two-edged swords," he wrote. "They give parties a short-term boost but raise expectations to a point where they are higher than the leader and the party can ever deliver. Remember Kim Campbell's honeymoon? It gave the Tories confidence in the early stage, but then their vote collapsed when she couldn't keep up the momentum. If Stockwell Day is only experiencing a honeymoon, we can expect many of his voters to return to the PC fold over time."

He liked the idea of a polarized battle between the Grits and the Alliance. "The truth is that the Liberals could benefit electorally from having one main target to campaign against, and contrast ourselves against. Especially a doctrinal target like the Alliance, with rigid views and thinking." Privately Marzolini was urging the Liberals to make abortion the wedge issue of this campaign, to play on the Alliance's vulnerabilities, especially in Ontario. If the Liberals' wavering constituency believed that an Alliance government would be socially regressive, the votes would stay with the governing party.

Some Liberals had looked on jealously as the Alliance replaced Preston Manning with a fresh new face. It was a summer of renewal for the Opposition, but more of the same for the ruling Liberals. Chrétien's answer was the same as it had been in 1993: the "nervous Nellies" were back; he had the confidence they lacked. He'd always been underestimated by his critics and this time was no exception. Just watch him.

Martin had expected to have plenty of time to make a final decision about whether to leave political life. He figured that by spring 2001 he would have a better sense of his post-politics job prospects. But he had learned never to discount the rumours. If there was a buzz about a fall election, the prospect must be a serious one at the Centre.

Without revisiting the resignation discussion with his advisers, Martin simply found himself drifting into another run for re-election. Herle was

The Board: On August 30, 2002, nine days after Jean Chrétien announced his resignation, Martin met with the team at Terrie O'Leary and David Herle's lakeside home. This was the group known as "the Board" or "Martin's PMO-in-waiting." They are, left to right, in the front row: Dennis Dawson, John Duffy, Paul Martin. Second row: Michèle Cadario, Scott Reid, Brian Guest, Tim Murphy, Pietro Perrino, Karl Littler. Back row: Ruth Thorkelson, Richard Mahoney, Mike Robinson, John Webster, Terrie O'Leary, Véronique de Passillé. At the rear, David Herle and Elly Alboim. (*Debbie Kotelniski*)

Mother and son: As a child, Paul Martin spent most of his time with his mother, Nell, while his father was pursuing his very public life. (*Courtesy of Paul and Sheila Martin*)

Go into politics, see the world: At the age of seventeen, Martin accompanied his father, then the minister of external affairs, on a trip to the United Nations. (*Courtesy of Paul and Sheila Martin*)

Happily ever after: Paul and Sheila Martin were wed in Windsor on September 11, 1965, and their marriage has been one of Martin's pillars. (*Courtesy of Paul and Sheila Martin*)

Family business: Three generations of Paul Martins were on hand for the ceremony in 1984 when one of CSL's ships was named after Paul Martin Sr. From left to right: Paul W. Martin, Sheila Martin, Jamie Martin, David Martin (front), Paul Martin Sr., Nell Martin, and Paul Martin Jr. (*Courtesy of Paul and Sheila Martin*)

Runner-up: Although he ended a distant second in the 1990 leadership race, which Jean Chrétien won on the first ballot, Martin believed that the convention week in Calgary was his team's finest hour. Here, he wanders the Saddledome trailed by reporters, with Richard Mahoney, shown left, shadowing close behind. (*Courtesy of Paul and Sheila Martin*)

Down on the farm: Martin's farm in the Eastern Townships is his retreat – a place to commune with the land or, in this case, move it. (*Courtesy of Paul and Sheila Martin*)

Why Finance? Despite his mother's reservations, and after a few days of debate with friends and advisers, Martin agreed to take the Finance portfolio in Jean Chrétien's cabinet and was sworn in on November 4, 1993. (*Courtesy of Paul Martin*)

Keeping a grip: Jean Chrétien and Paul Martin did not speak very often after 1995, and most of their exchanges were terse or formal. (*Diana Murphy, Prime Minister's Office*)

On the road: Martin's leadership team travelled with him all through the spring of 2003, during the Liberal leadership debates. From right to left: Tim Murphy, David Herle, Brian Guest, and Scott Reid share a laugh during some down time in the Yukon. (*Terrie O'Leary*)

The Machine: Martin's juggernaut depended on deep connections with Liberals in all parts of the country. Here, at Martin's farmhouse in late August 2003, the key organizers from all over Canada met to celebrate the victory that lay just weeks ahead.

Left to right, front row: Mark Marissen (provincial director, B.C.), Steve Mackinnon (provincial director, New Brunswick), Melissa MacInnis (provincial director, P.E.I.), Marlene Floyd (national youth director), David Herle (national campaign co-chair).

Second row: John Webster (national campaign, co-chair), David Brodie (director of operations), Pat Ferguson (provincial director, Manitoba), Paul Martin, Leslie Anderson (provincial director, Saskatchewan), Michèle Cadario (national campaign director), Jeff Copenace (aboriginal and northern liaison), Gord McCauley (national rules committee chair).

Back row: Mark Watton (provincial director, Newfoundland), Allan Sullivan (provincial director, Nova Scotia), John Bethel (provincial director, Alberta), Pietro Perrino (provincial director, Quebec), Véronique de Passillé (president, Young Liberals of Canada), Karl Littler (provincial director, Ontario). (*Jonathan Schneiderman*)

Miles to go: One of the survival secrets of political campaigning is to grab sleep whenever you can. Here, in a summer 2003 trip to Newfoundland and Labrador, Martin catches a nap in a Twin Otter while the local MP, Lawrence O'Brien, holding a water bottle, chats up staffers and local Liberals. Sheila Martin, shown with her back to the window a few seats back, catches up on some reading. (*Rick Madonik, Toronto Star*)

Read all about it: As an ex-finance minister after June 2002, Martin was a mere spectator to developments in the department now run by one of his chief leadership rivals, John Manley. (*Rick Madonik, Toronto Star*)

Coast to coast: By the summer of 2003, Martin had essentially won the prize he had sought so long, and campaigned only intermittently. There was none of the fanfare or attention that had been showered on him the summer before. Here, he takes a solitary stroll in Charlottetown, Labrador. (*Rick Madonik, Toronto Star*)

annoyed, believing Martin was putting the MPs' needs ahead of his own leadership interests. Martin admitted to him later that it was too difficult to turn his back on the caucus colleagues who had implored him to remain in politics.

In September, Martin received a clear indication that the prime minister was moving toward a fall campaign. Finance was asked to pull together an economic statement for delivery within weeks. Normally, Martin waited until late November to do the annual update in advance of a budget scheduled a few months hence.

In effect, Finance was being asked to do a full budget in all but name. The argument against a formal budget at this time was that the House would have to sit for several weeks after its introduction to see the bill passed. With some worried about an Alliance surge, the goal of the exercise was to outflank the Opposition on the issue of tax cuts, which was expected to be Day's leading election issue.

Before the date of the vote could be settled, however, the nation was shaken by the death of Pierre Elliott Trudeau. Trudeau's passing on September 28 was a significant moment in the country at large, but especially so for the Liberal party. His departure from the scene was the bookend to the era that began with Trudeau's "welcome to the 1980s" declaration at the Château Laurier Hotel. The party had been down for ten years thereafter but on a remarkable rebound in the decade that followed. The national mourning was an occasion to measure the depth and reach of Trudeau's legacy.

Chrétien was movingly eloquent in impromptu remarks made shortly after he received the news while en route to Jamaica. Once he landed, he spoke without notes to the reporters travelling with him. He described Trudeau as "an incredible companion in arms" and "a profound thinker."

"He made our country a country with great values, where people can trust each other, a generous country where people can share, a country where tolerance is a [matter of] great pride, a country that is welcoming citizens from around the world. . . . We have to keep on fighting for these values that make all of us so proud, when we are abroad, to say that we are Canadian."

In the wake of Trudeau's death, there was speculation that the election would be put off until spring to avoid any suggestion that the Liberals were exploiting the public's reawakened affection for the former prime minister. But it was too late to halt the momentum toward a fall campaign. In mid-October, Martin was driven to the prime minister's residence at Harrington Lake, in the Gatineau Hills, to film campaign ads. A clutch of school-children was on hand for the purpose. The ads depicted a smiling Chrétien and Martin, strolling through a bucolic scene of children laughing and playing – the very image of the happy couple. The irony was not lost on either man. They performed as good friends for the sake of those who would vote for this government as long as it was a joint Chrétien-Martin enterprise. As soon as the cameras stopped rolling, they retreated behind the walls of stiff civility that now characterized their face-to-face dealings.

Martin delivered his economic statement on October 18. As expected, the Liberals suddenly got religion on tax cuts. A five-year plan to reduce taxes by $58 billion was revised to achieve reductions of nearly $100 billion. Personal income tax rates dropped, from 17 to 16 per cent for lower-income brackets, and from 26 per cent to 22 per cent for middle-income earners. Martin also cut the capital gains tax in a bid to encourage private-sector investment.

Chrétien had saved one surprise for the eve of the election, welcoming a new star candidate – actually an old star – back into the federal fold. After serving as premier of Newfoundland since 1996, Brian Tobin was hoping to return to Ottawa. The prime minister expected him to help restore the Liberals' strength in Atlantic Canada, badly battered in the 1997 election. And he wanted Tobin's shrewd communications advice and friendship. Perhaps most important, Chrétien appreciated Tobin's designs on the federal leadership. As he had intimated to Frank McKenna in a similar pitch that summer, he could offer him a national platform and a little help from the boss.

Martin realized what was going on, but he could see the upside. The down-tools order could be lifted and, with it, his team's spirits. Essentially the prime minister was declaring the leadership race on, and if that was the case, the Martin team felt free to shift into high gear. When Heritage Minister Sheila Copps told Martin that Chrétien was urging her to assemble a leadership organization, he decided that the green light applied to him too, as long as he proceeded quietly, with no public fanfare. Rock was also organizing more openly now, and the Martin supporters knew that the ever-loyal Allan wouldn't do so without Chrétien's blessing. Herle and company were heartened by the prospect of having opponents other than Chrétien – then they would be portrayed as competitive rather than disloyal.

On Sunday, October 22, Chrétien strolled to Rideau Hall, the governor general's residence, and made the fall election a reality. As prescribed by Marzolini's poll analysis, and in keeping with the lingering sombre mood after Trudeau's funeral, the prime minister talked about vision.

"It is an opportunity for Canadians to choose between different visions and different values. This election offers two very different visions of Canada, two crystal-clear alternatives. The nature of that choice is now clear. And the right time to choose is now."

As for why he was calling an election at this early date, the prime minister bluntly acknowledged that his timing was predicated on an elementary political calculation: "I'm calling an election hoping to win."

This third campaign inspired little co-operation between the Martin and Chrétien camps. No one from Martin's office joined the national campaign war room, which was under the command of Warren Kinsella this time out. Kinsella had slipped into relative anonymity after Peter Donolo arrived as communications director, but he was enjoying a higher profile as a PMO adviser under Ducros's tenure. This spoke to the changed relations within the Liberal government, since Kinsella, unlike Donolo, regarded most of Martin's people as enemies within.

Perhaps the most obvious evidence of the unravelled Chrétien-Martin relationship was this campaign's hastily produced Red Book, a slim document that was issued midway through the campaign. When the first draft landed at the Finance Department, it took two minutes for Martin's staffers to notice a howling omission: no tally of the cost of the election platform. Scott Reid argued to Ducros that a Red Book without an accounting list would invite charges of cynicism or at the very least unpreparedness.

Reid and others from Finance huddled for the next few days with the Liberal research bureau, working up some semblance of a balance sheet for the back page of the booklet. *Balance* was the operative word. In these post-deficit days, the Liberals attempted to steer down the fiscal middle road by promising to devote 50 per cent of projected surpluses to debt reduction and 50 per cent to new spending. Many hours were spent trying to bring the numbers roughly within that range, not altogether success-fully. Karl Littler took his turn at the calculator but also found it difficult to make the equation work.

That problematic ledger had a serious flaw buried within it, one high-lighted soon after it was published in the Red Book by the party's star candidate in Markham, former Royal Bank economist John McCallum. McCallum told the media that when he toted up the numbers on the back page, he found a $2.6-billion deficit. Littler again stepped forward, this time juggling words instead of numbers in an effort to rub some of the sharp edges off McCallum's declaration, which was accurate. He explained that a deficit would be incurred only if the Liberals spent the maximum budgeted on these proposed programs, which of course, they would not.

These were sporadic interventions in the campaign by most of the Martinites, however, a far cry from the all-out participation of past elections. Mike Robinson was one of the few in the central campaign-strategy loop. He worked closely with Goldenberg and even with Ducros, who regarded him as a dove and therefore trustworthy. It was through Robinson that requests were channelled for Martin to do parallel cross-country campaigning.

Ducros once suggested to Robinson that Martin stand in for the prime minister at an event – proof, she believed, that reports of her hostility toward the finance minister were overblown. Mike Robinson's eyes widened. "You want Martin to go?"

"Sure, why not?"

Robinson pointed out that the media would play it as a leadership story: heir apparent stands in for Chrétien. Ducros said she wasn't bothered by such stories.

The finance minister spent very little time in his own riding of Lasalle-Emard, concentrating instead on risky ridings where his province could help the local candidate. He made a couple of joint appearances with Chrétien, taking an overnight flight on one occasion when summoned at the last minute to join the prime minister for an event in Vancouver.

MPs in Southern Ontario were especially eager that Martin bolster their campaigns in vulnerable constituencies. Even MPs who didn't want Martin to be the next leader, such as Bonnie Brown in Oakville, knew his drawing power. Martin turned up in Brown's riding in early November. Walking the main streets, shaking hands and popping into restaurants, Martin was inundated with questions he didn't want to answer. In one small gift shop, the store owner wouldn't relent. "You're the man, Paul," he said.

While Martin feigned interest in a brocade pillow, the proprietor persisted. "Is it that the team is strong or the leader is strong? Because my feeling, what I get, is that he's got a good team there, and how much of that intelligence really comes from Jean Chrétien?"

Such sentiments were being expressed all over Southern Ontario. Brenda Chamberlain, while having tea in a restaurant across from her constituency office, listened patiently while her waitress explained that the Liberals were running with the wrong leader. "Get Paul Martin in charge and then I'll vote for you," she said. A man walked up to her in a mall and said he would vote Liberal on condition that Chamberlain do all she could to "get rid of that S.O.B." – meaning the PM.

Party headquarters had shipped boxes of campaign pamphlets, the prime minister's photo prominently featured on the back cover. Some of those boxes languished unopened in campaign offices all over the country, while MPs made up their own brochures with pictures of Martin. Toronto MP John Godfrey, ever cautious, made room for both men in his literature. In the rural riding of Lambton, Rosemary Ur found a way to use the pamphlet: she just sheared off the back page. (Ur's devotion to Martin was fierce. In her Parliament Hill office, she had erected what could only be called a shrine to the finance minister, adorned with photos and mementoes.) And Roger Gallaway, from Sarnia, an outspoken parliamentarian known to be a maverick, said in a CBC interview that voters were asking him why Jean Chrétien was still in charge of the party.

After a particularly difficult day greeting voters at the St. Clair and Yonge subway station, Toronto MP Carolyn Bennett telephoned John Rae and told him the anti-Chrétien mood was "brutal." Rae wanted to know what the voters were saying. "They're saying he's arrogant, a bully, doesn't care about them," Bennett said.

"Well I don't think he's like that at all," Rae replied unhelpfully.

In the middle of the campaign, the provincial caucus chairs linked up in a conference call to trade tales from the election trail. Chamberlain talked about voter reactions in Ontario and her counterparts seconded that finding. Everyone, without exception, reported trouble at the doorstep for Chrétien. "The leader's a problem," was their polite conclusion.

Even among Chrétien's supporters, the truth of his unpopularity had to be confronted. At a private meeting in Toronto chaired by David Smith and David Collenette, Liberal MPs from the GTA were frank in their accounts of voters telling them that they preferred Martin to Chrétien as the leader. When news of the meeting hit the media, Chrétien snapped, "I am not contested. It is not the case.... Maybe it happened when one MP knocked on one door and one guy told him that he would prefer another one. It could happen, you know. I am not contested. It is an invention."

Chrétien took another hit – one that many considered fatal – on November 16 when the *National Post* revealed that the prime minister had called one of the directors of the Business Development Bank, a Crown corporation, in a bid to secure a loan to an inn in Chrétien's riding. The bank later approved a $615,000 loan to Yvon Duhaime, who had bought the inn from Chrétien and his business partners in 1993. The story raised the possibility that the prime minister was in violation of his own ethics guidelines. Chrétien brushed off the charges, saying he was doing his duty as an MP, but the controversy brought the "leader problem" to a sharp point.

"You call who you know, and I knew the president [of the bank]," said Chrétien. "I called him once or twice, he came to visit me at my home [at 24 Sussex Drive] with a group one day."

The negative attention made Chrétien strangely defensive, but still vague with respect to his political career.

"I'm seeking a mandate. I intend to serve my mandate, and if I were to decide not to go for another one, of course I will have to make a decision after three years or more so the party has a chance to select a new leader," Chrétien said. "I know there are no shortage of candidates to replace me."

A day later, Fisheries Minister Herb Dhaliwal reinforced the message. "I think in two or three years the prime minister would rather be out improving his golf game," he said.

Chrétien's popularity may have been waning, but his famed luck was not. To the Liberals' extreme good fortune, Stockwell Day and the Canadian Alliance fought a remarkably inept campaign. Day showed a mindless fondness for stunts, which too often backfired. A staged appearance at Niagara

Falls to decry the "brain drain" collapsed in hilarity when Day confused the direction in which the river flowed. A mid-campaign report revealed that the ultra-religious Day believed man had walked the earth with dinosaurs. Kinsella appeared on TV with a purple Barney dinosaur, joking that Stockwell was probably the only person alive who believed that *The Flintstones* was a documentary.

Ridicule, the most powerful weapon in politics, chipped away enough of Day's credibility to deny the party a breakthrough in Ontario. Without support there, the party would remain a Western protest rump. Joe Clark, the Conservative leader, had performed with unexpected confidence and kept the Tory party alive to fight another day. Clark's most adroit moves came in the leaders' debate, when he pointedly declared to Chrétien that he had changed, that he had lost his instinct for dealing with people. Clark observed Day's antics with ill-chosen props and joked that perhaps he was auditioning for game-show host.

Yet the opposition remained fractured and the Liberals prepared for yet another victory, despite the voters' misgivings about Chrétien.

One of the final events of the campaign was the traditional Toronto rally for Ontario Liberals. Eddie Goldenberg was there, watching intently for any signs of disloyalty among the restive bunch. He pulled Carolyn Bennett aside, telling her that his mother lived in her St. Paul's riding and that he couldn't help notice that the prime minister's picture was missing on Liberal pamphlets in her mailbox.

When the results came in on November 27, Canada's electoral map glowed Liberal red. The Atlantic provinces relented their anti-Liberal outburst of 1997 and sent nine more Liberal MPs to Ottawa than before. Tobin was back in federal politics, ready to position himself as a leadership rival to Martin. In Chrétien's home province of Quebec, the intended target of the Clarity Act's tough-love federalism had elected Liberals in thirty-six seats – almost half the entire province's representation.

The Liberals had increased their majority in this, the prime minister's third election as head of the party, to 172 seats. Chrétien was fond of saying that his favourite part of being prime minister was winning elections. Paul Martin and his increasingly impatient supporters could only hope that this win would be his last.

7

FRAYED RELATIONS

IN THE DAYS following the election, Jean Chrétien and Paul Martin were obliged to meet for one of the frosty exchanges that passed for conversation during their rare private encounters. The prime minister was assembling his post-election cabinet, a lineup that in the end looked very much like his pre-election roster. There was at least one major change on Chrétien's mind, though, as he had mentioned to Frank McKenna.

"You know, if I were you," he put it to Martin, "I'd move to Foreign Affairs." He said nothing more, allowing the hint to hang in the air.

Martin was not surprised by the suggestion; the word on the grapevine was that he would be uprooted from the portfolio that had been his for seven years. Some close to him didn't think Foreign Affairs was a bad idea, but Martin wasn't tempted. He didn't need to get his feet wet abroad; he'd been active on the international stage for years now.

Martin just shook his head no, he wasn't interested. The terse discussion ended there and Martin excused himself from the office. It was back to Finance.

Despite their larger numbers, the Liberal members' first caucus meeting of 2001 was a surprisingly low-key affair. Many MPs trudged into the

Centre Block on Parliament Hill unsure what the election had really accomplished. By their account, the party had won by default, narrowly escaping the electorate's growing antipathy toward Chrétien. The government was adrift; the only legislative items on the agenda were the leftovers and unfinished business of the last mandate. Those who had spoken out against Chrétien – Brenda Chamberlain, Roger Gallaway, the others who had been at the Regal Constellation – felt a gloom descend.

The sour atmosphere was similar to that of 1982, though the sinkholes of disaffection were slightly different. Quebec's alienation had eased: the Liberals had broken the Bloc Québécois's stranglehold on the province. But the West was still a problem – only fourteen MPs, less than 10 per cent of the caucus, had been elected west of Ontario. They resolved to make Western concerns a priority in this third mandate, setting up a caucus task force and considering a campaign to "reintroduce" Ottawa to the West, much as they had done in Quebec after the 1995 referendum.

In place of 1982's rebellious youth, there were malcontents of all ages registering familiar complaints about the wall between government and the party. This time the insider-outsider schism aroused an amorphous cry for "renewal," for parliamentary reform and for imagination and vision in Liberal politics again. Liberals talked about the distinction between management and leadership, muttering that there had been all too much of the former in the previous decade and an urgent need for the latter in this new century. Some of that hunger had been provoked by the death of Pierre Trudeau, and the sometimes overly rosy memories of his strong leadership.

The post-election mood among the Martin team and the many MP supporters who thought Chrétien would pass the torch in 2000 was one of exasperation. Herle stuck to his pessimistic view: this prime minister, like all others before him, would not leave office voluntarily. Only the prospect of defeat at the polls could push prime ministers from office and Chrétien had just survived that danger, thanks to a perpetually ineffectual opposition.

The optimists in the Martin camp clung to a faint hope: Surely now that the prime minister had his three election victories and his place in the history books, he could think of stepping aside. Publicly, Martin's supporters talked about how Chrétien had earned the right to choose his departure date, but they believed – prayed – that the prime minister would recognize his party was anxious for change. He wouldn't want to hang around until the hostility they'd witnessed at the voters' doorsteps spread all the way to Parliament Hill.

A different line of thinking was emerging from the prime minister's spokespersons: the third election victory was his vindication and a personal endorsement from the Canadian electorate. He had ridden victorious over all those nervous Nellies who had whined about "the leader problem" during the campaign. In the words of Eddie Goldenberg, "They were getting grief about the prime minister at the door, and after being in office for seven and half years, he won 170 seats. It is pretty hard to argue about the prime minister's success . . . after winning 170 seats and the majority of the votes in Quebec."

Moreover, according to his loyalists, Chrétien had earned the right to decide how long to stay. His mandate came from the voters and he could enjoy it for another four or five years if he wanted. Aline Chrétien's "four more years" could be prophetic.

There was one small bump on this long-term horizon. The Liberal party was due to hold another of their biennial national policy conventions in spring 2002. And because this would be the first party convention following an election, it would feature a leadership-review vote, as was the case in 1994 and 1998. The prime minister, like it or not, would have to subject himself to the scrutiny of his party. And unlike voters in the recent election, party delegates believed they had a real alternative: Paul Martin.

The Chrétien and Martin camps were polarized over the significance of the review vote and how its outcome should be interpreted. Chrétien and his supporters wanted it to be seen as a report card on the prime minister's accomplishments – a vote on where he'd been as opposed to where he was going. But the Martin people argued they'd been down this road before. "We gave him our grateful thanks in 1998 and he took it as an invitation to stay indefinitely," said Carolyn Bennett. "Not again." Herle was convinced that if Chrétien won the leadership-review vote, he'd seek a fourth term – no doubt about it.

David Smith, triumphant after another stint as the Liberals' national campaign chairman, believed Chrétien, characteristically, didn't want to close any doors too soon. A leadership review in little more than a year would force him to make some decisions. It would also require another internal campaign to whip up a positive vote. There were no signs that Chrétien was ready to press election-weary supporters into service on that front just yet.

The decision on precisely when to hold the next convention rested in the hands of the Liberal party's national executive, which was due to meet in Ottawa in January. Party president Stephen LeDrew was caught in the middle. Though he'd been viewed as a Chrétien acolyte, LeDrew knew the national executive was gradually becoming more Martin-friendly. Karl Littler's long-ago blueprint and analysis of the party rules, combined with the grassroots work of Michèle Cadario, had slowly filled the party's hierarchy with Martin supporters. Caucus chairs such as Brenda Chamberlain were known Martin sympathizers. So was the party's treasurer, Mario Cuconato, a long-time friend of Herle and O'Leary.

It was Cuconato who put forward at the national executive meeting the most forceful case for a spring 2002 convention and leadership review. When political parties are in government, Cuconato argued, they get cut off from the rank and file. Cuconato knew what he was talking about – he'd been one of those young Liberals who wanted to shake up things in 1982.

"All the party has is the Constitution and conventions," Cuconato said. "If we don't honour those, we are basically dismissing the Liberal party grassroots."

LeDrew, however, was under enormous pressure from the PMO to find a compromise. David Smith had already conveyed to him the prime minister's desire for a later convention. Regardless of where his loyalties lay, LeDrew was determined that the party and the prime minister should not be at odds. He advanced the case that Chrétien had earned the right to choose his own timing. Other members of the national executive agreed, arguing that Liberals did not push aside successful leaders.

Brenda Chamberlain, attending as Ontario caucus chair, could not believe that the party's executive was going along with this contrivance that the prime minister had won the endorsement of Canadian voters and a grateful nation would allow him to stay on without declaring his departure date. Wasn't it only a few weeks ago that Liberal candidates were being accosted by voters, warned that Chrétien had to go? Didn't anyone remember that conference call? Out of her briefcase, Chamberlain pulled a number of letters from riding presidents across Ontario, urging the national executive to hold a convention, and a leadership review, by spring 2002. Her message echoed Cuconato's: if the PMO controlled even simple matters such as when to hold a convention, what real power did party members have?

"We have a process, we have our grassroots, and we have the integrity of the party constitution to uphold," she said.

Herb Gray, the dean of the Liberal government, the loyal deputy prime minister and a thirty-eight-year veteran of the Commons, was sitting in the back of the room, monitoring the meeting. When Chamberlain threw the letters on the table, Gray turned white and walked out. The rest of the national executive lapsed into silence.

Intense as the discussions were, the debate at the table was a proxy negotiation. The real decisions were being made on the fourteenth floor of an office tower at 99 Bank Street, the home of the Fraser Milner law firm. For the better part of three days in late January, the genial mediators Richard Mahoney and David Smith sat in Mahoney's office and haggled over the timing of the review convention.

Smith warned Mahoney that aggressive positions such as those held by Brenda Chamberlain and Mario Cuconato would only push Chrétien into staying longer. With the down-tools order from Martin still ringing in his ears, Mahoney accepted the warning. "Okay," he said, "but we can't suspend the Liberal party constitution just because Chrétien can't make up his mind on when to leave. We're supposed to have a convention in 2002, but we might be able to bend and hold it later in the year."

Smith and Mahoney bargained back and forth until they both came to the view that the next convention could be held toward the end of 2002.

But after conferring with Chrétien, Smith came back with another proposal: January 2003. Mahoney shrugged. What was a month? This was fussing over a hypothetical event anyway, he figured. Chrétien was asking for a longer time so that he wouldn't have to face a leadership review. January 2003 might well become the date of a full-fledged leadership convention.

"You think so, do you?" Herle asked skeptically when he was consulted.

So January 2003 it was. Then at the last minute, Smith returned again to Mahoney's office. He sank into the soft leather chair in front of the desk with a sigh. "January's not going to do it. Gotta be February."

"Why February?"

"He needs a three," said Smith.

"Pardon?"

"He needs a three," Smith repeated. "The way he sees it, he got you on the Regal Constellation. He put you down in the election. Now, this is three – you have to wait until February 2003."

Mahoney snorted in disgust. It had come to this, a petty demand for another month. He threw up his hands. "Take it," he said. "Take your three."

Martin's supporters in caucus could not believe that Mahoney had given Chrétien this much latitude. They grumbled that these non-elected folk did not have to sit in caucus every day, enduring the chill of the prime minister's displeasure with all things to do with Martin.

But Martin himself was fine with the timing. He did not want a replay of the melodrama of the previous March. If this timing gave Chrétien his graceful exit, then so be it. Never again would the team be vulnerable to allegations of disloyalty or "coup" plotting against the leader. The charge that "Paul can't control his people" was also one that he was eager to avoid. Herle and Mahoney were ordered to clear all their statements to the media through Martin. MPs, though, were more difficult to rein in. Many were carping loudly about the prolonged stay granted Chrétien and some had no hesitation confiding their frustration to the press.

It turned out that Chrétien needed more than a three. In the weeks following, Martin loyalists suffered several defeats that they interpreted as vengeance. Nick Discepola, the Montreal MP and charter member of Martin's Italian caucus, ran a second time for the position of caucus chair, this time against the prime minister's favoured candidate, Paul DeVillers, from Ontario. With the help of a clutch of Chrétien-friendly senators, DeVillers won handily.

Brenda Chamberlain was voted out as Ontario caucus chair, the payback for her defiance of the PMO on everything from officials' presence at caucus meetings, to the NHL subsidies, to her intervention at the party's national executive meeting. Francie Ducros was on the phone to reporters before the meeting to elect caucus officers ended, characterizing Chamberlain's demise as the price of belligerent opposition to the prime minister.

Or, as Joan Bryden reported in Southam News the next day, the prime minister's loyalists had "lowered the boom" on people agitating for Chrétien's "early" retirement. "Insiders said the caucus elections signal an end to the Chrétien camp's 'passive' approach to leadership squabbling. From now on, Chrétien loyalists intend to fight back," she wrote.

Martin telephoned Chamberlain shortly after her caucus-election loss. She was at home in Guelph, huddled on her living-room couch. "I want you to know how sorry I am," Martin said. "I don't want to talk about it right now, Paul," she said. "I'll just cry." Martin agreed to call her again in a few days. When that conversation took place, a calmer Chamberlain was once more speaking in the voice of the collective. "The things I said and did were reflective of a lot more people than me," she told Martin. "It's important to me that you know that."

Ducros acknowledged that a decision was made to "aggressively put forth the coming agenda" – in other words, to assert the prime minister's authority over all and especially over the perpetually mutinous Martinites.

Warren Kinsella had returned to the PMO fold in the wake of the successful anti-Alliance campaign he'd waged from the war room. He was a weekly columnist for the *Ottawa Citizen* and at work on a new book, a primer on the hardball style of politics he so admired. Kinsella's *Citizen* columns, fiercely protective of Chrétien, witheringly dismissive of his foes, were studied carefully for clues of Chrétien's thinking.

The new triumphal tone of the PMO came through clearly in Kinsella's columns in early 2001. He seemed particularly piqued by a piece in the *Globe and Mail* by Edward Greenspon that had attempted to summarize the long history of personal tensions between Martin and Chrétien.

"The nagging questions that we had hoped the election would resolve, once and for all, are still with us. Being the most popular prime minister in the history of polling – and the first to secure three back-to-back majorities in decades – is, of course, not nearly enough. The sorts of stories most favoured by some in the Parliamentary Press Gallery (you know, the ones wherein the prime minister is nibbled to death by ducks) are back with a vengeance. . . .

"In a column recently penned by a *Globe and Mail* pundit who has built a veritable career upon anonymous (and carping) 'senior Liberal sources,' we are also told that one Terrie O'Leary is upset. Ms. O'Leary, in case you do not remember, is Canada's executive director at the World Bank. According to this breathless report in the *Globe*, the prime minister is 'well, petty' because he once did not send Ms. O'Leary an autographed picture of himself.

"Shocking as it may seem, the *Globe* also solemnly observes that invitations to state dinners have been 'few and far between' for Ms. O'Leary and her friends. Curiously, the same report declines to note that, in 1998, Ms. O'Leary was appointed to her World Bank post for a salary of $150,000 U.S. a year, tax free. It is, by all accounts, one of the plummest diplomatic postings extant. Curiouser still, the *Globe* scribe does not inform readers that one of the persons who approved the posting was the prime minister himself, who later attended one of Ms. O'Leary's going-away parties. (All of which prompts us to inquire: $150,000 U.S., tax free? Diplomatic status? Expense accounts? Where do the rest of us get in line for more of this prime ministerial 'pettiness'?)"

The implication was that O'Leary was an ingrate who nursed ancient grudges. She was livid that she'd been dragged back into the fray, by both Greenspon and Kinsella, from what she believed was the safe, neutral position of her World Bank post in Washington. Kinsella's barb signalled an escalation in hostilities – an indication of the Chrétien team's willingness to make examples of all of Martin's people, especially his nearest and dearest.

Certainly, the view that Chrétien had won the election single-handedly was a departure from the team approach that had been cultivated so carefully by Donolo. The leader's office was turning back to the insular, one-man driven strategy that had not been altogether successful in the early days of Chrétien's leadership.

At the same time, Kinsella was sending conciliatory messages to certain sectors of Martin support, most particularly to Maurizio Bevilacqua, the Toronto MP who had spoken so sharply to Chrétien only a year previously.

"The only people you make peace with are your enemies," Kinsella has said. "You don't need to make peace with your friends, because they're already your friends. So it made sense to me and a lot of other Chrétien partisans to try to work things out with Paul Martin's folks. . . . In political parties, disagreements are inevitable. But at the end of the day, we're all supposed to believe in a lot of the same things. At the end of the game, we all take off our jerseys and leave the rink together, you know? So even though I have a reputation for being someone who would take a bullet for Chrétien, which I would, I believe it's always worthwhile to talk."

Bevilacqua did not resist. Though he remained an avowed Martin supporter, he was too ambitious to be content forever with a supporting role in the growing cast of Martinites. Bevilacqua wanted recognition in his own right and credit for his own ideas. He wanted to be seen as a comer, one of a new generation of Liberals who aspired to loftier positions than that of organizer or supporting chorus for a well-connected WASP leadership. Chrétien, unlike Martin, was in a position to offer Bevilacqua the fast track to a serious role in this government. But not immediately.

With seven years of government behind them, ministers took a more relaxed approach to the Tuesday-morning cabinet meetings. Chrétien sat at the head of the table, flanked by Deputy Prime Minister Herb Gray. Martin faced him from the other end of the massive polished-oak table. Seated around the table, ministers would have their news clippings arrayed in front of them, perusing the stories while half-listening to one or another of their colleagues drone on about a particular agenda item. Once BlackBerry wireless e-mail devices became popular, some ministers would thumb-type messages to aides or officials while the meeting carried on.

Chrétien did not tolerate much freewheeling discussion at cabinet meetings. "Take that up at committee," he'd order if the conversation started down a specific policy or program path. Cabinet committee meetings, he felt, were the places for long-winded debate; Tuesday's full cabinet was about getting through the agenda and getting back to work.

Martin, a fan of the CMO-style of consultation, found these meetings almost intolerable and certainly boring. He spoke infrequently, occasionally making his views known or asking for more information from a ministerial colleague.

When cabinet met at the end of January, a couple of days after the haggling over the leadership-review timing, the "general discussion" agenda slot was dominated by leadership politics. Eddie Goldenberg had fretted to several ministers that this latest Chrétien-Martin tiff over the timing of the leadership review sent "unfortunate" signals about cabinet unity. Goldenberg hinted that it might be helpful to clear the air at cabinet, introducing the matter so that Chrétien could get his views on the table.

Human Resources Minister Jane Stewart lead the way. Stewart could always be counted on to speak up for the prime minister and, more generally, in favour of the Liberal party family. The family analogy was quite real to Stewart; her father, former Ontario treasurer Robert Nixon, was a close friend of Chrétien. The prime minister had stood by her, even stood in for her in difficult moments in 2000 when she and her department were under siege. It was Stewart who had put a protective arm around Chrétien when he broke down in front of caucus before the 1995 Quebec referendum vote, and it seemed she was throwing up that protective arm again against what she described as unseemly tactics by the Martin people.

John Manley chimed in. Martin's people were playing politics that were "divisive and unacceptable." Intergovernmental Affairs Minister Stéphane Dion added his comments in the same vein.

After the ministers had their say, it was Chrétien's turn. He reiterated that he was in charge, he wouldn't be pushed out, and that he would leave when he was ready. He turned to Martin, raising the very topic that was the subject of Kinsella's most recent column, saying, "What are your people complaining about?" The prime minister then tried to grasp, unsuccessfully, for O'Leary's name. "I gave that – that woman that job in Washington."

"Her name is Terrie O'Leary," Martin reacted.

Martin usually remained determinedly silent through these rants. Those who sat close could detect when Chrétien's tirades rattled him. The finance minister would radiate a palpable anger; his face would redden, his eyes would turn icy, and his posture would grow rigid. But he rarely took the bait, responding only when his people were attacked. Martin then would gingerly attempt to shut down the conversation. Most ministers found these incidents almost unbearable, similar to being in a classroom when the teacher deliberately humiliates a student.

On this occasion, Martin only muttered that he wasn't responsible for everything that appeared in the newspapers and agreed that the government should present a united front. Privately, he felt blindsided, particularly by Jane Stewart. Yes, she was loyal to Chrétien, but he also considered her a friend. They had worked together on the National Child Benefit and Martin had always hoped she'd support his leadership campaign. And hadn't he singled her out for special mention in the 2000 budget speech, in the midst of her troubles, against the strenuous advice of his aides?

In the days after this raucous cabinet session, Martin was surprised to see no mention of it in the media. If the incident was intended to teach him a lesson, the message would have been underlined by the usual anonymous sources, leaking the details to reporters. When no stories appeared, Martin assumed the fuss had died down. His relief was premature. Almost three weeks after the cabinet meeting, there was a double-barrelled hit over two days from Joan Bryden. Her first story was about Martin's flagging support, the result of impatience and erosion inside the front-runner's ranks. Quoting several former Martin supporters, the article claimed that the endless jockeying had chipped away at Martin's apparent invincibility.

The second story outlined, in remarkable detail, what had happened at the late January cabinet meeting. Leaks from Chrétien's cabinet were exceedingly rare. Leaks from caucus, yes – always. From in-camera committee meetings, certainly. But the cabinet had been the last bastion of government confidentiality. It could not have happened without a reason.

While the Martin team laid low in Ottawa, rival leadership organizations were gearing up with Chrétien's blessing. Allan Rock had slowly built a small but solid grassroots campaign, with support drawn from Chrétien-style Liberals who were unhappy with the rightward tilt of the measures in Martin's budgets. Rock also attracted those who simply didn't like the Martin organization, viewing it as too big and too arrogant. Cyrus Reporter, Herle's former roommate, was overseeing much of Rock's fledgling campaign. He had to move beyond the Liberal circles he had once travelled as a Martin supporter, cultivating those who were closer to Chrétien. Raj Chahal of Alberta, an impressive organizer who worked in the PMO, was one, and Warren Kinsella, who had committed his support to Rock, was another.

Brian Tobin was running hard to catch up to Martin and Rock. An expert in media bluster, Tobin counted on making a splash in the headlines, then using the momentum generated by a high public profile to attract leadership support. In spinners' lexicon, which borrows heavily from the military, this is called an air war, as opposed to a ground war. Tobin hoped to use the airwaves to build his standing in the contest. On the ground, though, Tobin had the backing of a powerful fundraiser, Steve Hudson of Borealis Corp., who had also bankrolled the wildly successful campaigns of Ontario Premier Mike Harris. It was an odd connection – a left-leaning Liberal and an ultra-right Tory sharing the same bagman – but Tobin was trying to reshape his image into a more business-friendly model, presenting himself to the corporate world as a Liberal in the Frank McKenna tradition. Tobin had managed to garner some organizational heft too with the support of Toronto union leader Tony Dionisio, who had ample funds and manpower to throw in the direction of a favoured candidate. Rounding out the team was Mike Klander, a respected manager at the Toronto offices of the Liberal party's Ontario wing, and David McInnis, a well-liked former PMO staffer who worked in Alberta with the Canadian Association of Petroleum Producers. McInnis was to steer the campaign as manager; Klander, to handle the organizational details.

What Tobin and Rock had in common was an initial conviction that they had been hand-picked by Chrétien to go up against Martin. Though not without bruises after carrying the tough Justice portfolio through the first mandate, Rock could comfort himself that Chrétien too had built his career by handling difficult files in the Trudeau era. The young Chrétien had been known as a firefighter, sent in to fix everything from the separatist threat to the unpopular National Energy Program.

Tobin, meanwhile, saw himself as a reincarnation of Chrétien's populist persona. Like Chrétien, Tobin fancied himself a modern-day street-fighter who did not shrink from controversy. Chrétien once fought separatists: Tobin now fought the Spanish fish trawlers. Each man took from Chrétien's reflected glory the shiny facets that served him best.

In May 2001, Jean Pelletier left the Prime Minister's Office, fuelling speculation that his boss's departure wasn't far behind. Pelletier went on record with the Quebec media to say that the prime minister had remained at the helm only because of the events of March 2000, contradicting others, including Warren Kinsella, who claimed Chrétien's motives went beyond spite.

Martin would soon lose two of his own key personnel, Ruth Thorkelson and Scott Reid. Both had decided to step out of the ministerial office, in part so they could play more active roles in the leadership campaign without antagonizing the ever-watchful Chrétien regime. Reid was headed for Earnscliffe's research and communications arm, to work with Herle and Elly Alboim. This would keep him in close touch with Martin's ministerial and political work. Thorkelson moved into the private sector, where she worked in government relations. They phased their exit so that Reid would leave first and Thorkelson would follow a few months later. The search began for their replacements, two people who would play the harder politics required in a geared-up leadership effort.

Herle had someone in mind for the executive assistant's position. Tim Murphy was the young lawyer who had served as Martin's Ontario campaign director in 1990. He had gathered considerable political experience since then, serving as an MPP in the legislature at Queen's Park from 1993 to 1995 and as president of the provincial Liberals in 1999. Currently with the prestigious Toronto law firm McCarthy Tétrault, Murphy had maintained a suitably loose connection to the Martin team. It was hoped he'd be seen by the Prime Minister's Office as new blood, someone untainted by the rocky relations of the past couple of years. At the same time, his familiarity with the Martin team, especially Webster and Mahoney, meant that he needed no education in the complicated, intertwined functions of the organization's other members.

Murphy's brief tenure as a provincial MPP was the value-added bonus on his CV. It made him a more credible link between Martin's elected and unelected advisers. Of all the members of Martin's inner circle, only Dennis Dawson, the former MP from Quebec City, had held elected office. But Dawson was keeping one foot firmly planted in Quebec and wasn't interested in becoming more deeply involved in the management of the Martin campaign.

Richard Mahoney put forward a candidate to replace Scott Reid in the communications post. Brian Guest was a communications director for Ottawa Mayor Bob Chiarelli but had once worked as an assistant to Mahoney at Association House. He stayed on at the firm for a few years after Mahoney left, learning consulting and communications under Jamie Deacey's tutelage. Guest had a particular expertise in communications technology and an eagerness to apply the new tools of e-mail and the Internet to politics. He was ambitious and entrepreneurial too, always pursuing sideline projects such as restaurants or Web-based publishing schemes. Though young, slight of build, and soft-spoken, Guest had earned a reputation at City Hall of being tough and aggressive. He had a take-no-prisoners approach to dealing with the media and, much like Reid, was known as a "hard spinner."

While Murphy and Guest settled in, Martin began to cast about, discreetly, for help in shaping the policy planks of his leadership platform. He relied heavily on expertise in caucus. Toronto MP John Godfrey was a fellow policy wonk who had contributed to the first Red Book. He was known as one of the more engaged MPs in terms of policy formation, spearheading the drive for the so-called children's agenda in the Liberal government. He'd somehow found the time to put down his thoughts in a book, *The Canada We Want*, co-authored with Rob McLean.

Carolyn Bennett had also written a book, *Kill or Cure?*, which encouraged Canadians to take a more active role in their own health-care treatment and to regard the various medical professionals around them as a team, with the patient as group captain. "But if I'm sick, maybe I don't want to be the captain," Martin said when she floated this notion past him. "Maybe I want to let someone else be the boss."

Bennett had been one of those asked by Martin to pull together some thoughts on parliamentary reform, along with Godfrey, Winnipeg MP Reg Alcock, and Hamilton-area MP Tony Valeri. Bill Graham, chair of the foreign affairs committee and the man in charge of the overall liaison body for Commons committees, offered his experience and knowledge of parliamentary practice. The backbenchers had taken to the task enthusiastically, preparing briefs for Martin and penning op-ed articles for the newspapers. Bennett kept a running list of ideas on her BlackBerry, button-holing Martin at every opportunity to elaborate on her thoughts.

Martin had fastened on the issue of parliamentary reform early on, prompted by what he was hearing from the backbenchers he consulted so frequently. He served notice of his dedication to the cause in a speech at Assumption College in Windsor, which had gone almost unnoticed by the media a year previously. It focused on what he'd learned through the budget process about the value of backbenchers and why elected representatives should be involved in developing policy and not used merely as sounding boards.

On the morning of September 11, 2001, Martin was at his farm in the Eastern Townships, reading the papers as he pedalled on the stationary bike when Sheila came to the door and told him that a plane had crashed into the World Trade Center in New York. Martin kept exercising, assuming that it was an unfortunate small-plane accident. A few minutes later, Sheila reappeared. "Another plane has flown into the World Trade Center," she said. "They're big planes. They're saying it's deliberate."

Martin raced up to his study, turned on the television, and watched the sights that were riveting the rest of the world. He sat in his leather chair, incredulous, as reports came in of a third attack, which destroyed an entire wing of the Pentagon. A fourth airliner had crashed in a field in Pennsylvania.

Martin stayed glued to the TV screen, while Sheila tried to make contact with their sons. Jamie, their middle child, lived in New York City; he managed to telephone early to reassure his parents that he was safe. David, the youngest, was in Montreal, and he too called quickly, registering his shock at the horrific attacks.

The Martins' worries extended to friends and colleagues: Terrie O'Leary's Washington office was not that far from the Pentagon. Martin reached

Herle, who told him that O'Leary was fine. She had been in a board meeting when the planes started hitting their targets. James Wolfensohn, head of the World Bank, had evacuated the building, but O'Leary wanted to stay. O'Leary was invited, if she chose, to watch the day's developments on the TV in Wolfensohn's office and she'd accepted the offer. "That's good," Martin said. (O'Leary's father was not so sure. "I'd rather she watched this with the janitor in the basement," he said later.)

Chrétien was at 24 Sussex Drive, meeting with Saskatchewan Premier Lorne Calvert over breakfast, when news of the World Trade Center attacks was delivered by his aide, Bruce Hartley. Calvert hurriedly took his leave, while Percy Downe, Pelletier's successor as chief of staff, and Francie Ducros sped to the residence in a government car. Eddie Goldenberg was there by the time they arrived.

For most of that day, the Centre operated out of 24 Sussex, as *National Post* columnist Paul Wells described in a detailed reconstruction of the Chrétien government's response to September 11. From the prime minister's official residence, a core team worked the phones with a network of emergency contacts, making decisions on border closings, grounding of all aircraft, shutdowns of official government business, and whether U.S.-bound planes, unable to land at American airports, should be diverted to Canadian landing strips. Rumours abounded of hijacked planes going astray over Canadian soil and of more attacks to come.

Chrétien and his staff were determined to maintain a calm and measured response to the tragedy. The prime minister delayed any public statement until U.S. President George Bush had addressed his nation. When Chrétien did speak later in the day, it was in a subdued scrum with reporters in the foyer of the House of Commons.

The Finance Ministry offices functioned that day in a state of distraction and stunned disbelief. Brian Guest, the man who prided himself on his high-tech sophistication, had seen the televised coverage of the second plane crash at the WTC and reacted with a low-tech holler.

"Did you see that?" Guest cried, running down the corridor. The unspoken understanding now was that the first hit could not have been an accident. He flew toward the phone to try to reach Martin. The finance minister meanwhile grasped the situation through professional eyes. "It was an attack on the World Trade Center, at the financial heart of the world," he said.

Martin hurried to the kitchen to use his phone, mentally making a list of the foreign finance chiefs he should contact: U.S. Treasury Secretary Paul O'Neill, Gordon Brown, chancellor of the exchequer in Britain, and Finance Minister Laurent Fabius in France. When he picked up the receiver, Sheila stopped him.

"You are not using the phone. I haven't heard from Paul yet," she said. Their eldest son was in Singapore, working for Canada Steamship Lines.

"Come on, Sheila," he said. "It's the middle of the night in Singapore. You're not going to hear from him for a while."

"I am not letting you use that phone until I've heard from all my sons. I'm their mother. I just want to hear from them," she said, her voice breaking.

Martin relented. He waited until they got through to Paul, then began the phone circuit of his international counterparts. From the top ranks of his own government, he was hearing nothing.

Like a number of other ministers, he was perplexed by the silence from the Centre on this terrible day. Industry Minister Brian Tobin was similarly out of the loop, sitting in a hotel in Quebec City, where he was taking a French-immersion course, watching CNN for the latest updates. No emergency cabinet meeting was called, no offer to brief the full cabinet on Canada's response to these extraordinary events.

Martin went about his business in the vacuum, turning his attention first to the immediate implications for the country's financial stability. The virtual sealing of the Canada-U.S. border and the shutdown of financial markets could have grave consequences for the economy.

"We had to get liquidity into the system," he explained later. "Think of it. There are hundreds of thousands of transactions which require liquidity, money from one side to the other, and suddenly nothing can be done. . . . There's paralysis. We had to get the central banks, not just in Canada, providing money."

Martin reached David Dodge, governor of the Bank of Canada, who was in transit, aboard one of the last planes allowed to remain in the skies that day. He conferred with officials in the United States, France, and

Britain. As the next host of the G7 annual meeting, it was technically Canada's responsibility to speak on behalf of the leading group of industrialized nations. Martin felt it was his duty to draft a communiqué that would serve as a joint statement of assurance from the G7 finance ministers and bank governors. He called up the official at Finance in charge of the G7, Jonathan Fried, to discuss the wording.

While they consulted, word came from the Centre. No ministers were to issue statements or news releases on their own. Everything was to be filtered through the Prime Minister's Office. Percy Downe made it clear to ministers that only Chrétien would speak. "There has to be one spokesperson for the nation and that happens to be the prime minister," he said.

Martin, though, had already told his international colleagues that Canada would handle the G7 statement and its release. The PMO would not approve public remarks of any kind. "Go back, tell them they're nuts. I'm not going to make a goddamn political speech," he told his staff, who prevailed upon the PMO again, but in vain, for clearance to make the statement. Thus constrained, Martin had to ask the outgoing G7 host country, Italy, to issue the few sentences that the Canadian government officials had written:

"We, the G7 Ministers of Finance and Central Bank Governors, condemn the appalling terrorist attacks carried out in the United States on September 11. Our condolences go out to those who have suffered and lost loved ones as a result of these cowardly actions. We are committed to ensuring that this tragedy will not be compounded by disruption to the global economy. Our central banks have indicated that they will provide liquidity to ensure that financial markets operate in an orderly fashion. We will monitor economic developments and financial markets closely and stand ready to take further action as necessary."

The gag order on ministers rankled. As finance minister, Martin felt he should have been encouraged to "tell the Canadian financial area that things are okay, and then basically tell the world, on behalf of the G7, that everything's okay. But I was told: 'Paul Martin, you can't speak.' I was stunned."

Martin's profile remained low in the days and weeks after September 11. He was not one of the ministers frequently on their feet in the House of Commons, though he was a member of the new ad hoc cabinet committee on national security, headed by Foreign Affairs Minister John Manley.

The international stage was increasingly his more comfortable political venue. The annual meetings of the International Monetary Fund and the World Bank, originally scheduled to be held in Washington, had been suspended because of security concerns after September 11. They were rescheduled for the weekend of November 16 to 18. Martin offered Canada's capital as an alternative site for the gatherings and the invitation was quickly accepted. Ottawa was deemed one of the few locales where all participants would feel secure.

Even on this occasion, though, leadership politics slipped into the heavily barricaded capital. At the same hour that Martin had scheduled a closing news conference to summarize the weekend's discussions among world economic leaders, Chrétien held a press conference to talk to reporters at the side of UN Secretary-General Kofi Annan. The media were left to choose the winner in the category of biggest international profile.

Tim Murphy had been warned before he joined Martin's office that handling tensions with the PMO would be a large part of the job. He assumed the ominous predictions were exaggerated.

"From Toronto, it sounded like one of those inside-Ottawa things, people being way too caught up in the politics of the place," Murphy says. "But once I got here, I was truly astounded by the degree to which we were being treated and portrayed as the adversaries – like we were the opposition. The atmosphere was as bad as advertised."

At Murphy's debut appearance at a meeting of all ministers' executive assistants, government-wide, Eddie Goldenberg jumped to his feet, introduced Murphy as an old friend, and cleared a spot beside him so Murphy could sit down. A prettier picture couldn't have been drawn of Martin-Chrétien solidarity in the staff ranks, but leadership politics soon became a constant undercurrent of their relationship.

There was a strain even in the minutiae of daily contact between Martin's office and the PMO, much of it in Murphy's bailiwick. It felt to him like a perpetual struggle, with the finance minister's motives constantly being weighed and evaluated. The PMO's weekly communications meeting was one such forum where these complex cabinet dynamics were on display. Ducros would lead the discussion and then go around the table, asking for input from the communications aides from the other ministerial offices. Aides whose ministers were friendly with Chrétien would banter back and forth with PMO officials. But a cloud hung over the Martin representatives. No matter who attended from Martin's office, whether it was Murphy, Brian Guest, or press secretary Melanie Gruer, people at the meeting noticed a subtle change in tone when they spoke up. Ducros and her colleagues became a bit more formal, a little less effusive about the matter at hand.

Not only were Chrétien-Martin rivalries at play, there were also prickly relations with the other undeclared leadership contenders. Tobin's star seemed to be rising as he attempted to displace Rock as the PMO favourite. The Liberal party itself appeared enchanted by all things Atlantic and Maritime, featuring East Coast music and beer at its pub nights in recent years. Tobin had successfully effected an image transformation. Now he leaned to the right, apologizing at the World Economic Forum in Davos in 2001 for his anti-free-trade position of the late 1980s in front of Brian Mulroney, no less. Tobin was playing his air war deftly, and the chatter around Parliament Hill was that he was becoming a larger threat to Martin than Rock was. This was evident in a change in relations between Martin and Rock's people: suddenly they seemed united in indignation about Tobin, exchanging eyebrow-raising tales of Tobin's over-the-top exploits at Liberal social functions.

Then in October, reports surfaced of an anybody-but-Martin movement. There were rumours that Rock and Tobin planned to join forces to fight Martin at the riding level in the Liberal heartland of Ontario. Karl Littler was in charge of Martin's Ontario organization in all but name and he quickly fashioned a plan to pre-empt any challengers: Ontario riding presidents would vote to make it more difficult to obtain membership forms for new recruits to the other teams. The forms would be distributed one at a time by the riding executive, so that no contender could take over ridings with batch sign-ups. Littler's idea had some appeal in the province, where most ridings were held by sitting MPs who were horrified by the notion that their own associations could be usurped by any leadership organization. Many of these incumbent MPs were already friendly to

Martin. At a meeting in Sarnia, Ontario, in late October, all the provincial riding presidents went along with the scheme to restrict the distribution of membership forms.

This skirmish paled beside a more serious challenge from a new contender. John Manley, the foreign affairs minister, had conducted an impressive air war of his own in the days after September 11. His public pronouncements had been empathetic and calming, his earnest yet controlled demeanour well-suited the crisis. A tax lawyer whom Chrétien had often called his smartest minister, Manley had scored valuable public-relations points for his straightforward handling of the tragedy.

Before September 11, Martin and the Finance Department had planned to deliver a budget in spring 2003. A fall budget was unlikely; none of the appropriate preparations had been made. The opposition was making much of the fact that it had been almost two years since the last full budget, but Martin pooh-poohed their complaints, arguing that the October 2001 economic statement had been a budget in all but name, and a powerful one at that.

The Commons finance committee was conducting its pre-budget consultations at a leisurely pace. Maurizio Bevilacqua, chair of the finance committee, had held a few exploratory hearings, so Martin could keep his options on timing open, but the general assumption was that they were working toward a February deadline. No "narrative" for the next budget had yet been decided, though there were vague ideas of an environmental theme, taking advantage of a new accrual-accounting system that would not regard environmental clean-up measures as liabilities for debt purposes.

But after September 11, the need for another narrative emerged. Suddenly *national security* and *confidence* were the buzzwords. Bevilacqua scrambled to schedule a raft of finance committee hearings on the economic fallout of the terrorist attacks, where the presentations focused on border security and its implications for Canada-U.S. trade. Martin felt pressure to deliver a full-fledged budget from the elite group of outside economists who had been advising him in a quasi-official capacity for the previous three years, as part of an effort to enhance the government's decision-making process. The economists and the opposition in the Commons argued that only a budget would serve as a statement of Canada's resolve not to go into deficit again in the wake of the post–September 11 economic decline.

"It was very clear that the country required a confidence measure," Martin says. "It was manifestly evident to me and to everybody else who could add two and two in the country that I had to do this confidence budget. And then, amazingly, the PMO opposed it."

The tussle was over its timing. No one would be sure until the last week of November, when Finance's panel of outside economists issued final figures for the third quarter, how September's events had affected Canada's economic picture.

Eventually, following meetings between Eddie Goldenberg and Martin's deputy minister, Kevin Lynch, the decision was made to issue a budget in the second week of December, shortly after the third-quarter's figures were known. Martin went to 24 Sussex Drive in late October to notify Chrétien that he intended to deliver a budget sooner rather than later. Goldenberg had prepared the ground to ensure that this encounter between Martin and Chrétien was a mere formality. The prime minister readily gave his assent.

Yet in Martin's mind, the fact that he had to argue over the timing of the budget represented a turning point in his relations with Chrétien. "That is when I began to say, boy, politics is intruding on my ability to do my job."

Ironically, Martin's problems at this point were rooted to some extent in a cabinet dynamic that he had been looking to change. In the first two mandates, this government functioned well on the creative tension between the prime minister and the finance minister. But now a third player had been inserted into the process at a time when the chemistry between them was becoming increasingly toxic. Chrétien had given John Manley overall responsibility for national security while Canada struggled to find its bearings in a scarier, more fragile world.

Martin's desire to do an early budget ran against Manley's inherent caution. He worried that budget-making would force decisions and commitments that the government wasn't ready to assume. While Canada and the rest of the world regained their equilibrium, it seemed a better idea to Manley – and to the PMO – to keep all options open on the spending front.

There are two varieties of broad ministerial function: making wish lists and making tradeoffs. They are the difference between theory and practice: deciding what you would like to do versus what you are able to do.

Every cabinet minister, in his or her own domain, sorts priorities on a daily basis. Department officials spend a lot of time designing the programs they would like to undertake and ministers make the hard choices of which programs are possible, politically or financially, within the dictates of pragmatism.

When they arrive at the budget negotiations, however, they come with a wish list of programs and projects. Only two ministers decide the tradeoffs and priorities from among these various lists: the prime minister and the finance minister. Chrétien and Martin had handled this, not without bumps but more or less adequately, since 1993. It was easier when they were in the deficit-cutting mode and co-operation meant only backing each other against the critics. It was more complicated when the government moved into a surplus position and Martin and Chrétien had to go back and forth on budget priorities. When Manley was introduced into the process, the situation became almost unworkable.

Manley was given the responsibility, much like Martin's and Chrétien's, for setting priorities under the umbrella of national security. Just as the prime minister had offered his full support to the finance minister when the objective had been deficit-reduction, he now gave his backing to Manley's choices, under the imperative of national security.

Manley's responsibility came without any significant increase in his staff or office infrastructure. He was head of a cabinet committee only and suddenly confronted with all kinds of new ministerial demands for "security" spending. Some of these were old ministerial wish lists dressed in new clothing – words like *innovation* replaced by *security*. Manley was charged with sorting through these lists to determine which proposals would genuinely help the government deal with its security concerns. He had to do so with a small staff and a slim support network. Furthermore, the funding of any proposals he endorsed had to be meshed with and delivered through a budget – a process controlled by Finance. Though Manley may have been nominally in charge of making national-security tradeoffs,

Martin's Finance was the only department with the resources to implement whatever he chose.

The inevitable clashes soon arose at cabinet meetings. Martin became more aggressive, pressing Manley to provide reliable numbers for his national-security ideas. Manley grew more stubborn in the face of Martin's demands. Other ministers stayed out of the verbal fisticuffs. This seemed to be an intensely personal feud.

Manley's people believed the fight over a national-security budget was driven by ego from Martin's office, that his staff were frustrated to be out of the spotlight and were desperately looking for a way back in. Martin, a would-be prime minister, didn't seem very prime ministerial in these months. Seen through the media's filter, he seemed to be absent or on the fringes.

Brian Tobin, also feeling sidelined in the post-9/11 world, had his own ideas about what this budget should accomplish. Tobin made no secret of his frustration with the government's security focus that fall. He believed it revealed a terrorists-have-won mentality, that it preyed on fear instead of courage. In his speeches, he invariably invoked the bravery of the New York City firefighters (his father had been a fireman), and how their heroic example of "rushing right in" to confront danger should inspire those left behind. Tobin came up with a nine-item wish list for the security budget and he made sure the world knew what he was seeking from Martin and Chrétien.

Industry asked for $1 billion over several years to bring high-speed Internet service – "broadband" as it is called – to every community in Canada. While Tobin was convinced of the program's merits, Martin and his people at Finance were doubtful. So too was Eddie Goldenberg, the prime minister's point man in budget negotiations. They were concerned that the government could pour millions of dollars into hard-wiring rural areas only to find that advances in wireless technology made the expenditure redundant. Skeptics believed that Tobin and his officials were simply putting a high-tech mask on the oldest political boondoggle in the world – paving roads. Or in this case, paving the information highway. Leadership dreams were also a factor. Tobin's broadband scheme was tailor-made to appeal to rural and remote areas where he hoped to build support to counter Martin's hold on urban constituencies.

Tobin took his case to the media, hinting not so subtly that he had the prime minister's support. This too played into the leadership story, as Tobin once again telegraphed the message that he was Chrétien's chosen successor. The fact that Francie Ducros was his former executive assistant also suggested that the industry minister was the man with the inside track. There was intense suspicion among those close to Martin and Rock that Ducros was a willing participant in floating this perception, a charge she would heatedly deny.

All of the policy and political ramifications of broadband were hammered out at Finance Department CMOs. Martin shared the general view that it was best to be cautious about broadband funding. With Goldenberg's agreement, it was decided that no money would go to broadband in this budget. Instead, funding would be committed in subsequent years, after its feasibility could be measured. Don't decide, just defer.

Finance was about to start its usual pre-budget leak strategy when it was caught off guard by media reports of the new budget's supposed contents. It was a leak that appeared to serve Tobin's purposes.

"$100 MILLION FOR BROADBAND PROJECT," the Ottawa Citizen brayed on its front page December 6, just four days before the budget was to be introduced. "BUDGET TO INCLUDE FUNDS FOR INTERNET ACCESS AFTER PM INTERVENES TO FORCE COMPROMISE."

The headline had Martin's people tearing their hair out. The story was not true, so they interpreted it as a public play to force Finance into going along with what the prime minister allegedly wanted for his favoured industry minister. Murphy decided the only way to confront the problem was head on, and he and Brian Guest asked for a meeting with Goldenberg and Ducros. The four sat down together over at Langevin Block that afternoon.

Murphy waved the headline. "This isn't going to work," he said. "We can't write a budget on the front pages of the newspaper." Mischievously, he added that this was a media campaign being conducted "without adult supervision." Unauthorized leaks, picturing ministers at odds with each other, didn't serve anyone's interests. Ducros agreed, as did Goldenberg.

On Monday morning, Guest was on his way to work when he heard an interesting item at the top of the CBC Radio news broadcast. Reporter Susan Murray listed every budget measure that Finance had held back for surprise on budget day. It was such an accurate report that Murray would be deflecting joking accusations all day that she had helped draft the budget over the weekend.

Guest knew that no one on his side had been working on the weekend, releasing information or making strategic leaks. Murray was known to be friends with Ducros, so Guest assumed that the PMO was behind this leak and that it was intended as yet another you're-not-in-charge message to the Martin team.

Good for Susan, he thought. Bad for us.

Murray, asked later about her report, naturally refused to identify her sources and denied that the information had been fed to her. "All I did was work sources hard . . . and I hit pay dirt. It's just that reporters are sometimes rewarded for their hard work, and I don't consider the result has even one iota of a connection with the leadership situation."

It was another example, though, of how much the news media were part of the escalating hostilities between the Chrétien and Martin camps. The two men spoke so little to each other, and there was so much distrust between the two camps, that national political coverage had become the medium by which they communicated. Staffers on both sides sifted through the daily news reports and broadcasts, looking for hidden messages; the Martin team searching for clues of Chrétien's plans, and the Chrétien team for evidence of Martin's disloyalty. Meanwhile, reporters were being fed stories by both sides. Most knew that they were being used, but decided it was worthwhile being the instrument of a Liberal feud, as long as they got the story before their competitors.

The feud was about to get worse, and thanks to the media's role, Canadians would have a ringside seat.

┤ 8 ├

THE POINT

OF TAKEOFF

BRIAN TOBIN HAD a blue Christmas. His high-spirited confidence had flagged over the fall, even while his air-war tactics appeared to make him Paul Martin's most serious challenger. But during the holiday break, he confronted an inescapable political reality: Martin was unbeatable. Already rolling in 2000, the Martin machine had grown to an intimidating size by 2002. Thanks to the rules adopted by the Ontario ridings in the fall, the Martinites controlled access to new membership forms in Canada's largest province. Martin-friendly party executives occupied most of the elected positions in riding associations across the country. A majority of Liberal MPs were sympathetic to Martin's undeclared leadership campaign. And backbench MPs had not warmed to the Newfoundlander's return to one of the precious cabinet positions. Most painful for Tobin was the realization that the prime minister would not be the helpful ally he had expected. The final disappointment was his failure to obtain the much-ballyhooed broadband financing in the December budget.

His resolve steeled, Tobin picked up the phone and asked for a meeting with Chrétien as soon as possible. On a cold evening early in the new year,

Tobin sat down with Chrétien at 24 Sussex Drive and told him he wanted to resign.

The prime minister thought Tobin was bluffing. He offered to acceler- ate the budget's provisions on broadband, giving the program an infusion of cash in the current fiscal year. Tobin just shook his head. "I'm serious," he said. Chrétien said he would exert some muscle to get Ontario's mem- bership restrictions lifted. "No good," Tobin said. "I'm leaving."

Tobin's resignation accepted, the two then shared a heart-to-heart chat, with Tobin candidly warning Chrétien that his hold on the party and the government was being eroded. The next day, Tobin said goodbye to that power's hold on him. He flew to Newfoundland, putting the press on notice to expect a statement and upsetting the PMO's plans for an orderly cabinet shuffle later in the week. As he headed home to make the official announcement, Tobin's assistant fielded angry calls from Ducros, who insisted that Tobin was not "authorized" to hold a press conference. Tobin, though still pals with Ducros, laughingly dismissed the warnings. "They don't get a say in this. I've quit! I'm gone!"

Tobin dropped the bombshell on live TV. He was leaving cabinet and abandoning the leadership race to spend more time with his family. Tobin played down any discontent that might have motivated his decision, breezily saying he had just decided, after a lifetime in the business, that a political career was not for him. Anyone who knew Tobin well recognized that this was a statement of "not yet" rather than "never."

Chrétien had been planning a cabinet shuffle, but Tobin's departure transformed a minor problem-solving affair into an all-out overhaul of the ministry. A number of cabinet members were being shown the door: Alfonso Gagliano, Chrétien's faithful Quebec lieutenant and public works minister, was in trouble over newspaper reports of alleged political inter- ference in his department. Two women ministers who had courted contro- versy were also headed for the door: Maria Minna, minister of international co-operation, was reported to have cast her municipal election ballot in a ward where she didn't live. Hedy Fry, secretary of state for the status of women and multiculturalism, had alleged in the Commons – falsely, it turned out – that racists were burning crosses in Prince George, B.C. As well, Martin's long-time junior minister, Jim Peterson, was returned to the backbenches, as was Gilbert Normand, another secretary of state.

The housecleaning revealed a prime minister now more willing to fire problem ministers in the midst of their difficulties. Chrétien had rarely done so during his previous seven years in office, preferring to defend his ministers while they were in the fire, then quietly move them when the fuss had died down. Gagliano's controversy was fresh in the papers, threatening to dominate Question Period when the House resumed in February. A former head of the Canada Lands Corporation had gone to the *Globe and Mail* with his complaints about the minister's political interference in that operation. Reporters were also sniffing around Gagliano's administration of federal advertising contracts and sponsorship programs in Quebec for evidence that Liberal friends had been rewarded with big money for little work. Chrétien reluctantly sent Gagliano on his way, appointing him ambassador to Denmark. With his departure and Tobin's, the prime minister had lost two of his most reliable allies in cabinet.

But prime ministers are never completely bereft of buddies. The lead news of the shuffle was Manley's ascent to the role of deputy prime minister in charge of national security and the infrastructure program, as well as chief minister for Ontario. Manley was being handed responsibilities that would make him the senior partner at the cabinet table, formalizing a status that had existed since last fall. Like Rock before him, Manley was being encouraged to see himself in the Chrétien mould as a fixer. And like Rock, Manley had leadership aspirations. When he donned the mantle of all-purpose troubleshooter, it seemed that he absorbed the PMO's antipathy toward Martin at the same time. Manley's aides, in private conversation, were frequently heard to make barbed remarks about Martin and his people.

Manley's promotion showed that Chrétien still believed in the effectiveness of the partnership system in cabinet. He just wanted to change the partner. Martin had been his lieutenant during the deficit wars; now Manley would be his lieutenant as the government's focus moved to international security and government-integrity issues. Francie Ducros was a proponent of the move, arguing that power should shift at the cabinet table to reflect the government's changed priorities.

"It isn't always your finance minister. It's your minister and your lieutenant that you need at the time," she said. Implicit in that analysis was the obvious corollary: Martin was no longer needed, at least not as a senior lieutenant.

Tobin's exit created a vacancy at Industry, a position coveted by Allan Rock and Anne McLellan, both of whom aspired to stretch themselves in economic portfolios. Rock won the title after a day-long personal lobbying effort with the prime minister. His interest in replacing Tobin was seen as an acknowledgement that the savvy Newfoundlander had picked the right portfolio from which to compete against Martin. Rock, like Tobin, wanted to battle Martin on his own finance and economy turf. What's more, no matter who held the portfolio, the industry ministers in this Liberal government always posted the largest annual receipts in political donations.

McLellan was shifted to Rock's former post at Health. Just as she had followed Rock to the Justice Ministry, now she would be the health minister, arriving at a time when the provinces were becoming increasingly bellicose in their demands for more federal cash.

To fill Manley's vacancy at Foreign Affairs, Chrétien reached into the backbenches. Bill Graham, the moderator of the 1990 leadership debates and chairman of the Commons foreign affairs committee, was named to the post. Graham was an international legal scholar, and a member of a wealthy Canadian family, whose cousin, Ron Graham, had ghost-written Chrétien's wildly successful memoirs, *Straight from the Heart*. He had long been known as a Martin supporter. He was a law-school classmate of Martin's and their wives were good friends, working closely on behalf of the literary community through the Writers' Trust and its annual Politics and the Pen dinner in Ottawa. Graham had languished on the backbench since 1993, one of the perils of Chrétien's having too many stars in his caucus. His elevation to cabinet was seen by most of his fellow MPs as an overdue, welcome development.

It was the appointment of another Martinite that set the cat among the pigeons. Maurizio Bevilacqua was elevated to a junior minister's post – secretary of state for science and technology – plucked from among the most active Martin supporters in the Liberal ranks to become part of the prime minister's cabinet team.

Bevilacqua had impressed Chrétien in the first days of the Liberal government, when the young MP had served as parliamentary secretary to Lloyd Axworthy during his attempt to overhaul social programs. Bevilacqua had assumed his cabinet chances were destroyed after barking at Chrétien during the Italian-caucus encounter in 1999, his outburst may have instead enhanced his standing with the prime minister. What Chrétien minded more than MPs who shouted at him were MPs who smiled to his face and then complained about him behind his back to the media.

So there were reasons to believe that this was a conciliatory gesture from Chrétien to Martin's troops, as Warren Kinsella billed it. But there may have also been an element of political calculation too.

One minister, loyal to Chrétien, had advised him to put Bevilacqua in cabinet because it would stir up jealousies in the Martin camp, especially among the so-called Italian caucus. "I told Chrétien, what better way to do it? Divide and conquer," the minister says. And that's exactly what happened; the sniping that Bevilacqua had sold out to Chrétien began almost immediately. Tony Ianno was among those who felt wronged. Like Bill Graham, Ianno had spoken to Chrétien a couple of years earlier and came away believing he would get into cabinet when there was an appropriate vacancy. Graham was chosen this time, but Ianno was forced to accept that he'd probably seen his last hopes for a cabinet seat evaporate with Bevilacqua's appointment.

The shuffle had dashed hopes among female MPs, who also felt left out of this round of promotions. All but one of the nine newcomers were men, the exception being Susan Whelan, daughter of Trudeau-era cabinet minister Eugene Whelan, who replaced Maria Minna as minister of international co-operation. Carolyn Bennett, the chair of the Liberal women's caucus, fielded many of the calls from dejected female MPs. She candidly told journalists that the cabinet shuffle had been a major disappointment to Liberal women. "I think the optics of the lineup of new secretaries of state [all men] is sort of upsetting to people," she said. "They just think it's a step backwards."

The ouster of former deputy prime minister Herb Gray provoked outrage beyond Parliament Hill and especially in his hometown of Windsor. Chrétien's dismissal of the faithful cabinet stalwart just six months shy of his fortieth anniversary in the Commons appeared to indicate that the prime minister was more attentive to his own anniversaries than anyone else's. (One of the oft-cited reasons for Chrétien hanging on so long was his desire to mark the fortieth anniversary of his election to the Commons in April 2003.)

Rumours had been circulating for months that Gray would be asked to step down. The mere suggestion offended Gray, especially when it was linked to his five-year battle with cancer of the esophagus, from which he had made an almost full recovery. Some of Gray's friends had urged him to offer to leave rather than be pushed out. Quietly, Gray had let Chrétien know that he would leave, provided he not be sent to the Senate or simply put out to pasture. He asked for the job of Canadian chairman of the International Joint Commission, a Canada-U.S. body that oversaw waters straddling the border. It was a perfect job for the Windsor-born Gray. Chrétien offered to keep Gray in the Commons so that he could mark his fortieth anniversary as an MP, but Gray demurred.

Chrétien held a rare news conference after the shuffle to talk about the meaning of the overhaul. Even as he spoke about the spirit of renewal he was trying to inject into his government, the scribes pressed him on the question of when he was leaving. Chrétien said only that he would probably do some more thinking, some other time. "I had a walk in the snow last night and I'm staying . . . I will go when I decide I will go. But as long as I'm prime minister, I am prime minister. Another day, another snowstorm – in July – I might decide to go."

On the Sunday afternoon before Parliament was due to reconvene in late January, the Liberal caucus gathered in the old Reading Room of the Centre Block. The top two officials of the Liberal party, president Stephen LeDrew and executive director Terry Mercer, had been invited to attend the session to talk about ways to pay down the party's $3-million-plus debt, incurred during the last stretch of the 2000 campaign when the Grits blew the budget on advertising.

One scheme to put the party back in the black involved siphoning off a portion of all money raised by MPs in their own ridings. Some had accumulated significant war chests, well over the approximately $50,000 they were permitted to spend during a single election campaign. Carolyn Bennett was among those who had argued that no money should be going blindly to Liberal party headquarters until MPs could see a financial plan and have a say in how the funds were being spent. In answer to that demand, just such a financial plan was placed on the MPs' chairs before they arrived at the caucus meeting. As debate began about the debt-reduction scheme, several MPs lined up at the microphone to air their frustration with LeDrew's proposal. Eventually Bennett got her turn. "If I'm going to go back to my riding and ask for more tithings to the central party, I need to know what the central party is doing for me," Bennett declared.

Chrétien, who had allowed LeDrew and Mercer to field most of the questions, suddenly snapped to life. "It got you elected, madame," he thundered. The prime minister then launched a diatribe on an unrelated subject, Bennett's public comments about the cabinet shuffle. "You were the only one to criticize me," he shouted.

Jaws dropped. Bennett's friends in caucus, many of them with the same complaint, were too shocked or intimidated to leap to her defence. Paul Martin, one of those friends, remained icily quiet, shifting in his chair uncomfortably, wanting to avert his eyes. Bennett went back to the microphone to restate her argument. She tried to hold to her ground, but the prime minister was unstoppable. For several uncomfortable minutes, he kept up his harangue, documenting all he had done to promote the cause of women in the Liberal party. Bennett made one more attempt to make her case on the tithing issue, but to no avail, and returned to her seat to await the end of the rant and the end of the meeting. One witness later told Bennett that it looked as if Chrétien wanted to stop himself but was incapable, as if he were possessed.

When Bennett went to an anteroom to collect herself, one of his aides passed her a press clipping from *La Presse*, the French-language daily. A couple of days earlier, Bennett had spoken to a reporter from the paper and confirmed that she did plan to raise the "unfortunate optics" of the cabinet shuffle at the Sunday caucus meeting. The paper couched her comments in the form of a warning to Chrétien, that he could expect some heat from Bennett and the other women in caucus. Bennett realized that if the prime minister had seen this *La Presse* article in advance, he would have assumed that the chair of the women's caucus had taken to the microphone for the sole purpose of attacking his cabinet choices. She sat down and wrote out a note to Chrétien, saying that only in retrospect had she seen this; now she understood why he had seemed so defensive. The prime minister did not reply.

As soon as caucus ended, Martin pulled Bennett aside. Would she join him and Sheila for dinner in the parliamentary restaurant? The symbolism couldn't have been lost on anyone who saw the group dining that night: the target of the prime minister's wrath had fled into the comforting embrace of his chief rival. Word of "the rant" had already reached the media; several MPs went straight from the meeting to their telephones to describe the outburst to reporters. The next day, the newspapers were filled with reports of the prime minister losing his cool. Typically, the complex story became an overly simple sketch: sadistic prime minister beats up on woman who has temerity to criticize him, reducing her to tears. The incident became fodder for the talk shows and a jumping-off point for discussion of the PM's bullying style of management and his iron grip on power.

For years, Chrétien's critics had tried to draw attention to his occasional temper tantrums as symptomatic of a larger PMO tendency to attack challengers. Beginning with John Nunziata's expulsion from caucus and including the APEC pepper-spray incident and the choke-hold on a Flag Day protester, his detractors claimed that this prime minister would rather crush dissent than debate it. The rant at Carolyn Bennett proved to be the tipping point. *Globe and Mail* columnist Jeffrey Simpson, who had written a 2001 book about Chrétien's centralizing tendencies titled *The Friendly Dictatorship*, began to joke that the word *friendly* would be crossed out when the paperback edition was issued. Chrétien had come a long way from being the little guy from Shawinigan, the politician who came first in Liberals' hearts; hereafter the popular perception was of a man who was first and foremost a bully.

It didn't take long for the Liberal caucus to register its protest over the shuffle and the Bennett incident. When it came time to elect the new chairperson of caucus, the Martin forces at last scored a victory. One of their own, Stan Keyes from Hamilton, emerged at the end of a hard-fought election as spokesman for the restive Liberal caucus.

The Martinites had been busy before this election. Tim Murphy had met with all of the candidates – Steve Mahoney from Mississauga and Sarmite Bulte from Toronto were the others – and asked directly whether they could be counted on to co-operate with "our agenda." Only Keyes had responded in the unconditional affirmative. The most ardent Martin supporters in caucus, especially Reg Alcock, Joe Volpe, and Tony Ianno, had then methodically tracked their colleagues' voting intentions and applied pressure on Keyes's behalf. Thereafter it would be Keyes who would meet privately with the prime minister every week to report on the important issues in caucus, and to whom the media would look for assessments of the mood of Liberal MPs. Keyes's election served notice that Martin's supporters were on the ascendancy.

Though Tobin was gone, Chrétien moved quickly to address the problems his old friend had laid at his feet during their candid conversation at 24 Sussex Drive in January. Tobin had persuaded the prime minister that there was a gap between what Chrétien wanted and what was being delivered by his government. Now Chrétien aggressively, if belatedly, reasserted his will over matters that hadn't gone his way in recent months, including the budget. Money was suddenly found for the broadband program, which Allan Rock would receive in this fiscal year. Goldenberg explained that the new-found funding was the result of a better-than-expected economic recovery after September 11. Tobin, however, told people that the change of heart had more to do with the prime minister's renewed desire to leave his stamp on government decisions.

Chrétien also hurriedly prepared legislation to reverse another of Martin's budget measures, the so-called Strategic Infrastructure Foundation. Announced in the December budget, this was an arm's-length agency established to finance much-needed improvements to crumbling roads, highways, and other public works across Canada. The funding for this agency was contingent on the size of the surplus.

Martin was fond of foundations, because they allowed the government a measure of predictability in the money doled out to any particular cause. The Canadian Foundation for Innovation was a model: the government turned over a committed sum to the foundation annually, and it was distributed according to merit by a panel of experts. The idea was also to eliminate political interference in the process and any suspicion of pork-barrelling.

Canada's auditor general, Sheila Fraser, did not share Martin's enthusiasm for government foundations – they were not subject to her office's scrutiny. By removing politicians from the mechanics of how the money was allocated, it was impossible to account for how it was spent, she argued. In at least one report to date, Fraser had criticized foundations for their lack of accountability.

The disagreement, while seeming dry and technical, turned on a fundamental question about the dual, sometimes conflicting roles of members of Parliament. When it comes to spending taxpayers' money, MPs are expected to influence decisions on how the money is allocated, either by lobbying individual ministers or tinkering with legislation before the Commons. At the same time, the public wants their MPs to serve as watchdogs on the federal treasury, to be vigilant that tax revenues aren't squandered on wasteful enterprises. They are supposed to exert their biases in the development of a government program and then dispassionately assess whether the program has delivered value for money once in operation.

The Liberal government had been toying with the infrastructure issue since 1993. One of the major commitments of the original Red Book was increased federal spending on roads, sewers, and a host of other services that make for a functioning community. Cynics called it political pothole repair, but many experts, including Lester Thurow, argued that a nation's economy is only as strong as the infrastructure that supports it. Martin and Chrétien had been persuaded by that argument and the Red Book offered to fund new infrastructure programs in three-way arrangements with provincial and municipal governments. Inevitably, though, the program came under pressure. MPs of all parties looked for creative ways to define their pet projects – sporting facilities, for instance – as crucial to their communities' infrastructures.

In the December 10 budget, Martin had offered to inject new money into infrastructure through a foundation, to circumvent the political problems that had arisen under the old program. Chrétien's people resisted the attempt to take MPs out of the picture. It was a strange irony: Martin, famed for his consultations with MPs, was chided for excluding them in this budget measure, while Chrétien, criticized for his aloof posture with parliamentarians, seemed to be actively defending their turf.

"We thought the auditor general was correct and that we should have more direct funding and accountability. [Martin's people] wanted arm's-length," explained Percy Downe. "Everybody who got on these foundations got on with the best of intentions, [but] after a while it was their money, not the government's, and they would decide. How is that accountable?"

In February, the government quietly introduced new legislation that essentially quashed the Strategic Infrastructure Foundation. Martin was mostly sanguine about the reversal, though he retained a preference for foundations, believing that the Human Resources controversy had weakened the public's appetite for mixing politics with government handouts. On this occasion, though, he was not prepared to get into a fight that would pit him against the PMO and the auditor general.

Yet this decision, along with the tinkering on the broadband decision, represented unusual backtracking for this government. Chrétien had put his signature to the December 10 budget before it was delivered, after all. But now he was issuing a second, edited draft. No matter how subtly it was done, it was hard not to see it as a rebuke of Martin. And there was another irony: unlike the case of the GST in 1996, the prime minister was eager to reverse "an honest mistake" this time.

Tobin's heart-to-heart talk had apparently moved Chrétien to try to undo some of Martin's handiwork in the party as well. Moves were initiated to loosen the membership restrictions that had been put in place in Ontario during the fall. Rock had been making the same point with the prime minister, but with little effect. Now Chrétien seemed motivated to do something about Martin's tight control over the party and – a third irony – to lecture the Martin team on the principles of open democracy. Here, though, Chrétien would begin to realize how much distance there was between the government he ran and the party he purported to lead. Twenty years ago, a similar insider-outsider schism had developed between the party and the government. In 2002, though, the outsiders were coalesced around a cause: Martin's leadership. Some of the Grit outsiders who had promised to shake things up were finally doing just that in Jean Chrétien's party.

The Chrétien team first tried tentative negotiations with the Martin group, hoping that "doves" such as Mahoney or Murphy would be open to a discreet retreat from the hawkish positions of Littler and Herle. But things had changed in a year. The previous January, the Martin team felt it had compromised on the timing of the leadership review, only to see the finance minister scolded in front of cabinet and accused in the media of disloyalty. When attempts were made to broker a compromise with Martin or Murphy on the membership restrictions, Chrétien's emissaries received the same reply: "Talk to David Herle." Strangely, no one ever did, though it was becoming evident that Herle was the all-but-official chairman of the unofficial Martin leadership effort. (Martin's was still an evolving organization at this point; only a month earlier, in December 2001, the team had appointed provincial campaign chairpersons.)

The next gambit was a personal intervention by the prime minister. Word was sent that Chrétien would pay a courtesy call on the party's national executive, which was meeting on the last weekend of January in Ottawa, and make the case for more open access to party membership forms. That idea was withdrawn when party president Stephen LeDrew warned that Chrétien's personal appearance before the executive would be interpreted as heavy-handed intimidation. It was yet another sign of Chrétien's crumbling influence with his own party.

The Chrétien side's last hope was to pull off a manoeuvre similar to the one that had worked the year before on the timing of the leadership review. The drill would be the same: a debate at the national executive meeting, with background diplomacy taking place at the same time through intermediaries. This time, the intermediaries were Tim Murphy and Eddie Goldenberg.

Goldenberg had been bending Martin's ear about the membership restrictions, but Martin was not eager to get involved. He told Goldenberg that he didn't want this to become a high-level fight and referred him to Tim Murphy to get the matter sorted out. On the weekend that the national executive was meeting in Ottawa, Goldenberg and Murphy were with their bosses in the heart of Manhattan, attending the World Economic Forum.

Normally held annually in Davos, Switzerland, it had been moved to New York in 2002 as a gesture of solidarity with the city after September 11.

Goldenberg invited Murphy to the prime minister's palatial hotel suite to discuss a deal on the membership limits. Goldenberg said he wanted the restrictions lifted, that the prime minister would not stand for such severe limits on party membership solicitations. Murphy allowed that there was movement toward the idea of distributing the forms five at a time – the procedure that had prevailed before the stricter regime introduced in the fall. But Murphy warned that there could be no complete retreat to the earlier rules. Grassroots Liberals would no doubt insist on some restrictions to address their concerns about potential takeovers in their ridings. Murphy was vague on what those restrictions might be, so vague, in fact, that Goldenberg didn't consider them to be of consequence or a part of their understanding.

Back at the Crowne Plaza Hotel in Ottawa, where the national executive was meeting, Murphy's talk with Goldenberg was interpreted as a Chrétien-Martin deal. Word circulated that Martin's forces were ready to back down and allow membership forms to be distributed five at a time again. The urgency and heightened import of this dispute was illustrated by the sheer numbers of Chrétien and Martin advisers milling around outside the national executive's meeting room. Chrétien had backed away from appearing personally, but his staff were out in force, an unusual sight at a meeting of party officials. Francie Ducros and several other PMO officials were on hand, talking with reporters in the hotel lobby. Karl Littler and Michèle Cadario hovered nearby.

When Littler heard the rumours of an agreement between Goldenberg and Murphy, he reached for his phone. He called Murphy in New York, who was still on the line with David Smith and others on the Chrétien side. Murphy tried – unsuccessfully, it turned out – to put the Smith call on hold while he spoke to an angry Littler. His end of the conversation was overheard by his other conference-call participants.

Littler told him he didn't have the authority to make a deal on behalf of the Martin organization. The party's executive wasn't going to back down just because he and Goldenberg had come to some kind of arrangement. Smith and the other inadvertent eavesdroppers smothered their laughter as they heard Murphy's irritated replies: "Fuck off . . . fuck off . . . fuck off!"

The national executive had no power to do anything but "urge" a compromise on the Ontario wing. It did so, in a formal vote that weekend, recognizing the rights of provincial wings of the party to set their own rules, but strongly recommending that membership forms be distributed five at a time. The next weekend, this compromise would be put to the province's 101 riding presidents, who were gathering to revisit the subject of membership limits.

On Friday night, Littler met with a group of riding presidents to explain an amendment he was proposing. Membership forms would be distributed five at a time, but the names and addresses of the five prospective supporters would have to be supplied in advance. It ensured, in other words, that Martin's rivals would still face bureaucratic hurdles trying to sign up large numbers of new party members. Littler's amended proposal was adopted on Saturday.

Goldenberg was apoplectic. "I felt betrayed, just felt betrayed," he said. "I am absolutely certain that we had an agreement that was not carried out . . . When they welshed on it, I felt my credibility with the prime minister and the prime minister's people was shot." Nor was he buying the argument that his understanding with Murphy had become tangled in the non-hierarchical network of Martin's supporters. "Do you really think the minutiae of rules comes from the grassroots?" he says.

While Goldenberg quietly seethed, Allan Rock cried foul in a very public way.

When his supporters on the national executive telephoned him and told him of the last-minute wrinkle inserted by Littler and others, Rock blew up.

"I'd had it," Rock says. "Here there was an agreement among the parties to the deal. They threw that overboard and then imposed a regime that made it terribly difficult if not impossible to do the very thing that is the lifeblood of a leadership campaign – which is to sign up members."

So he decided to make his frustration public.

In an exclusive interview with Joan Bryden, splashed across the front pages of Southam newspapers on Sunday morning, Rock declared: "I think this decision not only tears up the [party executive's] compromise last week but it's also an attempt to undermine the prime minister and anybody who would like to succeed him. What's worst of all, it really strikes a blow at the heart of the Liberal party. They're seeking to turn a flourishing, democratic vehicle into a country club for elites where only those who know the right password can get in. In my mind there's no doubt which group of people are behind this and what they're doing is they are sacrificing the democratic nature of our party on the altar of their own ambition."

Fighting words – which were endorsed with incendiary statements by Rock supporter Warren Kinsella. Kinsella homed in on remarks that had been made by Ontario caucus chair John McKay, who had argued in favour of even tighter restrictions that would bring the party's membership eligibility rules in line with the voter eligibility guidelines in the Canada Elections Act. McKay had said that if Liberals were choosing the next prime minister, it might make sense to exclude "children and non-citizens" from voting, as the Elections Act does. Kinsella jumped on these remarks as evidence of racism, apparently believing that "non-citizens" was code for ethnic groups. He called the McKay proposal the equivalent of racial profiling by Martin operatives.

"I have organized against racism for nearly two decades, and have written two books about the subject – one, I'm proud to say, a national best-seller. I criticize racism wherever it is found, whether it emanates in the Reform party or in the Liberal party. So when the chairman of the Ontario Liberal caucus publicly stated that 'non-citizens' should not be permitted a vote, I was angry," Kinsella later proclaimed.

"An attempt to undermine the prime minister"? "Sacrificing the democratic nature" of the party? Racial profiling? Something snapped. David Herle heard a different tone in Paul Martin's voice when they spoke by telephone that morning, reviewing the quotations in Bryden's story. Martin wasn't yelling or raving, but he was clearly furious. As the day wore on, Herle and others recognized that Martin wanted to go public with his own anger, that he wouldn't be content to respond to such inflammatory comments through his advisers.

Martin was due in Quebec City the next day, where a hastily arranged news conference, televised live early in the afternoon, was added to his schedule. The finance minister condemned Kinsella and Rock in terms stronger and more emotional than any he had ever used in matters of the leadership.

"This is the very worst kind of politics. It's destructive and it's personal. For my part, I am fed up with it," Martin said. "I am deeply troubled when the good faith of caucus and party officials is called into question. And I've had enough of having those who are close to me accused of disloyalty."

In the National Press Club in Ottawa, the lounge was packed with people returning from the funeral of long-time journalist Stewart MacLeod. The crowd near the television monitors fell into a hush when Martin's news conference came on. Veteran reporters and lobbyists blinked as if the screen might be deceiving them. "I don't believe what I'm seeing," said one slowly. It wasn't often that the pack was treated to an open slanging match between top-ranking ministers.

MP Dan McTeague, who believed the caucus had been too timid in defending Martin, grinned broadly as he watched the news conference. "Now we know that Paul stands up for his people and we should do the same for him," he said. Imagine, he thought, what would have happened if we'd shown this resolve in March 2000.

That night, David Herle was to attend a concert in Toronto with John Webster, Richard Mahoney, and John Duffy. He sat on the airport shuttle bus with a local Liberal from Toronto, a young woman and long-time supporter of Martin, who was exultant. "Finally, he stood up to them," she said. "This is a great day." Herle's BlackBerry buzzed with messages of celebration from the Martin network across the country. When he walked into the bar at the Royal York, Webster, Duffy, and Mahoney greeted him with cheers, toasting their candidate's display of courage.

The effect on Martin's troops was electric. Ordinary people on the street offered their congratulations. His plain-spoken words had been forceful and effective, and they were no act.

"Let's not kid ourselves, this isn't just Allan Rock speaking," Martin said. "This constant allegation that no matter what you've done for the party, and no matter how recently you've done it for the party, if you support Paul Martin, you're disloyal. . . . I just couldn't take that one any more."

Martin's show of defiance against Rock's accusations came only a couple of weeks after Chrétien's rant against Carolyn Bennett in caucus and less than a month after Tobin's dramatic departure from government. No one in Ottawa could remember a time quite like this, when cabinet ministers emoted so freely.

"I tell people I don't need a degree in political science to do this job, I need one in marriage counselling," Percy Downe was fond of saying.

Another heavily freighted notion entered the picture at this time. It was starting to be said in the media that Martin's people were not organizing simply for a future leadership campaign, they were plotting to *humiliate* Chrétien in the 2003 leadership review. The insertion of this word into the lexicon revealed an important shift in thinking about that review, on both sides of the Chrétien-Martin divide.

A year earlier, the Martin team had assumed that Chrétien wanted a delay in the leadership review because he didn't intend to go through with it. Mahoney and others had agreed to the later date, believing it was a way to allow Chrétien time to make a dignified exit before February 2003. At a cabinet meeting in the fall of 2001, the prime minister had assured his ministers that he would give at least five months' notice before he left office, to ensure a healthy leadership race. People had begun to count backwards: if Chrétien wanted to avoid the leadership-review vote, perhaps turn that policy convention into a full-blown leadership convention, he would probably announce his departure sometime around spring or summer 2002. If it was true that he had originally intended to leave in 2000, this put him two years beyond that, long enough to have taught the Martin forces a lesson about patience.

But over the winter of 2001–02, signs emerged of the prime minister's intent to go through the leadership review in early 2003. One was the increasing use of that word *humiliate* by Martin's foes. His leadership organization was seen as an immediate threat to Chrétien's rule, with anonymous sources alleging that the Martinites were shaming Chrétien simply by continuing to build their organization. That would be true only if the prime minister intended to stay in power and the Martin organization was an obstacle to his passing the review vote.

David Smith and Eddie Goldenberg spoke at this time about how the prime minister might fare in a leadership-review vote. Smith was surprised that Goldenberg seemed to be unaware of the sentiments at the Liberal grassroots. Goldenberg said Chrétien realized his high approval from 1998 would probably have dropped – maybe to as low as 80 per cent. Smith didn't know how to tell Goldenberg that the prognosis was rather more dire than that.

Martin continued to hope that Chrétien was merely bluffing, stringing out his decision for as long as possible before cancelling the leadership-review vote. When MPs approached him to ask, What if the prime minister goes through with the leadership review? Do we have the guts to bring him down in that vote? Martin tried to change the subject. He was repelled by the prospect of taking on Chrétien in a leadership review. Even if he won, he'd inherit a messy and divided Liberal party, probably too damaged to win another election. No one discounted Chrétien's taste for just such a street fight, however. Many of Martin's caucus supporters and organizers were in a mood to topple the prime minister if it came to that, and they redoubled their efforts to recruit new members in anticipation of a leadership contest, whatever its form.

Tobin's withdrawal turned out to be Martin's gain in the underground campaign. Tony Dionisio's Universal Workers' Union had thrown its considerable organizational heft to Martin in Tobin's absence, and plans were laid for Martin to appear at a Dionisio event, probably in late May, to seal the alliance. Tobin himself met with Martin soon after he left government and offered to support him in the race, though he wanted to keep his intentions private.

In late February 2002, Statistics Canada announced that it was changing the method by which it calculated equalization between the provinces. StatsCan had decided to alter the way it determined the value of residential property in Quebec, which would affect how much money the province was entitled to under the equalization formula. The changeover would reduce the payments to Quebec by almost $1 billion. Naturally, the separatist government there was ready to trumpet this outrage as another example of Ottawa's iniquity.

StatsCan's announcement was completely unexpected, and Martin did not like being surprised. He demanded that Finance's officials find out how this had happened without the federal government getting a heads-up, and he immediately convened a CMO to arrive at ways to handle this political hot potato.

As the meeting progressed, Martin kept popping out to speak to Pauline Marois, Quebec's minister of finance. She described to him in colourful detail the budgetary chaos that would be caused by a $1-billion shortfall in equalization payments. The officials around the table at Finance concluded that it was unfair to foist this on the province with no warning. Martin decided that the current system would stand for a year until all the implications of this abrupt change could be assessed.

On February 28, during Question Period, Martin summarily announced the solution. In full bureaucrat-speak, he caught many, including the prime minister, off guard with his answer to a question on the matter from NDP Finance critic Bill Blaikie. "It is the government's intention in terms of the first question to suspend any negative consequences of Statistics Canada's result for a period of a year so full consultations can take place. At the same time we are going to implement the positive consequences of that for those provinces concerned until such time as the final decision comes down," Martin said.

Word came back through Martin's deputy, Kevin Lynch, that the Centre was deeply annoyed with Martin for making this decision without clearance from the PMO. Martin should have consulted with the boss. Martin shrugged it off. It was his decision to make, he made it, and it would stand.

On the heels of this kerfuffle came another accounting problem, one with greater potential to upset the fiscal balance of the federation. Thanks to an accounting error by Revenue Canada, the federal government had accidentally paid out an extra $3.4 billion in equalization payments to four provinces: Manitoba, Ontario, Saskatchewan, and British Columbia.

Martin's first inclination was to write off the error as a costly mistake and be comforted by the fact that the money could be spent on health care in the affected provinces. But the mistake had wider implications. Equalization payments are calculated using Ontario as a base measure. If Ontario's numbers are skewed, so are those of the other provinces.

Discussing the problem with Intergovernmental Affairs Minister Stéphane Dion, Martin came to the conclusion that the principle of equalization couldn't be ignored. Perhaps they could come up with a scheme to retrieve the overpayment in full and then redistribute it to the provinces for health-care purposes.

Martin decided to test this solution with a small survey of cabinet opinion. He sought a meeting with some representative ministers: Dion, along with Anne McLellan from Alberta, Ralph Goodale from Saskatchewan, and David Anderson from British Columbia. Rey Pagtakhan was asked to attend as Manitoba's representative, and Revenue Minister Elinor Caplan was invited to represent the interests of her department and Ontario. But word soon came from the Centre: Martin wasn't authorized to call ministers to a meeting. Any such gathering would be chaired by Deputy Prime Minister John Manley. "What is this crap?" Martin asked. "Fine, I'll give Manley the file, it was a Revenue mistake, not our mistake, but I'm stuck with it."

Eddie Goldenberg relayed Chrétien's position: "The prime minister had very strong views on the subject. . . . If an error had been made the other way, he didn't think the provinces would all send their cheques to the federal government. If there was an error, [the provinces] should have known as well that it was there. And he didn't like the precedent."

After some to-ing and fro-ing, the meeting went ahead. A few adjustments had been made to Martin's invitation list, including the addition of Herb Dhaliwal, the natural resources minister, who was chosen to represent British Columbia. Manley called the meeting to order and put the problem on the table in simple terms. Dion argued that the government couldn't simply ignore the principle of equalization. Martin agreed, pointing out that the benefits of pulling the money back from the provinces would be far exceeded by the political and social costs of ravaging provincial budgets.

"The prime minister wants to get the money back," Manley said, then declared the meeting over. Martin wanted to stay at the table and work the problem through. He said so, with the heat that had come to characterize cabinet-table conversations between Martin and Manley over the past year. Stéphane Dion tried to pour water on the fire, telling Martin, "It's okay. We'll sort this out and have another meeting when we have some kind of proposal together."

Grumbling, Martin gathered up his papers and shuffled out of the room with the others. Over the next days and weeks, Dion and Martin cobbled together a proposal to redistribute the overpaid amounts among all the provinces, in line with the equalization formula, calling it a "health-care bonus." This time, they went into a meeting with Chrétien and Manley alone. They hit the same brick wall. The prime minister and his deputy wanted the money back, period. There would be no redistribution. Martin threatened to take the issue to a full meeting of cabinet.

Chrétien had other worries. The House of Commons was a riot of conflict-of-interest allegations, all focused on whether the Liberals had too-cozy relations with the advertising agencies who had been given lucrative government contracts to stamp the federal brand on the province of Quebec after the 1995 referendum. Dismissing Alfonso Gagliano from the Public Works Department had not bought Chrétien any peace. The opposition was looking into all of the Quebec ministers' relationships and those of Gagliano's replacement, Don Boudria, Eastern Ontario's man in cabinet and a fierce defender of Chrétien.

Boudria came to grief when it was eventually revealed that his family had enjoyed a deep-discount vacation at the chalet of one of the Quebec advertising contractors, Claude Boulay of Everest Group. Boudria produced an affidavit from a parish priest who swore that he had been transferred the Boudria family's cheque to cover the costs of the chalet rental – a cheque he hadn't cashed.

Cranky Liberal MPs were torn as they watched the spectacle. Their own government was taking a beating in the press, yet they weren't displeased that Chrétien and some of his most loyal cabinet allies were under scrutiny. Many of the Ontario MPs were resentful of the PMO's fixation with Quebec and smiled in quiet satisfaction as the opposition and the media peeled the covers off of the government's extensive operations in the province.

A new boldness pervaded the Liberal ranks, personified by Stan Keyes who, as caucus chair, did not hesitate to declare differences between the MPs and the PMO. Keyes and Chrétien had several private dust-ups over leaks to the media, each accusing the other of using the newspapers to undermine the Liberal team. "You talk too much to the media," Chrétien would tell Keyes. The caucus chair would complain about Francie Ducros's unhelpful spin against those MPs deemed too close to Martin.

The federal ethics counsellor, Howard Wilson, was a busy man, investigating and inevitably exonerating the offending ministers on the conflict charges. Wilson's habit of letting Chrétien's ministers off the hook enraged critics. He usually dismissed complaints by saying that no rules existed to cover the alleged offences, but a stricter code would be drawn up soon to take account of the new situation. In the meantime, ministers could hardly be punished retroactively, could they? This was the line Wilson had taken when it was revealed that Chrétien had phoned the director of the Business Development Bank. The fundamental problem was in Wilson's job description: he wasn't supposed to hold ministers to account, he was meant to keep them out of trouble in the first place – hence the title "counsellor" instead of commissioner. Wilson was more advocate than judge, and he answered to the prime minister.

This was another fundamental parting of opinion between Martin and Chrétien. The 1993 Red Book had called for an independent ethics commissioner, reporting to Parliament. Yet when it came time to form the government, Chrétien chose to establish only a counsellor, who would report to him. Martin had long vowed that if he became prime minister, the Red Book promise would be fulfilled. Yet he had mutely sided with the government in 2001 – and against the idea of an independent ethics commissioner – when the opposition had forced a vote on the issue in the Commons. It had not been worth sacrificing his job to break with the government, he decided.

Martin, a Quebec minister, almost managed to escape the storm of conflict allegations that spring. Various opposition attacks had been mounted over the years concerning his ties to Canada Steamship Lines or to Earnscliffe, but none of the volleys had dented his reputation. At least a dozen times during his tenure at Finance, Martin had been summoned to talk to Wilson about affairs at CSL, usually to be updated on developments relayed to Wilson by CSL's management team. They were quick affairs – the minister could have learned most of this information by reading the newspapers – and Martin and Wilson treated them as necessary chores. The encounters never produced a to-do list for Martin; he wasn't sure why he'd even attended them when they were over. Later he would rue the fact that he did.

"One of the advantages of not being part of the inner circle is that you're out of the inner circle," Martin dryly observed. But he was not so far out of the web that he couldn't be snagged.

One morning in March, Brian Guest received a call from Percy Downe, who said he and Goldenberg were on their way over to talk to Martin.

"What's this about?" Guest asked.

"I'd rather not say," Downe replied, apologizing for being cryptic, but stressing it was imperative that Martin be available. Less than half an hour later, Downe and Goldenberg walked into Martin's office and pulled out a cancelled cheque for $25,000, payable to "Campaign 2000." The project was stale-dated, but the cheque was not. It was from the TransAlta corporation, and had originally been sent to Calgary lawyer Jim Palmer, the party's official revenue chairman in Alberta, charged with raising money for the party at large. Although it was made out to Martin's blind trust, Palmer had inadvertently sent it on to the party offices in Ottawa. The faux pas had been brought to Downe's notice by two people who had warned him that Palmer was in a potential conflict of interest. As the cheque had been in his hands, he had obviously some role in raising money while also working as a consultant for the Finance Department. Palmer had been paid $75,000 in 2001 to provide legal advice to Finance and had continued to provide pro bono counsel after the contract ended. Downe had investigated whether TransAlta also stood to gain from Finance Department's decisions and had discovered that a small component of the firm, a coal-producing outfit, would fall into the category of companies affected directly by Finance's decisions.

Martin knew Jim Palmer well, politically and personally. For years, he had been a standard-bearer for the Liberal party in support-barren Alberta and in Calgary in particular. Well connected with the political and corporate elite in the province, Palmer had acted as a bridge between the Liberal government in Ottawa and party members in the province. Anne

McLellan had found him invaluable in her early days as natural resources minister in the first term of Chrétien's government. He was more than a fundraiser; he provided the government with strategic advice and looked to improve the Liberals' fortunes in the province.

Wincing at the mere sight of the cheque, which should have been directed to his blind trust, Martin agreed to fix the matter as soon as possible, the simplest way being to return the cheque and treat the whole thing as an unfortunate clerical error. Goldenberg and Downe left the office. But the errant cheque had not completed its journey. News of its existence found its way to Joan Bryden a few days later. Palmer was forced to step down as the Liberals' revenue chair and the headlines crowed about Martin being caught in an embarrassing conflict between his job and his undeclared leadership aspirations. Bryden's story also raised the question of why Martin was hoarding money for his own campaign, aided by a Liberal party fundraiser, when the party itself was $3.1 million in debt.

Martin was infuriated. This seemed to be another deliberate attempt to embarrass Martin's friends through the media. Alberta Liberals close to him were also annoyed. The prime minister's plans for a fundraising dinner in Calgary were thrown into disarray when the organizers of the event resigned in protest over Palmer's treatment. Stephen LeDrew had to announce the postponement of the Calgary dinner.

In the wake of the Palmer affair, Chrétien asked Wilson to draw up guidelines for ministerial fundraising activities. They were expected to be tough, requiring full disclosure of all contributions to any leadership campaign. And contrary to Wilson's usual practice, he was asked to make the rules retroactive, to cover past and future fundraising. This was worrying Herle and others. They had seen what happened to Jim Palmer, and feared that those supporting the finance minister would suddenly find themselves on the receiving end of prime-ministerial retribution.

By this time, leadership politics had made the Liberals a high-strung lot. An April Fool's Day joke on Pierre Bourque's popular political Web site, www.bourque.org, said that Martin had quit cabinet to raise rare ducks and prize cattle on his farm in the Eastern Townships. The news spread like wildfire on the morning of April 1. The Canadian dollar fell a third of a cent at the mere prospect of Martin's resignation.

A few days earlier, the Canadian Alliance had elected a new leader, Stephen Harper, forty-three years old and one of the founding members of the old Reform party. Harper came to office determined to inject professionalism and discipline into a party that had imploded under Stockwell Day's leadership. Harper swiftly ended any unite-the-right dalliances with the Tories and focused the party's energies on a spirited pursuit of the Liberals. That wasn't difficult. Canada's auditor general, Sheila Fraser, called in the RCMP in early May to investigate what she described as the "appalling" mess of the federal government's advertising and sponsorship program in Quebec.

To give Harper a chance to take a seat in the Commons and to fill vacancies left by the January cabinet shuffle, Chrétien called by-elections for May 13 in six ridings across Canada, including Herb Gray's in Windsor and Brian Tobin's in Newfoundland. Chrétien had appointed two short-serving members of his cabinet to the Senate – Ron Duhamel from Manitoba and George Baker from Newfoundland. Although one of the longest-serving MPs in the Liberal caucus, Baker had been passed over for cabinet many times before getting the nod in summer 1999. No sooner was he in than Tobin returned from Newfoundland and Baker found himself out once again. The Senate appointment in early 2002 seemed a much-delayed reward from Chrétien for his good sportsmanship. Raymond Lavigne, an obscure backbencher from Quebec, notable over more than a decade in the House only for two anti-Martin statements, also scored a Senate seat.

Going into the by-elections, the Liberals confidently predicted they would win all but the race in Calgary, where Harper was expected to gain his seat. Come voting day, however, the citizens of Windsor and Gander displayed an unexpected contrariness, returning a New Democrat in Gray's old riding and a Tory in George Baker's. It could hardly be called a coincidence that Liberals lost in two ridings held by well-loved party warhorses, summarily dispatched to political oblivion by Chrétien. The lesson was plain: whenever the Liberals' team ethic was ignored, their fortunes soon turned sour.

As May wore on, the opposition and the media kept finding more evidence of Liberals gone astray. Politics was turning into a morality play in the Commons and on the front pages of the newspapers. On Saturday, May 26, the *Ottawa Citizen* published a front-page exposé of the contract dealings of Art Eggleton, minister of defence. Eggleton had given a $36,000 contract to a former girlfriend, Maggie Maier, to study post-traumatic shock syndrome in the military. The photograph was almost more devastating than the story – Eggleton, wineglass in hand, a blonde on his arm.

The next day, reporters were summoned to Rideau Hall for what turned out to be a disciplinary cabinet shuffle. Eggleton was ejected from cabinet before he had received a hearing, let alone a phone call, from Ethics Counsellor Howard Wilson. Boudria was shunted back to his former job as government house leader. Ralph Goodale, Martin's oldest friend in cabinet, was handed the scandal-ridden portfolio of Public Works. Chrétien left Ottawa immediately after the shuffle, heading to a NATO summit in Italy. In the meantime, his officials were left to take care of the latest irritation with Martin, the so-called "new deal" for cities.

In 2002, the urban agenda was everybody's favourite public-policy project. The *Toronto Star* was championing a crusade to make municipal concerns a political priority and the federal government took notice. MP Judy Sgro, a former Toronto city councillor and a Martin supporter, had been put in charge of a caucus task force on urban issues.

On the day that Sgro's report went to cabinet for review in mid-May, Martin and Chrétien appeared publicly at odds over what should be done for cities. Martin was forthright with reporters, calling for a radical rethinking of how cities were financed. And he used the *Star*'s favourite phrase – a "new deal" – to underline the dimensions of the change required. "Property taxes, which take care of things like snow removal and garbage, are really not going to be sufficient to meet a number of the new responsibilities that provinces have given cities," he said. "In those circumstances, I think a new deal is required. I think that all options are on the table."

But the prime minister stuck to a far more conservative line. "The cities are under provincial responsibility. We don't deal directly with the cities. We are not in a position to give them more power. The cities are a creation of the provincial governments."

Martin's political staff regarded the urban agenda as one of the cornerstones of his future leadership platform, alongside parliamentary reform. The potential for revitalizing the cities had been driven home to Martin when he saw the miraculous recent transformation of Pittsburgh, a city that he had reluctantly visited many times during his days in private business. Its cityscape and its economic prospects had undergone a thorough makeover, thanks to a dedicated private- and public-sector effort. Closer to home, Brian Guest, with his experience in the Ottawa's mayor's office, was a strong influence on the minister's thinking. John Duffy, now a communications strategist in Toronto, believed that the next great leader in Canada would be the person who managed to shift Canadians' perceptions of their nation from a rural to an urban mindset. Louise Comeau, an environmentalist with the Federation of Canadian Municipalities, had contributed to budget consultations in the early years and she too offered fresh ideas about urban renewal.

And all of this policy enthusiasm was being poured into Martin's preferred outlet, a speech. On May 31, Martin intended to deliver a major address to the Federation of Canadian Municipalities, in which he would present the results of his ruminations on the urban agenda. Brian Guest would ensure that it was one of Martin's signature addresses of the year.

While Guest juggled draft after draft, the minister's office began to be peppered with requests from the Prime Minister's Office to see the speech. By the PMO's standards, this wasn't an unusual request; other ministers appearing at the FCM convention had their remarks vetted by the Centre; Rock had even made some minor changes to his presentation at the urging of the prime minister's officials. Martin's office resisted the PMO review at first, but finally relented. Shortly after Tim Murphy submitted the most recent version, a flag went up.

Francie Ducros believed that it was not helpful for Chrétien and Martin to be advocating contrary policy positions. Their differences inevitably were tangled with leadership politics, and in her words, a "new deal" automatically translated into a "big deal."

Paul Genest, the prime minister's policy director, was co-ordinating the ministers' speeches to the municipal leaders. Thoughtful and soft-spoken, Genest had known Chrétien since childhood through his father, a Toronto lawyer well connected to high-ranking Liberals. Genest appealed to Murphy to take out the phrase, but Murphy knew that his boss was determined to use it, as others already had in the same context.

That Martin was being muzzled in this way simply added to his building resentments. His frustration was very like that felt by Chrétien long ago, when he had moved from insider to outsider in John Turner's caucus. Martin was feeling the same urge to break from the Centre.

On the last Tuesday evening in May, Martin dined at a French restaurant in Gatineau, across the river from Parliament Hill, with his cabinet colleague Anne McLellan. Leadership manoeuvring was not Martin's preoccupation that night. Yes, he had heard that Stan Keyes and Joe Fontana had drawn fire for revelling in their fellow Liberals' misfortunes at a dinner the night before. Martin seemed destined to be tarred by the remarks of his supporters, and he knew he would have to make a call to Denis Coderre about Fontana's comments, but this too would pass. In the restaurant's private upstairs room, Martin talked about the state of Canada-U.S. relations in these difficult times and teased McLellan about the amount of money she was trying to coax out of him for health care. When she tried to raise the topic of the leadership, asking what he would do if Chrétien were to stay on for another term, Martin diplomatically excused himself from the table. When he returned, he introduced another subject and she decided not to press.

A couple of blocks away, at the Museum of Civilization, the Institute for Research in Public Policy (IRPP) was staging a gala thirtieth-anniversary dinner. The Montreal-based think-tank was known for its studies on everything from the Constitution to the future of health care and had been established in the heyday of Trudeau Liberalism, ten years before a band of upstart young Grits started to agitate for the democratization of the party. Gordon Robertson, the distinguished former clerk of the Privy Council and a one-time IRPP director, was the evening's honouree. Regarded as the ne plus ultra of Ottawa mandarins, the eighty-five-year-old Robertson elicited a respectful hush in the room merely by standing to speak. His audience knew that every word would be carefully measured and delivered.

Robertson had served four prime ministers during a long career and he remarked that most of his old bosses hadn't known when to retire.

"Now we have a successful politician wrestling with the same problem," he said. "A successful prime minister wrestling with the problem of when to quit.... I hope that Mr. Chrétien, wherever he is, is focusing a great deal on this question," he said. "My private guess ... is that he, too, will make the wrong decision."

Richard Mahoney and David Herle were among the attentive listeners. They looked at each other, then at Robertson. Had they really heard him correctly? Had the eminent voice of Ottawa's establishment just agreed with their assessment, the view of the perpetual outsiders?

With the cabinet meeting pushed to Thursday because of Chrétien's NATO commitments earlier in the week, many ministers planned to hurry out of town almost as soon as the weekly session ended. The prime minister was scheduled to fly to Winnipeg for a fundraiser that night. Martin would be off to Hamilton. Ontario ministers had cleared their agendas so they could be at the Regal Constellation Hotel in Toronto on Friday for the annual convention of the provincial wing of the federal party. Most intended to return to Ottawa on Saturday for the press gallery dinner. This week's cabinet meeting was expected to be a brief, touch-base affair, so that ministers could get on with their crowded calendars before Parliament wound down for the summer.

But when Chrétien walked into cabinet that morning, it was clear at once that this would not be a routine gathering. Angry, resolute, the prime minister delivered his orders on the leadership front: No more fundraising, no more organizing, no more "double-crossers" taking delight in the woes of their own government. The sources of any funds raised to date would have to be disclosed. Chrétien then declared that he would serve his full term in office and he would face the leadership review in February 2003.

Martin was expressionless while he scribbled the main points of the dictate. Allan Rock sat with eyebrows furrowed, relieved that the prime minister's directives would buy him some more time, but worried that the ban would freeze – and thus solidify – Martin's daunting lead. A few others nodded in encouragement of the prime minister's get-in-line command.

Phones began to ring at media outlets immediately after the cabinet meeting, notably at the *Globe and Mail* and at CTV News. Reporters all over

Parliament Hill were picking up hints of serious cabinet-level discord. And why was the prime minister so angry at the post-cabinet scrum?

Tim Murphy and John Webster had been fielding calls almost hourly from Chrétien's circle in the days leading up to the cabinet meeting. Percy Downe wanted to know why the PMO had not been notified of a speech that Martin intended to deliver on Friday in Toronto, not far from the location where Chrétien would be speaking at the same time. David Smith was telling Webster that Martin should think carefully about appearing onstage with Chrétien instead. Paul Genest continued to insist on changes to Martin's address to the municipalities.

As Martin, Tim Murphy, and Brian Guest rushed to the airport, they tallied up all the ways in which they had fallen into Chrétien's bad books in just a few days: the "new deal" controversy; the fundraising speech in Toronto; the leadership organizing, now banned. Martin tried to imagine doing another budget with this prime minister or accomplishing anything else that required negotiation with him. He couldn't see how it would happen. "I just don't know how it will work," he said.

That evening Martin spent hours on his cellphone in a round of conversations with more than a dozen people. David Herle and Karl Littler had heard about the ban on leadership-campaign organizing and Chrétien's intention to stay for the review in February. They had seen the story of the cabinet meeting interpreted as a warning to Martin in the media that night. Without exception, Martin's advisers were urging him to make a stand, to resist the leadership-organization ban and finally leave cabinet, as Herle and O'Leary had counselled more than two years ago. Martin searched out a contrary opinion among this crowd. There was none.

And yet a voice nagged at him. What about the G7? The time was approaching when Canada would play host to the summit meeting of the world's largest industrial nations. National leaders were to gather in Kananaskis, Alberta, while finance ministers would meet in Halifax. Gordon Brown, his good friend from the U.K., would be there, as would Peter Costello, the Australian finance minister who, like them, was the subject of frequent speculation about his leadership ambitions. Martin wanted to somehow catapult himself from this day to two weeks' hence, when he would be presiding over the influential forum.

Martin tried to buy time to make his decision. He told Murphy that he would consider changing his Friday-night plans so that he could introduce the prime minister at the Regal Constellation – provided Chrétien himself made the call. He was "fed up" too with intermediaries carrying accusations on the prime minister's behalf. Martin wanted Chrétien to confront him directly with allegations of disloyalty, rather than deliver them in coded messages through anonymous sources in the media or in provocative language through his loyalists.

But as the hours on Friday ticked by, the call never came. Chrétien's wishes continued to be transmitted through intermediaries. Martin stuck with his plan to attend a reception at a union hall in Toronto, where Tony Dionisio and others were waiting to introduce the finance minister to key labour and community organizers in Toronto. For all Martin knew, this event was precisely the kind of affair that was now forbidden by Chrétien's no-organizing ban. The appearance itself was a gesture of defiance. He would need a carefully worded statement to explain why he was flying in the face of the prime minister's dictate.

It took almost three hours for Martin and his group to arrive at the words that would bring him to the brink of resignation: He wouldn't quit – he would "review his options." This was the message he delivered to the media late on Friday night, minutes before most reporters' deadlines. He got in and out of the press encounter with only a smattering of questions from anxious journalists.

For almost forty-eight hours after Martin's declaration, it was the prospect of missing the G7 meeting that kept him from severing the last ties with Chrétien. Through countless telephone conversations that weekend, Eddie Goldenberg could sense the tug-of-war between Martin's feelings and his hopes.

"I am being facetious a little bit, but I think ... he wanted to resign from the Cabinet but would have liked to have stayed as minister of finance," Goldenberg said.

It could not be. Late in the day on Sunday, June 2, Paul Martin learned from CBC Radio that he was the former finance minister. John Manley, his replacement, would host the G7 summit in mid-June.

9

HARD TO
SAY GOODBYE

WAS HE FIRED or did he quit? It was a favourite water-cooler question among political junkies in the hours and days after Martin's departure from cabinet.

"We've been fired," the team proclaimed in a flurry of e-mails dispatched as soon as the prime minister scheduled the cabinet shuffle on the Sunday afternoon.

"No, I did not fire him. You heard his statement on Friday," Jean Chrétien said at Rideau Hall, after John Manley was sworn in as Martin's replacement.

Where one stood on this question clearly depended on where one sat – on the Martin side or Chrétien side of the struggle. Being fired positioned the former finance minister as the ill-treated and undervalued victim of a harsh, vindictive prime minister. Resigning put the onus on the ambitious Martin to explain his reckless flight from a top job in Chrétien's cabinet.

And then there were the jokes. Why did Martin quit? To spend more time with Brian Tobin's family. Or, why does it matter whether he quit or got fired? Two words: *employment insurance.* "Why do you think we let the

EI surplus get so large?" David Herle quipped when he heard that gag making the rounds.

Canadians were engrossed by the spectacle of the Martin-Chrétien blow-up. Just two days after the Sunday shuffle, Ekos pollster Frank Graves discovered a remarkable degree of public interest in recent political developments. A full 80 per cent of the 1,225 people polled by Ekos in the first week of June said they were paying close attention to the battle of the Liberal titans. "Ottawa has gone from boring to riveting overnight," Graves said.

But Graves also predicted that the fascination would be short-lived. The prime minister's prospects would rise, he wrote, when the excitement passed. "All in all, the Martin-Chrétien affair has provided spectacle and drama and has clearly wounded the PM, but there is little compelling evidence that the injuries are life-threatening," Graves wrote. "Mr. Martin's popularity does not appear to have dislodged the PM and in the absence of further difficulties, his popularity may have a waning influence as public interest in the issue declines and the public's impatience to return to national business rises."

Graves wasn't the only one who believed sympathy for Martin would be short-lived. On the night that Martin announced he was reviewing his options, Transport Minister David Collenette had shown up late at a private dinner in Toronto and confidently, even cheerfully, predicted that this was the end of Martin's leadership aspirations. "That's it," Collenette told his dinner companions. "It's over for Martin."

The miscalculation was based on the view that this was an old-fashioned power struggle. By all traditional measurements of power – rank, title, institutional authority – Chrétien held the advantage. But this view discounted the more ephemeral, non-traditional forces at work against Chrétien – the power of the party's grassroots, of public opinion, of the media, and of an increasingly defiant band of MPs. And all of these were on Martin's side. Their different power bases, in fact, were perfectly in sync with their different approaches to leadership. Chrétien's power, like his style of leadership, depended on chains of command and attention to long-established lines of authority. Martin's power and leadership style were rooted in loose networks of people who, like him, showed a stubborn refusal to defer to title or rank. The summer of 2002 was shaping up to be a power struggle between the traditional hierarchy and the open network.

The prime minister served notice early of his intent to fight for his leadership using his usual levers of power. Addressing reporters at Rideau Hall on Sunday afternoon, he used his mandate from the Canadian people as justification for his continued leadership. He wondered why he should have to face a leadership-review vote at all, after winning the 2000 election. "I'm surprised you would want to review with a mandate from the people of Canada," he said. "I find it a little surprising that someone be subject to a review while he was still prime minister."

This was a broad hint of Chrétien's first sally: put pressure on party president Stephen LeDrew to call off the entire review. Once a thorough Chrétien loyalist, LeDrew began to show an independent streak in the wake of Martin's departure, mirroring the party at large and its waning affection for the prime minister.

A vivid demonstration of that disconnect between Chrétien and the party took place on a June weekend soon after Martin left cabinet, when the fifty-four-member Liberal national executive met in Ottawa. On the Friday night, a social reception was held at the National Press Club. Party brass from around the country milled about the bar and lounge. LeDrew was sitting in a corner, talking to some journalists and politicos, when the door opened and Eddie Goldenberg walked in. The chilly blast of his presence could be felt in every corner of the room. LeDrew greeted Goldenberg curtly and then turned his back. "What the hell is he doing here?" he asked, loud enough for a few tables to hear. Other party officials sidestepped around the lounge to avoid the prime minister's envoy.

The disaffection was mutual, at least for LeDrew. Goldenberg had written off the party president as a self-promoter. "LeDrew loves to have his picture in the paper and his name in the paper," he said. But Stephen LeDrew did have enough clout to insist that the Liberals would not cancel a leadership review – unless, of course, Chrétien decided to call a leadership convention instead. And this did not appear to be his game plan at present.

Forced to accept that the review was unavoidable, the prime minister then pulled another traditional lever – his unilateral power to call an election and sign Liberal candidates' nomination papers. Two days after

Martin was gone from cabinet, the prime minister dared his rebellious MPs to defeat the government in the Commons and face an election under his leadership. It would take only nineteen contrary-minded Liberal souls – and there were plenty more than that – to vote with the opposition and bring down the government. "You know, they only have to vote on Thursday night to have an election," Chrétien told reporters. "If they destroy the Liberal party, the alternative is Harper."

Martin laid low for the first few days, staying out of the media spotlight but working the phones. He was besieged with calls offering help and support. He talked quietly to his friends in cabinet – Anne McLellan and Ralph Goodale among others – and assured them he didn't want anyone doing anything rash at this point. Like the people around Chrétien, he was taken aback by the momentum of developments and was far from sure that it would end well for him. He hadn't forgotten the lesson of Michael Heseltine in Britain.

"My advice was, you should just keep your nose clean and stay," Martin said. "I didn't see why I should damage their careers. . . . It was very, very important that my leaving carried with it a minimum amount of disruption."

To underline his play-it-safe message, Martin quietly showed up that week in the Commons for a vote, taking his new seat among the ordinary MPs in a dark corner of the front bench at the far end of the chamber. A bunch of red roses lay on his new desk. Chrétien and Martin exchanged the barest of glances as the voting began.

During these few weeks before the summer break, Martin turned Trudeau's maxim about members of Parliament on its head. This backbencher might have been a nobody on Parliament Hill, but he was a somebody a hundred yards away. At a concert hall a few blocks from the Commons, a little more than a week after his cabinet exit, Martin's team held a coming-out party for him. It was similar to the rally-the-troops event they had staged in the midst of the March 2000 fiasco. As a retrorock band blared its music from the stage, Martin pressed through the crowds of young and not-so-young fans. MPs discreetly hung back against the walls, wanting and not wanting to be spotted. Martin took to the stage, donned sunglasses, and made an unmusical swipe at a guitar chord.

Cameras whirred as Brian Guest and Scott Reid, the communications specialists, stood back and smiled. Martin's awkward attempt as a guitarist made for rotten sound but great visuals. The picture would show their man exactly as they wanted: fun, energetic, a man with rock-star celebrity and in touch with young people.

Chrétien, meanwhile, was settling into a bunker, flanking himself with loyal defenders. Loyalty was another of the traditional tools at the prime minister's disposal, and he was marshalling all the loyalists he could find. Now was the time for all good men and women to come to the aid of Chrétien. His cabinet stalwarts sprinkled the L-word (loyalty, not leadership) into every public statement, at every opportunity. At the leader's annual Maple Leaf dinner in Ottawa, just two days after Martin's rock-musician performance, Deputy Prime Minister John Manley gave an over-the-top accounting of Chrétien's many achievements. Then, addressing the prime minister directly, Manley said, "I'm for a leadership review. I think you passed. Thank you very much." (That weekend, CBC Radio's political program, *The House*, played Manley's tribute against a background of treacly love songs.)

The prime minister gave an interview to Don Martin of the *Calgary Herald* on the eve of the G7 summit in Kananaskis, Alberta, in mid-June. The interview was supposed to focus on Canada's expectations for the international meeting, but the *Herald* columnist pushed the prime minister to comment on the political drama unfolding in Ottawa. Chrétien vacillated between bravado and denial. "I know the Liberal party and I'm very confident that I will win the review," he said. As for Martin's prospects, Chrétien said, "We'll see if it [his 'resignation'] was good tactics or not."

As proof that Martin had resigned – and had not been fired – Chrétien talked about how Tim Murphy had been handing out his business cards at the Regal Constellation and how the shredding machines had been working overtime at Finance throughout that first weekend in June.

The prime minister did allow that he might have let the Liberal party itself get away from him. "I was not to run against myself. So the organization and who is president in what riding, it was my last preoccupation. As long as they were Liberal, I was happy. It was organized perhaps against the other candidates. Suddenly it became a problem for me. But at the time, I didn't give a damn. It was not my problem. They can have whoever they want as president of any riding, as long as they campaign for the Liberal party."

Then Chrétien revealed the grudge he had long held against those responsible for the events of March 2000, predicting that he would put down this insurrection the same way he had then. "It's the same thing as when they tried the putsch in 2000. They had a poll that very week, remember? It's always the same. All organized by the same guys. Arrive at the right time, with an editorial always from Peter Newman and a poll that arrives at the right time and a little scheme somewhere. I got 60 per cent at that time. I got more seats than the previous election. If the pattern is like that, I will have more seats next time. The more people want me to retire, the more they vote for me."

For their part, Martin's people also saw some parallels to March 2000 in the counterattack launched at them. An anonymous fax found its way to news bureaus in the capital, hinting that Canada Steamship Lines had received favoured treatment from the Royal Bank while Martin was finance minister. As with the memo and poison-pen letter of March 2000, the fax was riddled with errors, easily refuted by the journalists to whom it was sent. But it delivered the message that Martin had enemies who were trying to trip him with conflict-of-interest charges.

This blow-up was different from the March 2000 crisis in one very important way: This time, Martin's supporters had the means to force a confrontation with Chrétien. The February 2003 leadership review would be a moment of decision for Liberals, and many of those Liberal MPs who had spoken out against the prime minister in March 2000 were not hesitating to declare their allegiances. Tony Ianno had already begun to collect commitments from MPs to sign up one thousand members over the summer to vote against Chrétien in a leadership review.

Andrew Telegdi, the MP from Waterloo who had refused to stand onstage with Chrétien at the Regal Constellation, had been among the first to tell Chrétien publicly, even before Martin left cabinet, that his caucus might go against him in a leadership review. In the caucus meeting during that last raucous week in May, Telegdi pointedly recalled that Chrétien hadn't always believed that loyalty to the leader was synonymous with good Liberalism.

"I supported you in two leadership contests and I supported you in two leadership reviews. Further, I supported you in 1986 when I supported a vote for the leadership review of John Turner. Just as my voting for a leadership review in 1986 did not make me a bad Liberal then, voting for leadership review now does not make people bad Liberals," Telegdi said.

And on the day of Martin's departure from cabinet, MPs had willingly wired themselves to TV microphones, stared into the cameras, and spoken their minds. Stan Keyes was blunt: "The straw that maybe broke the camel's back is when the prime minister announced that he would be going for the leadership review, that in fact he would be staying on until 2003 and maybe even into 2004 . . . maybe even run in the next election campaign. Well, what room does that leave Paul Martin to advance in public policy if the prime minister had decided to stay on?"

"I think that we have finally come to a head, and I think it's unavoidable, considering Mr. Martin is Canada's best finance minister this country has ever had – including Jean Chrétien," said Tony Ianno, who had been organizing against Chrétien for many months. Now the campaign was, in the words of Carolyn Bennett, "organizing itself." People were dropping into MPs' offices and asking where to sign up to get rid of Chrétien. At the final caucus meeting before the Commons adjourned for the summer, several MPs stood and warned Chrétien that he could press them all he wanted, but the party membership had made up its mind.

"My riding association has given me a clear message that they want a leadership review," the Liberals' Ontario caucus chairman John McKay said. "That's not rocket science. That's not news. That's what people are saying."

Chrétien and his people were having to acknowledge, much like Tobin had earlier, that they were seriously outmatched on the ground. And like Tobin, their best hope was to mount an all-out air war against the ground campaign. There too, though, the Chrétien team was starting from behind. The Ekos poll showed they had lost the initial public-relations battle on the question of whether Martin was fired or had quit. A full 56 per cent of the respondents believed he had been fired, with only 7 per cent believing he had quit. More than 70 per cent of those polled disapproved of Martin's treatment at Chrétien's hands. Those around Chrétien decided that it would take the expertise of professionals to save his prime ministership.

In Toronto, at an office at the corner of St. Clair and Yonge Streets, Peter Donolo was working with legendary Tory pollster Allan Gregg at a firm called the Strategic Counsel. Donolo had returned from Milan in 2001 to take a job at Air Canada, where he stayed only a few months before deciding it was a bad fit. He was now offering his communications expertise to private-sector clients, contentedly living in Toronto with his wife and three children. For a year, he had been telling his friends in Ottawa that they had seen the last of Peter Donolo in active politics. He kept up his Liberal friendships, speaking occasionally with the prime minister and with Terrie O'Leary, among others, but he had no interest in being a player in the game any more.

Early one June morning he received a call from the PMO. Eddie Goldenberg and Francie Ducros were on the line together. "We'd like you to go on television tomorrow morning," they said. "There's an opening on CBC morning news and it would be great if you could speak up for the prime minister."

Donolo gave it a few moments' consideration. The sight of Chrétien under siege these past few months had been agonizing for him to watch. Discreetly, he had lamented the communications advice the prime minister had been getting; all the goodwill built for Chrétien over the years was being squandered on petty, internal politics. "Yes," Donolo said. "Of course I'll do it."

Donolo went on the air the next day with a spirited defence of Chrétien, but one that steered clear of attacking Martin. Privately, he sent out notes to friends in Liberal and media circles, serving notice of his intention to come to Chrétien's aid at this difficult time. He notified O'Leary by telephone, stressing that neither side should be drawn into a low-road, negative campaign.

John Rae was also pulled into service, making rare phone calls to journalists to talk up the importance of team loyalty. "The party has a winning tradition of loyalty, respect, unity, and support of the leader, and this leader has secured three majority governments," Rae told the *Toronto Star*. "Liberals are proud of that record and Canadians gave him a mandate in 2000. We have a review process and we will be working to ensure the winning tradition of the party is maintained."

The summer of 2002 proved to be a golden time for Paul Martin and his band of supporters. In some ways, they realized they might never have it this good again. Martin was at the height of his popularity, the darling of the public and the press, but under no obligation to say or deliver anything of substance.

Martin was free of his cabinet duties and no longer obliged to pretend that he wasn't interested in the leadership. He could catch up on policy reading, spend more time at the farm with Sheila, and play a little golf from time to time – when he wasn't on the phone. Martin lived on the phone that summer, carrying a cellphone in his pocket when he didn't have it attached to his ear. Out of the official loop, Martin relied on his contacts to keep him informed of developments in the party and in government. The calls came constantly.

In its first issue after Martin's departure, the *Hill Times* published the names of Liberal MPs and ministers under three headings: Martin, Chrétien, and "undecided/not known." A whopping ninety-nine members of caucus were listed under the Martin banner, including nine members of cabinet. Only forty-eight names appeared under Chrétien's name.

Reaction to the lists was instantaneous. Chrétien telephoned several of the people identified as Martin supporters, asking whether he could count on their support in the leadership review. Ministers in the Martin category were ordered by the PMO to have their names shifted to the list of the prime minister's loyalists. All dutifully complied, firing off letters of "correction" to the *Hill Times*.

But the game continued. For the next few weeks, the *Hill Times* ran revised versions of the list, as MPs flitted between columns, most of them under pressure from Chrétien, PMO officials, or fellow caucus members. The compiler of the list, journalist Angelo Persichilli, was invited to 24 Sussex Drive for a chat with Chrétien. For an hour and a half, Persichilli visited with the prime minister, who was curious to know how the list had been compiled, yet was careful not to apply any pressure directly. The session ended pleasantly, even as the PMO kept ringing the *Hill Times*'s office with more requests that the name of an MP be removed from the list of Martin supporters.

After five weeks and many revisions of the list on the *Hill Times*'s Web site, the PMO appeared to be satisfied when the final version put Chrétien's support in caucus at seventy-six, compared to seventy-three for Martin. The considerable angst and energy devoted to this exercise should have taught the prime minister's backers a lesson about the dangers of list-making in this atmosphere. Instead it seemed to have planted a seed.

Herle was alternately incredulous and disgusted at the fuss over the newspaper lists. He could not believe that the PMO was wasting its time on such an obvious and unconvincing public-relations ploy. Yet it was clear that there would be a real price for all to pay, now that the Chrétien-Martin feud was in the open. One example of the price exacted happened at Herle's own firm, Earnscliffe, which was now officially on the outs with Manley's Finance Department. Mike Robinson, diplomatically, had served notice to Finance that the firm would understand if the $277,130 contract had to be severed. Sure enough, on July 2, exactly one month after Martin's departure from cabinet, an internal memo to that effect went out at Finance. "As this is a very time-sensitive issue, would you please notify Earnscliffe by telephone before noon and follow up as quickly thereafter as possible with the formal documentation," stated the memo, which was obtained later under Access to Information legislation by researcher Ken Rubin. Earnscliffe's partners decided that they would say nothing publicly about this development. Why stir the pot when it was already boiling?

The Ekos poll in June had warned Chrétien that the government was vulnerable in another area, namely the public's disapproval of the money behind political campaigns. The PMO was already at work on an ambitious scheme to reform the system of election financing, but in the meantime, Ethics Counsellor Howard Wilson had put the finishing touches on the new rules for leadership contenders – the same rules that had caused the Martin team so much consternation before he left cabinet.

In early July, Wilson's guidelines were made public. All members of cabinet would have to reveal the contents of their blind trusts and return any contributions from donors who might have interests in their particular portfolios. As well, lobbyists working simultaneously for leadership contenders and for businesses with dealings in those contenders' ministries would have to choose one or the other.

Three cabinet ministers issued disclosure announcements in mid-July. Allan Rock offered the most detailed list, with total contributions at more than $1.12 million. It included a $50 donation he had received as far back as 1994. John Manley's list was much more modest, with total contributions of only $171,950, while Sheila Copps released a longer list of donors who made smaller donations, adding up to $54,489.

On Bay Street in Toronto, John Webster contacted the contributors to the Campaign 2000 blind trust. Gerry Schwartz sounded out the corporate donors he had been quietly rounding up since 1998. They met an almost universal wall of resistance. No one wanted to go public as a financial backer of Martin's undeclared leadership campaign. Many ran businesses that had extensive dealings with government; others were Liberals hoping for a chance at a government appointment or lawyers with dreams of becoming federally named judges.

Martin deemed the retrospective aspect of these rules unfair. People had donated money to his campaign on the assumption that full disclosure would not be required until thirty days before a leadership vote. Further, he preferred not to know the sources of these donations. Now these contributors were being asked to adhere to a totally different arrangement, possibly for no other purpose than to embarrass or discredit them. The decision was made: Martin's blind trust would remain blind.

But non-declaration carried risks. Martin would almost certainly be accused of base motives – protecting a secret network of people who had gained favourable treatment from Finance in return for their largesse. So if he couldn't be candid about his donors, he would have to be frank with reporters about why he was bucking the new regime.

"Many people harbour fears that disclosure of their names at this time and in the current political climate will put them at a disadvantage – particularly concerning their relationship with the federal government," he told reporters.

This comment – an accusation of vindictiveness levelled against Chrétien and his government – outraged John Manley. "I think it's ridiculous, quite frankly," he said. "According to that justification, contributions to opposition parties shouldn't be disclosed, because who knows, somebody may be vindictive about it. If he doesn't want to disclose because he doesn't feel it's fair to people who contributed . . . that's one rationale. But to suggest there will be some kind of action taken against them, I don't think that's an adequate explanation."

Donolo was similarly unamused by the talk of potential retribution, believing that Martin had stepped off the high road. Privately, Donolo speculated that Martin was revealing the real reason he had wanted out of cabinet: to avoid full disclosure of his campaign war chest. "It's a phony and groundless claim," Donolo told the *Toronto Star*. "I think he's grasping at straws to find reasons not to disclose the information." Shortly after he made this remark, Donolo heard from Terrie O'Leary. "Paul wants to know when you started working with Warren Kinsella," she said.

Herle had emerged as the chief of the Martin campaign, though he had no formal title. Co-ordinator was as close as anyone could come to describing his role. Nor did Webster, in charge of the national organization, have any title. Martin's staffers had no fixed job descriptions in their changed circumstances. Tim Murphy liked to joke that in one year he'd gone from being a high-priced Toronto lawyer to a backbencher's executive assistant. It was easier to describe him simply as Martin's right-hand man.

Titles or no titles, Martin's leadership team wasn't prepared to go into full campaign mode when he left cabinet. Earnscliffe became a temporary bunkhouse for many of the former Finance Department staffers who were left unemployed on June 3. The severance payout for the entire ministerial staff was more than $300,000. Brian Guest and the others lived on this temporary payout, using Earnscliffe's offices and telephone lines while the team scrambled to find more permanent headquarters and a budget for salaries.

Thérèse Horvath, Martin's long-time secretary, had given a nickname to the tight-knit group of people around Martin: she called them the

Board. Some worried that the moniker made Martin's inner circle sound like a shadowy corporation, manipulating a grand plan for the nation. Nevertheless, the name stuck. Board members included David Herle, Terrie O'Leary, Richard Mahoney, John Webster, Dennis Dawson, Tim Murphy, Karl Littler, Scott Reid, Brian Guest, John Duffy, Ruth Thorkelson, Elly Alboim, Mike Robinson, Véronique de Passillé – the president of the young Liberals – and Pietro Perrino, one of the latest members of the Martin team, a veteran organizer from the Quebec Liberal party.

In the weeks after Martin left cabinet, he would consult the Board constantly, individually and collectively, in cacophonous conference calls where everyone tried to speak at once. All politicians have extensive networks, but in Martin's case, the number of close advisers was almost staggering. And the Board represented only the tip of the iceberg. Depending on the issue being discussed, many others across the country might join in the conversational free-for-all and their advice often weighed heavier with Martin than that of those closer to home. If the team was discussing something that touched on Martin's interests in his hometown, for instance, the conversation had to include his constituency assistant, Lucie Castelli, who had worked in his Lasalle-Emard office since he was first elected. If Western issues were up for debate, the team would pull in John Bethel from Alberta or Mark Marissen from British Columbia – two of the Liberal partisans who had put their vocal chords to such controversial use in the 1990 Montreal leadership debate. Bethel and Marissen headed the Martin teams in their respective provinces, working closely with provincial Liberal party presidents, who were also Martin-friendly: Kent Davidson in Alberta and Bill Cunningham in British Columbia.

Martin regarded this sprawling network as a band of friends. Sheila Martin treated them as an extended family, as did the Martins' sons. The test of admission, Martin was fond of saying, was whether he could contemplate spending a free weekend with them.

"None of these are acquaintances. None of these are friendships of convenience," he said. "I have a lot of confidence in their judgment. Mostly, they all have a better sense of political judgment than me."

There were three objectives in the early days of this campaign: One, keep Martin in the public eye. Two, get a policy platform underway. Three, find the money.

On this last point, the team had to scramble to put a budget in place and push the fundraising operation into a higher gear. This was Webster's domain. For a couple of years, the campaign had not required much money beyond Michèle Cadario's salary. Now there was a fleet of people to put on the payroll. Martin was determined that none of his dozen political staffers from the minister's office would find themselves unemployed and it was decided to pay these people on a par with their salaries as Martin's employees. Tim Murphy's old law firm, McCarthy Tétrault, kicked in $10,000 to make up the difference between his ministerial-office salary and his lower paycheque as a backbencher's executive assistant.

Replicating the ministerial operation was not just a matter of preference. Martin had been a cabinet minister for almost ten years and a certain degree of professionalism was expected from his operation. His speeches had to be accompanied by a published text and translation; a squadron of advisers had to be available to answer policy or strategy questions. Normally all of this would have been handled by his ministerial or departmental staff, but now he was an ordinary MP with a much more modest budget.

In terms of policy, Martin had only the beginnings of a leadership platform. Thanks to the work of a few of his backbench colleagues, he had some ideas on where he was heading with parliamentary reform. His advisers had found a catchy phrase to link Martin the fiscal manager with his passion for parliamentary reform – he would slay the "democratic deficit." Martin also had his "new deal" for cities sketched out in broad terms, thanks to his intense focus on the issue that spring. His international experience gave him some notions about foreign policy, though it was more focused on finance and aid issues than on matters of peacekeeping or armed conflict. But he needed something comprehensive, a wide-ranging series of positions on policy.

Herle contacted John Duffy, now a consultant in Toronto who had worked with the provincial Tories on Mike Harris's Common Sense Revolution campaign. For Martin, Duffy would take charge of something known as "policy positioning." It would be his job to shape all the ideas whirling around the Martin network into a coherent package. It was similar to but more ambitious than the work Duffy had done a decade earlier on the Red Book.

Herle gave Duffy four themes, reflecting Martin's core interests, and told Duffy to go wild. The four themes were: Cities, Democratic Reform, Health Care, and something loosely described as "Learning." Duffy soon found that this task, as he put it, "was not for the faint of heart." The priorities began to change as Martin's attention ricocheted among more immediate policy questions: aboriginal issues, because he was addressing the Assembly of First Nations chiefs in July, or the environment as the Kyoto air-quality protocol came forward for debate.

As for keeping Martin in the public eye, that task was taking care of itself. He was besieged with requests to appear at events across Canada, mostly from MP supporters and Liberal friends at the provincial level, especially in Ontario. His first foray was to Southern Ontario in late June. Martin popped into Carolyn Bennett's riding early one morning in Toronto to meet a cheering throng at a breakfast meeting. Then it was off to Hamilton, where, in Stan Keyes's riding, he was once again treated as a conquering hero. It met the same reception in Ancaster, Strathroy, Sarnia, and London.

Martin's speeches on these occasions were largely content-free, with occasional, gently worded hints of opposition to Chrétien. "Surely we are not here to congratulate ourselves on what we've done," he'd say in a veiled reference to the leadership-review vote. "You're only as good as yesterday's headlines," he told the crowd in Hamilton. And in London he told Liberals, "If you clean up your balance sheet, you don't do it because it's an end in itself."

What was also apparent was the number of MPs who were eager to stand at the side of Martin the renegade. Some of those cajoled into de-listing themselves from the *Hill Times*'s Martin column were proudly outing themselves as supporters in their home ridings. In London, a knot of long-time Liberals in the crowd sported paper silhouettes of martini glasses on their shirts to signal their loyalty to Martin. Every event featured a sign-up table for new Liberal party members.

In early July, it was off to British Columbia and Alberta for Martin and his team, to visit with Sikh supporters in Vancouver and to attend the

Calgary Stampede with the Western Liberals he had so assiduously courted all these years. His base of support remained grounded in the West, in his home province of Quebec, and among young people – those pockets of alienation first identified two decades earlier.

In Bragg Creek, Alberta, Martin spent an idyllic afternoon at a youth camp, aptly named Camp Finally Free. Clad in jeans and new cowboy boots, he sat on a picnic table, fielding questions from young Liberals about everything from globalization to a lower voting age.

Herle had come along on this trip. Martin spoke to the young Liberal partisans about their role in keeping the party renewed and reformed. "But be careful," he said, pointing to Herle, lying back on his elbows, soaking in the sun. "See that guy there? That's what young Liberals look like when they get older."

"No," Herle snapped back. "This is what someone looks like after spending twenty years of his life with one candidate, waiting for something to happen."

Frank Graves's bold predictions about Chrétien's ability to recover while Martin's prospects faded were not borne out by the anecdotal evidence of these early days of the non-campaign tour. A body of opinion had taken hold, fed by images of Chrétien on the news.

In a cab in Calgary one hot summer day in July, the driver was keen to know why he was carrying so many fares to the university. Told that Paul Martin was in town, he asked: "Oh yeah. What happened with that guy anyway?" The driver then went on to say that he sympathized with Martin. He too once had a boss who yelled at him all the time, and he had been forced to quit. "You can't put up with that," he said.

This cab driver had no knowledge of any yelling matches between Martin and Chrétien – mainly because there were none. The two men barely spoke. He was responding to what he had picked up through coverage of Chrétien in the media, transposing it to the Liberal cabinet feud. The accumulated evidence was that Chrétien was an angry man, if not vindictive. He'd yelled at Carolyn Bennett in January. He'd dispensed with Herb Gray. He had proved himself remarkably sensitive to criticism. He had said extraordinary things before the cameras: "Leave me alone or I'll stay." These pictures had turned Martin into a victim in the mind of a Calgary cab driver. Why would anyone stay and put up with it?

Martin wasn't prepared for this reaction. He had expected to enjoy a brief blip in the polls, then drop into the political has-been category. This had been part of his calculated risk, weighed over and over during that agonizing weekend of decision in early June. But it wasn't happening.

Herle wasn't surprised. Earnscliffe had tested public opinion too in the wake of Martin's departure from cabinet and, contrary to Frank Graves's conclusions, discovered just how much Canadians' mood seemed to have soured on the prime minister. From surveys with approximately one thousand respondents in late June–early July, Earnscliffe estimated that 60 per cent of Canadians regarded Chrétien as a bully to some degree. A full 78 per cent agreed strongly or somewhat strongly with the perception of the prime minister as "power hungry." The knockout question was whether Canadians thought it was time for a change of leadership. Only 20 per cent said Chrétien should stay in the job. A whopping 76 per cent said the Liberals should hold a leadership convention.

As much as Herle admired Martin, his hard analysis led him to the observation that Canadians weren't so much flocking to the finance minister as they were deserting Chrétien. The crumbling of the prime minister's power rested, Herle concluded, in three things: the aimlessness of government, the hardening of Chrétien's personality, and the inattention paid to all-important political relationships in the past few years.

Had Chrétien kept Martin waiting too long? That summer, Martin turned sixty-four, the same age Chrétien had been when Martin's own supporters had begun to build the campaign to succeed him.

In terms of public perception, Martin's advisers weren't that worried about his being seen as too old. About a year earlier, Herle had conducted focus-group testing of reactions to Martin's age, relative to other potential leadership contenders. The groups were shown TV clips of Martin, John Manley, Brian Tobin, Allan Rock, and Sheila Copps. Martin, at least ten years older than any one of the others, tended to have his years seen as a positive, synonymous with experience or wisdom. Rock scored well in these focus groups too, with respondents registering surprise at how articulate he was. Manley did not do so well, with people confused about what he stood for. Copps and Tobin were seen as performers over all, and not taken too seriously.

Martin himself took the age issue to heart. Before the cameras, he was careful – sometimes too careful – to keep his head tilted slightly upward, so as not to appear jowly or fatigued. At Herle's urging, Martin had started to work with a personal trainer in spring 2001. Martin had been fond of sports in his youth, fancying himself a potential medalist in everything he tried. An overconfident foray into boxing had left him out cold, on the mat, within his first minute in the ring. But as an adult, in business and in politics, Martin spent most of his time either behind a desk, in meetings, or on the road. His only exercise came in the summer, when he golfed and swam in the pond on his farm. Nervous energy, fuelled by the vats of coffee he drank every day, helped keep his weight down year-round. Martin also liked to walk, and he often sent his driver home early when he was at an event in Ottawa, happy to stroll an hour or more back to his apartment. Every now and then, he'd find himself with unexpected walking companions when someone recognized Canada's finance minister, with his slightly pigeon-toed gait, striding homeward on foot late at night.

His trainer's name was Rick Roy, a local Ottawa physical-education expert who ran a small gym near Parliament Hill. Herle had been seeing Roy himself, embarking on a weight-lifting program at the suggestion of his old boss, Ralph Goodale, who kept to a rigorous fitness regimen. Herle, playing to Martin's natural competitiveness, told him that if Goodale could remain fit and strong while a cabinet minister, so could he.

Martin, somewhat reluctantly, was put on a beginner's schedule of biking, weights, and stretching exercises. He found the thirty- to forty-five-minute routine boring and distracting from the phone calls or reading he'd prefer to be doing, but at the farm that summer, Martin began his day on the exercise bike or treadmill, reading the newspapers while catching the morning news programs.

There was something to read about himself almost every day. Martin and his people found themselves on the right side of the media's insatiable hunger for change. Chrétien's defenders claimed that Martin was getting a free ride from the press.

Martin approached the media with naive bafflement and curious admiration. He would be amazed to find a complex, convoluted discussion with a reporter written up the next day in a clear and succinct fashion. He would be similarly startled to see reporters garble concepts or ideas that to him seemed simple. Martin knew only one rule for handling journalists: Don't call them if you're angry at their coverage or disappointed in their mistakes. Reporters get those calls only from politicians at the losing end of contests.

Martin was intensely interested in every aspect of the leadership campaign except one: the organization. Until he left cabinet, he had been dimly aware only of the size of his leadership machine. Its structure had been finalized just six months earlier when Herle, O'Leary, and Webster met in Toronto in late December 2001 and chose the provincial directors of the undeclared campaign. Still, Martin recognized its importance, a lesson learned from the hard experience of 1990.

"In 1990, we were clearly the underdog. I had no idea just how important Jean Chrétien's organization was. It was overwhelming," Martin says. "I had far better people than he did. But he had a much better organization."

There were three principles at the heart of Martin's organization: First, it had to be "flat," in keeping with Martin's non-hierarchical management style. Second, it would be built with the long view in mind – not just one victory, but several. Liberal party memberships were sold on a one-year or two-year basis, so the team had grown accustomed to renewing its strength and adding to it annually. This was Webster's influence.

The third guiding principle was known as the "big-tent" approach. Every Liberal in Canada, and a considerable number of potential Liberals as well, should be given a chance to climb aboard Paul Martin's leadership bandwagon. This was largely O'Leary's cause: she did not want it said that Martin's people took supporters for granted or rejected new participants. She was extremely sensitive to charges that Martin's organization was arrogant or too established to offer meaningful roles to new recruits. It would have amounted to a renunciation of all that she and the others had wanted to achieve in the 1980s.

The job of garnering support in the ridings had been carried out almost single-handedly by Michèle Cadario, who had racked up one million Aeroplan miles and recorded thousands of contacts in her trusty BlackBerry by the time Martin left cabinet. Herle, travelling around the country making his own contacts for Martin, would often be asked whether he worked for Cadario.

Cadario was young, in her early thirties, tall, with an almost shy demeanour but a no-nonsense approach that some MPs found off-putting. She had worked in Martin's office when she was only nineteen years old, leaving for a while to live in Alberta, but returning in 1999 to become the first paid, full-time employee of the Martin organization, operating out of Webster's Maple Trust financial firm in Toronto.

Cadario possessed innate skills at networking. She had begun her task under Webster's supervision, with a collection of the various lists of supporters that had been kept over the years by O'Leary and by MPs such as Joe Volpe and Joe Fontana. "For the first bit, it was catch-up, just getting in touch with people who wanted to stay involved, to make sure they weren't forgotten," Cadario says. She methodically built the network from there, riding by riding, working with the local Liberal MP if he or she was friendly, working independently or with the local riding association members if there was no elected ally in the area. Though Cadario kept an apartment in Toronto from 2000 to 2002, it was little more than a wardrobe-change station. She travelled light, never checking any luggage, and she knew her territory well – where the support was most likely to be found, where other leadership candidates would try to make inroads.

Cadario appointed "captains" for Martin's campaign in every riding. These were usually highly motivated fans of Martin who could commit enough time to do the networking required. Some were veterans of the last campaign, others were new Liberals. Cadario was the link between Martin Central and the ground, and she approached her duties like a motivational coach, generous with praise and encouragement for the smallest of victories. When a riding captain signed up a few dozen new members, Cadario would send blanket e-mails across the system, lauding the achievement. She ensured that people knew that Martin himself appreciated their efforts.

What made her job easier – and a departure from the campaigning of previous times – were the technological gadgets at her disposal. The youthful bent of Martin's team made them early aficionados of BlackBerry wireless e-mail devices and much of their communication whizzed about through the pocket-sized gizmos. It was not an exaggeration to say that the BlackBerry had helped transform the modern political organization. Martin himself had only a nodding acquaintance with the gadgets, preferring his ever-present cellphone and the fax machine. But the team around him lived on their BlackBerries. A typical scene on the road would be of the candidate, working on a speech, his briefcase spilling over beside him, sitting amidst his team of road warriors, huddled over their tiny keyboards, madly thumb-typing messages that could be mass-mailed to dozens if not hundreds of addresses across the country. Occasionally, one aide or another would hoist the little BlackBerry screen for Martin to see an interesting news clipping perhaps, or a list of new members in a far-flung region. Martin would peer at the device, holding it as a foreign object, smile, and then return to pen and paper to revise his speech.

There were some parts of the Martin machine, though, that relied on the techniques and campaign styles of the late 1980s – ethnic-recruitment drives, for example. Tony Ianno, Joe Volpe, and Albina Guarnieri were masters of this style of organization. Summer, with its picnics and festivals and outdoor get-togethers, is the perfect time to cultivate these groups, and Martin's people were busy touring the social circuit this season, passing out membership forms.

There is a term in political-organization speak for community members with broad networks of their own: "bingo players" – a relic of the old church-basement style of recruitment, perhaps rooted in the days when Irish Canadians, with strong ties to the church, were recruited in droves to political parties. That wave had been replaced by the Italian Canadians in the 1970s and 1980s, who then too slipped into the mainstream, to be replaced by Sikh and East Asian immigrants.

With strong attachments to their local temples and communities, Sikhs were the prize bingo players of the 1990 leadership. This resulted in some bitter fights, especially in British Columbia, where Natural Resources

Minister Herb Dhaliwal, a Sikh and the minister in charge of B.C., had positioned himself as a Chrétien loyalist. This was a risky gambit by Dhaliwal, who could not have been unaware of Martin's strength in the province.

Karl Littler was living on the road in Ontario that summer, moving from town to town and city to city, signing new members. He travelled almost exclusively by car, listening to books on tape en route, wandering into local bars in the evenings and indulging in pub-trivia contests to keep himself amused. Herle joked that Littler was the Colonel Kurtz in this *Heart of Darkness* drama: even when the campaign ended, Littler would remain at large, fighting for the cause.

Young people were also vital to the Martin organization, as they had been in 1990. Thanks largely to Ruth Thorkelson, Martin was regularly in touch with the under-thirty set. The president of the young Liberals, Veronique de Passillé, was an intense Martin supporter much in the tradition of the young Martinites of the previous campaign. Martin's touring days often ended in pub nights with young Liberals, rollicking affairs with plenty of beer and loud music. Here, as at other events, Martin would be treated like a celebrity, signing autographs and posing for pictures with young fans. Gone was the awkward manner of the 1990 campaign. He'd glide from handshake to handshake, stopping to toss an arm around someone's shoulder, twinkle his eyes for the camera, and then move on to the next group. He knew the two cardinal rules for political performers at rallies: don't dance and don't wear headgear. He'd only sway as the music played and, if given a hat, he'd whisk it off his head and wave it in the air. The sight of him wriggling out from under oversized white Stetsons during Calgary's Stampede Week amused and relieved his handlers.

While Martin's parade on Main Street was noisy, a puzzling silence hung over the Centre. A new communications adviser had been hired, the affable Jim Munson, a former CTV reporter who had been unceremoniously fired a few months previously in a cost-cutting move at the network's Ottawa bureau. Munson was well liked by his former parliamentary press gallery colleagues. Observers speculated that sympathy for his poor treatment at the hands of his CTV employers might translate into sympathy for a prime minister getting a rough ride from his own party.

That was the only news from the Centre this summer. The official line was that a robust effort was in the works to pull out the vote for Chrétien at the leadership review. John Rae, Peter Donolo, and others were working the phones, but neither the numbers nor the sentiment was there. Riding presidents responded that their associations weren't prepared to give Chrétien a positive endorsement in the leadership review. Some said they didn't want a review at all, they wanted a leadership convention.

Stephen LeDrew knew that it was his job to tell Chrétien about the degree of antipathy toward him among the Liberal rank and file, but he didn't look forward to the task. LeDrew made the drive to 24 Sussex Drive from a cottage in Temagami, Ontario, a yellow legal pad on the seat beside him. Periodically, he'd scribble down notes or facts to bolster the bleak prognosis he intended to deliver. Shortly before he reached his destination, a gust of wind blew in through the open car window, sending all his notes fluttering down the highway.

Noteless, LeDrew arrived at the prime minister's residence in time to greet Art Eggleton, who was just leaving. Eggleton, still recovering from his sudden ouster from cabinet, was being pressed to help out in the campaign to defend Chrétien in the leadership review.

LeDrew walked in and sat down with Chrétien. "Prime Minister," he said, "I have a duty to tell you this. If you go through this leadership review, you're going to be severely embarrassed." LeDrew took him through the numbers, province by province. In Nova Scotia, British Columbia, and a number of provinces in between, Chrétien could not hope to win much more than 10 per cent of the membership's votes according to LeDrew's estimates.

"See that corner over there?" LeDrew pointed. Chrétien craned his neck to look. "I don't want you to be painted into it."

Chrétien dismissed LeDrew's analysis, launching into a chapter-and-verse recital of all the times he had defied the critics, beaten the odds, and proven the nervous Nellies wrong. The party president took his leave, mission not accomplished.

It was a difficult summer for David Smith too. The son of an Anglican minister, ever the team player, Smith often described the Liberals as a family. This felt like a divorce to him, and a messy one at that. Truly fond of Chrétien, it saddened him to see an embarrassment looming for his old friend.

In early August, shortly after an impromptu meeting of about thirty close allies in Toronto, the Chrétien team came up with a plan to prepare a "loyalty list," a pledge of support for Chrétien in the leadership review, to be signed well ahead of the event by Liberal members of Parliament. The Martin forces were alerted early by MPs reporting strange calls from John Rae, Peter Donolo, and others. The pledge was read aloud to the MPs over the phone. Nothing was committed to paper, for fear of it falling into the wrong hands. Scarborough MP Derek Lee, hearing the proposed wording, said he wouldn't sign it because it committed him to rallying the support of his riding, something he could not guarantee. Other MPs voiced the same concern. Rae offered to change the wording, to make it less specific. It was clear that the caucus now held the upper hand.

Richard Mahoney knew about the loyalty list and the increasingly desperate attempts to secure signatures. But he was taken aback when David Smith called him with a peculiar proposition. Smith asked for the Martin team's help in the list campaign. Would they consider asking their loyalists to pledge support for Chrétien in the leadership review? In return, they would receive assurances – probably in the fall – that the prime minister would step down before the next election.

"Why would we do that?" Mahoney asked, incredulous. "Haven't we gone through this before?"

It was Chrétien's intention to announce an exit plan sometime in September, possibly in a speech around the date of his forty-fifth wedding anniversary. He would lay out a timetable and to-do list before his resignation from elected politics. Goldenberg had been working on the agenda, drawing on ideas that the new clerk of the Privy Council, Alex Himelfarb, had been soliciting from the bureaucracy all summer long. Vacations had been cancelled, special policy teams set up, and department heads directed to regard this period as one long brainstorming session. Martin would not be permitted to claim a monopoly on the notion of change and activism.

Martin liked to trot out a line from his father when he felt he was going on too long with a speech. "Just to conclude . . . ," he would say. "My father taught me that if you're going on, just tell them you're going to conclude and then you can keep going forever." As August wore on, the prime minister and his loyalists were working up a way to apply this oratorical device to the larger question of Chrétien's future. The principle was the same: buy a little more time by announcing that you're winding things down.

Peter Donolo flew to Ottawa in August to advise Chrétien that his only option was to announce a departure date and avoid the leadership review. David Smith, crushed at having to tell the prime minister that the party was not with him, quietly did the same. But it was Chrétien's former mentor and $1-a-year adviser who made the recommendation public. Summoning a reporter to his office in the Langevin Block less than a week before the Liberal caucus was due to meet in Chicoutimi, the gentlemanly Mitchell Sharp laid out the blueprint for Chrétien.

"While the prime minister has not stated exactly what he's going to do for the rest of his political term, the likelihood of him wanting to run again is so slight," Sharp said, "I would have thought that what he would like is to complete his work that he has before him and then leave in a graceful way, you know, with the thanks of the people for making the efforts he's made."

Sharp had no private insights into Chrétien's immediate intentions; he had barely seen him all summer. Nor had Sharp consulted with Goldenberg or David Smith before making this public intervention. Sharp was simply looking for a way to help a friend in his time of need.

However, Chrétien was still not abandoning his options. Acknowledging the bleak outlook for a review vote, the prime minister's team moved up the timing of the "defend-the-agenda" speech. It would be delivered in Chicoutimi, to the Liberal caucus and the media, in the hopes that its detailed blueprint for the months ahead would quash speculation that Chrétien was not prepared to fight the leadership review.

On the weekend before the caucus retreat, David Smith held his annual party at his summer place in Cobourg, Ontario. What had started as a sedate men's weekend for Smith and a few cronies had ballooned over the years into a gathering of Liberal party backroomers. Stephen LeDrew was a regular guest, as were Peter Donolo and pollster Michael Marzolini. Richard Mahoney and John Webster both usually attended as well.

The discomfort at this year's gathering was palpable. Few jokes were made about the Martin-Chrétien standoff. The situation was well beyond humour.

Mahoney and Donolo stepped outside at one point for a candid chat. "What's going to happen, do you think?" Mahoney asked. Donolo shook his head; he didn't want to venture a guess. It didn't look like anyone was prepared to back down, that much he knew.

The loyalty list was unveiled with fanfare on Sunday afternoon, at a news conference in the National Press Theatre in Ottawa. Chrétien's staunch cabinet and caucus allies were up on the podium: Government House Leader Don Boudria, Justice Minister Martin Cauchon, and three MPs: Dominic LeBlanc, Mac Harb, and Bonnie Brown. They had 94 names on their list, representing a little over half the 170-member caucus. It wasn't a landslide, exactly, though it was billed as a statement of the MPs' "overwhelming" confidence in the prime minister.

But within twenty-four hours, as MPs arrived in Chicoutimi to take part in a local fundraising golf tournament, the list began to shrink. John Cannis, travelling half a world away, telephoned reporters to say he had never been consulted. Others came forward with the same story – their support for Chrétien had been assumed, wrongly, it turned out in at least five or six cases. If this kept up, the prime minister's support would soon fall below 50 per cent. It was turning into a massive public-relations disaster.

Stan Keyes and Joe Fontana, the dissenting duo in Chrétien's caucus, stood outside the Montagnais Hotel heaping scorn on the loyalty list. Keyes called the tactic "distasteful and divisive." Fontana was scathing: "It looks very much like a pathetic and desperate move on the part of some of these people around the prime minister . . . I don't think you should ever ask or demand loyalty. Loyalty is earned and the moment you have to start to demand it, you've lost it."

Winnipeg MP John Harvard, normally a mild-tempered supporter of Chrétien, publicly implored the prime minister to put an end to the summer of strife. "I beg, no, I implore, the prime minister to spare us this trip through hell," Harvard said, calling for an "unambiguous, irreversible, and irrevocable" resignation announcement from Chrétien.

Chrétien was not due in Chicoutimi until late on Tuesday afternoon, after an appearance in Toronto with Microsoft founder Bill Gates and various captains of Canadian industry. The event highlighted the issue of corporate governance and ethics in the private and public sector. Chrétien made a speech in which he promised an increased focus on ethics when Parliament resumed in the fall.

Maurizio Bevilacqua was in attendance in his capacity as junior minister of science and technology. In recent days, he had attempted to play an intermediary's role between Chrétien and Martin, placing calls to Martin and Herle, sounding them out on their willingness to strike an agreement with Chrétien on a departure date. "Is there no way that Martin would agree to some timetable to let the prime minister leave with dignity?"

Herle spoke to Bevilacqua as an ally, explaining that no backroom deal was possible. Liberals, and moreover Canadians, he said, were tolerating this summer of strife because they believed it rested on a matter of principle. If they saw it being resolved with some cozy exchange of power between Chrétien and Martin, they would rightly condemn them both.

After the Microsoft event, Bevilacqua hitched a ride to Chicoutimi with the prime minister, as did David Smith. Francie Ducros, travelling with Chrétien as well, was getting regular bulletins from the caucus meeting about the crumbling loyalty list and the ugly mood rippling through the opening days of this retreat. Summer had only heightened the belligerence toward Chrétien. MPs such as Karen Redmond were feeling ragged and torn, angry that they had to choose between supporting the current leader and the leader-to-be.

Talking to reporters after the Toronto event, the prime minister took a shot at Martin's popularity. "I remember in 1993, you know, we had a great star all summer that we called at that time a shooting star. She had a summer job. It was Kim Campbell," Chrétien joked. Martin responded later in the day: "It's been a long time since he called me a star, shooting or otherwise."

As soon as the scrum broke up, Chrétien ducked out for a private lunch with Eddie Goldenberg at the Four Seasons Hotel in downtown Toronto.

Quietly, unemotionally, over their meal, they came to a decision on what the prime minister would say to the caucus in Chicoutimi. The leadership review could not be won. It was time to announce that Chrétien would not run in the next election. These two, who had worked together as masters of the open-ended political decision for almost four decades, had to accept that at least one option was no longer available.

"You write the statement," Chrétien told Goldenberg. "But don't write it in front of everyone else on the plane." Goldenberg found a seat at the back of the government jet, near the RCMP officer accompanying the prime minister's entourage. He drafted the text alone while the others remained oblivious.

Chrétien arrived in Chicoutimi that evening and delivered the speech, one couched in his trademark ambivalence. "I am setting out this evening on an ambitious agenda," he said. "It is an agenda that cannot be put in place overnight. It will take some time, and possibly two budgets of Manley, to set the legislative and fiscal framework which will put this agenda firmly in place."

The prime minister didn't mention Martin by name, but he registered his opposition to causes that were known to be Martin's, including parliamentary-reform proposals, saying they would lead to the Americanization of the system.

"Our parliamentary system is different from that of the United States, where there is no party discipline; where members of Congress do not run on national platforms; where special interests pour money into individual congressional races; where the administration cannot deliver an agreement on softwood lumber because it has to give in to the wishes of some senator who owes his election to American lumber producers and who threatens to use his power as chairman of the Senate Finance Committee to block other legislation of importance to the president. We don't have a system where important judicial positions remain vacant for years because of the political games and ideological tests of Congress. We don't have a system where the administration tells the world it doesn't like the Farm Bill, but has to give in to congressmen, who are subject not to party discipline, but to the discipline of lobbyists and the money of special-interest groups." Using

Martin's own catch-phrase, Chrétien added: "Now that is a real democratic deficit. And we don't need it in Canada."

Many interpreted the activist agenda as a sign that Chrétien intended to hang on to power, perhaps even run for another term. But privately, Chrétien had begun to call in the aides and ministers closest to him to tell them of his plans for the next day. Francie Ducros spent an emotional forty-five minutes with the prime minister. Martin Cauchon and Denis Coderre, Chrétien's two Quebec lieutenants, sat quietly in his darkened hotel room as dusk settled, solemnly talking about the need for strong Liberal federalists from the province to carry on the good fight in Ottawa.

The next morning, while the smaller regional caucuses were meeting, the Martin team picked up a more purposeful mood in the Chrétien ranks. They assumed the Chrétien side was about to turn up the volume. Tim Murphy and Brian Guest were sure that it involved some plan to pit Maurizio Bevilacqua against Martin in a public forum, a scheme hatched out on the plane they'd shared from Toronto. The Board decided that Martin would launch a pre-emptive volley in late morning. The former finance minister waded into a scrum after the Quebec caucus meeting and pointedly took issue with the prime minister's words on parliamentary reform the night before.

"The role of individual MPs is not simply to follow the directives set out by the Prime Minister's Office," Martin said. "There is a democratic deficit and I'm going to speak about this a number of times over the course of the next months."

Outside the hotel, a government car pulled up and Aline Chrétien climbed out. A few reporters and MPs lingering in the foyer raised their eyebrows at her sudden appearance, but it wasn't unusual for spouses to show up at the summer caucus retreat. Then Jim Munson began to circulate through the corridors and restaurants, alerting the media that Chrétien would be holding a news conference in the next hour.

Martin arrived at the caucus room seconds after Chrétien. As he walked in, a Liberal caucus staffer pressed a folded note into his hands. Martin didn't even glance at the note; he shoved it into his pocket and hustled over to a seat near the back of the room.

Keyes, unaware that the prime minister was preparing to make a significant announcement, took his time with the opening remarks. He gave effusive thanks to André Harvey, the MP for Chicoutimi and, as such, the host for the gathering. Keyes rambled on casually, urging MPs to applaud.

Finally, Chrétien got his chance to speak. As soon as he stood, Martin recognized with a start that the moment had come. Chrétien pulled out the text that Goldenberg had written on the plane and read:

I entered public life for one reason and one reason only. To serve our country. To make it a better place. Our responsibility, all of us, each and everyone of us, is to focus on our agenda. To implement our commitment to Canadians. In short, to govern. This summer we have not been focused on governing. We are not doing our job. Canadians don't like that. Liberals don't like that. None of us in this room is comfortable. I certainly am not. Aline has always been by my side. I have always called her my Rock of Gibraltar. Two years ago, we agreed that I would not seek a fourth mandate. Indeed, shortly after the last election, we took an option on an apartment in Ottawa that we would live in when I had finished my work. It was my view that it would not be in the best political interests of the Liberal party for me to signal my intentions publicly until later in our term. Over the course of the summer, I have spoken to many of you. Some have asked me to run again. Some have told me not to run. All have told me to finish the job we were elected to do. You have also told me to make my intentions known publicly as soon as possible. I have heard you.

"Last night I spoke about my duty to the country, to the Liberal party, and to the office of prime minister. For forty years the Liberal party has been like family to me. Its best interests are bred in my bones. I have reflected on the best way to bring back unity. To end the fighting. To resume interrupted friendships. I have thought about how much time it will take to finish the job we were elected to do. To complete the agenda for governing which I set out last night. For children in poverty. For aboriginals. For health. For the environment. For urban infrastructure. For public-sector ethics. I have taken into account my duty to protect for my successors the integrity of the office I hold from the Canadian people. An office that is non-negotiable. Here is my conclusion: I will not run again. I will fulfill my mandate and focus entirely on governing from now until February 2004. At which time my work will be done and at which time my successor will be chosen. This will be after three of the opposition parties have chosen their new leaders. So Liberals will know what they are facing. And it will be early enough to give a new prime minister all the necessary flexibility to choose the date of the next election. Everything we have achieved since we formed the government has been because of the unity of our caucus. I owe a debt of gratitude to each and every one of you. I thank you from the bottom of my heart. But our journey is not over. We have a lot of work to do together for Canada over the next eighteen months. I will need all of you to complete our work. And then, at the age of seventy, I will look back with great satisfaction as I take my rest secure in the knowledge that the future of Canada is unlimited.

The prime minister was then hustled out of the room to drop the same bombshell at a formal press conference with the media. His Liberal caucus was left to absorb the shock. Immediately, a crowd of MPs pressed in on Martin. A smaller group on the other side of the room – Chrétien's loyalists in caucus – simply glared in reproach at the commotion. Some of Chrétien's supporters wiped tears from their eyes.

Leaving the caucus room Maurizio Bevilacqua spotted Nick Masciantonio, one of Martin's former youth supporters and someone to whom he had always been close. Bevilacqua was bitter and angry. "I hope you guys are happy," he said.

Chrétien's announcement brought events at the caucus gathering to a standstill. Martin immediately went off to huddle with his advisers. Trying to duck the cameras, he accidentally took refuge in a women's washroom and, more than once, nipped into the hotel's swimming-pool area to flee the scribes. Two people in the pool giggled as they watched Martin trying to escape. "You can't hide from us anywhere, Martin," yelled David Collenette, who was paddling about the water with his wife, Penny.

Brian Guest did not want Martin to wade into a wild free-for-all scrum at this moment; he would appear besieged or desperate, he calculated. Guest scrambled to find a room where Martin could stand or sit at a microphone and take questions from the press. When Guest looked into the room where Chrétien had held his press conference, he found it already being dismantled.

Martin finally retreated to his hotel room, where he drafted a formal reaction to the announcement. The big question was whether to indicate a willingness to go along with Chrétien's incredibly long goodbye. Martin and most of the Board were prepared to accept it. Herle and O'Leary were on the phone to Chicoutimi, stressing the need to be gracious. "Six months ago, we didn't know when or whether Chrétien was leaving. Now we do. That in itself is a victory," Herle said. Tim Murphy also counselled the group not to be put off by the eighteen-month timetable. They had been counting on a leadership convention to take place in spring 2003; now it would be held either later that year or early in 2004. "Are we going to go to the wall for a matter of months?" Murphy asked.

Beyond Martin's circle, though, many MPs were not pleased. Some of the hard-line Martin supporters in caucus were holding their own huddles, whispering to reporters that they were going to find a way to force Chrétien from office long before 2004.

Martin debated whether to take questions from the media, which could almost certainly trap him into a discussion about how and whether he had caused the prime minister's downfall. Guest and Reid argued that Martin could get away with a brief statement, pleading that this was Chrétien's day in the spotlight. In the midst of the discussion, Martin pulled a scrap of paper from his pocket. It was the note he had been handed going into the caucus meeting. Opening it, he realized it was from the prime minister.

In French, Chrétien had written simply: "I am making this statement to help heal divisions within the Liberal party."

Nearly four hours had passed since Chrétien's news conference. Reporters were simmering – what was taking Martin so long? Other ministers had been lining up at the microphones all afternoon, filled with praise and tributes for Chrétien. Near 6 p.m., Martin finally entered one of the backrooms of the hotel and made a terse statement: "I can tell you that none of us in the government would have enjoyed the success that we did without his support, without his leadership. Jean Chrétien is a man who has shown courage all of his life. He is a man for whom I have the highest respect." And with that, Martin walked out of the room. Reporters stood aghast. It took four hours to put together those words?

While the Montagnais Hotel bustled with the fallout from Chrétien's resignation announcement, TV reporters solemnly intoning their standups before the cameras, the parking lot a sea of satellite trucks, Martin and his team quietly left by a back door and headed to an out-of-the way country restaurant near Chicoutimi to savour the moment in private. Ralph Goodale joined the group. When Murphy discovered the restaurant was a bring-your-own-wine establishment, he quickly went back on the road in search of a depanneur.

Martin stood outside in the driveway with Brian Guest. Resting one hand on the mini-van, his eyes taking in the countryside, he turned to Guest. "We're going to get this thing done, eh?"

Guest nodded, then leaned closer to hear Martin mutter: "Just can't screw it up."

10

THE UNOFFICIAL

OPPOSITION

ON AUGUST 30, 2002, ten days after Chrétien's surprising announcement at Chicoutimi, Martin met with the Board at O'Leary and Herle's lakeside home in the Gatineau Hills. It was a gorgeous day, with the sun sparkling on the water.

They were seventeen in all, clad in casual summer clothes, gathered around the long, rustic dining table. John Webster sat at one end of the table, Martin at the other, with David Herle beside him behind stacks of paper. As the team settled into its seats, exchanging wisecracks, Martin said a few words to open the day-long meeting.

"Don't all bow your heads and shuffle in your seats," he began. "I've got something to say." The team gave him its full attention. "Look around. What we have here is the best group of political people ever assembled. We are in the middle of something historic, something unprecedented. I just want to say that I'm so glad that I'm going through it with each and every one of you."

Martin handed the meeting to Herle, who quickly got down to business. "We have a lot of ground to cover," he said. They would have to look at the big and smaller pictures: where they stood in terms of overall communications strategy, organization, and policy formation. They would have to decide when Martin would announce positions of substance. Pacing was crucial – they were facing a marathon and had to make sure their energy and momentum would last a year and a half. True to his nature, Herle reminded the group that there were traps and trouble ahead. With Chrétien out of the way, Martin, as front-runner, would be the new target.

Webster then spoke up. In the newspapers in the days after Chicoutimi, one anonymous "Martin adviser" had been quoted as saying that the leadership contest had already been won.

"That's not how we should be talking, and that's not how we should be seen," Webster warned. "We're almost there. We're going to win this thing. But if we get into trouble, it's going to be because we get too arrogant."

Herle distributed charts and diagrams, which laid the political landscape. Chrétien's resignation announcement had changed everything. Polls told him that Liberals, torn by the summer of strife, were now in the mood for peace. Martin had to be seen as a unifying force. The group agreed that it was best to ignore any comments about Chrétien's long goodbye hobbling the Martin campaign. They knew that if they reacted, they would just open themselves up to charges of Martin being the "arrogant front-runner." Slow, steady, and humble would win this race.

As for potential leadership rivals, the group was primarily concerned with just one: Allan Rock. The summer disclosure announcements had illustrated that Rock had already accumulated a substantial campaign war chest. Karl Littler, in his intensive tours of Ontario over the summer, had encountered significant pockets of support for Rock.

The team discussed whether John Manley or Sheila Copps might also throw their hats in the ring. They were baffled that Chrétien had reasserted the ban on ministers campaigning when he made his announcement at Chicoutimi. Did he not realize that this just left the field clearer for Martin to build even more strength on the ground?

"I hope Manley enters the race," Martin said. "I hope Copps does too. I don't want to spend the next eighteen months campaigning against Chrétien."

At the tail end of the afternoon, Sheila Martin along with more campaign workers and their families began to descend on the country home.

About fifty people in all joined the team for a bigger party. The barbecue was fired up, beer bottles uncapped, and the most exuberant among them whooped and dove into the lake. Martin stood in the centre of the throng and delivered an address similar to the one he'd given the Board that morning: This was the best damn group of people around. This was history in the making. Let the adventure begin.

Now the campaign tour could begin in earnest, with Martin free to declare his ambitions. Almost immediately after Labour Day, Martin went on the road, heading west to Manitoba and British Columbia.

The sheer size of Martin's organization was most evident when he travelled. He had an official tour operation, headed up by yet another staffer with Earnscliffe, Charles Bird, who had been among Martin's spirited youth brigade in the last leadership. It was Bird's job to manage all the logistics, taking into account the leadership candidate's desire for punctuality and no surprises. Bird was the discreet fellow in the background who knew where protesters were lying in wait and how long it took, to the minute, to get across a city in rush-hour traffic. He worked hand in hand with Jim Pimblett, who was known affectionately as Martin's "wallet." Pimblett was constantly at Martin's side, guiding him through crowds, minding every one of his possessions, including his comb and wallet.

In every town, a crowd of local volunteers awaited his arrival. The tour was conducted with professional attention to scheduling, backdrops, and media availability. Reporters tailed him, peppering him with questions on everything from Canada-U.S. relations to his personal use of drugs. Had this sixty-four-year-old man, product of a generation before the baby boom, tried drugs? Well yes, as a matter of fact, he had. Back in the mid-1960s, a friend of the newly married Paul and Sheila Martin came to visit from the United States, carrying a lump of hashish. The only thing any of them knew what to do with hash was to bake it into brownies. So Sheila went to the store, picked up a box of brownie mix, and crumbled the hash into the batter. The three friends sat around the kitchen, sampling the finished product. They ate one each, then two, then three, and waited for the effect. Nothing happened.

In Vancouver on an early-September stroll through a Taiwanese cultural fair, Martin was asked again whether he had experimented with drugs in his youth. He had his answer ready: "It is possible that I had the experience once when I was in my twenties. Actually, if I remember correctly, it didn't have any effect on me at the time. But I must say, I like brownies."

As if to prove that there are no safe answers in politics, Martin heard the very next day from the anti-brownie constituency. Community leaders in Nanaimo light-heartedly took a poke at his oversight of the local delicacy – Nanaimo bars – urging him to judge them superior to brownies.

On the way to Nanaimo, Martin and his team had received word on the timing of the leadership convention. It would take place in November 2003 – a full three months ahead of the prime minister's announced resignation date of February 2004.

The convention date was, in many ways, a result of the same kind of negotiations that took place over the timing of the leadership review in the wake of the 2000 election. But this time, the outcome was reversed. Back then, Chrétien and his people had succeeded in persuading the Liberal national executive to push the date from November 2002 all the way to February 2003. In this negotiation, during a weekend meeting in Ottawa, the elastic snapped back, in Martin's favour.

Stephen LeDrew found the executive in no mood to grant Chrétien all the time he needed. Even the moderates on the fifty-four-member body said it was too much to expect the Liberals to delay a supposedly biennial convention another full year. If they went along with Chrétien's preferred timing, February 2004, the Liberals would not have held a convention in almost four years.

Eddie Goldenberg had telephoned Stephen LeDrew before the meeting, assuring him that if he proposed to hold the leadership convention in February 2004, the national executive would go along with it. LeDrew made his own inquiries, then talked to David Smith, his old friend and constant broker with Chrétien. "Tell Eddie that it's not there," LeDrew said. "There's no way this bunch is going to go along with that. Some of them even want to push for June."

The push for June 2003 was also based in those earlier tense negotiations over the timing of the leadership review. Some members of the national executive felt that Chrétien had implicitly, if not explicitly, made a deal in 2001: The executive had agreed to delay their biennial convention by a year, on the understanding that Chrétien would probably resign late in 2002. When that happened, they would just scrap the February 2003 leadership review and hold the convention to choose a new leader in June of that year.

Smith got the word back to the Prime Minister's Office: The Liberal party brass needed to hold a convention by the end of 2003, probably sometime in November, on a weekend that wouldn't conflict with Grey Cup weekend or municipal elections. Chrétien and his people were surprisingly sanguine about the timing of the convention, though Francie Ducros told reporters that the February 2004 resignation date was firm and non-negotiable.

LeDrew emerged early from the weekend meetings in Ottawa to declare that the next leader of the Liberal party would be chosen in November 2003. The exact dates and the location would be worked out after various cities put in their proposals. The question of the long transition time would be something to mull over later.

Martin, sitting in the boarding lounge of the Vancouver airport, merely shrugged when he heard that the Liberals were going to choose a new leader three months before Chrétien was leaving office. "Doesn't make much difference to me," he said.

Later that day, while waiting for the seaplane that would take him back to the B.C. mainland and another three events, Martin fell into a reflective mood. He looked around at the nearly dozen people with him, all talking on their cellphones, planning the most mundane aspects of his itinerary ahead. This was a leadership campaign, in earnest. Walking down the gangplank, Martin remarked on how far he and his campaign had come since 1990. "This time, it's big." He paused. "It is, isn't it?"

A few hours later, Martin was ready to state publicly, for the first time, the worst-kept secret in Canadian politics. Standing in a driveway of an upscale home in West Vancouver, Martin told reporters, "The balloons aren't out yet. But certainly I'm going out across the country talking about the issues that I think are important. And I really do believe that's what Liberals want and that's what Canadians want."

Of course, this didn't stop reporters from asking repeatedly, in every town and city Martin visited in the days and weeks ahead, whether he was running an official leadership campaign. Martin grew so weary of the question he whittled his answer down to two words, "No balloons," before he breezily went on to the next question.

Martin, like every politician, has his idiosyncracies about travel. His predilection for punctuality was legendary – a five-minute delay or a last-minute addition to the itinerary would agitate him. He phoned Sheila at every stop, letting her know where he was and what had happened in the hours since his last call. In turn, she would tell him about news she'd seen or read, always referring to the campaign as "ours." Sheila joined him on the road only infrequently, pouring her time into work with the Writers' Trust and frequent lunches and dinners with the spouses of Martin's political friends. Anyone who knew Martin well knew that Sheila was the centre of his world, as much as Aline Chrétien was the prime minister's Rock of Gibraltar. Interestingly, in all the years that Martin and Chrétien served together in cabinet, the two couples never socialized except as part of larger gatherings. Sheila and Aline's usual conversation was limited mainly to inquiries about mutual friends or brief discussions about children and the Chrétiens' grandchildren. The Martins had no grandchildren, to their oft-spoken regret. Their three sons were all childless. To compensate, Sheila often invited friends with small children to visit them at the farm.

In this leadership campaign, only David Martin, the youngest, was an active participant. Paul W., the oldest, was now living in Singapore, working for Canada Steamship Lines. Jamie, the middle son, was the most apolitical of all, but regarded by the rest of the family as the most creative and talented. He lived in Toronto, though he planned to enter screen-writing school at university in Los Angeles in the fall of 2003.

David lived in Montreal, where he worked for Merrill Lynch. As the campaign heated up during the fall and winter of 2002–03, he began to take time off work to help his father. He did some travelling of his own on behalf of the campaign, doing interviews with local papers across the country. He was twenty-eight, exactly the same age as his father had been when Paul Martin Sr. campaigned for the Liberal leadership in 1968. Many, including Sheila, saw David Martin as a chip off the old block – similarly impassioned about politics but also sometimes naive and overly competitive. David had become close friends with many of the young Martin supporters. He often showed up at their parties, keen to grill politicos and the occasional journalist about how they regarded his father's chances. He had devoured his grandfather's memoirs and was fiercely protective of the Martin family reputation.

On the road, Paul Martin's discipline was religious – literally. Everyone who organized his schedule on the weekends, from the 1990 campaign all the way through to this campaign, knew they had to build in time for him to get to church. He had rarely nagged his sons, Sheila said, but when he had, it was on the issue of their accompanying him to church when they were teenagers. In the 1990 campaign, the leadership debates had been held on Sundays, so Martin would go to mass the previous night before going out to dinner with his team and journalists. In 2002, his team planned ahead when organizing trips across Canada, locating a Roman Catholic church for him to attend if he was going to be away from home on the weekends.

There is a parallel between Martin's attitude toward religion and politics. He is driven to adhere to them, for reasons that he has trouble articulating. He goes to church, he says, "because I believe. Simple as that." Then he will wriggle out of a further explanation with a joke. "Sheila always says it gives her an hour away from me."

Martin regards his religion more as a foundation for his behaviour than an operating set of principles. "I'm probably a fairly typical Catholic, in that I believe, I go to church, but I make my own decisions and my own rules. Both my parents went to church, they were believers, but they made their own rules," he says. "I suspect my values are much the same as most people who don't go to church. We all make judgments, we all grew up in more or less the same society and we have those same values. To a certain extent, people who don't go to church have [similar] values and traditions by virtue of the fact that this is a Judeo-Christian society."

The Martin organization could now be more open about raising funds, and accepting them. On the tour, people frequently approached Martin himself, pressing business cards into his hand and offering financial backing. Jamie Deacey, who had served as a communications director in the 1990 campaign, was put in charge of the public fundraising efforts. These would operate on a standard formula: one hundred invitees, asked to pay a thousand dollars each. The gathering would usually take place in someone's home. Deacey had no trouble rounding up paying guests for these events. He had a small group of local volunteers on hand in each major city to handle the invitations – usually ten people, selling ten tickets each.

The first was held in Toronto in late August, with Martin a reluctant guest of honour. But he warmed to the format after the first few events. His famed punctuality had long been a problem at receptions where he was the featured guest. Because he would get there early, guests would arrive to find the would-be prime minister already loitering at the table of crudités, denying them a grand entrance. By now, however, the lesson had been drilled into him. He'd arrive a few minutes after the start, mingle with guests for a while, then say a few words to open a question-and-answer session. Two hours later it would all be over, and another $100,000 would be on its way to the campaign coffers.

Brian Tobin's old labour supporter, Tony Dionisio, hosted one of the few large-scale fundraisers of the campaign at the same Toronto union hall where Martin had announced his review of options in June. The Dionisio event, in mid-October, raised almost $800,000. Another large event, in Montreal the following spring, raised a whopping $1 million in one fell swoop. Serge Savard, the former Montreal Canadien, was the celebrity host for the event.

All of these donations were disclosed in bi-monthly statements around the eleventh of each month. Unlike the blind-trust donors, who were still telling Webster and Gerry Schwartz that they were nervous about revealing their support right now, with Chrétien staying in office for another year, these Martin backers agreed up front that their names could be disclosed.

It didn't take Deacey long to recognize that one of these events would beget another. "I enjoyed this. I'd like to organize one myself," one of the guests would inevitably say as the evening wound down. The fundraisers virtually organized themselves. A significant number of the attendees were new Liberal donors, many of them refugees from the Conservative party.

Deacey and Webster realized that they would probably raise as much money publicly as they would through the blind trust – $4 million to $5 million in each domain, around $10 million in total. This was about five times the amount they had raised in 1990 and well over the $4 million campaign-spending limit the Liberal party was expected to set. Money over the limit, they decided, would be poured into the party, to silence the perennial accusation that Martin's fundraising operation was diverting cash away from the debt-ridden Liberal party.

The Martin team would end up spending well over the $4-million limit, for a variety of reasons peculiar to this strange leadership contest. First of all, the limit applied only to the official campaign period, which wouldn't get underway until February 2003. As well, the limit did not apply to the costs of travel or polling. The exclusion of travel, one of the most expensive items on any campaign budget, addressed the inequity of having ministers and non-ministers in the race. Cabinet ministers, it was reasoned, could get around travel limits by adding one or two political events to trips on government business. In any bid to enforce limits, it would be impossible to determine whether a minister-candidate was in British Columbia, for instance, to make an official announcement or to rally the troops.

Politicians on tour don't get much of a chance to eat. Their perpetual hunger is a cosmic joke visited upon those who seek the approval of the electorate. Political events revolve around dinners, lunches, barbecues, and cocktail parties. Fleets of caterers are kept busy trucking their wares to campaign events, big and small. Yet almost inevitably, the star attractions at these events leave without even a morsel of food passing their lips. They are too busy shaking hands and cruising the room. If they do succumb to the temptation for a nibble, their handlers are on them at once, checking for crumbs on their lips or food stuck between their teeth. Of such things, failed politicians are made, the handlers assume. In Martin's case, Melanie Gruer, his press secretary, kept a watchful eye on the candidate at all times for just this.

Martin, racing through the British Columbia leg of the trip in September, began to complain about being perpetually hungry. Someone thought it was a good idea to take him to a fancy sushi restaurant in Vancouver. Martin hates sushi, so he ordered a sampling of tempura items, most of which were devoured by the rest of the table.

The next day, he hurried through a breakfast, a lunch, a coffee-and-doughnuts in Vancouver and on the island. Martin didn't eat a thing. He began to talk dreamily of a dinner of ribs at his beloved Tunnel Barbecue in Windsor. The day carried on. There were more events – more food tables, and then a barbecue in the ritzy neighbourhood of West Vancouver. Still, Martin got no chance to eat. The team decided to squeeze in a quick stop at a Vancouver restaurant before an evening appearance at a young Liberals' pub night. If they organized this right, they figured, they could stuff themselves with appetizers. The restaurant was obliging, quickly serving plates heaped with deep-fried morsels. Martin did it again. He offered the food to the dozen people at the table with him, leaving little for himself.

By the time the pub night was over on Granville Island, Martin was famished. But his team had organized a treat – a trip to a rib-restaurant franchise, where Martin could finally eat something he liked. As his car pulled into the parking lot, Martin leaped out of the car, beaming. Tim Murphy held the restaurant door open for him. "Okay. We've taken you for your fucking ribs. Are you happy now?"

Martin stopped. "Hey. When I'm prime minister, you can't talk to me that way," he said. He paused, blinked, realizing what he'd just said. For twelve years, Martin had been extremely cautious about voicing his leadership aspirations. But this day had seen his outlook grow increasingly confident. In the morning, he had talked about his goal in conditional terms. "You know," he'd said, sitting in the foyer of Vancouver's Wall Centre Hotel, "if I'm . . . if I . . . if this thing ever turns out, I won't want to have the RCMP around me all the time." That afternoon, he had told reporters that the campaign was official. And now, here he was at day's end, telling Tim Murphy that things were going to change when, not if, he became prime minister.

Overconfidence and, paradoxically, overcaution were Martin's two chief enemies during fall 2002 while he had the campaign field to himself.

Martin's detractors liked to say that his organization was composed primarily of zealots who had never accepted the last leadership loss. Indeed, the core team was composed largely, but not exclusively, of the key figures from the Martin leadership bid of 1990. But in terms of its strategy, the Martin campaign was also using the lessons learned from Chrétien in 1990. Now campaign workers were amassing a large grassroots organization and a huge block of caucus support. By fall 2002, Martin already had the support of about 120 Liberal MPs – an astounding 70 per cent of the elected caucus.

The Martin campaign also shared a feature with the front-running Chrétien campaign of 1990: an exasperating tendency to play it safe with public pronouncements. Martin was quickly gaining a reputation for a frustrating level of caution and ambivalence. He was the candidate in a bubble – a reality he acknowledged wryly on an autographed picture Brian Guest later hung over his desk. "When are you going to let me out of the bubble?" Martin had scribbled across the photograph.

He spoke to the parliamentary media only occasionally. He never showed up for Question Period. "Because I don't answer any questions," he'd say when asked why his seat remained empty. "What am I going to do? Question Period has got nothing to do with the bubble. I'd go to Question Period if I could answer any questions."

The peril in conducting a front-runner campaign lay in its failure to recognize that times had changed. Caution, at least in the public eye, had been devalued during Chrétien's low-key managerial reign. Now a wary politician looked like a cynical politician.

The silence also ran directly at odds with the style of leadership Martin was vowing to bring to federal politics. He was promising to be an open, accessible leader, yet the media was seeing him only behind a phalanx of fiercely protective aides, much as Chrétien had been in 1990. It was insider-brand politics, a risky approach for someone aspiring to lead a Liberal party that traditionally handed the crown to the person who spoke for those outside the Ottawa political establishment.

A vivid picture of the tension between Martin's roles as insider and outsider took place in late September 2002, at a Toronto conference organized and attended by many of the backroom players from the Trudeau era. Tom Axworthy, former principal secretary in Trudeau's powerful PMO, organized the weekend talkfest titled "Searching for the New Liberalism." The need for such a conference spoke volumes about what had happened to many of the former Liberal insiders. Since the 1980s, they had been on the outside, left out of the fold during both Turner and Chrétien's times at the helm. "Every generation has held to their old truths but adapted them to new realities," Axworthy wrote in an essay that outlined the reasons for the conference. "Liberalism in Canada is at such a divide today: the philosophy still has resonance but its application to today's problems and opportunities needs a fundamental rethinking."

Martin popped into the conference on Sunday morning and ended up staying most of the day. On this second day of the conference, the lament against the current state of Liberalism was sharpening to a point. Speaker after speaker stood up to condemn the cynicism and drift within the party. Even Richard Mahoney took to the floor to complain that the only thing he knew to do with new members was sign them up; there was no real outlet for them to contribute their ideas and thoughts to the party's vision.

It was the Liberal party's policy director, Akaash Maharaj, who put it most articulately: "The party itself, in our elected wing and in our civil wing, must exercise meaningful political leadership to quash what I feel has been a disease galloping through our ranks for the better part of a political generation – and that is a fundamentally illiberal impulse to equate dissent with disloyalty. I believe everyone in this room will agree that meaningful dissent is not merely the right of every person; it is the responsibility of every thinking person to expect that. A system that does not recognize that truth is simply today a system which will inevitably and rightfully collapse in on itself. Our loyalty as Liberals is to one another, but our loyalty as Liberals is first and foremost to the ideals that we represent."

A hush fell over the room. For a moment, it was almost possible to imagine that this was not the Munk Centre at the University of Toronto on a brisk fall day, but the Château Laurier in 1982. Almost exactly twenty years later, the critique was the same – the party was out of touch with the grassroots, too interested in power for its own sake.

Tom Kent, who as a former journalist and policy director to Prime Minister Lester Pearson was a voice from an even more distant Liberal past, spoke out against the influence of corporate power on the party. "I've no doubt that this is the moment of opportunity," Kent said. "A for-the-time-being prime minister has only to raise his hand. To cleanse political financing, to revive the heart of Liberalism, would be very different from a deathbed conversion to neglected social schemes for which there's little money today and his successor may or may not stick to. By contrast, financial reform of politics would be the least costly, yet firmest and finest of legacies."

The group gave Kent a standing ovation. Kent intended his address as a dare to Chrétien, unaware that just such a piece of legislation was in the works, and had been since May, when the prime minister, under siege over the latest ethics controversy, decided to mount a more aggressive fight. Indeed, legislation to impose strict limits on corporate financing would be one of the so-called "legacy" projects of Chrétien's final year, along with other controversial moves to put the capital L back in Liberalism.

Martin did not handle the emotion of this day particularly well. All through the sessions, he scribbled notes, nodding in agreement at various points. When Maharaj spoke out about how loyalty trumped dissent, Martin nudged others around him in whole-hearted assent. Yet when it came time for him to speak, he chose to speak in vague, cautious language about the need for parliamentary reform. It sounded for all the world like the perfectly bleached, focus-group-tested remark that any politician, including Chrétien, would make. Nothing in his "spontaneous" intervention was intended to inspire or even to acknowledge the passionate Liberalism felt by many in the room. It was an opportunity missed.

At Herle and O'Leary's home, during that all-day planning session at the end of August, Martin had strongly and repeatedly stated his aversion to becoming Canada's unofficial opposition leader during Chrétien's long goodbye. Had he wanted to take on the prime minister, he had more resources to do so than anyone else in the Commons. He had more support among MPs than the Canadian Alliance, the Conservatives, and the New Democrats combined. The power sat uneasily on him. He believed the battle against Chrétien was now all but won. He didn't have the stomach or the inclination to injure the prime minister in the time being. "I take a position and immediately it becomes a wedge issue. I don't want to hurt the government, so why would I create a wedge issue? I obviously have a wide range of areas in which I don't agree with the government. And those are going to come out," he said. "We're dealing with a year-and-a-half-long campaign. . . . I don't think it's in the country's interest that I be out there for a year and a half as an alternative government to the government. I'm going to wait until the campaign really starts."

He knew that eventually he would have to be seen to represent change from the current regime. He couldn't just blithely agree with Chrétien for the next eighteen months. Martin and his unwieldy team of supporters would spend the fall trying to juggle the contradictory strategies and the strategies of contradiction. Much as they would have liked to believe that the battle with Chrétien was over, there was still enough tension in the air to make this a very difficult period.

Chrétien spoke to his staff as a whole soon after his return from Chicoutimi. He reassured them that he was not a lame-duck leader, but a "liberated" leader, free to do all the things he wanted to do in his remaining time in office. It would be a time of activism on all kinds of fronts. The Prime Minister's Office was preparing a Speech from the Throne that would lay down formally the goals he had outlined in his Chicoutimi speech. These included a vow to ratify the Kyoto Protocol by year's end, promises to make the health-care system more accountable to Canadians, increased aid to Third World nations, and a variety of measures aimed at strengthening the federal government's role and reach in Canada. On the day the speech was delivered by Governor General Adrienne Clarkson, the last Monday in September, Martin made sure he was part of the cheering squad. "The Speech from the Throne is the result of a great deal of serious work," he said to a crowd of reporters who had waited more than an hour to hear his reaction. "And I think it certainly demonstrates the direction that Canadians want to see us take."

The virtue of the Martin organization was also, at times, its vice. Its sheer size made it daunting to challengers, but also difficult to manage. Borrowing the lessons learned from the successful early days of the Chrétien government, this team had to learn to speak with one voice, or at least in many voices in harmony.

A major part of this mission was reconciling the elected with the unelected. The chasm between these two bands of Martin support had been at the root of the debacle in March 2000 and, more recently, the dissonant reactions to the prime minister's long-goodbye announcement in Chicoutimi. If the Martin team was going to hang together through this slow, arduous goodbye, MPs and the inner circle – the Board – had to sing from the same page of the strategy song sheet.

There was another important consideration too: members of Parliament, who had been less important to the campaign during the drama of the summer, were now a significant part of the organization, now that a leadership convention, not a review, was scheduled.

The two are very different, requiring distinct tactics and strategy. In a review vote, every member's vote counts: every single Liberal across the country gets to cast a ballot, voting Yes or No. The ballots are then counted at a convention, where delegates are permitted to vote again. Because the question is such a stark one and the voting mass so large, this is where the so-called air war is more important. The person who has the best handle on party opinion at large usually prevails.

But in a leadership convention, the issue is ultimately decided by delegates elected by the riding association. The question is more complicated, too – it's not should the current leader stay on but which person, among a field of contenders, would be the best leader. Although all party members are eligible to elect delegates to represent their riding, plus the various clubs for women, youth, and aboriginal Liberals, it is only those delegates who get to vote for the leader. This makes leadership campaigns more of a ground war. MPs, with their connections to the ground, become a significant force. The MPs who supported Martin realized this, and strategized throughout the fall on how to use this leverage for Martin and against Chrétien.

All through fall 2002 and into the winter, a small band of devoted Martin supporters among the Liberal caucus met most Tuesday nights in one or another of the MPs' offices.

Much of these meetings was spent articulating their simmering frustration over Chrétien's long goodbye and their own sense of powerlessness. Joe Volpe, Albina Guarnieri, and Roger Gallaway were particularly irked by Chrétien's threat of an election to keep them all in line. Volpe had suggested to the media that the governor general might not let Chrétien call an election, especially if it could be proved that Martin enjoyed the confidence of a majority of MPs.

Martin came down hard on this public musing by Volpe, snapping to reporters: "That's not going to happen."

More than a few of Martin's supporters in the Commons were uncomfortable with the go-slow, low-profile approach of his advisers. They believed, not without justification, that it was they who were largely responsible for forcing Chrétien's hand in the summer. It was their boldness, their refusal to be cowed into signing the loyalty letter, that sent the chilly blast into the prime minister's hot summer of denial. And here they were, having pushed the confrontation almost to a conclusion, only to be told by advisers that now was the time to proceed with caution. The angriest MPs felt hung out to dry – that they had been used to get Martin onto the trajectory toward 24 Sussex Drive and now they were being told to just hang tight, keep quiet, and adjust to their role as pariahs until February 2004.

Tim Murphy began to pop into these Tuesday-night sessions, if only to offer some visible demonstration of the connections between Martin's elected and unelected supporters. Michèle Cadario kept in close touch with the MPs as well, spending more time in Ottawa and less on the road. Their presence was not always a soothing force. Murphy and Cadario were constantly trying to prevail on the MPs to keep the long game in mind, and the MPs felt that the game had already gone on long enough.

It was Martin himself who was caught in the middle of the widely divergent approaches toward this interregnum period. "There is something about having to get elected, having to sell yourself, that gives you a unique perspective," he said. "On the other hand, the people who are closest to me have a national perspective. They bring in far more other elements. My view is, my basic job is to pick the best of both."

The Board, meanwhile, had its own, more subtle dissonances with which to contend. As a microcosm of Canada, it had a few gaps. For instance, no one with any deep connection to Atlantic Canada was in Martin's inner circle – an indication of how that constituency had remained loyal to Chrétien during his time in power and the unease many Liberals out East felt about Martin's reputation as a right-wing Liberal. The Board's "national perspective," as Martin liked to see it, was more focused on the West and Quebec – and on younger people. Most of the Board was between the ages of forty and forty-five. Only Dennis Dawson, Elly Alboim, and Mike Robinson were over fifty.

Martin advisers were now hot commodities on the pundit circle. CTV's Ottawa bureau chief, Craig Oliver, was particularly aggressive in his pursuit of Martin advisers, urging them to come out of the shadows and serve as commentators on CTV's various news programs. Freed from the restraints of the past few years, the Martin advisers happily complied and leaped on to the airwaves. For the communications director, Brian Guest, this just meant new chaos. Now he never knew when he turned on the TV at night which Martinite was going to be speaking for the group. Would it be one of the MPs, a group over which the organization had very little control? Would it be a Martin adviser who had spontaneously agreed to pop by a TV studio and spout the collective view of the organization?

Guest thought it was a good idea to get some professional analysis of the Board's individual skills in punditry. Tapes were gathered of various performances: Tim Murphy on CTV, David Herle on CBC, Richard Mahoney on TVO, Mike Robinson on CBC Newsworld's *Politics* show. The tapes were sent to Jack Fleischmann, a veteran television specialist and founder of a slick corporate-communications TV studio in Toronto called News Theatre. Fleischmann reviewed the tapes with Elly Alboim at Earnscliffe, and then the two conducted their own mock interviews with the pundits-in-training.

The results were enlightening – almost serving as character studies. The analysis mirrored what all those close to the Martin team, including Martin himself, assessed as the individual strengths each contributed to the organization.

David Herle, whom Martin depended upon to pinpoint the "defining moment," brought the same attribute to his public performance. Herle, it was decided, should only be put before the cameras at momentous occasions, as a symbol of the Martin team's strength and determination. He was just too intense on TV, easily provoked. It hadn't helped that Alboim, who had worked closely with Herle for a decade, knew exactly which buttons to push in the mock interview.

Scott Reid, similarly, was seen as too hot. Quick with a turn of phrase, sharp with criticism, Reid was also viewed as someone the team would want to use mainly for spirited defence.

Mahoney, on the other hand, was viewed as charming to a fault. True to Martin's initial impression back in 1990 – "Richard is his own best schmoozer" – Mahoney's TV presence spoke volumes about his own personability, but not as much about the message that Guest and others wanted to put out.

Robinson was the master of velvet punditry, combining no-nonsense talk with a no-problem demeanour. He came across as the personification of Liberal party authority, using "we" more often than "I" or "them." He could fend off attacks with a friendly laugh, but he was less effective at pushing a hard message or counter-charge.

Tim Murphy shone in the punditry test. His famed stubbornness was an asset for the Martin organization on TV, because he could not be distracted from his message. He gave the impression he was listening to contrary views or questions, but then he would turn around those remarks and simply go back to his main point.

Brian Guest ruled himself out. Asked by the team to go on TV, to present the younger, more energetic side of the Martin organization, Guest rehearsed at home one night, asking himself questions and then trying to give answers he would approve. He would get three questions into the self-interrogation and then, exasperated with his non-answers or information slips, start all over again. After a few tries, he simply crossed his own name off the roll of potential pundits. They had more than enough talking heads to sate TV's hunger for commentators.

Terrie O'Leary didn't participate in the exercise. She was still at the World Bank, serving out the last few months of her second term as Canada's representative to the international body. But the real reason she abstained was her unique position in the pantheon of Martin advisers: everywhere and nowhere in particular but, ultimately, at the top. She had no aspirations to see her name in the paper, regarding any public mention as a violation of her privacy. Martin had long described O'Leary as the brightest mind on his whole team, someone who grasped all aspects of the organization, people, and policy process and was able to bring it coherence.

"A lot of them have their own opinion," Martin says. "Terrie is able to have her own opinion. She is also able to seek out other opinions and then she brings it all together. And one of the reasons that I think she is so good is that she's able to hear the fourteen conflicting forces and use them to get the bottom answer."

Since June, O'Leary had been reporting to John Manley, the new finance minister. Given the deterioration of the relationship between Martin and Manley and the fact that government appointees are rarely given more than two terms, few expected O'Leary to be in Washington for much longer. Sure enough, she learned in a roundabout way in October that she was about to be replaced. O'Leary would return late in the year to live at the lake in the Gatineau Hills and take a more active, if discreet, role in the areas of strategy and policy.

By early fall, commentators across Canada were starting to wonder when Martin was going to say something substantial. He had been out of cabinet for more than three months and had yet to deliver any major policy pronouncements. Part of his reticence was purely strategic. Dennis Dawson and others had been advising him for weeks that a long leadership campaign needed to be paced properly. If everything was thrown before the public at once, critics and foes would nibble the platform to death before the race even started. But Martin and his team wanted to flesh out the proposal to reform parliamentary procedures so that he could do more than talk in vague terms when he went around the country, pitching the importance of making the Commons relevant again.

A small team of advisers on this issue was pulled together from the caucus and from the world beyond Ottawa. Patrick Monahan, a law professor and constitutional expert at York University's Osgoode Hall, quietly worked on a series of reform proposals. MPs such as Carolyn Bennett and Tony Valeri fed him their ideas and comments. Much of the consultation took place by e-mail and conference call, in keeping with the networked, wired style of the Martin campaign.

On October 21, Martin appeared at Osgoode Hall in front of a couple of hundred law students and outlined his ideas on parliamentary reform. It was a highly scripted performance, one that saw Martin trying to straddle the line between being a loyal Liberal MP and promising change from the Chrétien style of leadership. Naturally, the media were drawn to the latter, especially given the snappy lines that Martin delivered in a not-subtle reference to the prime minister: "We have permitted a culture to arise that has been some thirty years in the making, one that can best be summarized by the one question that everyone in Ottawa believes has become the key to getting things done: 'Who do you know in the PMO?'" he said. "This is unacceptable. We must change that reality." That was the media's fifteen-second sound bite for the day.

Martin's six-point plan was modest in scope, drawing on ideas that had been discussed in parliamentary-reform circles for several years. He proposed to ease up on the use of the party whip, to allow MPs more leeway to change the principles of bills in committees, and to increase opportunities for private members' bills to be introduced and passed by the Commons. More ambitiously, he vowed that committees would have the power to review appointments to the Supreme Court and foreign postings. He called for an independent ethics commissioner, reporting to Parliament, just as the original Red Book had stated. He also urged that committees be allowed to choose their chairs by secret ballot, ending the practice of their being chosen and removed at the prime minister's discretion.

The most intriguing line in the entire speech, though, was one that foreshadowed events soon to take place: "There will be disagreements. There will be reports that caucus is divided. From time to time, the government's legislation will be defeated, leaving ministers, even the prime minister, looking discomfited."

The Canadian Alliance had been playing wedge politics, as Martin would put it, for several months now. Mischievously, even in the days after his departure in June, the Official Opposition had pored over stories of Martin-Chrétien disagreements and pushed during Question Period to get the prime minister to contradict his would-be successor.

Martin's Osgoode Hall speech gave the Alliance another round of ammunition for this game. In a complicated procedural wrangle, the Alliance had managed to guarantee a Commons vote on the issue of the secret election of committee chairs. Chrétien served strong notice that he was against the idea, emerging from a cabinet meeting to douse the notion with cold water, saying it would harm the prime minister's prerogative to balance regional and gender interests among the caucus leaders.

"Having one hundred members from Ontario, you have to work for the balance, and the question, too, of gender opportunities, but at the end of the day, it's always members who vote. It's not the cabinet," he said. "But there's always ministers who are talking with the whip and others, because you have to keep in mind, too, who should be on the committees." The next day, Chrétien met privately with Government House Leader Don Boudria, looking for a way out of the vote in the Commons.

Stan Keyes, the Liberal caucus chairman, called for an emergency meeting of MPs, to figure out how to avoid being drawn into the Alliance's wedge game. The meeting ended with an agreement – a classic example of pragmatic Liberal tactics – to defer the whole matter until the next time committee chairs had to be chosen. In all likelihood, that would mean that the issue would be moot for the remaining time Chrétien was in office.

In response, the Alliance simply pushed harder, forcing a Commons vote on the issue, a vote set for November 5. Now Martin was on the spot. If he voted with the government, he'd be accused of hypocrisy or cowardice – selling out one of the main planks of his parliamentary-reform proposal for the sake of peace with Chrétien. Neither the Canadian Alliance nor the prime minister seemed keen to make life any easier for him, digging further into the trenches as the day for the vote loomed.

Martin flew out to B.C. over the weekend before the vote, mulling over his options. He decided he would vote against the government. Naturally, given the extensive nature of Martin's consultations on all matters, big and small, the word got out. Martin's MP supporters gleefully looked forward to the vote as their chance to stand up with their preferred, unofficial leader in the Commons. The prime minister was furious, telling Keyes privately that he had whipped this issue up to a frenzy by calling an emergency caucus meeting. Keyes snapped back that if Chrétien hadn't raised the stakes by voicing his opposition so publicly, the Liberals wouldn't be divided.

On the day of the vote, the prime minister told his cabinet that while it would be treated as a free vote, ministers should be very careful about opposing his wishes. British Columbia's junior minister, Stephen Owen, regarded this as an order and conspicuously absented himself from the Commons. Rumours swirled that Chrétien was finally losing control not just of the caucus, but of the cabinet. (Owen later allowed that he might have misinterpreted the warning. He was never punished for abstaining.)

As the vote took place, Martin stood up with fifty-six fellow Liberals – not all of them his supporters in caucus – in favour of the Canadian Alliance motion. It passed by a vote of 174 to 87. If this had been a vote of confidence, the government would have fallen. It was now clear that in any contest between Chrétien and Martin, the prime minister could no longer count on winning by persuasion. Only the threat of a snap election would now keep the caucus in line.

The affair left Martin quite unhappy. The sight of Liberals divided may be diverting in the short term, he reasoned, but the Canadian electorate could punish the party at the next general election for putting its open wounds on display for month after month in this long goodbye. Martin resolved that he would not vote against the government again. Yet that decision flew in the face of his own words during the Osgoode speech, in which he argued that real reform depended on bold leadership, unafraid of risking discomfiture and division.

"I don't want the government to look bad," Martin said. "I'm a member of this government. I want this government to win the next election."

His troubles weren't over yet. The new problem was Chrétien's determination to have the Commons ratify the Kyoto Protocol, which Canada signed in 1997 as part of an international treaty to cut greenhouse gases and improve air quality. The cuts contemplated were significant. When Canada had initially signed five years earlier, it was largely on the basis of Chrétien's stated determination to go beyond the Americans' commitments. The Clinton administration had ended up agreeing to larger-than-expected cuts, which Canada then outmatched. Since then, the new Bush administration had pulled out of the protocol, but Canada – and, more particularly, Chrétien – remained firmly in favour. Liberal MP John Godfrey, a close friend of Martin and a staunch supporter, had been leading a charge in caucus to have the Kyoto Protocol ratified by the end of the year, collecting a number of MPs' signatures to back his pro-Kyoto campaign.

Martin was annoyed by the unilateral way in which Chrétien had approached Kyoto. He believed it was folly to commit to a plan without preparing the ground first. It was the opposite of the successful team approach that had worked during the deficit-cutting years. "If you're going to make substantial cuts, you first have to have the plan in place," Martin said.

He knew that many Western cabinet ministers, who represented the region most nervous about Kyoto, had been caught flat-footed when Chrétien announced in Johannesburg that Canada would ratify the deal by year's end. Health Minister Anne McLellan, representing oil-rich Alberta, heard about Chrétien's declaration on the news. Natural Resources Minister Herb Dhaliwal had assured the media before the Johannesburg trip that the prime minister was not contemplating any such announcement.

Martin had long regarded himself as a strong environmentalist and a supporter of the Kyoto Protocol. He had attended the 1992 Earth Summit in Rio de Janeiro as the Liberal environment critic, and had taken part in the early international negotiations that led to Kyoto five years later. Yet now he was also hearing some fierce opposition from the West, even from his long-time supporters out there. He spent a great deal of time wrestling with what to do when Chrétien put the vote to the House on Kyoto. It was yet another tug-of-war between his contradictory desires to be a loyal Liberal at the same time as being a critic of Chrétien's style of governance.

In the end, he resolved the contradiction through a show of both defiance and compliance. He let it be known that while he supported ratification, he would not go along with any attempt to end debate on the motion in the Commons. The Chrétien government regularly used closure in the Commons to get motions put to a vote. Kyoto was no exception. Martin decided to be conspicuous by his absence from the House, effectively abstaining from the vote, rather than accidentally leading another charge against Chrétien. As the opposition shouted, "Where's Paul?" the government side voted to close down the debate on ratification. Martin showed up later in the Centre Block and nervously circumvented reporters' questions about where he stood in relation to the prime minister on this question.

"My position on parliamentary reform is that closure should be the exception, not the rule," he said. "I also believe that, given the necessity of establishing a very wide national consensus in order to ensure the implementation of Kyoto Protocol, that it might have been better if a bit more time had been given for the debate."

This was all he would say. The lines were rehearsed, and the press encounter was brief. He looked terrified of saying anything that could even remotely be construed as criticism of Chrétien's determination to get Kyoto passed. Martin knew that this wasn't his finest hour. "As Terrie says, I'm not very good at dissembling," he later acknowledged.

The Liberals seemed to be still at war. Every day in the media there were new stories of Liberals turning on each other. Chrétien was the usual target, but Martin came in for his share of anger.

An aggressive ground war was underway in British Columbia between Martin's forces and the supporters of Herb Dhaliwal, who had emerged by this point as one of the more vocal critics of Paul Martin inside the cabinet. Dhaliwal, the minister representing B.C., had had designs on running for the leadership, but his anti-Martin stand had not gone down well with rank-and-file members of the B.C. wing of the Liberal party, who were largely Martin supporters. In June, Stephen LeDrew and others had assessed British Columbia as one of the provinces where opposition to

Chrétien was running the highest. Dhaliwal's reaction had been to rush to support the prime minister, using increasingly vitriolic language aimed in Martin's direction.

Dhaliwal's temper boiled over when his riding association was taken over by Martin supporters. He had been outside the country when the meeting was held and was caught off guard by the takeover. Dhaliwal went public with his rage, which he directed at Martin personally.

"He is responsible. It's his organization," Dhaliwal told reporters. "He needs to come out whether he condones this type of action, and whether he thinks embarrassing me helps the Liberal party or helps him in his campaign."

Chrétien flew off to Prague in late November, for an international summit of NATO leaders. The most pressing issue on the agenda was the Americans' growing insistence on fighting a war with Iraq. Chrétien was determined to speak up against U.S. unilateralism. But NATO meetings were turning out to be a jinx on domestic matters for the prime minister. The last time he'd attended one of these summits, in late May, all hell had broken loose inside his cabinet and caucus. This time, the trouble would explode in his own tight PMO circle.

In a media briefing room on the opening day of the summit talks, Francie Ducros was talking to CBC Radio reporter Chris Hall within earshot of other reporters. Flippantly, she referred to President George W. Bush as "a moron." *National Post* reporter Bob Fife overheard the remark and put it in his story, anonymously sourced, to illustrate the mood of Canadian officials toward Bush's fixation on Iraq. Back in Ottawa, the anonymous quote immediately set off a stir among the chattering class. Who had been so impolitic as to describe the U.S. president so dismissively? Ducros was "outed" by all major media the very next day.

Ducros's aggressive defence of the prime minister over the previous three years had taken its toll on her relationships with the media. The "moron" remark reflected all that political reporters and even Liberal caucus members had resented about Ducros's approach to communications, which was to demonize and ridicule the enemy. By outing her they vaulted an inside-Ottawa scandal on to the international stage, and the story of the remark drowned out news of any developments at the summit.

The U.S. media seized upon the slur, and Ducros's name became notorious on the American talk-show circuit.

Chrétien initially stood by his communications chief, refusing to accept her resignation and insisting that the comment had been taken out of context. The prime minister also denied that there was any bad blood between the two leaders. "He is a friend of mine. He is not a moron at all," he said, breaking a cardinal communications rule: never repeat a contentious remark, not even to deny it. The pile-on continued until Ducros was forced to insist on leaving the PMO.

Her departure was greeted with enormous relief by most political reporters, who believed that her overly partisan approach to Martin, his people, and the media had only aggravated the destructive atmosphere on the Hill in this very bad year for her boss. Martin and his advisers, especially Scott Reid, who had worked closely with Ducros, were more cautious in response to her ouster. They had come to believe that she was less of a cause of the tension than an agent of it. Reid thought it was folly to pin all the blame on Ducros, or to assume that all the problems between Martin and Chrétien would magically disappear when she was gone.

As if to prove that point, the internal atmosphere in the Liberal caucus only degenerated further as the year drew to a close. In early December, with tempers fraying over the ratification of Kyoto and the PMO still rattled by the Ducros controversy, Canada's auditor general, Sheila Fraser, issued a scathing report on cost overruns in the federal firearms registry, set up when Allan Rock was minister of justice. Original estimates for the registry had pegged the costs at $2 million, but the auditor general's scrutiny revealed it would probably cost more than $1 billion by 2004–05.

The revelation reignited all the angry resentment of the anti-gun-control forces during Chrétien's first mandate. Old animosities came back to haunt the Liberals, when they already had more than enough current troubles. Rock, now at Industry, mounted an aggressive defence, saying he would not allow this news to knock the government off its determination to have effective gun control. "They're using this as an opportunity to attack the law," he said. "What I say is, Over my dead body."

At the time, Rock was expected to be Martin's strongest rival in the leadership race. But the fiasco of the firearms registry costs put another dent in his already severely damaged political armour. Never a favourite with the caucus, especially since the membership fracas of the spring, Rock now found that Liberal MPs were calling for his resignation. Benoît Serré, a Northern Ontario MP who had always opposed gun control, said Rock should be "gone, gone." Joe Comuzzi, one of Martin's Italian caucus, also said Rock and McLellan, currently responsible for the registry, should quit if it was found that they had authorized the out-of-control spending. Other MPs with strong Martin ties, such as Judy Sgro, were publicly distancing themselves from Rock and the registry mess.

Martin decided he would do interviews with the media to try to remove leadership politics from the fight. "Definitely there were questions that should have been asked, follow-up that should have been done by all of us," he said. "As far as I'm concerned, the responsibility is one that we all share, and as I mentioned, I certainly bear my share of that responsibility. I don't think this is an issue in which people should be trying to defer blame. This is one where we all have collective responsibility."

But Rock saw this comment as yet another salvo from Martin and lashed back. It didn't do him any good. Rock's reputation was taking a battering. In British Columbia, a passerby in the airport yelled at him, "Give me back my $1 billion! You stole $1 billion from us." Rarely before had Rock been assailed so virulently in public. The incident rattled him. He began to wonder whether he could be a credible candidate, at least this time, against such a powerful foe as Martin. Quietly, he asked his organizers around the country to begin making a realistic assessment of his chances. If he could not get 20 per cent of the delegates, he would have to reconsider his candidacy for the Liberal leadership, a project he had pursued for the better part of the last five years.

During the pre-Christmas chaos on the Hill, Martin's MP supporters were growing bolder. They had spotted another opportunity to revive the calls for Chrétien's resignation they had been trying to make since 2000. Many of the same gang that put their necks out during the March 2000 controversy were back in the newspapers, angrily urging the prime minister to step down.

Nick Discepola of Montreal told the *National Post*: "On the record, my constituents are saying the same thing [that Chrétien must go]," he said. "Not only my constituents but good friends and long-time Liberals are saying that our credibility is now starting to erode as good sound fiscal managers, especially with the gun registry."

Albina Guarnieri, one of Martin's most staunch, long-time supporters, said, "People are worried that this country cannot afford another fourteen months of legacy building." Ontario MP Dan McTeague condemned the "aimless drift" of the Chrétien government. In all, seven MPs, including Roger Gallaway, Joe Volpe, Paul Steckle, and Quebec MP Hélène Scherrer, spoke out as they prepared to head home for the long Christmas break.

Chrétien barked back. At a news conference in his office to mark the official signing of the Kyoto Protocol, he said, "No, I am leaving in 2004, in February. I said that very clearly. I have been elected by the people of Canada to run a government – not to leave."

Once again, he dismissed the MPs' dissent as the product of raw ambition and predicted that they would remain disgruntled under Martin. Just as Eddie Goldenberg believed that Martin's advisers would be silenced if they were hired to work in Langevin Block, Chrétien appeared to think that the only thing that the MPs wanted was to be in cabinet. "You know, it has been going on since 1990, and, you know, many of them from a year and a half from now, you will write about them and they will be former future ministers," he said.

Martin in the meantime was publicly putting distance between the MPs' remarks and his own attitude toward the long goodbye. "The schedule is set out by the prime minister, and the party is very clear, and I'm happy with that," he told supporters at a Christmas gathering in his riding.

Fine words, perhaps, but this *annus horribilis* for the natural governing party was ending almost as badly as it had begun, with MPs howling for Chrétien to leave and Martin still in slow-motion pursuit of his leadership goal. The heir apparent seemed no more free to talk openly now about his aspirations than he had been before he left cabinet, but now the gag was largely self-imposed. Peace between Martin and Chrétien had not been bought, yet both the party and the government were paying a price. The cease-fires hadn't come cheaply either: both had been forced to walk away from their jobs in 2002 in circumstances neither chose, according to timing not entirely of their own making.

It may have been that peace was particularly difficult to achieve between the two rivals because no one could really figure out when or why the enmity started. Some pundits said it started in June 1990, in the noisy audience of the Montreal leadership debate. Others said that the two men stopped working with each other as soon as the 1995 budget was completed and that, once the books were balanced, they had lost any reason to work together at all. Without another Aylmer conference to give them a mission, they had drifted back to their old rivalry. Still others believed that the whole government went off the rails somewhere between the summer of 1999 and the fall of 2000, when Chrétien made his fateful decision to seek a third term. But no one was sure why that happened, either. Sheer vindictiveness, Martin supporters believed, arguing that the prime minister's only goal since 1990 had been to block Martin's succession. Sheer treachery, said those around Chrétien, adding that if Martin and his team hadn't displayed their impatience with the March 2000 meeting at the Regal Constellation, the leadership succession would have happened much sooner, in a far less messy fashion. And that brought the whole argument back full circle to the ugly Montreal debate: Did Chrétien believe in anything but winning power? Why can't Paul control his people?

Nor could anyone put their finger on any substantial reason for their differences, beyond their personality traits and approaches to leadership. No great policy differences separated them. There was no clash of visions, for neither one had displayed any great attachment to any set of ideas in their twelve years of working together.

The simplest explanation was probably the most accurate: This was raw political rivalry between two fiercely competitive men, who each viewed the other as an obstacle to their ambitions. It was fuelled by the competitive people who surrounded them and fed by a news media keen to find drama in the often dry world of government and politics.

In their differences of style, though, there was perhaps a clue to how Martin and Chrétien could begin to forge a peace. Martin placed a great emphasis on words, in the power of language to make a lasting imression. It was why he fretted so much over speeches and why it took him so long to come up with even the simplest responses to reporters' questions. For his part, Chrétien believed in deeds. His decisions weren't always explained, but they were carried out, sometimes too hastily. If Martin's greatest weakness was his hesitation over words, Chrétien's weakness lay in barrelling right past them. Martin's biggest worry was that he'd say too much or say the wrong thing. At his most frustrating, he prompted his critics to beg him to say something. Chrétien's fears, on the other hand, appeared to be that he'd do too much or do the wrong thing. He was most frustrating to his critics when he wouldn't act.

For Chrétien, then, peace would have to come through a gesture. And late in December, as the holidays loomed, there was a small one. A Christmas card landed at the Martins' Montreal townhouse. It was the standard-issue prime-ministerial holiday greeting, featuring a smiling Chrétien on the cover. Inside, a simple signature, short on words, but pointed in significance.

"In friendship," the card read. "Jean and Aline."

It was not a grand gesture, but it was a start. In the weeks and months ahead, Martin would have to find the words to put the rivalry to rest. It was time to move on.

11

FADE TO FINISH

THE CLOCK TICKS slowly in the federal Liberal world. The party governs for longer than other parties do, grudges linger over decades, not years, and it takes an eternity for a Liberal prime minister to say goodbye. It took Pierre Trudeau two resignation announcements, in 1979 and 1984, to make the break permanent. Jean Chrétien needed two tries over six years to become prime minister and, after eleven years in power, carved himself an exit strategy that would take eighteen months from resignation to actual departure. Paul Martin waited more than thirteen years, and tried twice, to win the Liberal crown. And, if history is the judge, it takes twenty long years to shake up things in the Liberal party.

Winning, losing, vindication, letting go of grudges – these all take place in the Liberal party at glacial speed. Yet in the early weeks of 2003, the thaw and the transformation was clearly underway.

All through the Christmas season, even as he vacationed with his family in Hawaii, the taunts of the heckler at the Vancouver airport had echoed in Allan Rock's ears. "Most affecting," Rock would later say. The holiday had put Allan and his wife, Debby Hanscom, in an almost wistful mood as they reviewed his nearly ten years in elected politics and recalled the early, heady years of power and their old friendships with the Martins and the Martinites, now frayed, if not in tatters. A decade had taken its toll: the leadership campaign had exacted very personal costs.

In early January, after his return from Hawaii, Rock got on the phone to supporters across the country and asked them to deliver a hard-headed assessment of his leadership chances. These were difficult calls to make. Rock was asking people to contemplate putting an end to their own aspirations as well as his own. All were volunteers; most had joined his campaign fully aware of the uphill struggle they would face against the front-runner. Their underdog status was a point of pride, their resentment of the Martinites' sheer force in numbers intense. But Rock needed his team to put aside their emotions and give him a realistic forecast.

Rock already knew in his gut that the outlook was bleak. Provisionally, as he put it, he had decided over Christmas to bow out. On a cold Sunday afternoon, January 12, Rock's "board" assembled around the dining table in his downtown Ottawa house. Cyrus Reporter was there with his wife, Johanne Senécal, who worked as a Quebec adviser in the PMO. About a dozen others were on hand, including almost all of those supporters on Parliament Hill who had been with him since the beginning of his campaign.

Rock asked all of them to speak, in turn. Everyone knew where the discussion was headed. Each of them had evidence of the dim prospects, though all stressed they were willing to jump into the race at the word *go* from Rock. He wasn't going to say it, though. Debby, Rock's highly political wife, nodded pragmatically at each bleak prognosis. A few people around the table started to shed quiet tears. At the end, Rock offered his crestfallen troops the same reassurance he later gave to his teenaged children when he told them the news: "It's not over forever. It's just over for now. There will be a next time."

The next day, Rock held conference calls with organizers across Canada and set the wheels in motion for his withdrawal from the campaign. There were speeches to cancel, fundraisers to halt, hopes to put on hold.

On Tuesday, January 14, exactly one year after Brian Tobin pulled out of the leadership race, history repeated itself. Rock paid an early-morning call at 24 Sussex Drive and told Chrétien his intentions. The prime minister was neither surprised nor disappointed, though he was solicitous about Rock's disappointment. Rock then phoned Martin. Their conversation was brief, yet warmer than any they had had in recent years. Martin praised Rock as a formidable candidate and said he looked forward to being friends instead of rivals. By mid-morning, Rock was ready to make his way to the National Press Theatre, to tell the media that yet another industry minister and leadership candidate had come to the conclusion that Martin was unbeatable.

"For many reasons, this is not our time," he said. "Paul Martin is the most popular politician in the country. He's a tough candidate to beat. That's the reality." For the first time in many years, Rock seemed relaxed, sanguine, self-deprecating, more like the private man his friends and associates knew.

"Á la prochaine," Rock said as the news conference closed. Until the next time.

His leadership hopes were still alive, but Rock would postpone them for now. Instead, he would pour his energies into being a good minister and try to overcome his reputation of being disaster-prone. He would try to relax more in front of the cameras, show his audiences a little more of the man people saw at the news conference or in private.

"There's no doubt there's a close link between how you perform as a minister and how you're perceived as a candidate," he said after the press conference. "One of the reasons for Paul's strength as a candidate is that he performed so well as a minister of finance. And I think that while I'm very proud of things I've achieved as a minister, I had a lot to learn when I arrived in 1993. And I learned it in a very public way. . . . It was period-ically painful, but I have learned a lot and that process of education will continue."

Rock's announcement was good news and bad news for the Martin jug-gernaut. Much of Rock's organization and support went to the Martin team – even Rock himself eventually, despite his initial pronouncements about remaining neutral. Cyrus Reporter soon left Rock's office to work with none other than Richard Mahoney at the Fraser Milner law firm. The tense, no-politics cordon was also lifted in the friendship between Reporter and Herle. The "suspended friendships," in Martin's words, could be resumed. Even Debby Hanscom and Sheila Martin picked up their friendship, meeting for lunch soon after Rock pulled out of the race.

The bad news was that Martin was now alone in the field of contenders, just as he had been through the difficult fall.

The party's national executive had decreed that the official leadership campaign would begin on February 24, 2003. With Rock out of the race and no other strong contenders set to emerge, Martin and his team began to worry that Chrétien would remain his primary opponent all the way to the November convention. It wasn't clear whether Heritage Minister Sheila Copps would enter the contest, nor was Finance Minister John Manley displaying any great enthusiasm about running. Even if one or both of these ministers did decide to take the plunge, their campaigns would be starting from well behind. If neither Rock nor Tobin had been able to mount a serious challenge, with far more time and organization, why would anyone take the risk now to run a distant second – or worse, a distant third?

Stéphane Dion, the Quebec minister closest to Chrétien, delivered an intriguing speech to a Liberal party convention in Alberta in early February, which appeared to argue that no race at all might be better for the Liberal party. A race for the sake of appearances might result only in a chipping away of the next leader's credibility and reputation. This view was shared by Herle and others close to Martin, but they knew that if they had advanced it publicly, they would look arrogant. Dion had put his finger on a tension between Martin's short-term leadership and long-term election goals. In the short term, Martin would benefit from a lively leadership race, because it would inject some vitality into a Liberal party increasingly viewed as complacent. In the long term, though, during the future general election, Martin would have to present himself as the leader of a strong, united party. If the leadership race was run against Martin, there was a chance that voters would remember all the negative things that his own colleagues said about him. The Liberal party, and Martin, could be diminished by such a contest, maybe all the way to a minority government.

But the splits in the Liberal party were already glaring. The Chrétien-Martin rivalry had seared this into the public's imagination. And, even if there were no other leadership candidates, Chrétien would continue to be seen as Martin's main rival.

The Martin team's spirits sank at the prospect of a continuing duel with Chrétien in the absence of any other debate; a shadow-boxing match from which neither would emerge looking better to the public eye. It would only stretch the patience of grassroots Liberals – the people who held the power to choose the next leader. As it was in the fall, everything that Martin said would be measured against the prime minister's position. Any declaration for change would be taken as a disavowal of the government in which he had been a senior partner. As well, John Manley was getting ready to deliver his first budget, and Martin dreaded the prospect of being hounded by reporters with questions about how he would have done things differently.

Martin had not managed this situation well so far. The media was growing increasingly critical of his attempts to evade any question that put him at odds with the prime minister. He knew that his duck-and-cover approach to Kyoto in November had made him look guilty, or at least cowardly. "But what can I do?" he repeatedly asked his advisers over the Christmas break. "I'm a Liberal. I don't want the government to look bad."

Terrie O'Leary was now back from Washington, but she shied away from any visible role in the campaign. Behind the scenes, however, she was totally immersed in strategy discussions. Her assessment of any situation or person was quickly embraced by the organization as the prevailing wisdom. Meetings of the Board took place throughout the winter and spring in hotel meeting rooms on the Quebec side of the river – where smoking was still permitted indoors – largely to accommodate O'Leary. She didn't take an office in the Ottawa headquarters, though, as Herle and Murphy had, preferring to operate from the house in the Gatineaus. A few smart alecks in the organization began to describe her – much to her annoyance – as "Canada's most powerful homemaker." Herle and O'Leary had a second telephone line installed at their home, solely dedicated to calls to and from Martin.

More than the others, O'Leary worried that Martin would be personally damaged if he spent the next few months on the defensive against Chrétien. Typically, she argued for openness; a strategy that would see Martin putting his dilemma on the table and candidly acknowledging his difficulties in running a campaign against the sitting prime minister. Why not just tell the media how hard this was?

On January 30, while campaigning in the hamlet of Sherwood Park, east of Edmonton, Martin made a full statement to reporters. He said he wanted to talk about how the leadership race could be conducted without dividing the party.

"I'm going to take a bit of time to answer," he said, clearing his throat. "The fact is that the last few months, certainly the few months before Christmas, were awkward. They were pretty uncomfortable for a number of us. The current situation is without precedent. There's no playbook that we can refer to for what we're going through. We've got to find a way to make the transition work a heck of a lot better. Candidates for the leadership have got to be free to express their views on where they would take the country. They've got to highlight what the course forward – that they want to advocate – would be."

All the leadership candidates, Martin said, had to be able to state their platforms without being labelled as disloyal. "In the coming months, all of us as Liberals are going to be confronted with this challenge: How do you champion new ideas without damaging the integrity of the government?"

His public statements echoed what he had said in private discussions with his team. "I think I have a particular role to play in this because, I'm going to tell you, I am not running to become the leader of the Opposition. I was born and bred a Liberal, and I want the current government to succeed as much as I want the new government to succeed."

The Liberal party needed the renewal that a lively debate would provide, he said. "We cannot permit a self-imposed silence on controversial positions that would deny the party, deny the government, and deny the country a very much-needed debate as to where we're going to take the country. . . . But I want you to understand that these are policies that I would implement as prime minister. They are not demands on the current government. There can only be one prime minister at a time and the current prime minister, Jean Chrétien, is the leader of the party and of the government." There it was. He had uttered the name of his rival, in deferential tones. Did Canadians need any further evidence that a truce had been declared. In a small way, this was Martin's reply to Chrétien's "in friendship" Christmas message.

Martin's statement was duly reported in all the national media, and the team held its collective breath, waiting to see whether the lay-it-on-the-table approach had worked. Sure enough, as budget day loomed in February, Martin appeared to have bought some peace from media questioning. Reporters who did try to probe Martin's budget priorities were simply referred to what was now being called the "Sherwood Park statement." It seemed to dampen the journalistic hunger for tension between Martin and Chrétien.

On February 18, 2003, for the first time in ten years, Paul Martin and Jean Chrétien did not enter the Commons together on budget day. The prime minister made his entrance with Manley. Martin slipped into the chamber and into his seat at the far end of the front row ready to play the role of backbench cheerleader.

Graciously, Manley singled out Martin in the opening line of his budget speech: "I am proud and honoured to stand in this House today to present to the people of Canada this government's sixth-consecutive balanced budget, and our sixth in a row that will reduce the nation's debt burden – a result of the determination and discipline of the prime minister and my predecessor as minister of finance, the Honourable Member for LaSalle-Emard."

The budget provided an 11.5 per cent increase in spending immediately and 20 per cent over three years, with new initiatives in several federal government departments. Much of the new spending commitments were multiyear programs, meaning that Martin, should he become prime minister, would have to pass legislation to undo any of the measures and risk offending the various interests – farmers, families, and so on – who had benefited from Chrétien's largesse. The theme of this budget was also this year's buzzword: *accountability*.

As soon as Manley had finished his speech, Martin and Chrétien made their way over to shake his hand. The three men – prime minister, loyal deputy, and would-be successor – stood together. Martin shook Manley's hand. "Thank you, Paul," Manley said. Then Chrétien extended his arm toward Martin. The two clasped hands, ever so briefly, but significantly.

Outside the Commons, the foyer and corridors of the Centre Block were transformed as is usual on budget day into a gigantic media circus. TV anchors had set up their desks outside the Commons door; representatives of interest groups of all stripes hawked their one-line critiques to every microphone in sight. The immediate reaction to the budget was not good. Commentators were seizing on the spending commitments, speculating on how much Martin's hands would be tied by the multiyear promises. Don Drummond, a former finance official turned Toronto-Dominion Bank economist, who had attended more than his share of CMOs during Martin's tenure, was one of the experts being sought out for reaction.

"It's literally whatever lobbyist group or individuals have asked for in the last ten years. If you haven't already got it, you pretty much got it in this budget," Drummond said.

Scott Reid and Brian Guest had served early notice to the media that any reaction from Martin would be limited to generalities. "It's Manley's day," they said – a line that Martin echoed immediately after the budget was delivered. When he talked to the horde of reporters awaiting his comments in the Commons foyer Martin limited his comments to generalities and faint praise, calling the budget "ambitious" and uttering platitudes about the importance of fiscal prudence. "It's very important that the government, at the same time, control its spending and expenses."

Privately, Martin and those close to him regarded Manley's budget as an opportunity missed and more evidence of a government adrift. They saw Chrétien's – or, more to the point, Goldenberg's – fingerprints all over the brokering between the lines of the budget. There was a little something for everyone, but no focus or direction. Unlike the previous eight budgets, there was no "narrative" or overarching theme. Martin believed that the country needed a health-care budget. He had watched in frustration a few weeks earlier when a first ministers' meeting on health care dissolved in confusion and recrimination. A focused federal government, he believed, would have gone into that first ministers' meeting with a targeted plan to improve health care and a budgetary vision to back it up. Why, he wondered, had Manley not laid out how government would reduce waiting times for medical treatment – an issue of deep concern to Canadians?

For Martin, the health-care discussion that February was a good illustration of the main difference between his style of governing and that of Chrétien. While the prime minister believed in managing across the wide spectrum of government, covering all bases adequately and brokering between priorities, Martin believed that the job of prime minister was to concentrate on a few areas and do them well. Health care, democratic reform, Canada's position in the world – these would be his priorities. Chrétien's announce-now, deal-with-the-critics-later approach (which had become more pronounced since the prime minister proclaimed himself "liberated") ran counter to Martin's way of dealing with issues. He was an advocate of first preparing the ground for a deal, then implementing it. This had showed up in their different stategies over Kyoto, and it was also reflected in their different ways of handling the Liberal party itself: Chrétien, from the top down; Martin, from the roots up.

But by the early months of 2003, as the rivalry with Chrétien wound down, no one in Martin's circle was eager to state these differences. They thought it better that people drew their own conclusions on how Martin would represent change from the current prime minister. No more battles with Chrétien. Enough was enough.

One price of détente with Chrétien, though, was the way the media began to treat Martin. For many years, he had benefited from being seen as the underdog, but now that he was the front-runner, the media was interested in chipping away at him. This changed attitude began to be seen in the media's closer scrutiny of his links to Canada Steamship Lines and their search of his record in government for any hint of conflict or favoured treatment of the shipping industry in general.

Glen McGregor at the *Ottawa Citizen* had devoted the most ink and attention to this issue in the past few months. And now, in February, McGregor revealed an interesting, up-to-now unknown fact: Martin had received regular briefings on his business dealings from Ethics Counsellor Howard Wilson.

This revelation was buried in a story about CSL's links to a power project in Indonesia, run by the son of the ruthless former dictator, Raden Suharto. But the opposition and pundits picked up on the tidbit and wondered what this signified about Martin's alleged blind-trust arrangement. Conservative Leader Joe Clark gave the best one-liner, calling Martin's CSL connection a "Venetian-blind trust" – one that allowed him to peek through the window whenever he chose.

As a backbencher, Martin could not respond directly to any of the attacks in the House. Moreover, he was still not showing up for Question Period. But as the pursuit of Martin became more relentless, Chrétien chose to handle many of the opposition questions himself. "The minister of finance of the day followed all the rules and ensured he was not in a conflict of interest," Chrétien said. Day after day, the prime minister rose to his feet to portray his former nemesis as a scrupulously ethical minister. "It was a family business run by trustees in the interest of the company and the minister of finance of the day who was doing his job properly without any conflict of interest."

The "liberated" prime minister appeared to be freeing himself from the antagonism of the past few years. He was also pulling together an ambitious, activist set of legacy projects, including the ban on corporate financing in politics and legislation to decriminalize marijuana. Skeptics speculated that Chrétien's new position on corporate financing was a deliberate attempt to punish Martin for his huge leadership war chest. As the legislation barrelled ahead, even over the protests of Liberal party president Stephen LeDrew, Martin reluctantly agreed with the scheme.

While the tone of Martin-Chrétien relations appeared to improve, those with Manley seemed to worsen. The pattern was continuing: Martin and his team reserved their greatest hostility for their most formidable opponent. Rock had felt it, so had Tobin. Now it was Manley's turn. Martin and his advisers saw all challengers, not without some justification, as proxies for Chrétien. The most loyal deputies to the prime minister were the most resented opponents. Grudges don't disappear quickly in the slow-motion world of the federal Liberals.

It appeared that Manley was seriously considering entering the race, assembling a small but seasoned group of Liberals to lay the foundation of a campaign. Two well-known and well-liked Ottawa lobbyists, Doug Kirkpatrick and Herb Metcalfe, were working almost full-time on building a Manley organization. Alf Apps, the man who had authored the resolution against backroom operatives in 1982, and who had been part of the delegation that invited Martin to the youth convention, was assembling a healthy Toronto contingent to back Manley. Ironically, Manley's core team included Ian Davey, son of the legendary "Rainmaker" Keith Davey, who had been the main target of Apps's resolution.

On a personal level, the relationship between Martin and Manley sank to a nadir. They had begun to be chilly toward each other in the wake of the September 11 attacks and had turned even frostier in the tussle over who said what in that contentious phone call during the June 2002 weekend of Martin's exit from cabinet. Relations had degenerated into near-hostility over the subsequent summer of strife, as Manley grew more intensely defensive of Chrétien. The deputy prime minister had begun to radiate an attitude of disapproving scorn toward Martin – in response, his aides said, to the Martinites' portrayal of the prime minister as vindictive and vengeful.

The moral tone of Manley's disapproval seemed rooted in the background and character of this dutiful, earnest young man who had grown into a loyal, if not showy, Liberal politician. Growing up in public housing in a disadvantaged section of Ottawa, across from a tuberculosis sanatorium where his father was hospitalized, Manley had been raised under his mother's tutelage a strict, evangelical Christian. The young John Manley – like Allan Rock, who grew up in similarly modest circumstances in Ottawa – pursued a legal education on an ambitious track. He served in the prestigious position of clerk to Supreme Court of Canada Chief Justice Bora Laskin, before going into private practice and carving out a successful career as a tax lawyer. After entering politics in 1988, Manley had built upon his earnest reputation, though friends said his serious demeanour was tempered by an off-the-wall sense of humour. But few people outside his immediate circle saw this side of him. In all, there were many parallels with Rock: a modest Ottawa upbringing, a desire to be seen as earnest and loyal, and a role as inheritor of the Chrétien team's indignation and opposition to Martin. Unlike Rock, however, Manley was considering a run at the leadership in this campaign.

Until his entry into the Liberal leadership race, Manley had only rarely flirted with controversy. He'd emerged mostly unscathed through the NHL-subsidy fiasco of early 2000, but he had caught some heat for ill-timed remarks against the monarchy in Canada through the years. One such remark was made on the eve of the Queen's visit to Canada in 2002, which critics seized upon as proof of his lack of political instincts.

The prospect of Martin's coronation appeared to rile Manley as much as the fact of the monarchy, if not more so. He became chippy with reporters whom he believed were in league with Martin. His criticism of the Martin team's methods veered toward moral outrage, using words such as *unprincipled*. His reputed sense of humour was nowhere in evidence.

The main target of Manley's indignation, like Rock's and Tobin's before him, was Martin's stranglehold on the party apparatus. Again like Rock and Tobin before him, Manley vowed to champion the cause of open party membership, but the Martin machine was so deeply entrenched now that most efforts were in vain. In the first of what would be several missteps by the Manley campaign, a few members of the team talked to the media about having Elections Canada take over for the Liberal party. This only enraged grassroots Liberals, for the implicit suggestion that they were too corrupt to conduct a fair campaign. It was a classic political gaffe – attacking the supporters of his opponent instead of the opponent himself.

Sheila Copps, in a more low-key fashion, was also now pulling her team together, despite the odds against her. She too was vowing to rattle Martin's lead by attracting new, left-leaning liberals into the party fold. Joe Thornley, her campaign chief, billed Copps as the candidate who would speak for "progressive" Liberalism, while Manley and Martin fought over the narrow field of right-leaning, fiscally obsessed ideology. The big surprise of Copps's campaign, in the eyes of the Martin team at least, was that it was being fought on the high ground. Throughout 2002, Copps had launched several verbal and personal salvoes in Martin's direction, accusing him of hard-hearted fiscal policies and arrogant political tactics. But her tone had shifted in recent weeks, and the notoriously loose-lipped Copps was refusing to be drawn into any negative comments about the front-runner.

As the start date of the official campaign drew near, Copps appeared to be the most eager candidate, filing her nomination papers, paying half the $75,000 campaign deposit, and hitting the road almost as soon as the bell sounded. Manley, on the other hand, kept assuring questioners that he would most likely be in the race, but first he had to finish his post-budget tour and take some time to reflect on his prospects.

Martin, meanwhile, was planning a little surprise for his official entry into the race. Throughout February, his team gathered the signatures of Liberal riding presidents all over Canada, which they appended to Martin's nomination papers as a show of his deep ties to grassroots Grits. On March 5, the papers were delivered to Liberal party headquarters on Metcalfe Street in Ottawa by Martin's own riding president from LaSalle-Emard, Jean-François Lalonde. A whopping 259 riding presidents had put their signatures to Martin's official declaration. Evidence of the rampant success of the old "twinning" program was found among the signatures: Martin's organization controlled the Liberal riding association in virtually every one of the 171 ridings in Canada held by the opposition parties. The original team of MP supporters had tended this non-Liberal territory well, aided by Michèle Cadario's constant attention to the Grit wilderness.

Manley was still officially undeclared in early March, though his supporters, especially Apps and Kirkpatrick, were now telling reporters that his candidacy was all but a certainty. "I intend to run," was Manley's stock answer by now. He ended his post-budget tour and then went off on a sailing vacation to make his final decision. Among the guests on the voyage were Ed Lumley, the Trudeau-era minister of everything, as he was called, and Gordon Giffin, former U.S. ambassador to Canada. The guest list refuted Martin's view of leadership campaigns as a time of suspended friendships: Lumley and his wife were good friends of the Martins, as were the Giffins. In leadership contests, as David Herle and Cyrus Reporter had learned, sometimes friends go separate ways.

The media's main complaint about Martin was about his front-runner's style of campaign. Martin was now dubbed "bubble boy" by most of the Ottawa press corps. Jokes began to circulate that he was hiding out in a cave somewhere, releasing the odd video or audio tape, like Osama bin Laden. Even when Martin did appear in public to say a line or two, his pronouncements were couched in so many conditional tenses and vagaries that it was impossible to figure out where he stood. His harsher critics, especially those within the prime minister's circle, argued that this had nothing to do with being a front-runner and everything to do with Martin's notorious indecisiveness and desire to be all things to all people. Herle and the team urged his supporters not to take the bait: slow, steady, and careful would win the race.

The Martin team had to make sure that Martinite MPs were following the same strategy. After all, this campaign had been punctuated by not-always-welcome diversions in opinion between the elected and non-elected since the bleak days of 2000. The Tuesday-night meetings were still taking place on Parliament Hill when the Commons was in session, but a collective quiet had fallen over the Martinites in caucus. Nothing they could do or say was going to hasten Chrétien's departure. They weren't happy about the corporate-financing bill, which they thought would doom the Liberals to eternal debt, but caucus chairman Stan Keyes failed in his attempts to delay the legislation. Tim Murphy and others made clear to the MPs that internal fighting in caucus only made life more difficult for Martin. Slowly, and with some bumps, the open agitating against Chrétien waned. Some MPs, such as Roger Gallaway, still simmered at the election threat the prime minister hung over their heads, but a resigned attitude descended on the once-restive Martinites. It became evident, though it was never articulated, that the potential of future Martin cabinet ministers would be measured by their ability to hold their tongues. The usual suspects began to disappear from the cluster of MPs ready with off-the-record comments to the media after caucus meetings. Winning Liberals play the long game. Would-be ministers keep their mouths shut.

Just as O'Leary had a decade or so earlier, Brian Guest and Scott Reid decided to break Martin out of the bubble with a series of off-the-record dinners with groups of journalists from the major media outlets. During late February and early March, Martin met at small gatherings with reporters and columnists from the *Toronto Star*, the *Globe and Mail*, and the *National Post*, as well as several broadcast outlets. These inevitably turned into charm offensives, with Martin amiably arguing with the scribes and trying to pry more information out of them than he was giving. But this wasn't enough. Martin bristled at the "bubble boy" nickname. He wanted more to be done.

Martin's invisibility wasn't all due to strategic caution, however. Among reporters and even the public, there was a feeling that no one really knew who Martin was or what he stood for, even when he was in the spotlight. Part of this was undoubtedly caused by his famed reticence to speak about himself or the things that were important to him. On the deepest matters of importance to him – religion, family, and his own ambitions – he seemed incapable of finding words to explain himself. Martin's greatest lapses to date as a politician were his failures to communicate. On issues he found personally difficult, he would second-guess and rewrite himself into paralysis or simply duck the moment all together.

Brian Guest recognized this weakness, but he also knew that almost everyone who met Martin in person came away charmed There had to be a way to get Martin talking about his deeper self before the cameras. Then he thought of something. While the snow still clung to the ground in Ottawa, Martin got behind the wheel of a car and subjected himself to an interview with Earnscliffe's Bruce Anderson and his wife, Nancy Jamieson. The two fired questions at him on everything, from his beliefs on family to his definition of success and what it means to be a Canadian.

Martin, always comfortable babbling and driving at the same time, spoke more freely as he drove leisurely to Wakefield in the Gatineau Hills, back into Ottawa, and down the road by the canal. Canadians, he said, were more generous than Americans when it came to government, but Americans were more philanthropic. Canadians didn't appreciate fully the emotional impact of September 11 on ordinary Americans.

Martin also confessed that he didn't like to be alone, unless it was in a house full of people – a revealing insight into how he managed to stay at the centre of the chaotic conversation that characterized his leadership campaign organization.

The would-be prime minister even danced around the subject of his age – he would be sixty-five by the time the leadership convention was held in November.

"I'm really getting quite hostile to the contemplation that [my life] is more than half over," Martin said, looking away. "And that's being generous," he added with a grin.

Once Guest and O'Leary looked at the raw footage of the impromptu interview, they decided not to edit or package the conversation, believing that Martin "unplugged" would sell himself. They took the questions and replaced them with bold black-and-white titles, then slapped the digitally recorded conversation on to hundreds of CDs and mass distributed it to

Liberal partisans. The last black title read: "What does it take to become a great prime minister?"

"Conviction," he said. "An ability to seize the moment."

Martin was still under daily siege about CSL. He realized, in retrospect, that he should have simply refused to attend the dozen or so sessions with Howard Wilson. He was growing resentful of the implication that he was corrupt. The skirmishes in the House had drilled into the public's mind that he was wealthy and Canadians got squeamish about rich guys in politics. The newly elected leader of the New Democratic Party, Jack Layton, was enjoying himself before the cameras, describing Martin as "a coal baron" for the alleged environmentally unfriendly cargo that CSL ships were carrying. Martin was angry that he was under attack from career politicians and media pundits who didn't know what it was to risk all to buy and run a multinational firm. He was starting to take all of this very personally.

He decided to enter the debate, knowing that it would require him to overcome his famed reticence and speak about himself and what was important to him. He gave an interview to the *National Post*, in which he poured out his passion for CSL in particular and the shipping industry in general. This had been his life's work and his dream, he explained. He would not, he could not give it up. To sell CSL now, he said, would be "to turn a dream into a nightmare."

The interview bought him a smattering of positive commentary, notably from pundits and business people who agreed that if Martin was forced to give up CSL, it would be a disincentive for any other business person to run for public office. If the price of elected office was total divestment, who would give it all up for the fickle fortunes of a career as a politician? But O'Leary, Herle, and Tim Murphy knew that the opinion balance had tipped against Martin. No matter what he said, the public wouldn't be happy until he put some neutral space between himself and his precious shipping firm. Martin bucked the advice. He didn't want to give up the company.

The opposition attacks continued, though, and Martin reluctantly came to the conclusion that his dreams for CSL and the Liberal leadership could no longer co-exist. On the first weekend in March, the team held a conference call and came up with the salvage plan: Martin would pass the firm on to his sons. It was the compromise between keeping CSL and selling it outright. Paul W., his eldest son, was already working for the firm. Martin went to the National Press Theatre to make his announcement, which ran over several pages, detailing the technicalities and rationale of turning over the firm to his grown children.

"It has always been my intention to pass control of the company onto my sons one day. The combination of circumstances indicates that that day has arrived. There has been an excellent management team in place for some time now. My sons are ready, willing, and able to support them.

"Thus, Sheila and I have decided that, whether or not I win the leadership, we will dispose of all our shares in Canada Steamship Lines and thereby will have relinquished ownership and control of the company to our three adult sons. The bottom line is that I will completely sever all ties with Canada Steamship Lines. Furthermore, I will have no forward interest in the company, as I will also relinquish any future claim to reacquire control when I retire from public office. I raise this today because I have heard the concerns that have been expressed and I want Canadians to know that if I should become prime minister, my only business will be the public's business."

The announcement bought Martin the peace he sought, though it caused a flurry of media interest in the family, especially the children he had tried to shield from the spotlight. David had been doing some campaigning for his father in rural and small-town Canada, out of the glare of the media, but the two other sons, especially Jamie, had no interest in becoming public figures. Still, after a few days of stories about the Martin boys, the story and the controversy, it seemed, faded away.

All of the developments on the domestic political front in the spring of 2003 were dwarfed by events on the world stage. The United States, under President George W. Bush, had been spoiling for months for a war with Iraq, proclaiming this as the next stage of the post–September 11 war on terrorism. He accused Iraqi leader Saddam Hussein of complicity in anti-American terrorism campaigns and of possessing weapons of mass destruction. But the United States was having a difficult time proving those allegations in the international court of opinion. Only British Prime Minister Tony Blair had emerged as a committed ally. Canadians, according to the polls, were hugely skeptical of Bush's reasons for a war with Iraq. Chrétien and Foreign Affairs Minister Bill Graham had been trying to put the brakes on the Americans' enthusiasm for an attack, lobbying at the United Nations and with allies abroad. In the end, the United States, backed by Britain, decided to go to war. Chrétien announced that Canada would not participate, stirring a furor at home and south of the border. Americans denounced Canada on open-line talk shows. U.S. Ambassador Paul Cellucci gave a speech in Toronto, expressing his government's displeasure at Canada's non-participation. President Bush cancelled a scheduled spring visit to Canada.

Through all this, Martin wanted to lie low. He thought that non-participation could have been better communicated to the United States and worried about the long-term damage to Canada-U.S. relations. Several of Martin's strongest caucus supporters, including Tony Valeri and Joe Fontana, conducted their own quiet diplomacy in the United States to smooth some of the friction caused by Chrétien's decision. Martin remained deliberately out of the fray. His old friend from the Clinton administration, Larry Summers, now president of Harvard University, had invited Martin to talk about Canada-U.S. relations at the university in late April. Quietly, Martin decided to scrub the appearance, concerned that it would present another opportunity for the media to jump on the differences in his and Chrétien's positions.

As the weeks wore on, more and more toxin drained out of the long Chrétien-Martin feud. Martin remained steadfast in his support of every Chrétien declaration on Canada's non-participation in the Iraq war. Canada needed to speak with one voice, he said. In early April, Martin went out of his way to congratulate the prime minister on the fortieth anniversary of his first election to the Commons. Talking to a journalist by phone from a car stuck in the middle of a late-winter blizzard in Southwestern Ontario, Martin carefully praised his old rival.

"Well, I think that, certainly, forty years of public service, his entire adult career devoted to politics, is an achievement in itself, and I think is virtually unparalleled," he said. The politician in Martin, however, could not resist exploiting the opportunity to talk about his own achievements.

"I think that the fact that he gave me such strong support through what were the decisive years in dealing with the nation's finances, I think that that was incredibly important. Finance ministers cannot do it without the prime minister."

Asked how Chrétien would be remembered by Canadians, Martin offered this homily: "I think that he was such a strong Canadian and that he felt so deeply about the country. I think that is his hallmark. That he was such a strong Canadian – that's always been his hallmark."

Martin had not spoken to Chrétien since that fateful Sunday in June 2002 beyond a hello or the brief budget-day handshake, but he acknowledged that the tension was slowly receding.

"Yes, I think so. Things are unfolding pretty well, as they should. Transition periods are never easy."

Whether it was a slip of the tongue or a deliberate description, Martin's use of the phrase *transition period* accurately captured not just his relationship with Chrétien, but the whole tenor of the leadership race. Even before the official debates began, Martin was seen – and had begun to see himself – as the leader in waiting. The race itself was starting to look like some bureaucratic red tape or a distraction on the route to 24 Sussex Drive. The media was feeding this perception by paying only cursory attention to any policy or political differences between the contenders. News reports repeatedly described Martin as "the front-runner" or even, the "next likely prime minister." Ottawa's chattering classes talked not about Martin the candidate, but about Martin the leader-in-waiting.

Despite protests to the contrary, the Martin campaign had started to organize around this principle too. The campaign was focusing on two targets: first, the Liberal partisans who would decide on the next leader, and second, the Canadian electorate, who would be indirectly voting on Martin as the next prime minister, probably sometime in 2004. Webster had long urged the team not to forget the long game; this was part of that approach.

A massive policy-development operation had been underway in earnest since January, with literally hundreds of advisers and experts putting their insights at Martin's disposal. The size and scope of this consultation spoke volumes about how far Martin's organization had come since the lean days of 1990. Mark Resnick, the policy chief from that campaign, was involved in this effort too, but now he was co-ordinating the work of multitudes, as opposed to the five or six people who had formed the policy nucleus of Martin's first leadership bid.

Academics, business people, social-policy advocates, and others with ideas to share were all busily writing policy papers for Martin. In total, about three hundred volunteers lent their insights to the policy process. Their papers were posted on one of a series of twenty-two policy Web sites, accessible only to the few participants at each of the Internet round tables. These Web sites featured chat sites too, so that the experts could bat around various proposals. One person at each round table was designated as the chief "wrangler" – the person responsible for harnessing the discussion into a coherent policy for Martin. Resnick was the top wrangler, overseeing the entire system. Martin's MP supporters linked into the discussions too. Stan Keyes, Joe Comuzzi, and Joe Fontana worked with the transportation group; Joe Volpe worked on immigration issues; Carolyn Bennett took an active role in the health-care discussions. Other caucus members continued to fine-tune Martin's parliamentary-reform ideas, devising ever more ways to make the role of individual members of Parliament more relevant. The candidate himself often dipped into the policy discussions, especially when he had a speech looming that touched on one of the various areas of interest. On foreign policy, for instance, Martin consulted with about a dozen experts, including Mike Pearson, grandson of the former prime minister, and with academics across Canada.

The attraction of contributing to the Martin leadership campaign was rooted in future considerations, naturally. All of these people knew that what they did now could have an influence on a future Liberal government. Martin and his team were laying the groundwork now for governing more than for the debates.

This was also the thinking behind an ambitious, unprecedented series of "town-hall" meetings that were being slotted into Martin's campaign schedule for late April and May. In conjunction with several think-tanks around the country, such as the Canada West Foundation and Quebec's Chantier de l'économie sociale, Herle and the campaign team pulled together groups of non-partisan Canadians for a free-wheeling, unscripted question-and-answer session with the future prime minister. Martin would play to his strengths, which he usually demonstrated on his feet, in CMO style, and prove that he wasn't afraid to face tough questions.

Martin went into intense preparation for the town-hall meetings and the campaign debates right after Easter, pitching himself and his advisers into a flurry of rehearsals.

By now he had memorized a dizzying array of facts. He would leave nothing to chance. What were the hydro rates in Quebec? How much was a loaf of bread or a jug of milk at the grocery store? Knowing the price of groceries was a legacy of other campaigns. George Bush Sr., during his unsuccessful run at presidential re-election in the United States in 1992, had famously not known the price of a quart of milk. No such error would trip up this candidate.

The team closeted itself at headquarters, peppering Martin with questions. Then they went into full dress rehearsal, with Elly Alboim playing the role of John Manley and Terrie O'Leary playing Sheila Copps.

That week, Richard Mahoney met with Brian Tobin for lunch and told him about the plan for the first week. He rattled off all the events, described the emphasis on the town-hall format, and lauded Martin's strengths at question-and-answer rehearsals. Tobin, a master communicator, approved. The town-hall thing, though – had the Martin team ensured that the questioners were friendly?

"Nope," Mahoney said. "We're going in there cold."

Tobin stared at Mahoney. "You're crazy," he said.

Martin worked extensively with his team of advisers on the statement he would make to launch his campaign, which Scott Reid and Brian Guest insisted to the media was not a real launch at all, since Martin had really been campaigning for the better part of the previous year. Martin himself tried to play down expectations for the campaign unveiling, saying to the rare reporter with whom he spoke these days: "When I do announce, do you think anyone will be surprised?" Behind the scenes, the team was calling it the relaunch. It would, in keeping with Martin's abbreviated answer of the fall, have "no balloons."

There was a bit of a tussle between Martin and his advisers over how he should position his campaign. He had to symbolize change from the Chrétien regime. Canadians, Herle was convinced from his polling and focus-group analysis, were not in the mood simply to grant the Liberals a fourth majority. Martin had to speak about those issues he would handle differently. And that meant voicing criticism – careful criticism – of Chrétien. It meant risking reopening the rivalry to position Martin's campaign for the future general election. Martin resisted, but the team pushed back. They knew that while Martin was no longer interested in being portrayed as the anti-Chrétien man, the media still was looking for ways to tell that story. Herle and O'Leary had to push Martin hard before he agreed to an opening statement critical of the current government. "We've got you this far," they told him. "You have to trust us."

On April 27, Martin, looking a little nervous, made his way to a darkened room at Montreal's Intercontinental Hotel, where an unfamiliar crowd of about one hundred people sat stiffly in beige and chrome chairs, illuminated by stark TV lighting. The only friendly face in the crowd was his wife's. Sheila Martin had accompanied her husband and sat intensely watching every minute of the event.

The show began. Martin issued his opening statement, and, bowing to his team's advice, described the Chrétien government as adrift. "I am proud of what we have accomplished in the past decade as a government. But in recent times a kind of complacency – a certain amount of drift has set in. We've lost some of the energy and enthusiasm that Canadians are looking for." In the media room next door, reporters scribbled and marked the time on their recording devices. This would be the next day's headlines. The tension may have been leaving the Martin-Chrétien relationship, but the media wasn't done with that story yet.

Questions began to fly; most of them in French. Martin seemed stiff and rehearsed at first, but relaxed a little as the first hour passed and began to get into give-and-take with the audience. Now, with a decent interval of time since the February budget and the first ministers' conference on health care, he gave careful voice to his frustration over what Ottawa hadn't said or done about long waiting lists for medical treatment. Martin sketched out the broad lines of a policy he would elaborate on in the weeks ahead, by which Ottawa would collect up information on waiting times and set in place a system of standards.

"What we have got to do is put in place a structure whereby Canadians will be guaranteed that within a certain period of time you get to see this kind of a doctor or, if not, you can go to another province where they will be able to provide it."

Just past the banks of chairs, standing against the darkened back wall of the hotel ballroom, Martin's friends were out in force, at a discreet distance. Nearly the entire Board was in the room, as well as several people from the old 1990 campaign. While the front-runner scrummed with reporters, David Herle and Dennis Dawson, those old CSL employees, stood against the wall, talking to each other but keeping their eyes fixed on every move of the candidate they had virtually invented so long ago. Richard Mahoney sat on a chair in the wings watching the line-up of people waiting to be charmingly spun. Jean Lapierre, the old co-chair of the 1990 effort, now a radio talk-show host in Quebec, came as a media delegate, smiling and whispering with Martinites who waded into the corner where the scribes sat.

O'Leary, true to form, determinedly avoided any appearance at the event, staying in a private room downstairs where the inner circle had monitored the debate by closed-circuit TV.

Martin's launch week followed much the same path as his 1990 launch, but with much more polish and attention to timing. It started in Montreal, but this time with no missteps over Meech Lake or anything vaguely constitutional. Instead of trying to race to Toronto and Windsor the same day, Martin went first to Ottawa for interviews with the national media.

Then it was off in a small charter plane to the Martin homeland of Windsor, where a small but devoted crowd was waiting for him at the Ciociaro Club, on the rural fringes of the border city. There was no snowstorm this time to hold Martin up, no need for anyone to open up the bar and keep the crowd happy with free drinks. Most of all, though, there was no Paul Martin Sr. waiting among the Windsorites. His son was on his own this time. In a gesture apparent only to the closest of Martin-watchers over the years, Paul Martin Jr. was introduced to the crowd by Carl Quenneville, son of Martin Sr.'s former riding president, Fred Quenneville. (Quenneville Sr., patriarch of the respected Windsor Liberal clan, was in the audience too, only a couple of months away from his death, as it turned out. Martin delivered the eulogy at his funeral during the Canada Day weekend 2003.)

It was his mother's absence Martin felt most, however, as was always the case when he came to his hometown. Nell, the matriarch, remained a large presence in her son's memories.

The next few days in Toronto were a buzz of high-profile events, all aimed at pulling Martin out of the bubble. There was another town-hall discussion at a downtown Toronto bar, more meet-and-greet sessions with influential Bay Street Liberals, and a major foreign-policy address to executive journalists with the Canadian Newspaper Association.

The speech to the journalists would turn out to be the signature policy piece of the Martin campaign. Martin used the occasion to lay out his thoughts on Canada-U.S. relations, the hottest topic in the country in the wake of the Iraq war. But his address also spelled out his idea of where Canada could make a difference in a larger international context.

"Canada boasts a set of enviable values and interests and skills, values such as freedom, tolerance, and mutual respect, an acceptance of others, a belief that democracy and pluralism stand side-by-side. We have our interests too. We have joined alliances to preserve and protect them. We have fought wars to defend them. And we have worked diplomatically for an international system that embodies and extends them. We are internationalist in outlook, humanitarian by disposition, pragmatic in implementation, and always mindful of the limits of acting alone." Martin was comfortable making this speech. Canada's attributes mirrored what he saw as his own best traits – some saw those characteristics as weak and fuzzy; others saw them as mindful of complexity and consensus.

Martin appeared to gather energy with each event during the launch week. A small contingent of his closest confidantes accompanied him everywhere, including Herle and O'Leary. Their lunches with local organizers took place at huge tables in restaurants, with Tim Murphy, Brian Guest, and Scott Reid barking into their cellphones or madly thumb-typing on their BlackBerries to stay in touch with headquarters or journalists in Ottawa. Martin was the bemused observer at these lunches for the most part, if he wasn't fretting over getting to the next engagement. His team treated launch week as much as a celebration as work. High-spirited dinners would turn into late-night parties resembling the raucous 1990 campaign. Martin, thirteen years older now, would usually excuse himself early from any of the post-event gatherings, retiring to his hotel room to fret over speeches or policy briefing papers.

The first of the six leadership debates took place in Edmonton on May 3. Although it took place onstage at the Citadel Theatre, there was very little drama or excitement in the performance. Manley, Martin, and Copps all stuck to their tightly scripted lines, with few sparks or exchanges, for a mind-numbing ninety minutes. The audience was heavily stacked with Martin supporters. Manley attempted a few jabs at Martin's blind trust and refusal to divulge the names of his contributors, but the Martin-friendly crowd didn't respond. For the entire debate, reporters sat slumped in their chairs, yawning or looking at their watches.

Back in Ottawa the following week, the group at the central campaign headquarters was gearing up for a rally-the-troops party in the capital. The event would serve two purposes: First, it would give the workers closest to home a taste of the excitement that other loyalists around the country got when Martin popped in for a rally. Second, it would be a show of force on Manley's turf, vividly illustrating the enormity of the gap between the front-runner and the deputy prime minister from Ottawa South. Word of the party had spread among the MPs and senators too; the event was shaping up to be the first major gathering of Martin's impressive support on Parliament Hill.

On May 6, at the Corel Centre, home of the Ottawa Senators NHL hockey team, the crowd began to file in early. More than twelve hundred people milled about the stadium, watching as each MP and senator walked on to the stage, one at a time, as his or her name was announced. All the usual suspects were there, but also some caucus members who had kept a low profile so far. In total, more than one hundred names were called out as the crowd's cries grew wilder.

Martin, backstage, kept peeking through the curtain at the growing mob on the platform. He started to worry they wouldn't all fit. As each MP's name was called, the Martinites onstage pushed ever closer together. Joe Fontana, Joe Volpe, and other members of the original band of Martinites in caucus gulped with emotion as they saw, for the first time, the size of the team they had helped build. Newer members of the gang – Andy Scott from New Brunswick, Reg Alcock from Manitoba – realized the magnitude of the effort they had joined.

Martin walked onstage last, with Sheila at his side. "This tops everything," he said. "Tonight, we are beginning a new march, one that will bring us to the convention in November."

Down on the floor, Herle and O'Leary beamed. Richard Mahoney caught his breath. Who would have believed that all those small evening gatherings at his office would have led to this sight? Who would have predicted, in the dark days after the March 2000 debacle, that it would ever be a moment of great joy for MPs to stand onstage, in public, and declare their allegiance to Martin? Here it was – the parliamentary equivalent of the 259 riding presidents who had signed the nomination papers, and a similar testimonial to all those years of effort and heartache and tension. Martin's support in caucus and within the party was about as close to unanimous as any leadership candidate could boast. This was more than a team. This was a juggernaut.

After that high point, the "race" dragged on. It was a contest with very little spark. Martin's lead was so great and his organization so solid and extensive, there was little point for the media to treat the race as a serious leadership contest. Martin believed he was saying things of substance along the campaign trail, but unless he spoke against Chrétien, his words were almost never reported. Few national reporters accompanied him on the trail, partly because of lack of interest, partly because the news media had blown their budgets covering the Iraq war. Yet there were five more debates to go and forty-five days left for candidates to sign up Liberal members.

The first debate in Edmonton had set the pattern for the rest. They were all stiff, unmemorable events, held in Whitehorse, Charlottetown, Vancouver, Ottawa, and finally, in St-Hyacinthe, near Montreal. The only thing the final debate shared in common with the 1990 campaign was the province in which it was held. Unlike in 1990, the Montreal debate was yet another dry, dull affair, attracting little media interest. The whole Liberal leadership contest had slipped to the back pages of the newspapers. Manley's campaign stumbled and faltered along, plagued by infighting among his team and the abrupt resignations of key advisers such as Alf Apps and Ian Davey. Manley appeared to be inheriting Rock's accident-prone reputation. Most of the news about his campaign was bad. Copps hovered below the media radar, keeping to her high-road rhetoric for the most part, but gathering only a modest band of followers. Neither of the challengers was turning in any great numbers of membership forms, even after the party's loosened restrictions had put a thousand more forms in each riding. The Martin team kept scooping up most of the new members, doubling the party's numbers to nearly 500,000 from about 250,000 a few years earlier. More than ever, Martin's victory was seen as a fait accompli.

Over the weekend of May 31 to June 2, the anniversary of Martin's exit from cabinet passed without much notice. Martin was on his way back to Ottawa from Regina, where he had made a stop after the Vancouver debate. He went to church on the Sunday morning with David Herle's mother, Magdalena. That evening, he attended a wedding shower in Ottawa for Kevin Bosch, a young Westerner who oversaw policy operations at head-quarters. Every now and then over the weekend, Herle or O'Leary or one of the gang would note the date and marvel at how far they had come in a year. Martin's leadership team was now posting a countdown to the mem-bership cutoff date on its Web site, but there was no sense that there was any need to scramble to seal Martin's win. Copps and Manley had gathered up respectable numbers of new members but not enough to make any difference.

The deadline for signing up new Liberal members was June 20. When all the forms were sifted and processed, the size of the juggernaut came clear.

According to the candidates' own estimates, Copps had signed up 32,000 new Liberals; Manley, about 45,000. The rest of the more than quarter-million new members belonged to Martin. And this was on top of a base that largely belonged to him anyway, thanks to the long years of work in the trenches by Cadario, Littler, and others. Now people could see for themselves why Tobin and Rock had vacated the field.

On a slow summer news day in mid-July, John Manley joined the ranks of ex-candidates when he announced he was pulling out of the race. In the same basement room on Parliament Hill where he had announced his embarrassing reversal on NHL subsidies a few years earlier, Manley read solemnly from a prepared statement. "A finance minister needs to be pretty good with numbers, and it is clear that the numbers just aren't there for me this time. I have offered the party a choice, and it is clear to me that the party has chosen and that Paul Martin will be the next leader of the Liberal party and the next prime minister of Canada."

The tone of the press conference was grave; no self-deprecating smile played across Manley's face, as it had during the NHL-subsidy reversal. Manley deliberately left hanging the question of whether he would even run for office under Martin's leadership, saying only that he would work to help the Liberals to another victory. It left the impression that something permanent and irrevocable had happened to the two men's relationship, even if Manley was offering his backing to Martin.

Manley's followers, like Rock's and Tobin's supporters before them, were expected to line up behind Martin. To the victor goes the spoils. Manley had telephoned Martin to give him advance notice of his decision, yet Martin decided not to speak to the media that day. He was at his farm, Guest told reporters, and would only issue a written statement. It took two days, in fact, for Martin to appear in public and make any comments about Manley's departure from the race – shades of Martin's characteristic reluctance or inability to seize the moment. If he was grateful for Manley's statement of confidence in him, he didn't show it.

Copps remained in the fray, vowing to stay in the contest right up to November 15. "You can take that to the bank," she told reporters immediately after Manley's announcement. To signal her seriousness, she even released her own Red Book of policy positions the following week, outlining the ways in which she would speak for a more progressive Liberalism than Martin was promising.

But Manley's departure made the leadership race even more lopsided in Martin's favour, if that was possible. Three candidates in the race had meant that it was remotely possible there would be more than one ballot in November. On a second ballot, Liberal delegates would be free to change their votes maybe some of Martin's committed support would bleed away. It was a remote possibility, but it kept hopes alive among the also-rans. But now, with the contest reduced to a single round, the result would effectively be known as soon as all delegates were chosen on the super voting weekend in September. Martin would become the next leader, in all but name.

Really, though, hadn't people known for some time that Martin was the winner? The real battle, in many ways, had been won a year earlier, certainly by the time the Liberal caucus had arrived in Chicoutimi the previous August. The fight was never against future contenders; it was always against the past rival – Chrétien.

And what of that rivalry? It had been laid to rest by the summer of 2003. There were occasional echoes: a couple of days after reports of Chrétien's seeking a future role at the United Nations, it was announced that Martin had found himself a temporary position at the UN, on a blue-ribbon international panel dedicated to boosting the private sector in the Third World. Few commentators were small-minded enough to point it out openly, but with this appointment, Martin had outdone Chrétien again. Martin's willingness to take on a new international responsibility also spoke to his confidence about his status in the race. Chrétien went to Florida on vacation in the middle of the 1990 campaign; Martin spent the summer of 2003, on the brink of victory, dabbling in international affairs and vacationing at the farm.

Their rivalry had always been a simple one: it was about ambition. It was settled as soon as each of them got what he wanted, more or less. Chrétien got to stay on long enough to hammer a legacy of sorts into place: a ban on corporate financing in politics, an initiative on aid to Africa, a bid to legalize same-sex marriages and marijuana, an increasingly independent foreign policy vis à vis the United States. All of these projects showed Chrétien attempting to mould Canada into a more progressive nation.

Reviews of his leadership improved in his final year in office, and Canadians grew increasingly reluctant to brand him a simple manager without vision.

But Martin and Chrétien had still not spoken to each other in person, beyond brief greetings, since June 2, 2002. Would the day ever come when the two men would speak again? Martin said that conversation would come "when the occasion presented itself."

Perhaps the strongest indication of the end of the truce came when both sides quietly began their transition plans in the spring and summer of 2003. Mike Robinson at Earnscliffe started to work discreetly on the blueprint of the Martin government machine, in consultation and with co-operation from the federal bureaucracy. Chrétien gave a discreet nod to the Privy Council clerk, Alex Himelfarb, to work with Robinson and the Martin forces to ensure as smooth a changeover as possible. Robinson and Himelfarb started to meet every couple of weeks to review some of the bigger issues that would pass from Chrétien's watch to Martin's. Manley and other ministers began to acknowledge that Martin would need to be consulted on any major decisions in the period before he officially took office. All this talk of transition made Martin's team very nervous. The more they were seen as participants in Chrétien's final days, the less they could claim to represent significant change in Liberal government when they took over. Still, quietly, they began to draw up plans for the future PMO, even sounding out people for various positions in the office. Not all the members of the Board were destined to end up in Martin's PMO, but without exception they would be important players in the new Liberal regime.

The only question that hung in the balance, leading up to the November leadership vote, was how long Chrétien would stay on after Martin was named his successor. There was every reason to believe that Chrétien would stay until his promised exit date of February 2004, and the long transition period could be seen as mutually beneficial to both of the old rivals. Chrétien would leave at a time of his own choosing, while Martin would have plenty of time to make the adjustment from heir apparent to king. Once he gained the power he had sought for so long, he would have to worry less about the enemies he had made than the friends he had gained along the way. More to the point, Martin needed time to figure out how to handle all the expectations invested in him by so many people over the years. He was about to win a prize that was founded on ambition – his own and all the others with him. And ambition requires continuing rewards. As Mahoney had warned on that sparkling weekend after Chrétien's resignation announcement, the journey would be more fun than the goal. The hard part would lie in deciding how to wield the power the team had long sought.

The prospect of cabinet building loomed before Martin. It was the most unoriginal and oft-repeated question thrown at him and his team during the time they had amassed their impressive support. How would he pick and choose among all the backbenchers who saw Martin as their ticket to cabinet post that had eluded them during Chrétien's tenure? The jokes had been around for years: Martin would need to hold cabinet meetings in the Corel Centre. Or, as Chrétien had remarked to more than one reporter, the media would start to hear gripes from Martin's "former future ministers" as soon as his successor took power.

The members of the Board could be certain of influence over whatever shape the new regime took, but the future did not look so clear for many MPs. Some of the Martinites would get into cabinet, but many others would have to content themselves with the beefed-up role for backbenchers that Martin had promised. Still others would have to clear out of the Commons all together before the next election, to make way for the team that Martin wanted to recruit. In other words, backroom supporters of Martin were more likely to be rewarded for their support than were the current MPs who had worked for the cause. That loomed large as a headache for the future prime minister. MPs had always taken the greater risks, yet their future influence in Martin's world had always been doubtful. It was also another reason why Martin would appreciate a long transition period, if only to handle the numerous expectations he was going to have to fulfill or dash.

Martin tried to avoid being drawn into premature cabinet-making. "I have made no promises, no commitments to anyone," he said. "If you make one, you might as well make twenty. If you make twenty, you might as well make a hundred. I'm just not going to get into that."

He bristled, too, at the characterization of his supporters as simple cabinet wannabes. "To say that we've only got people who want to get into cabinet, that would be true if we had twenty caucus members. It's sure as hell not true when you've got well over a hundred."

If he wasn't so sure of who would be in his cabinet, however, he was a little more certain of how it would be run. The Chrétien style – short, terse, businesslike – had its virtues, but Martin dreamed of a PMO that would be run more like a CMO.

"What Chrétien did was very good: he essentially said, You're the minister, run your department, and, as a result, cabinet meetings had really very little discussion. . . . The problem is that cabinet rarely dealt with substantive issues."

Martin also wanted to hold cabinet meetings across the country, maybe even set up satellite operations of the PMO in other regions, notably the West. The inspiration for this idea, he said, came from former Alberta premier Peter Lougheed, who sawed off the competition between Edmonton and Calgary in his province by setting up premier's offices in both cities. Martin was convinced that alienation – from the West, Quebec, from young Liberals – would be the force that would undo him if he didn't pay attention. All politicians fight the last war.

There is a pattern to how Canada's most recent prime ministers started their mandate and how they left. Call it a curse, or the contrariness of fate, but all of the prime ministers over the previous forty years are remembered for the opposite of how they wanted to be seen. Trudeau came to office with a desire to push his ideas and an alleged disavowal of public affections. He ended up a popular icon, his ideas secondary to his principles and panache. Brian Mulroney wanted to be liked; he ended up the most unpopular prime minister, but his ideas – free trade, more power to the provinces – endured. Chrétien came to office as the "straight from the heart" little guy from Shawinigan, only to be called a dictator in his later years in office. If the contrary curse continues, Martin would also be remembered for the opposite of his pre-prime-ministerial reputation. In his case, competence was his trademark. Will he ultimately be thought of as incompetent?

Challenges to Martin's future leadership were already lurking, even before he won office. Thirteen years in the public eye had made Martin a darling in public opinion. He gave every indication that he would be a far more open prime minister, one who would jettison the traditional command-and-control model of government and introduce consensus and consulation. But the exposure had also highlighted some weaknesses too: his inability to address issues of symbolic or emotional significance and his over-reliance on advisers.

Leadership is a complicated blend of paying attention to people, ideas, and organization. Yet the Martin juggernaut was built almost completely on the strength of organization alone. The style of the Martin machine – tough, aggressive, with the brute strength of numbers and reliant on the party hierarchy – was at odds with his team's avowedly more democratic, networked approach to people and ideas. Martin's promises to revitalize the Liberal party and address the "democratic deficit" faced this contra-diction – if his victory was built on raw organization over all, where was the incentive to adopt a new approach to people and ideas? What does a potential successor to Martin learn from the example set by his large-scale takeover of the Liberal party structure?

The media, so long a tool of Martin's leadership ambitions, if not an ally, was bound to turn on him too. Already, in the summer of 2003, the tone of reporting was changing, and more columns and punditry were devoted to chipping away at Martin the invisible and invincible. In the last half of his mandate Chrétien had learned how the media likes to gang up on the one with all the power. Martin, not overly adept at handling hard questions on his feet, was now having to handle a more aggressive media too.

By far the largest challenge for Martin, though, would be coming to terms with the trail he blazed to 24 Sussex Drive. For twenty years the winner of Liberal leadership contests has been haunted by the second-place finisher. Turner's six years as leader in the 1980s were almost totally consumed with fending off challenges from Chrétien and his followers. Chrétien's leadership was ultimately undone by Liberals hungry to see Martin in office. When the would-be successor and his people feel aggrieved, the leadership of the Liberal party is imperiled.

Martin's over-arching goal, then, would be to ensure that he contained his potential successors' ambitions without forcing them outside the Ottawa establishment. Thanks to Chrétien's and his own example, Martin knew all too well how revolt can spread like wildfire at the grassroots. By the summer of 2003, Martin had managed to draw most of the obvious would-be successors – Brian Tobin, Allan Rock, Frank McKenna – into his leadership tent, and even John Manley had pledged his support. Only Sheila Copps remained as a rival, possibly to test Martin's ability to treat a second-place finisher as he had been treated after 1990.

Martin believed that succession planning was not something he needed to worry about, at least in the short-term. "Nobody will start to do that in the first mandate," he said. "Some might through the second mandate. . . . They're going to ask themselves, Is he going to run for a second?" Even so, Martin said, as long as he didn't turn the race into one between old and new, the pattern wouldn't repeat itself. The Liberals need not be victims of their past. "As long as I am genuinely neutral, there is not going to be a lot of activity. I never wanted to take Chrétien on. Chrétien won the convention. Most Liberals supported Chrétien. Why would I want to take Chrétien on?"

Martin ultimately did take Chrétien on, of course, because he could – and because the how-to manual had been written in the twenty years since a bunch of young Grits had vowed to shake up things in the natural governing party. John Turner and Jean Chrétien had used the same manual in their runs for the leadership: the status of the heir apparent, a strong grassroots organization not afraid to buck the Ottawa establishment, and a team with a knack for keeping the candidate constantly, but enigmatically, in the public eye. The fact that Martin built himself a bigger, more formidable machine from this manual is explained simply by the fact that he had more time to do so – time handed to him by a rival who refused to step down. In this way, the juggernaut was set in motion as much by Chrétien as it was by Martin and his team. And by the late summer of 2003, the juggernaut had rolled in. Martin had won the crown.

ACKNOWLEDGEMENTS

AT A MERE 350 or so pages, *Juggernaut* doesn't even begin to reflect all the time and effort that interviewees gave to me. First and foremost, my thanks to all of the people who agreed to talk and help me sift through more than twenty years of Liberal history.

The book initially was intended to appear as a Macfarlane, Walter, and Ross publication. Unfortunately, this jewel of a publishing firm is now gone, though Jan Walter stayed with this book as editor almost to the very end. I am enormously indebted to her for believing in this book in the first place and for all she has done to teach me about writing and for trying to rein in a big, sprawling story. I also want to thank my new publishing home, McClelland & Stewart, especially Doug Gibson and Dinah Forbes, for seamlessly picking up the project and for their support for the book. It was Doug Gibson who came up with the title, *Juggernaut*, and so far has been the only person who knew off the top of his head that the word was Hindi and had nothing at all to do with ships.

My lawyer and old friend, Peter Jacobsen, continued to protect my best legal and personal interests, as he has done for so many years.

David Zussman at the Public Policy Forum kindly and patiently read through the text before it went to print. His suggestions were incorporated with much gratitude, and if there's a smart insight or two to be found among the many words in this book – especially with regard to the reality of how government works – chances are pretty good that it comes from Zussman.

Someday I'll really have to thank Richard Mahoney for introducing me to the Martin gang many years ago. David Herle and Terrie O'Leary and nearly every member of that famed Board were incredibly patient with my endless requests for information and stories. It was Thérèse Horvath, Martin's private secretary and probably one of the most pleasantly efficient people I've encountered on Parliament Hill, who named this team the Board. I now refer to them as more than mere acquaintances – a phrase that carries its own freight.

As for my colleagues in the journalistic trenches, it is impossible to list all those who helped me out in this enterprise – from the bosses who encouraged me, to the guys around the daily lunch table at the National Press Club. Let me just name a few members of the media, though, who were an important part of this book and supported me throughout the project. Don Newman, the dean of political reporting in Ottawa and anchor of CBC Newsworld's *Politics* show, was especially helpful. So too were two of my colleagues at the *Toronto Star*, Jim Travers and Graham Fraser. From his listening post in Victoria, columnist Norman Spector prodded and challenged me. The CBC Radio journalists on Parliament Hill, especially Anthony Germain, Jennifer Fry, and bureau chief David Taylor, treated me as part of their work family. Institutionally, I owe the *Globe and Mail* thanks for my early opportunities to see Liberal politics close up; the *Ottawa Citizen* and the *National Post* for later years; and now the *Toronto Star* for giving me a new platform from which to watch how Martin uses the power he fought so long to win.

Closer to home, I have friends and family who have put up with an awful lot of blathering from me over the years about this book and, before it, the stories within its covers. My cherished friend Jan Lounder often knows what I am trying to say before I do, Susan Harada and Rita Mezzanotte have walked along this path so long with me that I often forget where one of us leaves off and the other starts. Jessie Chauhan, Elaine Collins, Geoff Norquay, and Graham Fox, all Tories, remind me regularly that not all the best stories are Liberal. To all of these friends, I can only say thanks, and I promise I will go back to being a normal human being again.

The same has to be said to my parents, John and Vera Delacourt, and my younger brother, John, who showed me, long before I saw it in politics, the value of loyalty, sticking by your people, and, most of all, keeping a sense of humour and perspective about it all.

The most supportive man in this whole project and, indeed, my entire life is my husband, Don Lenihan. Spouses not only see the sacrifice and focus needed for a project this large, they share it. Any good things to be said about this book should be directed to him too. Any criticism should come to me alone. It will probably come because I've failed to take his advice on something. The best and biggest thing I can say about Don with regard to this book is that he cared, in every way that mattered.

INDEX